P9-CCQ-170

PLAYING TO
THE EDGE

PLAYING TO THE EDGE

AMERICAN INTELLIGENCE
IN THE AGE OF TERROR

MICHAEL V. HAYDEN

PENGUIN PRESS

New York

2016

PENGUIN PRESS
An imprint of Penguin Random House LLC
375 Hudson Street
New York, New York 10014
penguin.com

Copyright © 2016 by Michael V. Hayden
Penguin supports copyright. Copyright fuels creativity, encourages diverse voices,
promotes free speech, and creates a vibrant culture. Thank you for buying an authorized
edition of this book and for complying with copyright laws by not reproducing, scanning,
or distributing any part of it in any form without permission. You are supporting writers
and allowing Penguin to continue to publish books for every reader.

LIBRARY OF CONGRESS CATALOGING-IN-PUBLICATION DATA
Names: Hayden, Michael V. (Michael Vincent), 1945-
Title: Playing to the edge : American intelligence in the age of terror /
Michael V. Hayden.
Description: New York : Penguin Press, 2016.
Identifiers: LCCN 2015044201 (print) | LCCN 2015049127 (ebook) |
ISBN 9781594206566 (hardback) | ISBN 9780698196131 (ebook)
Subjects: LCSH: Intelligence service—United States. | National security—United States.
| United States. Central Intelligence Agency. |
United States. National Security Agency. | BISAC: BIOGRAPHY &
AUTOBIOGRAPHY / Political. | POLITICAL SCIENCE / Political Freedom &
Security / Intelligence. | HISTORY / United States / 21st Century.
Classification: LCC JK468.I6 H39 2016 (print) | LCC JK468.I6 (ebook) | DDC
327.1273—dc23
LC record available at http://lccn.loc.gov/2015044201

Printed in the United States of America
1   3   5   7   9   10   8   6   4   2

Designed by Meighan Cavanaugh

This does not constitute an official release of U.S. Government information. All
statements of fact, opinion, or analysis expressed are those of the author and do not
reflect the official positions or views of the U.S. Government. Nothing in the contents
should be construed as asserting or implying U.S. Government authentication of
information endorsement of the author's views. This material has been reviewed solely for
classification.

To my wife, Jeanine,

who lived this as fully as I did,

but who sacrificed more along the way

CONTENTS

FOREWORD: WHY THIS BOOK?

I had just walked out into the glare of the hot sun of the Australian outback, made even more harsh by the darkened light and digital screens of the windowless operations floor I had just departed. I was in Pine Gap, almost in the middle of nowhere. When you land at the local airport and travel the short service road to the main highway, you are greeted by a road sign. The closest town, Alice Springs, is a little more than ten kilometers to the right. Go left and the next important land-mark, the near-mystic and locally sacred Ayers Rock (Uluru), is 450 kilo-meters away.

As we shielded our eyes from the sun, I turned to my Australian coun-terpart and asked if he ever wanted to explain to his citizens, and espe-cially to his critics, the quality of the work we had just witnessed inside the facility. Actually, I said something along the lines of "Wouldn't you love to be able to show people exactly what we do?" He quickly responded that he would.

Critics, observers, and just average citizens don't know as much about intelligence as they want or should. A goal of this book is to help ad-dress that.

Okay. We can't go to the outback, but we can go behind the scenes. These pages are my best effort to show to the American people what their intelligence services actually do on their behalf. No Jack Bauers or Jason Bournes here, though. Just hardworking and dedicated Americans whose labor deserves understanding, appreciation, and even occasional criticism. This is a memoir, so I have to tell the story through my eyes, but I hope those about whom I write see it as their story as well.

Of course, there are limits. Classification and such. Frankly, there are too many limits and that hurts the community I served and still love, and the republic it serves. But I have pushed as hard as prudence and the law (and CIA's Publications Review Board) allow.

Even with stops as an ROTC instructor and some stretches in policy, I can still rightly be described as a career intelligence officer: reading out satellite imagery as a lieutenant at Strategic Air Command headquarters; supporting B-52 operations in Southeast Asia from Guam; head of intelligence at a tactical fighter wing in Korea; an overt intelligence collector as air attaché in Communist Bulgaria; chief of intelligence for US forces in Europe during the Balkan Wars; commander of the air force's intelligence arm based in Texas.

I enjoyed nearly every minute of those jobs, but this book is less about them than about the last ten years of my government service, the decade I spent at the national level as director of the National Security Agency (DIRNSA), the first principal deputy director of National Intelligence (PDDNI), and director of the Central Intelligence Agency (DCIA).*

There were policy and international issues aplenty in those years (1999–2009), and most of them touched on and were touched by intelligence. Many are recounted here from the perspective I had from those positions. The narrative reflects the always important, but sometimes delicate, relationship between intelligence and the policy makers that it

---

* As opposed to the DCI. Prior to 2005, the director of CIA was also the head of the US intelligence community and called the director of Central Intelligence, or DCI. I just headed one agency, hence DCIA.

serves. There's a healthy dose also of the even more delicate relationship with congressional oversight.

There's a chapter or three on bureaucracy as well. After all, the budgets of the agencies I headed are measured in the billions of dollars, their personnel counts are in the tens of thousands, and their presence is global. Organization, budgets, and personnel decisions matter, not so much in their own right, but as enablers of performance and mission success. Getting the overall structure right has been a pursuit of American intelligence for more than a decade.

Anyone running a large organization will understand how limited the tools of a CEO or a commander or a director really are. He or she can move (or get more) money, move boxes on an organizational chart, change out people, and exhort and inspire. That's just about the whole toolbox. I've always found it difficult to actually finish reading a book on management or leadership, but I've nonetheless laid out my experiences here.

Then there's the spooky stuff—espionage, covert action, and the like. There's a lot of that even if there's more to be told that's not tellable now. A lot of the spooky stuff is about terrorism, but NSA and CIA have global responsibilities, so other topics will appear as well.

The telling is largely chronological, starting with events at NSA and proceeding through the ODNI (Office of the Director of National Intelligence) and CIA. Once engaged on a topic, though, I sometimes play it forward and play it back. The chapter on cyber, for example, comes naturally during my time at NSA, but to tell the tale properly I have to begin in Texas in the 1990s and play it forward through my time at CIA and beyond. There's some of that with detentions and interrogations too.

Since this is a memoir, its center of gravity is the past, which will perforce drag in issues like renditions, detentions, interrogations, and the badly mislabeled "domestic surveillance" program. But in the writing I was struck by how much my experiences pulled me toward the future, toward things like the cyber domain and its challenges, a domain of conflict and cooperation whose importance seems to grow by the hour.

And, perhaps even more important, I was pulled toward the challenge of the long-term relationship between American espionage and the American people in an era of shrinking trust in government and expanding global threats.

I could be accused of grading my own work, but I believe that despite our flaws, we're actually pretty good at this spy stuff. We need to preserve that capacity. The world is not getting any safer, and espionage remains our first line of defense.

The growing difficulty of that challenge helped prompt the title of this work: *Playing to the Edge.* The reference is to using all the tools and all the authorities available, much like how a good athlete takes advantage of the entire playing field right up to the sideline markers and endlines.

In espionage, that often proves controversial, and I fear we will not be able to do that in the future without our public's deeper understanding of what American intelligence is and does, without our doing (at least metaphorically) what I suggested to my Australian counterpart that sunny afternoon. So I committed to tell this story, a story shared by the thousands of folks with whom I have worked.

At bottom, it was a blessing to be part of such a noble enterprise.

ONE

THE SYSTEM IS DOWN

FORT MEADE, MD, 1999–2000

The call came after dinner on a cold Monday night, as I was watching the TV news at home. There was a computer problem at work. A software failure had knocked out the network of the National Security Agency.

"Give me a sense," I asked the duty officer over the secure line. "What are we talking about?"

"It's the *whole* system."

A result of overloading. One of my technicians later described us as victims of a "data storm." The sheer volume of collection had overwhelmed the capacity of our networks as they had been configured. It wasn't unlike a nor'easter overwhelming what seemed to be sturdy docks, breakwaters, and seawalls on the nearby Chesapeake Bay.

Not *entirely* our fault. NSA had experienced years of declining budgets, a shrinking workforce, an aging infrastructure, and little new hiring. Running hard just to keep up, we had let the network become so tangled that no one really seemed to know how it worked. There was no real wiring diagram anyone could consult. Picture Darren McGavin's character plugging in the tree in *A Christmas Story*. That was us.

It was January 24, 2000. I was a three-star air force general and I was just finishing my tenth month as DIRNSA, the director of the National Security Agency, America's largest and most powerful spy agency. I was still relatively new, but I didn't need the duty officer to explain the magnitude of the problem.

Signals intelligence, or SIGINT, is a continuous process, a kind of espionage production line where communications are collected, processed, analyzed, and reported twenty-four hours a day. At that moment satellites and earthbound collection points around the world were still intercepting communications, their vast take—telephone calls, faxes, radio signals— still pouring into memory buffers. But once in hand, the data froze. We couldn't move it. Nobody could access it. Nobody could analyze it. It wouldn't take long for intelligence consumers to notice something was wrong. They could tell it when their morning take showed up light or didn't show up at all. For all intents and purposes, NSA was brain-dead.

I nervously called George Tenet, the director of Central Intelligence, on a secure line and broke the news to him. There was nothing either of us could do but get out of the way and let the technicians try to figure out what was wrong. As keepers of the nation's secrets, we now had another one to keep—a secret Saddam Hussein or Osama bin Laden or any other enemy could have used to great advantage.

The next morning, the only consolation I had was the snow: a record blizzard had blasted the Washington area and shut down the federal government, giving our gathering army of computer engineers and techies some time—without the workforce around—to bring the agency out of its coma. But despair deepened as two full days passed without progress. The full complement of mathematicians and linguists and analysts reported back for duty Thursday morning, only to find a handwritten message taped to all of the doors and badge readers. With amazing understatement, we announced: "Our network is experiencing intermittent difficulties. Consult your supervisor before you log on."

The crash had now become a genuine security crisis. By noon, at a hastily called town meeting, I walked onto the stage of the agency's Friedman

Auditorium (named after a married couple, William and Elizabeth, both pioneers of American cryptology) and told thousands of employees—in person and on closed-circuit television—what had happened. "We are the keeper of the nation's secrets," I said at the end of my grim presentation. "If word of this gets out, we significantly increase the likelihood that Americans get hurt. Those who intend our nation and our citizens harm will be emboldened. So this is not the back half of a sentence tonight over washing the dishes that begins, 'Honey, you won't believe what happened to me at work today.' This is secret. It doesn't leave the building."

The computer crash was the perfect metaphor for an agency desperately in need of change. Antiquated computers were a problem. But the reality was actually worse.

NSA was in desperate need of reinvention. Heir to America's World War II code-breaking heroics, NSA was created in secret by Harry Truman in 1952. Many consider signals intelligence even more valuable than human intelligence or satellite imagery, because the quantity and quality of the potential take is so much greater.

But it's also fragile. Spies are often hard to ferret out, but an adversary can neuter even a carefully crafted SIGINT system by just hanging up the phone. Intercepting communications and breaking codes requires absolute secrecy, so NSA took secrecy to extremes. Most Americans had never even heard of the agency for decades after it was established.

And then many of them heard about it in the worst way. In 1975, a Senate committee headed by Senator Frank Church revealed that NSA had exceeded the foreign intelligence mission envisioned by Truman and had been spying domestically on the likes of Jane Fonda, Joan Baez, and Benjamin Spock.

The revelations led to laws and regulations that strictly limited what NSA could do, especially when it came to what the agency calls "US persons"; as a practical matter that meant anyone in the United States and US citizens anywhere. The agency lived by those rules, so much so that it came under criticism in later years for being too cautious.

The agency's success throughout the Cold War had rested on massive budgets, superior technology, and the luxury of having a single main adversary—the Soviet Union—that enjoyed neither of those first two advantages. Now all those pillars were crumbling. Still one of the largest employers in the state of Maryland, NSA had lost 30 percent of its budget and an equivalent slice of its workforce during the 1990s. And instead of one backward, oligarchic, technologically inferior, slow-moving adversary, the agency found itself trying to deploy against elusive terrorist groups, drug cartels, and rogue states, all using cell phones, the Internet, and modern communications technology. And that was in addition to the full slate of traditional targets like Russia and China and North Korea.

More and more communications were being encoded with powerful new commercial encryption that was proving virtually impossible to break. Then there was the exploding volume of global communications as more and more messages were moving through hard-to-tap fiber-optic cables. And broadband fiber-optic cables were being laid around the world at the rate of hundreds of miles an hour. The modern data stream was threatening to drown NSA in a roiling sea of 1s and 0s.

In this new world, it was private industry and commercial investment that fueled technological advances and NSA had been isolated from the dynamism of the market by its own cult of secrecy. In 1999, the House Permanent Select Committee on Intelligence declared that NSA was "in serious trouble," desperately short of capital and leadership. In my first meeting as DIRNSA with Porter Goss, the chairman of that committee, he told me, "General, you have to hit home runs in your first at bats."

At the same time, civil libertarians, privacy activists, and encryption entrepreneurs—not to mention the European Parliament and thousands, perhaps millions, of ordinary Europeans—questioned the continuing need for such an agency, describing NSA as an "extreme threat to the privacy of people all over the world," in the words of an American Civil Liberties Union Web site.

In 1997, two years before I became director, the European Parliament had commissioned a report on something called Echelon. That report had concluded that NSA and its Anglo-Saxon partners were capable of intercepting every fax, phone call, and e-mail in Europe and were stealing European companies' secrets and passing them on to their competitors.

Beyond industrial espionage, the Europeans also worried about individual privacy, because the US laws and regulations that keep NSA from spying on Americans provide no similar protections for foreigners. By 1999, this controversy had attracted the attention of civil libertarians in the United States, who were concerned about NSA spying once again on Americans.

The irony was powerful: NSA was an agency that was simultaneously being accused of omnipotence and incompetence. It was going deaf *and* it was reading all of your e-mails.

The computer crash in January only confirmed the worst fears about the agency's antiquated technology and its leaden bureaucracy. After my town hall meeting, I called all of the agency's top technicians and engineers together and told them just how serious the meltdown had become. The President's Daily Brief was getting pretty thin.

In reality, about a third of SIGINT production was continuing. That was the fraction produced by allies or by American collection stations that could do their own processing. But two-thirds was still sitting out there, fallow, in our buffers.

Tenet was still giving us plenty of room to fashion a solution, but pressure was building "downtown." The NSAers understood. As veterans who loved the agency, they understood perhaps even better than I.

Things began to break Thursday night. It happened to be my thirty-second wedding anniversary. That night, with the system showing some signs of life, I took my wife, Jeanine, to an inn west of Frederick called Stone Manor for dinner. On the drive home, Bob Stevens, the deputy director for technology, called to say that he needed to talk to me "secure." I called him back on a secure line as soon as I got home.

The system had been dysfunctional for more than seventy-two hours. It was back up to about 25 percent capacity, Stevens said, but he didn't think the techies were on the right path.

Multiple nodes were involved, each of them supporting different customers. We were trying to bring the network up node by node, prioritizing the most important ones. Parts of the network were recovering, but this was through extraordinary means that we could not sustain. We were not driving to a workable or stable solution. Everything was still fragile. We were accelerating down a dead-end street.

Bob wanted permission to take the entire system down and start all over again. He said that he needed to rationalize each of the nodes and to make them compatible with one another, not work them as one-offs.

I gave my OK, and with the system completely shut down, he began installing a massive hardware and software upgrade. By Friday morning, the system was coming back to life.

George Tenet came out to visit Friday night along with his deputy, General John Gordon, to personally thank the engineers who now looked like their eyeballs were about to fall out from fatigue. George was good at this. He personally and genuinely thanked them. There was mutual appreciation all around. America was back in the SIGINT business.

I owed George a lot too. I've always characterized my immediate superiors as transmitters, amplifiers, or buffers when it came to bureaucratic pressure coming at them. George was a buffer. He had also had his air assets fly through the blizzard earlier in the week to bring in some badly needed parts. We had trouble driving to the airport, but his guys flew through the storm. I met them later, worthy heirs of Air America, CIA's swashbuckling Vietnam-era air force.

The next day, Saturday, America's global SIGINT enterprise worked through the backlog. No coverage had been lost; all of it had been buffered at the point of collection. (Imagine the computer storage space that would have been required at our collection points if we really were vacuuming up everything out there, as some were alleging. The inherent contradiction went unnoticed.)

There was still two feet of snow on the ground, so I decided to unwind by cross-country skiing with my wife on Fort Meade's thirty-six-hole golf course. Near dusk, as we were gliding near one of the post's roads, an

NSA patrol car began to stalk us and then pulled ahead of us and stopped. An officer climbed out of the driver's seat, looked at me, and said, "Mr. Director? I need to take you to the ops center."

I hadn't had a patrol car stalk me since I was about thirteen years old. I threw my skis into the trunk and left Jeanine to slush home on her own.

ABC News' John McWethy had the story of our blackout. Secrecy had a short shelf life. He was going to go with the story that night and he wanted to talk with us.

With Tenet's reluctant permission, I confirmed that we had been down for about seventy-two hours, but were now up and running.

McWethy was skeptical: "That all sounds good, but how do I know that it's true?"

"Would I have taken your call if it wasn't, if we weren't back up?"

"Good point."

I watched the story that night on the evening news.

The blackout episode helped me better understand what was ahead of me. I had been cautious. NSA was a national treasure and my first task had been to do no harm. Now it was clear to me that no course of action I could set out on would be as dangerous to the agency as standing still.

Had I known what awaited me—and America—a year and a half down the road, I might have been even bolder.

But the broader lesson stuck. Caution isn't always a virtue. Not if you're serious about doing your duty.

TWO

A NATIONAL TREASURE . . .
FOR HOW MUCH LONGER?

FORT MEADE, MD, 2001–2005

I once described NSA as "a big ship with a small rudder." I could have added, "With a temporary captain and a temporary navigator."

I never expected to be DIRNSA, the director of the National Security Agency. I was in Korea in 1998, serving as the deputy chief of staff for US and UN forces there following command at the Air Intelligence Agency in Texas. The Korea post was not an intelligence job. As deputy chief of staff, I kept things running smoothly for the American commander in Seoul, stayed in touch with our Korean allies, and (in my UN role) negotiated with the North Koreans at the truce village of Panmunjom.

Such was my life when my wife interrupted my shower on a bright fall morning in Seoul to tell me that Mike Ryan, chief of staff of the air force, was on the phone.

"Mikey," he began, using a form of address he had developed for me a few years earlier when I headed up US intelligence in Europe and he was running the air war over the Balkans.

"Mikey, we're going to nominate you to be the director of NSA. You're not going to get it, but we'll bring you back, you can make the rounds, and then you'll be well positioned when the director of DIA [Defense Intelligence Agency] position comes open next summer. That's the one we're really shooting for."

Not exactly a ringing vote of confidence, but at least the chief was interested in my career, and I was happy enough to get a trip home. Actually it was a circumnavigation. I flew to Hawaii for a promotion board, continued to Washington for the job interview, and then went on to Geneva as the Korea Command representative to the four-party talks between China, the United States, and the two Koreas before I returned to Seoul.

I had only one interview for the DIRNSA job. It was with George Tenet at the Wye River Plantation on the Eastern Shore of Maryland as Tenet was shuttling back and forth between Yasser Arafat and Bibi Netanyahu trying to broker a peace deal in the Middle East.

I was picked up from Bolling Air Force Base, where I was staying, and climbed into the backseat of one of those large black Suburbans that seem to populate most spy movies. We crossed the Chesapeake Bay Bridge, and the security detail deposited me in one of the Wye Plantation's spare lodges, where I awaited the DCI and fought off jet lag.

George came in about an hour later, all energy, seemingly happy to talk about something other than Israel and Palestine. I had not met him before, but the conversation was relaxed. We talked about intelligence in general and a bit about NSA in particular; since I had never served there, I relied a lot on what I had learned at the air force component of NSA, the Air Intelligence Agency, which I had commanded in Texas in 1996–1997.

About a month later, now back in Korea, I learned that I was going to be the next director of NSA. I doubt that I had overwhelmed George, but his new deputy was air force general John Gordon, and John and I had served in the same office on Bush 41's National Security Council staff. Stuff like that happens in Washington.

Before my appointment was publicly announced, my wife and I took in a Friday night movie at the Yongsan army garrison base theater. It was

packed with GIs for the popular thriller *Enemy of the State*, in which Will
Smith battles an omniscient and malevolent National Security Agency.
As the plot twists and turns, a career NSA civilian aspiring to the deputy
director position actually kills a US senator. I was sinking into my seat as
my wife whispered in my ear, "What did *you* have to do for this job?"

I was sworn in for the NSA job in late March 1999. The day after
the ceremony, my new agency put me into a reclining chair, hooked up
sensors to my body, and asked a series of questions about my trustwor-
thiness. All of NSA's people have to be polygraphed. It's the cost of admission. And if Snuffy has to do it, so does the new director. Apparently, I
passed.

I arrived during NATO's bombing campaign in Kosovo. The agency
was providing solid direct support for the combat operations, as it had
done in the Gulf War eight years earlier. Nothing surprising there. NSA
was a national treasure. Since its founding by President Truman in 1952,
it had been tasked, broadly speaking, with intercepting communications
that contain information that would help keep Americans free and safe
and advance our country's vital national security interests. That is mostly
the communications of adversaries, but it could also include the communications of others, not protected by the Constitution's Fourth Amendment (which is not, after all, an international treaty), who happen to be
talking about things we need to know. Picture the foreign travel agent
innocently passing on the travel schedule of a terrorist or an arms traf-
ficker.

NSA's closest counterpart is its best friend, Britain's GCHQ, which is
only about one-fifth its size.

By 1999, though, NSA had a problem, as we have seen. It had grown up
in an era in which it was the lead for a host of computer and telecommunications breakthroughs. But the outside world had passed it by in many
areas. John Millis, who headed up the House staff overseeing the agency,
commented that "technology has been the friend of the NSA, but in the
last four or five years technology has moved from being the friend to being
the enemy." The cultural habits built up in a world where the trouble with

SIGINT was that there was too little, and it was too hard to get, were now counterproductive in a world where the trouble was in the category of too much, too hard to understand. NSA was appropriately obsessive about secrecy, but the gates and high walls that provided twentieth-century security cut the agency off from innovation as it approached the millennium.

Then there was the question of the director, described as "Christmas help" by one senior* (and he was a friend). Even in a public setting it was not unusual for NSA leaders to refer to the occupant of the eighth-floor suite as "the *current* director." It was a challenge for a career military officer to sit atop a pile of civil servants who knew that they were right and everyone else was wrong, and who were fully capable of and well practiced at waiting out change that they opposed. That description didn't apply to everyone, but it applied to enough.

Former director Bobby Ray Inman is a revered figure at NSA. (I once compared his status in retirement to that of the reverence shown to the off-camera Randolph Scott in Mel Brooks's *Blazing Saddles*.) Early on, I made a pilgrimage to Austin to seek Inman's advice. He warned me about the isolation of the eighth-floor director's office. "They'll want to put you in a sedan chair, carry you around like Pharaoh, and keep you as far away from decisions as possible."

It's an opaque place too. Rather than calling an office, say, the Balkans collection division, that shop is given an impenetrable alphanumeric designator. NSA employees routinely answer the phone with the last four digits of the office number: "3685. Can I help you?" That's all good operational security, but it makes the place hard to understand, even from the inside. One officer later told me that I tried to penetrate the workforce like the agency tried to penetrate a target. I spent one of my first Saturdays just walking through the empty halls trying to decipher office symbols and locations.

---

* The American intelligence community has a near-impenetrable maze of abbreviations to describe civilians whose rank is comparable to that of general in the armed forces: SIS, SES, DISES, DISL. Collectively they are just referred to as "seniors."

And the agency had a pretty fixed culture. A veteran compared the prevailing views to that of Tevye in *Fiddler on the Roof*: "Tradition!" In the face of unprecedented change and challenge, tradition was comforting, tradition was stabilizing.

But outside observers believed that NSA was a burning platform. A group called the SSCI TAG (the Senate Intelligence Committee's technical advisory group) was composed of high-tech gurus who warned that only about ten years of global technological advance separated the agency from operational deafness, and the clock was running.

For a signals intelligence agency, we had surprisingly antiquated IT systems, both for ourselves and to target our adversaries. Shortly after I arrived, I asked, "How do I send an e-mail to everybody?"

"Oh, we can't actually do that," was the response.

"But didn't we kinda invent the computer here?"

On the mission side, according to one estimate, 70 percent to 80 percent of reporting was still coming off traditional voice intercepts. But even here we weren't keeping up. Al-Qaeda and other targets were migrating to a new form of satellite communication. Chasing the signal required an infrastructure investment that NSA refused to make, so CIA did it on its own. When that agency briefed me on its program, I asked, "What measure of NSA sin would have caused you guys to build your own SIGINT system?"

And this was in a world in which digital communications—e-mails and the like—were also exploding. NSA largely went after non-voice data only when it was encrypted (suggesting its importance) and even then largely in fax and telex rather than e-mails.

Prior to this, e-mails had been generally limited, dedicated, point-to-point communications that came to a program loaded on your machine. Without the appropriate software, you could neither read nor send a message. We were now on the cusp of Web-based e-mail systems that promised far greater convenience and thus far greater volumes. Toying with the old point-to-point e-mails had us shooting way behind the target.

Trying to escape the tyranny of expertise (aka the existing organizational structure), I sought opinions from an outside group of experts and a group of young Turks from within the agency. They gave me a variety of recommendations and observations, the most telling of which was that the agency was less than the sum of its parts (many of which, they emphasized, were really quite good).

The outside gang went out of its way to be generous, commenting on NSA's world-class competencies, its critical role, its response to crises, and the agency's deep commitment to the institution and its people. It then catalogued poor systems for communication, decision making, financial and personnel management, requirements development, and business processes. It predicted rapid technological obsolescence, the product of an inward-looking culture and a leadership team that many (including some of the leadership team) believed was not up to the challenge.

The inside group, the "New Enterprise Team," was equally scathing. They began their report with a quote from Darwin on the relationship between adaptability and survival. Then they hammered the institution and its leadership, saying that NSA's customers had already begun to separate NSA's products and services (which they still treasured) from NSA the institution, which they now viewed as a threat to the continued availability of those products and services. The workforce, they said, had been carrying the agency on its back for a decade.

They agreed that we lacked leadership, a strategic plan, a decision-making process, and the ability to manage our resources. What we did have, they pointed out, was a lot of committees. One of their "quick hits" was to eliminate all working groups and committees where a single individual could make decisions. I eliminated all of them by fiat and then challenged chairmen to petition for reinstatement if they still thought the panel was essential. When we were done, we had cut over a third of an amazing total of more than 450 *internal* panels.

Next was the inevitable reorganization; it's what government agencies do, after all. And there's a reason for that. Given cumbersome restrictions on budgets and personnel, there really aren't a lot of other tools available.

I tried to simplify things on the organizational chart, identifying two large operational boxes, one for offense (SID, the SIGINT Directorate) and one for defense (IAD, the Information Assurance Directorate). We pulled enabling functions—things like research, IT, training, logistics, human resources—out of the operating units and moved them to direct reports under me. Flattening the organization that way gave me a challenging span of control, but also let me directly use these agency-wide support activities as tools for change.

One office that was critical to get to my level was the Foreign Affairs Directorate. We had lots of partners, but for all but a few of them, relationships were managed at a fairly low operational level and decisions about them were largely based on whether or not the affected NSA office felt they needed any summer help. I wanted these ties based on strategic considerations, not just on who could or could not cover discrete targets, languages, or radio frequencies.

All the reorganization helped, but the real plus was the chance to put new leaders into a bunch of the newly created posts. We reached deep within the ranks, betting that most of these promising rookies would learn to hit a major-league curve ball soon enough. Most did.

We institutionalized that approach, setting up a one-man senior personnel shop just down the hall from my office. Federal bureaucracies are dedicated to *process* in promotions and assignments, committee upon committee deciding who advances, when, and to what job. That's designed to reduce favoritism (and lawsuits) and to enhance stability. We didn't want stability; we wanted disruption, and I was hell-bent to favor some over others.

We eased out a whole generation of leadership and skipped over a big chunk of their obvious successors. These were good people. They didn't deserve this. At the time, I thought of air force general Curtis LeMay's legendary ruthlessness when it came to shortcomings. "I can't tell the difference between unlucky and unskilled because the results are the same," he once said. I knew that these people were quite skilled, just unlucky. It was a tribute to the agency and to these individuals that they handled this with grace, even though their only offense was being at the wrong place at the wrong time.

My most disruptive choice was my new deputy director. Barbara McNamara was in the position when I arrived and stayed on until June 2000. Barbara was career NSA and loved the agency with every inch of her being. She had started as a linguist and worked her way up the ranks. She was tough as nails and took nothing from her male counterparts. Her middle initial was "A," and her signing off on countless papers over the years caused everyone to address her simply as BAM.

Barbara was badly treated in a November 1999 *New Yorker* article by Seymour Hersh, he of My Lai exposé fame and chaser of real and imagined scandals ever since. The lengthy article was a pretty stern critique of where NSA stood (accurate enough), but it then singled out McNamara. "Hayden gets it," Hersh quoted one intelligence committee aide. "But he's parachuted in there, and faced with a deputy director whose job is to foil what the director wants to do."

Not true, but Barbara would never be a ruthless change agent; she was approaching three years in the job, and as a thorough Anglophile she was happy to end her career representing us in London to our British partner.

There was talent in the senior leadership, but no obvious choice for a new deputy, and there was no one in the lot who was close to being the bomb thrower I wanted. So I scoured the alumni association for anyone who had left recently and who had left angry. Bill Black's name quickly popped up. Bill had been my predecessor's special assistant for information warfare (see chapter 8) and had resigned from the agency three years earlier. Since entering NSA in 1959, he had been at the heart of the agency's traditional mission targeting the Warsaw Pact, but he had been frustrated by the slow pace of transformation to a new age. He was also a bureaucratic knife fighter; if he was deputy, I knew he would have my back.

I invited Bill to lunch at a nondescript Korean restaurant outside the back gate of Fort Meade. Over bulgogi and kimchi we covered the state of the agency and his views on what could be done about it. He was firm, but not especially vindictive. It went well. My executive assistant, who was with us, later said that I was the most relaxed she had ever seen me during the meal.

We chose the off-base Korean restaurant to keep all of this quiet. But NSA as a social group permeates eastern Maryland. The next day Bill received an e-mail from a retiree in California asking him how his lunch with the director had gone.

Bill was the choice, but I had one last question. I invited him to my base quarters for a Sunday dinner for just the two of us. My wife was traveling, so I opted for simple roasted vegetables over couscous.

I told Bill that I wanted him to be the deputy, but I had one concern. I knew he could make things happen; he was notorious for his back-channel expertise. "But, Bill," I said, "we've got to institutionalize this. This has to work even if you and I don't show up for work." He agreed. We had a deal.

Bill was a great choice. He stayed on for six years and served as acting director after I left. I owe him a great debt. After 9/11, though, in a private moment, I confessed that up to then I should have been thanking him for being there. "Now," I said, "you need to thank me." He didn't argue. He would have died of frustration if he were confined outside after the attack.

To reinforce the shake-up, we hired from the outside to create crosscurrents within our own culture. We were being intentionally disruptive. At the time, I didn't think there was sufficient expertise in the private sector to delegate mission responsibility to newcomers from the outside, so I didn't. The closest I got to that was the 2000 decision to outsource our IT to a private consortium in the $2 billion ten-year Groundbreaker program.

In retrospect, I may have missed an opportunity, since American industry was already breaking new ground in what came to be called the cyber domain, and the more I learned, the stronger the parallels became.

But my caution certainly did *not* apply to a host of support tasks. The new chief financial officer came from Legg Mason, the Baltimore investment firm. We got our new inspector general via an ad in the *Wall Street Journal.* We created the position of senior acquisition authority and filled it with a former deputy assistant secretary of the navy with thirty-five years of acquisition experience. The chief information officer came from the Federal Trade Commission (and NASA). The chief of legislative affairs had been an executive assistant on the Hill for five years.

We even went outside for some direct mission support tasks. Working through a member of the advisory board who was an Academy Award winner in Hollywood, we recruited our new chief of research from the R&D department at Walt Disney Imagineering.

Another advisory board member with deep experience in telecommunications hooked us up with a tech- and business-savvy outsider who became our chief of IT. I interviewed him personally, without fanfare, then simply introduced him and his mandate to a meeting of seniors still trying to decipher the IT meltdown of January 2000.

There was nothing easy about this. We had to transform, but I didn't want to make war on the agency either, and I certainly did not think that I was the anointed one sent to bring it salvation.

I think I was open to advice, but I had to decide on my own. Folks were candid and insightful, but in an organization as compartmented as NSA, most people viewed issues from their own vantage point and not the broader field of view I had from my office. We had to get off the *X* of inaction,* and waiting to build consensus or accommodating all concerns would have been a killer.

I had to be really careful with my language. I had been at NSA less than a year; a lot of people had been there (and usually nowhere else) for decades. I always used first person plural: "We're going to do this." "We're going to try that." Never first person singular. And never, never, never second person. The routine use of "you" would have deepened the chasm that was always threatening to open between me and a talented workforce.

Beginning in November 1999, I communicated regularly in a series of director's e-mails that we called DIRGRAMs to announce and explain

---

* The *X* in this case is the point of maximum vulnerability. A common phrase in the intelligence community is "We have to get off the *X* here."

changes and keep an open line for comments and critiques in return. By the time I left in spring 2005, I had issued over four hundred. This made sure that the message got through unfiltered and probably accelerated our pace, but as a career military officer I knew that I was jumping the chain of command, communicating directly with all echelons, eroding the real or perceived authority of intervening layers of leadership.

NOT ALL OF OUR PROBLEMS were internal or self-inflicted. We also had a public relations problem that threatened our future. Even as some members of Congress and outside experts were accusing us of incompetence and being on a path to deafness, some civil libertarians and European parliamentarians were characterizing us as omniscient, stealing industrial secrets and invading personal privacy. The catchphrase for all of this was Echelon, to the Europeans an Anglo-Saxon cabal to steal economic advantage; to groups like the American Civil Liberties Union, "[T]he government . . . once again spying on American's private communications."

Never officially or precisely defined, the concept of Echelon was a convenient all-purpose bogeyman for any critic who wanted an audience. The transatlantic handwringers seemed to reinforce one another even if their grievances weren't exactly the same.

The American handwringers were more important to us. We had to take them head-on. We needed more money, and we weren't going to get it unless the American people and their elected representatives had a level of trust in us. Trust was especially important, since we were telling our overseers that the signals we were going to chase were no longer confined to isolated target networks, but were on international networks commingled with other, innocent communications, including those of Americans.

As for the Europeans, they were a self-righteous nuisance; I refused to meet with them. They spent more time researching us than their own security services, several of which actually did conduct economic espionage. And the reason that they researched us was that American espionage is far more transparent than European. Talk about looking for your car keys under the lamppost. I suppose we were a little contemptuous. Looking back now, that still feels about right.

We convinced Porter Goss, chairman of the House Intelligence Committee, to hold an open hearing on all this. In April 2000, George Tenet and I testified, as did Congressman Bob Barr, a Georgia Republican passionately committed to civil liberties.

In front of a packed gallery for a full two hours, both George and I freely admitted that we collected information on foreign businesses when it came to things like arms sales, chemical trading, money laundering, and drug trafficking. But we adamantly denied that NSA spied on European companies to collect industrial secrets and pass them on to US companies.

I talked about the challenges NSA faced because of the volume and variety of modern communications and the velocity with which they changed. Anticipating the cyber challenges then beginning to unfold, I said, "Our ability to collect may have increased, but it has increased at a pace far slower and smaller than the explosion of the ones and zeros that are out there."

With regard to US privacy, I stressed our lawfulness and observed that if Osama bin Laden crossed the bridge from Niagara Falls, Ontario, to Niagara Falls, New York, provisions of US law would kick in, offer him protection, and affect how we could cover him. At the time, I was using this is a stark hypothetical. Seventeen months later it was about life and death.

EVEN IF WE SUCCEEDED in building some public trust and squeezing a few more dollars out of Congress, we still had the technical challenge of signals that were growing more complex, more numerous, and more encrypted. How to tackle that?

Our answer was Trailblazer. This much-maligned (not altogether unfairly) effort was more a venture capital fund than a single program, with our investing in a variety of initiatives across a whole host of needs. What we wanted was an architecture that was common across our mission elements, interoperable, and expandable. It was about ingesting signals, identifying and sorting them, storing what was important, and then quickly retrieving data in response to queries.

And all of this at speeds and volumes no one had ever seen before. One very prominent captain of the IT industry visited me in my office one evening, and when we explained our volume challenge to him, he slowly exhaled before observing that what we were discussing was bigger than anything he had ever encountered.

Despite his caution, we still believed it was important to engage industry on this, even though it stretched industry with its technological challenges and stressed our ability to manage a contract with deliverables beyond just billing for time expended and materials consumed.

Our program office had a logical progression in mind: begin with a concept definition phase, then move to a technology demonstration platform to show some initial capability and to identify and reduce technological risk. Limited production and then phased deployment would follow.

It looked good on paper, and there is no doubt that we got a lot out of the effort, more than just by-products like Velcro and Tang in NASA's space program. Trailblazer advances were integrated into mission systems, and they contribute to this day.

But there is also no doubt that the overall results were disappointing and took far longer than we wanted. We found that when we went to industry for things they already knew how to do, we got impressive results. When we went to them for things nobody had done yet, we found that at best they weren't much better or faster than we were. And that was true even with a team that included such defense giants as SAIC, Boeing, CSC, AT&T, and Booz Allen Hamilton.

We were also trying to do too much, too quickly. Trailblazer comprised multiple moon shots. We ended up like a lot of big federal IT programs—like the FBI's Virtual Case File and DOD's Navy Marine

Corps Intranet. We would have been better advised to pick our spots and work incrementally, trusting to spiral development to eventually get us to where we wanted to be.

We also had to deal with guerrilla warfare. There was a group of talented technologists within the agency who had developed a tool, Thin Thread, to collect and sort metadata (the facts of a communication such as number calling, number called, time, duration, and the like) and then to point analysts to the rich veins of SIGINT ore within a mountain of information.

Thin Thread wasn't the program of record when I arrived at the agency. I didn't make it the program of record during my time there, and neither did my successor. We all could have been wrong, of course, but we had our reasons.

Thin Thread technology included e-mails, which was very good, since the volume of global e-mails was about to take off. It had a good packet processor, which meant it could assemble the individual packets that comprise e-mail messaging. It also had very good "session reconstruction," which enabled it to put communications back together from the individual packets.

A third aspect of Thin Thread was software to actually detect meaningful traffic via the metadata of a massive communications stream (e-mail or voice). By studying the pattern, frequency, and length of calls, the system intended to point to the communications whose *content* should be explored. Of course, all data streams are different, so the system had to be trained within a particular data stream to pick out the valuable from the other information flowing by.

We gave it a try and deployed a prototype to Yakima, a foreign satellite (FORNSAT) collection site in central Washington State. Training the system on only one target (among potentially thousands) took several months, and then it did not perform much better than a human would have done. There were too many false positives, indications of something of intelligence value when that wasn't really true. A lot of human intervention was required.

As a FORNSAT site, Yakima was also dealing with a data stream nowhere near the volume of modern cable traffic. A good rule of thumb for FORNSAT speed is about 150 megabits per second. Microwave intercept pushes you over 600. We expected cables, where most traffic was now going, to have multiple strands of fiber, each working at a minimum of 10 gigabits per second, each about 70 times the FORNSAT pace. Even if Thin Thread had performed better, the requirements of space and power for the system would have made applying Thin Thread technology to the mass data flows of cable cost-prohibitive.

The best summary I got from my best technical minds was that aspects of Thin Thread were elegant, but it just wouldn't scale. NSA has many weaknesses, but rejecting smart technical solutions is not one of them. In the end, parts of Thin Thread were merged with parts of Trailblazer to create new systems that were indeed quite successful and were used for years.

But the developers of Thin Thread, Bill Binney, Kirk Wiebe, and Ed Loomis, were messianic in their approach, and they had an ally in Diane Roark, a staffer from HPSCI (House Permanent Select Committee on Intelligence) who monitored the NSA account. They were later joined by Tom Drake, a senior outside hire who entered the agency almost as the twin towers were crumbling.

The alliance with HPSCI staffer Roark created some unusual dynamics. I essentially had several of the agency's technicians going outside the chain of command to aggressively lobby a congressional staffer to overturn programmatic and budget decisions that had gone against them internally. That ran counter to my military experience—to put it mildly.

In April 2000 I sent a message to the workforce that laid out my thoughts. I was simultaneously angry and careful. "Some individuals, in a session with our congressional overseers," I began, "took a position in direct opposition to one that we had corporately decided to follow. This misleads the Congress regarding our agency's direction and resolve. The corporate decision was made after much data gathering, analysis, debate, and thought. Actions contrary to our decisions will have a serious adverse effect on our efforts to transform NSA and I cannot tolerate them."

After endorsing full participation in our internal decision-making process, I went on to say that "once a corporate decision has been reached, I expect everyone to execute the decision to the best of their ability. I do not expect sheepish acquiescence, but I do expect the problems necessitating course corrections will be handled within these walls."

I then reminded everyone that "openness and candor are critical to our future success and I do not want anyone dealing other than with total honesty with our congressional monitors. Further, anyone suspecting that any activities at NSA constitute a violation of law, regulation, or ethics must notify proper authorities. However, when policy, resource, or operational decisions are properly arrived at and promulgated by agency authorities I expect each of us to carry out their part of the program."

The note was unclassified, so the Hill was certainly aware. Surprisingly, the phone didn't ring. They had their responsibilities. I had mine.

Most never saw the whole Thin Thread dispute as anything other than a technical argument; I never encountered any other senior who seemed to think or act otherwise. But the small group of passionate Thin Thread supporters have elevated this into a sort of digital age morality play.

First of all, they claimed a kind of operational equivalency and then compared their program's relatively modest price tag with Trailblazer's substantial costs. Even if it had been able to scale, Thin Thread was addressing a fraction of the issues that Trailblazer was designed to take on. The comparison is specious.

Since then, they have also argued fraud, waste, and abuse, pointing not only to Trailblazer's troubled procurement history, but to the fact that SAIC, where Bill Black had worked while away from the agency, was the prime contractor on Trailblazer's technology demonstration platform. SAIC is indeed where Bill worked—and where he left when I asked him to come back to serve—but that had nothing to do with the contracting process.

Finally, Binney, Roark, Wiebe, Drake, and Loomis have claimed an ethical and legal superiority. Binney has flatly accused NSA of lying. In 2012 he charged that "George Bush, Dick Cheney, Tenet, and Hayden combined to subvert the Constitution, the constitutional process, and any number of laws."

Such comments gained steam and a larger audience after NSA's retention of American metadata was made public by Edward Snowden. Thin Thread would have made all of that unnecessary, they argued.

I don't see how, even setting aside the operational issues. They argued that Thin Thread would have collected the data but would have immediately encrypted it and would have made it accessible only through strict protocols. But the issue with NSA's retention of massive amounts of American metadata was *not* that NSA had misused it, but rather that NSA *had* it, a condition that would not be ameliorated by encrypting it.

Sometime before 9/11, the Thin Thread advocates approached NSA's lawyers. The lawyers told them that no system could *legally* do with US data what Thin Thread was designed to do. Thin Thread was based on the broad collection of metadata that would of necessity include foreign-to-foreign, foreign-to-US, and US-to-foreign communications. In other words, a lot of US person data swept up in routine NSA collection.

But NSA's protocols required that US person information be filtered out at every step of the intelligence process. Avoid collecting it if possible; if collected, avoid retaining it, and so on. Thin Thread required collecting, retaining, and then *using* US information for its success.

Binney and company insisted that encrypting and controlling access to the US data solved this problem; they told us that Roark, NSA's overseer, agreed. NSA's lawyers didn't, and when they briefed the House Intelligence Committee's staff, the lawyers from both sides of the aisle sided with the agency.

It wasn't that we weren't trying. As we approached the millennium with 1999 rolling over to 2000, we were all deeply concerned about a potential terrorist attack in the homeland. Our fears were justified; an alert border agent later detained a terrorist trying to enter the country on a ferry in Puget Sound.

At NSA, we were pulling out all the stops. The operations folks were proposing a new course of action. Like all of us, they were concerned about terrorists entering or already inside the homeland. The head of operations wanted to try the Thin Thread approach, retain US metadata that we were collecting in our foreign intelligence activities, encrypt it, limit access to it through a kind of "two key" protocol, and then (when indicated) chain through the metadata to other contacts.

It was operationally sound, but my lawyers remained very suspicious of its legality. They demanded a meeting with me. After a session with both the ops and legal teams present, I decided to force the issue. "Press Justice," I said. "Tell them we want to do this."

Let me be clear. This was me arguing for a limited use of the Thin Thread approach prior to 9/11.

The answer from Justice was also clear: "You know you can't do this." When that was reported back to the HPSCI staff, Roark accused NSA of just not being forceful enough with Justice, a charge that brought a barely suppressed laugh from a Democratic staffer.

So Thin Thread did not moot the US person issue, as some later claimed when condemning President Bush's Stellarwind program (chapter 5). The US person issue was mooted only after the president in *that* program specifically authorized NSA to acquire US metadata after the 9/11 attacks. That would indeed prove a controversial decision (controversial even though NSA continued to acquire US metadata through the summer of 2015), but Thin Thread would have required a similar authorization. Inexplicably (at least to me), the Thin Thread team has continued to hold up its approach as a lawful alternative to the president's "unlawful" Stellarwind.

Put bluntly, prior to President Bush authorizing Stellarwind, Thin Thread's intricacies and processes did not meet the requirements of US law. After Stellarwind was launched, Thin Thread's scalability problems simply caused us to choose a different system.

Thin Thread's advocates filed an IG (inspector general) complaint against Trailblazer in 2002. After I had left NSA, in late 2005, Siobhan Gorman published a series of articles in the *Baltimore Sun* bitterly critical of Trailblazer. They were later sourced to Tom Drake, who had apparently already despaired in 2005 that the new DIRNSA, Keith Alexander, would reverse course on Thin Thread. The subsequent FBI investigation of the leak led to heavy-handed raids on the homes of practically everyone in the Thin Thread group. Drake was later indicted under the Espionage Act, a heavy and blunt instrument, and not surprisingly, the case ultimately collapsed of its own weight.

To be clear, I had nothing to do with that. I didn't even file the crimes report that precipitated the investigation. Drake overstepped and the rest of them were a pain in the ass, but that's hardly grounds to ruin lives. This was a matter better handled administratively, like revoking clearances, for example.

The Thin Thread folks weren't done, though. When a team of Americans went to Moscow in 2013 to present Edward Snowden with the Sam Adams Award for Integrity in Intelligence, Tom Drake was in the group.

Then in the summer of 2014, Drake and Binney showed up in front of the German Bundestag's commission looking into NSA's activities there. Binney asserted that "they [NSA] want to have information about everything. This is really a totalitarian approach. The goal is control of the people." Drake, after claiming that NSA wanted to punish Germany for harboring the 9/11 hijackers, added that NSA's "monitoring regime has grown into a system that is strangling the world."

Like I said, they were messianic. I wonder what they would have been like if we had bought their widget.

THREE

GOING TO WAR . . . WITH SOME HELP FROM OUR FRIENDS

FORT MEADE, MD, 2001–2003

We all remember that Tuesday morning, crystal clear, not a cloud in the sky along the East Coast. September 11, 2001, the end of the world as we knew it. I had stayed up late watching *Monday Night Football*. The game was in Denver, the opening of the Broncos' new stadium, and I was coming into my office on about six hours' sleep. I started around 7:00 a.m., as I always did, this day running down to the agency barbershop for a quick haircut. On the way back I stopped at my operations center, the NSOC, for an update. Pretty normal. Nothing special on the horizon.

Back in the office, I was working my way through some routine appointments when my executive assistant, Cindy Farkus, came in and said, "A plane hit the World Trade Center." Like practically everyone else, I thought it must have been an accident, probably a small plane, and I continued with my meeting. Then Cindy came in again and said, "A plane hit the other tower."

"OK—get the head of security up here," I responded as I adjourned the meeting. Just as Kemp Ensor, the security chief, was coming through my office door, Cindy came in again and said, "There are reports of explosions on the Mall," a garbled version of the third plane hitting the Pentagon. Ensor still hadn't said a word. "Tell everyone, all nonessential personnel, to evacuate," I ordered.

I then directed that those remaining (probably more than five thousand) move out of the two high-rise headquarters buildings and into the original ops building, a long, low-riding three-story structure that would present a tougher target for an aircraft. That's where my ops center was, so I moved there as well.

My executive assistant came with me. The rest of the office staff evacuated, but before they did, one of them, Cindy Finifter, who religiously kept my calendar, hammered out an entry in her log:

NOTE: ATTACK ON AMERICA—EARLY DISMISSAL—
PM MEETINGS WERE CANCELLED

Attack on America. DCI George Tenet called me before the morning was out, asking what we had. Like everyone else in the intelligence community (IC),* we knew it was al-Qaeda, but I had the benefit of having real evidence and was able to report that we were getting the communications equivalent of celebratory gunfire on al-Qaeda networks. George responded with a resigned "Yeah."

One group that we could not move out of the high-rise buildings was our counterterrorism team. Fort Meade is more than just the headquarters of NSA; it's also its biggest field station, and a significant portion of America's SIGINT is produced there every day—including its counterterrorism intercepts and reports, and this was one team whose work we could *not* disrupt to move it to a safer location.

---

* IC (pronounced "eye-see") refers to the confederation of sixteen agencies now more or less under the direction of the director of National Intelligence (DNI). The community ranges from well-known members like NSA and CIA to more obscure ones like the small intelligence shops in the Drug Enforcement Administration or the Department of Energy.

It was getting close to dusk when I went up to their offices. Most of the team were Arab American, so the national and professional trauma of the attacks was even more personal for them.

They were hard at work. I didn't interrupt them. I just walked from station to station, not even pausing for them to take their headsets off, gripping a shoulder, nodding my head, an occasional "hang in there" or words to that effect.

While I was there the maintenance staff was tacking up blackout curtains over the windows. It felt surreal. Blackout curtains in eastern Maryland in the twenty-first century.

When I finally got home that night, my wife was waiting for me and gave me a warm hug. We joined the national mourning as we both broke into tears. I had not spoken to her since a quick call that morning asking her to locate our adult kids. She had taken calls from her mother and from my brother and had assured them that I was not at the Pentagon when the plane hit.

There, in our hallway, Jeanine and I acknowledged that tomorrow was going to be a very different day.

It was, and so were all the days after it during my time at NSA. For one thing, with more people and more money and a relentless focus, we could mass our resources on decisive points. On 9/11 we had about 250 mission areas we were required to cover. Within weeks of the attacks and without objection I had suspended over 10 percent of them and degraded another quarter. Increased resources and focus also allowed us to accelerate the transformation already under way. The week of the attack, I asked our gathered seniors what effect 9/11 should have on our transformation program. Their bottom line was, "Change nothing. Accelerate everything."

There was anger as well as resolve in our response. Before the week of 9/11 was out, I could see bumper stickers all over CIA with the last known words of Todd Beamer, one of the heroes of Flight 93 over Pennsylvania: "Let's roll." Jeanine suggested a similar theme for NSA after we unwound late one night looking at a replay of a national concert commemorating 9/11 losses. It was Tom Petty's "I Won't Back Down." With Mr. Petty's generous permission, we plastered NSA facilities around the world with the thought and the music for the next several years.

Operationally, the counterterrorism chiefs at NSA narrowed their work down to three clear tasks: follow the money (terrorist financing); follow the stuff (arms, precursor chemicals, and the like); and, above all, follow the people.

SIGINT was invaluable for this. Time and again the intercept of communications told us what we needed to know. An example: Eliza Manningham-Buller, head of Britain's MI5, called me in March 2004 after her service and the British police had raided twenty-four locations, made eight arrests, and confiscated half a ton of ammonium nitrate. She thanked me for the NSA SIGINT that was an "absolutely crucial building block for the whole operation."

I put that out to the entire NSA workforce and got a grateful e-mail in return. It seems that a local Maryland radio station had been waxing eloquent about the British takedown, contrasting it to the bumbling ways of American intelligence. The e-mail writer had been understandably offended and was very heartened to learn of the NSA role. It was a reminder that, in intelligence, you often don't get to publicly sign your own work.

In pursuit of terrorists, we also mastered geolocation and metadata, a bit different from traditional reporting on the *content* of targeted terrorist, diplomatic, or even military communications. If you had enough metadata—the pattern of how a communications device was used (whom did it call, who called it, when, for how long)—you could pretty much determine what the owner of a device was up to. Some of this would later be the topic of debate when it came to collecting American metadata, but here it enabled NSA to burrow in on a dirty phone and determine its user and his contacts even with limited knowledge of content. Then, using all the tools available, we could precisely fix *where* the phone was.

We had struck pay dirt, almost haphazardly, early on in Afghanistan, killing an al-Qaeda leader and several of his lieutenants as they were fleeing Kabul. The strike was enabled by combining imagery and intercepts in real time. After I was briefed on the operation, I asked, "Why can't we do that all the time?" and put some bright minds on figuring out how to institutionalize the approach.

We set up an effort, the Geocell, staffed it with smart young folks, teamed them up with imagery analysts from the National Geospatial-Intelligence Agency (NGA), and then wired them directly to tactical units in the field.

Old SIGINTers will tell you that this was just a version of what they used to call traffic analysis. If it was, it was on a massive dose of steroids.

We put the Geocell in the basement among the heating ducts, fork-lifts, supplies, and other detritus of our industrial base. When visitors passed through the cypher-locked door and entered the secure work area, though, they could see huge screens with current imagery and watch Fort Meade analysts in multiple chat rooms throughout the war zone, advising combat forces in real time and living up to their self-described role: "We track 'em, you whack 'em."

In early November, the US government took a shot from a Predator drone at a Taliban compound north of Kabul based on Geocell input. We were under way.

This kind of activity was first confined to the war zone in Afghanistan, but then, beginning in late 2002, NSA SIGINT was married to real-time imagery and other intelligence to support actions against al-Qaeda elsewhere.

Time magazine was skeptical. In reporting on such strikes, *Time* opined that "the idea of targeting terrorist quarry from the skies far from the open battlefields of Afghanistan is, of course, a different proposition and it's unlikely to become the norm."

Wrong.

Around this time, George Tenet and other intelligence luminaries were at Fort Meade to celebrate the fiftieth anniversary of the founding of NSA by President Truman's (secret) executive order in 1952. A lot was said about the origins and importance of the agency. It put a nice exclamation point on our current successes.

The operational success of SIGINT-imagery cooperation shouted out for more and stronger linkages. Jim Clapper was an old friend and mentor, and now headed NGA, the clumsily labeled National Geospatial-Intelligence Agency. NGA merged imagery intelligence (IMINT) with traditional mapping and tried to live its motto, "Know the earth. Show the way." Our two disciplines, SIGINT and IMINT, lived parallel lives in terms of their technology and their speed. Both of us were collecting and producing electrons.

Over time we linked our databases and our IT systems and were sharing exploitation techniques. In the fall of 2004 Jim and I were onstage together for an hour in New Orleans, briefing our collaboration to thousands in our contractor base. Anyone who doubts the significance of that scene just doesn't know enough about the traditional culture of the American intelligence community.

Jim and I were united in the knowledge that this was an intelligence-driven war. All wars are, of course, but this one especially. We had spent most of our professional lives in the Cold War. Intelligence then was hard work, but it was difficult for our adversary to hide the tank armies of Group Soviet Forces Germany or the vast Soviet ICBM fields in Siberia. That enemy was pretty easy to find. Just hard to kill.

This was different. This enemy was relatively easy to kill. He was just very, very hard to find.

Seems simple, but it inverted a lot of conventional thinking. That's why later, when some intelligence programs became controversial, I argued that restricting our intelligence in the current effort was like unilateral disarmament in the former. You were voluntarily surrendering the key elements of success.

It inverted some concepts of operations too. Intelligence professionals are accustomed to operators demanding information so they can go do something important. I was having dinner at the house of Charlie Holland, the commander of Special Operations Command (SOCOM), early in the war. Charlie was a good friend. We had been together in something called CAPSTONE, DOD's finishing school for new brigadiers, and while on that program's class trip had jogged together through the capitals of several Latin American countries. Over dessert Charlie turned to me, tapped the table, and said, "Mike, I need actionable intelligence."

I assured him that we were working on it, but then said, "Charlie, let me give you another way of thinking about this. You give me a little action and I'll give you a lot more intelligence." In other words, we needed operational moves to poke at the enemy, make him move and communicate, so we could learn more about him. Operations could be designed to generate information. Over time we more and more settled into that pattern.

AFTER 9/11, a lot of people wanted to help us, especially our closest friends, what NSA calls second parties—those English-speaking democracies, the members of the Five Eyes community (Australia, Canada, New Zealand, the United Kingdom, and ourselves) whose SIGINT roots go back to Bletchley Park and breaking the German Enigma code in Europe or to similar efforts and locations in the Pacific.

These loyalties run deep. There is a general consensus between British and American SIGINTers that the two countries' special *political* relationship began in the parlor office of the Bletchley manor house when American cryptologists arrived and were briefed by their British counterparts on what they knew (and did *not* know) of the Enigma code.

On 9/11 a new arrival in the New Zealand liaison section was in his Fort Meade office. He was directed to evacuate. He refused to leave and continued to keep his capital updated. "Friends do not leave friends at moments like this," he later told me.

Almost within hours of the attack, the heads of Britain's intelligence services came to the United States. They needed special permission and even a special escort to penetrate American airspace. On landing they went to Langley, where they met with George Tenet and others of us on his team. The instructions to our guests from their prime minister were clear: help the Americans however you can.

There are permanent structures to facilitate this cooperation. Every year, the Five Eyes intelligence services customarily get together; the United States is represented at these meetings by the heads of CIA, NSA, and FBI. Not every partner parallels our structure; we routinely have thirteen agencies there from the five countries. The first meeting after 9/11 was in March 2002 on New Zealand's South Island. New Zealand's hosting had been long planned, but the session had been delayed and then stripped of much of its social agenda. We narrowed the staffs who would attend too. Security demands would be high; we didn't need to make them a nightmare.

We all knew one another. Despite the disparity in budget and size and power among our organizations, personal relationships reflected a professional egalitarianism. There was no superpower strutting. Except at the airport. The heads of CIA and FBI arrived in their own jets, setting off rampant speculation in the local papers about who these guys were and what might be going on.

We quickly dove into the work. How could we best keep our citizens safe? There were operational conversations to be sure, but also something more. All of us were both the defenders *and the products* of democracies. Eliza Manningham-Buller, then deputy head of Britain's MI5 with extensive experience working against IRA terrorism, struck a chord with her blunt description of our operational and constitutional challenge. How were we to deal with the not-yet-guilty? After all, we were in the business of preventing terror, not just punishing it.

Implicit in her question was a potential recalibration of the traditional balance between liberty and security. Indeed, in September 2005, following the London Tube bombings, Manningham-Buller (now chief of MI5) advocated that "there needs to be a debate on whether some erosion of civil liberties we all value may be necessary to improve the chances of our citizens not being blown apart as they go about their daily lives."

I realized later that (at least American) political elites were not really anxious to take on Manningham-Buller's question. Far easier to criticize intelligence agencies for not doing enough when they feel in danger, while reserving the right to criticize those agencies for doing too much when they feel safe again.

That's a pity. Avoiding the hard choices creates a whipsaw effect, based on the perceptions of the moment, and ultimately costs us both freedom and security.

As close as the Five Eyes nations are, there are differences. En route home from Queenstown, I stopped in Wellington and met with Prime Minister Helen Clark. She could not have been more gracious or more supportive—mildly surprising, since she had been largely responsible in the 1980s for New Zealand's nuclear-free policy that had strained the ANZUS alliance to near dysfunction. Now she was supportive, but with a cautious concern about the contours of American counterterrorist actions. She feared that aggressive moves on our part would erode the international norms and processes on which small nations like hers depended. No specific issues. Just discomfort. Looking back, I/we could have been more sensitive to such concerns.

We later had a more dramatic discussion with, of all people, the British. Folks in GCHQ, Britain's NSA counterpart, were apparently conflicted (as some of the NSA workforce would be) about the wisdom of the war in Iraq. In early 2003 one of them, Katharine Gun, leaked to the London *Observer* what appeared to be an e-mail exchange between NSA and GCHQ calling for SIGINT coverage of UN delegations in the run-up to a crucial Security Council vote authorizing war. Gun referred to herself as a kind of "third culture kid," a term that describes children raised in a culture outside their parents' culture for a significant portion of their development years. She thought of herself far more as a citizen of the world than of Great Britain, having spent her early years living in Taiwan. Indeed, it was her Chinese-language skills that made her attractive to GCHQ.

Katharine Gun should have been a sign about changing mores in our societies. We didn't pick up on it. It became a lot more clear a decade later with Edward Snowden.

The Gun incident was far more an irritant than a crisis, at least for us.

Even if her allegations were true, intercepting diplomatic communications to achieve a political objective was hardly novel. Britain's use of German foreign minister Zimmermann's telegram in 1917 to goad the United States into war comes to mind. And we could hardly condemn a foreign partner for an occasional leak, not with our own challenges in that area. (Good thing, too, since little more than a decade later, American Edward Snowden dumped a ton of GCHQ secrets into the public domain.)

But in 2004, my GCHQ counterpart David Pepper confided to me that he had moved some people off the Iraq mission because of their personal discomfort with it. He proposed a discussion of "values" at an upcoming bilateral meeting.

I think a Brit would have described me as gobsmacked at the concept that people in a SIGINT agency could opt out of missions in wartime. Admittedly we had some linguists reluctant to voice-identify targets for a kill (see chapter 4), and GCHQ was completely civilian and under the Ministry of Foreign Affairs, whereas NSA was 50 percent military and a combat support agency within the Department of Defense. I quickly agreed to David's proposal, as much out of curiosity as friendship.

NSA and GCHQ senior leadership meet annually, alternating which side of the Atlantic would host. GCHQ generally finds a country estate near London and hosts us in elegance. Coming this way they are lucky to get a Motel 6 in Glen Burnie, although one year we did stay at a Sheraton adjacent to the Gettysburg battlefield, which formed a nice backdrop to our discussion. I still recall our partners' reaction when the US Army War College docent, about to lead us along the path of Pickett's Charge, reflected, "In the next ninety minutes here, more Americans died than would die at Normandy eighty-one years later."

Our 2004 meeting was held at Chevening, a beautiful English country house. Benjamin Franklin had really enjoyed its charms, judging from the thank-you note he had sent his host, still on display there. We filled our day with the usual operational and technical discussions and then, after dinner, retired to the library with brandy glasses in hand for David's requested discussion.

It was truly among friends but, on balance, we Americans spent a fair amount of time explaining ourselves. Such as explaining our views on the use of force in international relations. Differences were more stark with many Continental Europeans, of course, but we were representing a government and (I think) a people with, let's say, a more robust view of the utility of force than even our British cousins.

One surprising aspect of the discussion was movies, specifically one movie, *High Noon*, which shows up routinely on American lists of great films. The movie's protagonist, Marshal Will Kane (Gary Cooper), is one of the American Film Institute's top five cinema heroes of all time. Although the film was little known to our partners, this classic western plays to American mythology about itself. Kane—with a murderous gang descending on him, his new Quaker wife, and the town—rejects compromise or flight, acts against the prevailing view, and in the end relies on righteous violence to survive. Not exactly contemporary European fare.

Near the end of the evening, as we were draining our brandy snifters, I summarized some cultural differences with a bit of hyperbole: "Most Americans own a gun and most Americans go to church on Sunday."*

It was a good evening. If any air needed clearing, we cleared it. Besides, GCHQ was having its own issues with Britain's growing "Europeanness." The overlay of the European Convention on Human Rights onto British law, policy, and practice was a broad issue for the government. For GCHQ it meant additional administrative burdens and procedures to be able to demonstrate compliance.

The Australians suffer from no such European overhang. I once volunteered to Prime Minister Rudd that this was the most comfortable intelligence relationship we had, bar none. I don't know if that devolved out

---

* Since we've never had a gun in the house, only the "going to church" theme applied to me personally. We were so committed to the latter that we actually brought our parish priest along on a family vacation during our first tour in Korea. In retirement I combined the themes during a graduation address at the Franciscan University of Steubenville when I talked about sniper fire in Sarajevo. I told the graduates that if they were tempted to sleep in and miss Mass on a Sunday morning, they should ask themselves, "Are there snipers on the way to church?" "If the answer was no," I told them, "get out of bed."

of parallel immigrant histories, similar frontier experiences, or common pragmatic cultures. Whatever it was, it worked. The Australians were good, and although their services were small, they had more than enough critical mass to be well worth our time.

Through a careful division of labor, NSA relied on reporting from DSD (Australia's Defense Signals Directorate) for certain areas of the world. We even bent NSA collection pipes on some overseas regions to Canberra, to be worked there, and although the possibility of sweeping up US person communications wasn't quite zero, we had full confidence that DSD analysts would respect the US person privacy protections on which we had trained them. It's hard to have more confidence in a partner than the proposition "If he screws up, I go to jail." (In October 2014 the Australian ambassador hosted a reception commemorating the sixtieth anniversary of Canberra's relationship with CIA. Not every country commemorates that sort of thing.)

We had other trusting relationships. One of our Northern European partners once inadvertently intercepted an American government fax that revealed sensitive details about presidential travel. The partner had enough confidence in the relationship (that we would not assume that they were intentionally targeting us), that they actually showed the fax to us, warning that if they were able to intercept it, others could too. We thanked them and alerted the Secret Service. That's a pretty good friend.

We were a good friend too. We helped a European ally when several of its citizens were taken hostage in North Africa. We worked hard at it. In the end they said that we acted like the hostages were Americans.

I thought that we could do more. One of my predecessors had organized key NATO countries in a more cooperative SIGINT relationship targeting the Soviets. Although the Soviets were long gone, the construct— called SIGINT Seniors—continued. Meetings were held annually rotating among the members, and with each trying to outdo the other in hospitality, they were always delightful. Progress on operational matters, however, was glacial or, as one perceptive wag observed, it was measured in what he called "NATO time units."

The director of NSA was permanent chair of this group, and although it wasn't our turn to host, I called an out-of-cycle meeting in early December 2001. We would host it, not in the United States because of security and travel burdens, but at an installation in Europe that NSA used for logistics and technical support. It would be on European soil and the Europeans were fully supportive. The British were not the only services that had quietly slipped into the United States after the attacks to offer help.

There was no ceremony, fine food, or wine at this particular session. We were candid and tactical and operational to an unprecedented degree. It was pretty much our transmitting what we were doing. We told our friends the details of terrorist-related communications we had discovered entering or leaving their countries. Let me repeat this, in light of the furor over Edward Snowden's later revelations: we were telling our European friends what numbers in *their* countries were in contact with numbers we believed were associated with terrorism. Their response in 2001 was to take notes.

We covered our collection posture—where we thought we were strong and where we needed help. We didn't have to convince them to put their shoulder to this wheel. Of course, they would all have to do this consistent with their laws and their own political guidance, but we got the result we wanted: everyone was ready to help.

Over time in Afghanistan we developed something called Center Ice, an American initiative to tie these SIGINT partners into a single tactical network. Our investment wasn't much more than laptops and secure communications, but it allowed us to coordinate and de-conflict collection across national units.

We also didn't hesitate to be creative about our choice of partners. Even before 9/11 we approached some Central Asian states for cooperative relationships. The Soviet Union's old site at Termez in Uzbekistan looked right down the throat at Mazar-i-Sharif in northern Afghanistan. Even with parts of the site still tied into the Russian SIGINT system, geography mattered.

Beyond SIGINT, NATO took a dramatic if largely symbolic step in the fall of 2001. The alliance invoked Article 5, which states that an attack against one is an attack against all, and deployed NATO AWACS (an airborne command and control platform) to North America for this continent's defense. I had spent thirty years thinking about how to move military power in the other direction, and the first real-world example of common defense was Europe coming to our aid. Strange feeling.

OF COURSE, at NSA we also had to tend to our own defense. The agency has always had people in harm's way. SIGINT aircraft have been shot down by the Soviet Union and North Korea in the past, and the Israeli Air Force strafed a SIGINT ship in 1967. But we had always figured that being in garrison, like being at Fort Meade or some other field station, was also being in sanctuary. The 9/11 attack showed that this was no longer true.

The traffic jam generated by my order to evacuate nonessential personnel on 9/11 showed very clearly that we were not prepared to defend in place. And too many of our buildings were too close to public lands and highways.

Many of our people sensed that. I know that their families did. I tried to allay some of the concern with a letter we sent home with all of our employees. "Please be assured," I wrote, "that . . . every effort is being made to ensure the safety of our employees. We will protect ourselves—but, most importantly, we will protect the nation."

Fortunately, we had a program called PSAT (perimeter security antiterrorism) already under way, so we accelerated that. We were moving to treat NSA as a secure campus (like CIA), rather than isolated buildings each approachable via public roads. Now, in addition, large boulders were placed all around our perimeter so that vehicle-borne explosives could not get close to our structures. We enlisted local reserve units to intimidate would-be attackers with the visibly threatening presence of armored personnel carriers, weapons mounted, at our vehicle entrances. Our youngest son was courting his now wife at that time, and one of her first introductions to the family was going through such a checkpoint to get to our quarters.

The state of Maryland worked very hard to protect us, particularly our buildings near Route 50, which they eventually rerouted. We also pumped up CONFIRM, the system that recorded the badge swipes of people entering and leaving our facilities. Now such data would be kept off-site. In the event of catastrophic destruction, we could at least determine who was and was not in our buildings.

But this had to be about more than protecting our physical plant or even our personnel. We also had to protect our digital infrastructure and our intellectual property. What would the nation do if we lost our computer complex or our source code to a determined attacker?

We never wanted to have to answer that question, so we set out to build an alternative facility where much of this would be preserved. We got a boost from Congressman David Obey from Wisconsin, who earmarked money to preserve our supercomputing capacity. It was no accident that the congressman was from Wisconsin, where our Cray computers were built. It was still a very good idea. But we also knew that preserving our supercomputing capacity was not enough. We had to preserve our assets from end to end. The challenge was how to duplicate NSA. Quickly.

We hurried to set up an alternative site, a physically separate complex that allowed us to replicate about 80 percent of NSA's capability with about 20 percent of its capacity. That wasn't a perfect world, but at least it preserved us against catastrophic failure. We decrypted our first message at the new facility in late September 2003. For us it felt a little like driving the golden spike at Promontory Summit in 1869. It let us breathe a little easier.

We had one final option to exercise for continuity of operations. As we approached one holiday season with a particularly high quotient of background terrorist chatter, I called David Pepper of GCHQ to tell him that in the event of catastrophic loss at Fort Meade, we would entrust the management of the US SIGINT system to him and to our senior representative in London. The long pause on the other end of the secure line betrayed both the gravity of the threat and the enormous burden I was imposing on a friend.

WHILE WE WERE WORKING the present and preparing for the future, Congress wanted to question us about the past and how the 9/11 attack could have happened. The House and Senate Intelligence Committees organized themselves into something called the Joint Inquiry Commission (JIC) and began to hold hearings, both open and closed. This was the beginning of a wave of inquiries (the 9/11 Commission, the WMD Commission, and later, similar looks at CIA interrogations) that burned up big chunks of time for some of the intelligence community's best people.

The big open hearing for the JIC was in October 2002, where George Tenet, FBI director Bob Mueller, and I were at the witness table together. It was an all-day event, and there was later a *Time* magazine cover photo of all three of us with our right hands in the air being sworn in.

It wasn't as bad as it might have been. The chairmen, Congressman Porter Goss and Senator Pat Roberts, kept a pretty tight rein on things. In the hearing I admitted that, sadly, NSA had no prior knowledge of the 9/11 attack and that we were challenged by a global telecommunications revolution. We had competed successfully with the Soviets. "Now we had to keep pace with a global telecommunications revolution, probably the most dramatic revolution in human communications since Gutenberg's invention of movable type." And we weren't doing very well.

I complained that our resources and people had been cut by about a third in the preceding decade, the same decade when "mobile cell phones increased from 16 million to 741 million, an increase of nearly fifty times. . . . Internet users went from about 4 million to 361 million, an increase of over ninety times. Half as many landlines were laid in the last six years of the 1990s as in the whole previous history of the world. In that same decade . . . international telephone traffic went from 38 billion minutes to over 100 billion. This year [2002], the world's population will spend over 180 billion minutes on the phone in international calls alone."

I admitted that I had under-resourced the counterterrorism mission when it came to linguists and analysts but pointed out that "if these hearings were about a war that had broken out in Korea or a crisis in the Taiwan Straits, if we had been surprised by conflict in South Asia, if we had lost an aircraft over Iraq, or if American forces had suffered casualties in Bosnia or Kosovo—in any of these cases I would be here telling you that I had not put enough analysts or linguists against the problem."

I ended by congratulating the committee for prompting a needed national dialogue on the balance between security and liberty. It was an oblique reference in open session to the challenges created by the Stellarwind program, a secret collection effort (see chapter 5) then under way but known to fewer than ten people in the crowded committee room. "I am not really helped by being reminded that I need more Arabic linguists or by someone second-guessing an obscure intercept sitting in our files that may make more sense today than it did two years ago. What I really need you to do is to talk to your constituents and find out where the American people want the line between security and liberty to be."

There, in October 2002, I summed up the question of a decade later pretty well: "In the context of NSA's mission, where do we draw the line between the government's need for CT [counterterrorism] information about people in the United States and the privacy interests of people located in the United States?"

After Edward Snowden's revelations in 2013 (chapter 21), NSA was accused of indifference to and wanton violations of American privacy. Neither accusation was true. By the way, my 2002 question to the Congress went unreported (and largely unanswered).

I was pretty defensive; after all, the subtext of the questioning was pretty clearly, How did you guys let this happen? But I needn't have been as defensive as I was. They were really going after George Tenet.

They were hammering George hard over CIA's losing lock on a terrorist pair who had attended a meeting in Kuala Lumpur and then continued on to San Diego. The pair had lived in California in true name and ended up being two of the muscle guys on the American Airlines flight that hit the Pentagon. The record wasn't clear about who knew what, or when and what CIA did or did not pass to the FBI. A few members were pressing George for the name of the analyst who had been most involved. George refused. At one point he feigned leaning over to reach into his briefcase, which was on the floor between us, and as his mouth passed by my ear, whispered, "I'm not giving her up. I'm not giving her up."

It was a daylong hearing. No breaks. For us, anyway. Members came and went. Some got sandwiches from the cafeteria, brought them back, and ate them at the dais. At two o'clock, George turned to his legislative liaison chief and complained, "Are they ever going to feed us?"

They weren't, so the chief sent out for egg salad sandwiches from the Senate cafeteria. When he delivered them to the three of us still at the witness table and still testifying, it seemed that every cameraman in Washington suddenly appeared in the well between our table and the dais ready to snap a potentially classic shot of witnesses chowing down. The sandwiches remained unopened and we remained unfed.

On the way out from the long day, I was intercepted by a family member of a 9/11 victim. She was still visibly grieving, and the day's events surely gave her no comfort. I chatted with her for a short while, saying something like we were all doing our best. It was all I had to offer.

The closed session with the JIC was a bit bizarre. It was held in the secure hearing room on the House side with a lot of senators denied space on the dais and instead sitting at small tables and on small chairs in the well. They looked like parents sitting in their children's grade school classroom.

In this session Senator Richard Shelby from Alabama led the charge against NSA for two intercepts that were made on September 10 but not processed, translated, and reported until September 12. One cut contained "The match is about to begin," while the other observed, "Tomorrow is zero hour."

The communicants were affiliated with al-Qaeda, but were not senior-level folks. The phrases were oblique and embedded in lengthy conversations about a variety of things.

They certainly did not predict that an attack would take place and did not contain any details on the time, place, or nature of what might happen. No New York. No Washington. No airplanes as weapons. The longer we studied them, the more they looked like they might have been about the aftermath of the assassination of Ahmad Shah Massoud, head of the Northern Alliance in Afghanistan, who had been killed on September 9.

In any event, throughout the summer of 2001 we had had more than two dozen warnings like this that something was imminent. We dutifully reported them, yet none of them subsequently correlated with attacks.

Sometimes the absence of an attack was because of what we had reported. In July we tapped a communication between Afghanistan and Saudi Arabia. It was a discussion of a soccer match, and when asked where the match would take place, the Afghan side said, "Somewhere in your region." We, of course, alerted Americans in the region; some DOD units took appropriate precautions. Later, we intercepted the same communicants, and when asked if the match had taken place, the reply was no, because the spectators were not there.

I tried to explain to the committees how SIGINT works, that "thousands of times a day, our front-line employees have to answer tough questions like: Who are the communicants? Do they seem knowledgeable? Where in the conversation do key words or phrases appear? What is the reaction to these words? What world and cultural events may shape these words?"

I explained that NSA rarely listens to a conversation while it is taking place. Intercepts are collected, stored, and sorted, and then a linguist works his or her way through the queue. That's what happened with the September 10 intercepts. And the work plan to handle the existing backlog would surely have been affected by shifting priorities as the attacks of 9/11 unfolded.

Now, you might think that the intelligence oversight committees would already have a pretty good idea about all this. But you would be wrong. They weren't even buying the explanation now.

Pretty much exasperated, I actually pulled out the transcripts (not the reports, the transcripts) of the conversations we had intercepted. I read them in their entirety, including the small talk, greetings, and a lengthy discussion about needing batteries. "Real batteries," I said. "These aren't code words for anything."

When I was done, I put the paper down and looked at the dais. "So you tell me. Strategic warning or two Bubbas pumping gas at 7-Eleven?"

We actually took a short break for lunch in the closed hearing, and we hurriedly downed some sandwiches as the members scattered. When we resumed in the afternoon, we started to pick up the "tomorrow is zero hour" theme again. But now George and I were getting notes from our staffs that details of the morning's (closed) session were playing on CNN, including the ominous September 10 phrases.

As luck would have it, Congresswoman Jane Harman was lamenting the leaking of classified information in general when George and I interrupted our testimony to tell Porter Goss, who was chairing the session, what was happening. He was genuinely irate, and said so.

During the hearing we were inaccessible to the press, of course, but back at our headquarters the phones were ringing off the hook with journalists looking for comment—which, of course, could not be provided, since this was still top secret stuff. It was never officially determined where the leak originated. But one correspondent who called NSA did submit a curious question: "What does Shelby [the senator who had interrogated us on the intercepts in the morning] have against you guys?"

EVEN WITH THE JIC DISTRACTION, we were sharpening our game against al-Qaeda and, frankly, were getting pretty good at it. In March 2002 CIA and Pakistan's Inter-Services Intelligence agency (ISI) rolled up Abu Zubaida, the first of many al-Qaeda senior leaders we would capture, and later George Tenet was kind enough to call me at home to both alert me and thank me as Khalid Sheikh Mohammed met a similar fate.

By this time, though, Iraq was also on the front burner. I must admit the occasional dark moment when I asked myself why we were doing that. Saddam was dangerous, but he wasn't going anywhere. I wasn't a policy maker, though. I focused on getting any war there over quickly.

FOUR

GOING TO WAR . . . AGAIN AND AGAIN

So, as we were sorting out the aftermath of 9/11 with Congress, we were running up to the war in Iraq.

For better and for worse, NSA had a powerful role in that as well. Clearly there were those in the administration who believed that 9/11 justified an assault on Saddam's regime. To buttress their case they often suggested a connection between the Iraqi government and al-Qaeda and would sometimes call for more detailed analysis of specific pieces of signals intelligence that they felt supported their case.

It happened often enough that I feared some of our stuff might be taken out of context, so I directed our Iraq folks, whenever they were asked to do that, to put an overall caveat in their reporting along the lines of "Taken in its entirety signals intelligence neither proves nor disproves an operational relationship between the government of Iraq and al-Qaeda."

Intelligence services, especially those like Saddam Hussein's, have contacts with a lot of people. Those contacts aren't a prima facie case of collaboration, cooperation, or subordination. I'm not saying it was unfair or somehow unethical to recommend the hypothesis or to look for evidence to prove it. In the end, though, there just wasn't a case for it.

But we all thought that there was a case for weapons of mass destruction. I was in George Tenet's conference room when we voted on the now-infamous National Intelligence Estimate (NIE). I voted yes—on all counts. I was comfortable with the vote, then. I had earlier told Condi Rice, the national security advisor, in a private conversation, that I had a roomful of evidence that Saddam had a WMD program. "A roomful of evidence," I confided, "all of it circumstantial."

That was often the nature of SIGINT, indeed the nature of a lot of intelligence. Years later Michael Morell, then deputy director of CIA, was briefing President Obama on the likelihood that Osama bin Laden was at that Abbottabad compound. It turns out that some in CIA viewed the odds at no better than fifty-fifty; others handicapped it at nine out of ten. When pressed by the president as to why the large spread, Michael replied that those who had been involved in the Iraq NIE were the most conservative, while those whose only work was counterterrorism and al-Qaeda were most optimistic. Michael added that in both cases the evidence was circumstantial—and that we may have had more of it for the Iraqi WMD question than we did for Abbottabad.

The intelligence guy is actually most at risk when he is telling the policy maker things he wants to hear. And there is no doubt that Saddam's linkage to weapons of mass destruction gave the Bush administration its clearest public argument in articulating the case for war. Paul Wolfowitz, the deputy secretary of defense at the time, has said as much. It was the case most easily articulated. It was just wrong.

Years later, discussing this very issue, NSA's historian surprised me by linking it to the great Civil War battle at Antietam, still the bloodiest day in American history. Union forces there were led by General George McClellan, an incredibly cautious man who always believed that he was outnumbered by Lee. In truth, in this fight he outnumbered Lee two to one and had the Army of Northern Virginia pinned with its back to the Potomac and only one usable ford behind it.

But McClellan was wary and his intelligence chief, Allan Pinkerton (of detective fame), fed his caution with reports of imaginary legions that

Lee had brought with him across the river. Neither man was dishonest, but their tendencies so strongly reinforced each other's that it is still unclear who was really misleading whom. In any event, McClellan fought scared, committed only a part of his army and then only piecemeal, and allowed Lee to survive to fight another day.

The NSA historian's clear lesson: when the intelligence is making a policy maker too happy, he ought to challenge it, and when he doesn't, the intelligence briefer needs to launch a red team against his own conclusions to see if they can stand their ground.

And the intelligence officer with the unhappy message needs to insist, really insist, the way the State Department's Carl Ford (unsuccessfully) did when we were arguing over Saddam's aluminum tubes and nuclear program in late 2002. Carl was stubborn to the point of being damn near obnoxious. All he got for it was a footnote that State Department's intelligence shop disagreed with some of the NIE's conclusions.

We compounded our error by stating our conclusions in the NIE in language that was far too categorical. No reader of the final product could conclude other than that we were firm in our judgments, despite some thin sourcing of our human intelligence and signals intelligence that (as noted) was circumstantial, at best.

The urban legend has it that we were pressured by the White House, and especially by Vice President Cheney, to write a case for war. I never experienced such pressure, and when I got to CIA and talked to those more directly involved, they reported that they felt no such pressure either. We just got it wrong.

As I was about to leave government, I mentioned to Leon Panetta, who was coming in at CIA, that I had read some of his commentary on Iraq while he was in private life. "Leon," I said, "this wasn't the White House. This was us. We just got it wrong. It was a clean swing and a miss." The IC had lowballed its estimate of Iraqi WMD before the first Gulf War. Now we overcorrected.

NSA also had a role in Secretary Powell's ill-fated call to arms in front of the UN in February 2003. Three NSA intercepts related to Iraqi WMD were played during the speech. I had to clear their release (a formality) and make damn sure they were right and accurately translated (they were).

There was a fourth intercept that was in the stack of possible entries for the speech. This one was in some ways more explicit and detailed than the others. Playing it in New York would have been incredibly effective. But it would also have been incredibly misleading. Although it was highly suggestive of WMD use and while it was indeed from Iraq, it was not from the part of Iraq under government control and we saw no evidence of linkage to Baghdad.

I sent our best linguist to Langley to make the point. He did. There was no pushback. The cut was removed.

Later, as 2003 turned to 2004, it was very clear that we had gotten the WMD wrong. There were no weapons of mass destruction. We did a lot of soul searching. What do you do when you are wrong? Obviously you look to your tradecraft. We did.

But there was an even larger dimension. Shortly before Christmas 2003 an NSA historian developed a case study about another national decision that had been based on flawed intelligence: the Gulf of Tonkin Resolution, which launched a major US escalation in Southeast Asia. The case seemed to fit our current circumstance. Perhaps too well.

The historian e-mailed me a concern: although this was an "extraordinarily powerful and richly textured" episode, he began, "because of possible accusations of a 'cover-up' of intelligence errors, and what some might see as rough similarities to the current controversy over intelligence reporting related to the issue of WMD in Iraq, we want to make sure you believe it appropriate to use this particular case study this time."

I responded the next day. "I don't see a problem—sounds like a great way to use this historically rich material to address concerns that still exist today." And so we did.

On August 2, 1964, North Vietnamese torpedo boats had attacked the US destroyer *Maddox* in international waters as that ship was supporting raids on the North Vietnamese coast. SIGINT had warned of an attack, and the torpedo boats were repulsed. Score one for SIGINT.

Then, two nights later, in the midst of Johnson administration warnings to North Vietnam about further action, SIGINT misread North Vietnamese reporting on their continuing recovery operations from the first night as a second attack and issued a CRITIC (a kind of global warning). Subsequent US Navy evasive action and firing at some spurious radar hits were duly noted in North Vietnamese shore-based communications, which were in turn picked up by NSA and errantly catalogued as further evidence that a second attack was under way. President Johnson ordered air attacks against the torpedo boat bases, and Congress delivered the Gulf of Tonkin Resolution, authorizing the president to take "all necessary steps" to halt Communist aggression in Southeast Asia.

In the aftermath of the resolution, NSA stuck to its story that a second attack had occurred. It's unclear if the agency's subsequent investigation was careless, misguided, or just consciously ignored evidence. But it is clear that the August 4 reporting was wrong.

Tonkin and Iraq's WMD were sobering lessons.

SURPRISINGLY, AS DIRECTOR OF NSA, I received no formal guidance to prepare for war with Iraq. But it didn't take a rocket scientist to know that we were going to war, so we moved around what we later estimated to be about $400 million to get ready for the conflict. The deputy head of our SIGINT Directorate, a Gulf War veteran, directed the team we set up to prepare for war to read the agency's history of the first Gulf War. He then conducted what the army calls a "rock drill" to synchronize what various tactical and national SIGINT units would do to support one another.

Linguists were a perennial challenge, even before the demands of this war. A year earlier, in 2000, with al-Qaeda strengthening and with information on their plans sparse, CIA had outfitted an early model of the Predator with electro-optical and infrared cameras to hunt al-Qaeda in Afghanistan. The agency was looking for bin Laden, his close associates, training camps, and any evidence of weapons of mass destruction. It was tough getting this under way; a whole infrastructure of people and equipment had to be built to handle the streaming video from the UAV (unmanned aerial vehicle).

Those early missions did not carry SIGINT packages, but that didn't let NSA entirely off the hook. As weak as Afghan air defenses were, we still didn't want the political embarrassment of losing a drone, so we could not simply ignore the Taliban's limited radar coverage and its handful of MiG-21s. Any Afghan detection of the Predator was deemed sufficient to scrub the mission. So we couldn't fly without monitoring the air defense network, and that required linguists. Actually, we were so limited in Pashto speakers, it required *the* linguist, who would be dedicated to this task whenever the Predator was in Afghan airspace.

The Afghans finally did attempt an intercept, but the Predator was so small and so slow that the unlucky MiG-21 pilot reported that he could not find it—a conversation duly reported by NSA. In truth, the actual intercept was a little oblique. Something along the lines of the "birds spotted a pigeon but lost it." A good object lesson for anyone who thinks it's OK to "talk around" classified data on the phone.

Great work, but we were going to have to get a whole lot better to support full-scale conflict or rather, as it turned out, several conflicts: Afghanistan, al-Qaeda, soon-to-be Iraq. We began to pull Arab linguists off mission in order to sharpen them in the Iraqi dialect. All accounts, except for CT, suffered.

There was no magic lever to pull here. Good language analysts are a rare and special breed, since they have to be masters of so many skills.

First and foremost, they need to know the language and the culture. They have to be target smart: Who is related to whom? What is the overall context? What code words do they use? Who lies to whom on the phone? Finally, they've got to know the SIGINT system. Intercepts don't come to you on a platter. You have to be a hunter far more than a gatherer.

In ways not widely understood—taking a communication not in your language, between two individuals not of your culture and perhaps not quite able to distinguish the world as it is from the world as they would like it to be (common in messianic groups like al-Qaeda)—taking all of that and turning it into something actionable is high art and science.

In one instance, analysts were puzzled by the continued references to a specific household article from a known terrorist group. One linguist decided to stay at work for a weekend to listen intently to all the available cuts. Analysts usually scan cuts to get to the important ones; otherwise they would never get through the queue. But by giving up a weekend, this analyst listened to everything and gathered references to this household article and a variety of colored accessories. By Sunday night he had it. The household article symbolized passports. The accessories were visas. Their colors signified specific countries. Breakthrough.

The last time NSA intercepted bin Laden was in 1997, but that wasn't the last time it heard him. In 2000, one AQ intimate of bin Laden's was calling another and using a harsh tone, almost barking orders, in a way that seemed very inappropriate to the language analyst. The cut was puzzling. Why the odd tone? When the analyst finally turned up the volume to a very high level, there, identifiable in the background, was the voice of bin Laden himself telling the first communicant what to say.

Only a few days after 9/11, Russia passed us a warning about al-Qaeda possibly using "the big one" based on an intercept of a communication between two terrorists. We immediately thought nuclear and hunted throughout our system to find a copy of the cut. We succeeded, and luckily it was of very high quality. With George Tenet demanding answers fast, I put our very best linguist on it. Within thirty minutes he reported that the targets were certainly players in the terrorist network, but the question was whether or not they were talking about a nuclear attack on us or whether they were talking about our taking dramatic action against them. It was indeed speculation about our response to them. False alarm, this time.

So language skills really mattered. I upped the required standard for our military linguists. In an earlier world, where we were intercepting heavily formatted military messages, basic fluency would suffice. A ground controller directing a fighter to turn left or turn right or to ascend to a certain altitude was pretty easy to follow. Al-Qaeda didn't talk that way. They were elliptical, metaphorical, indirect, nuanced . . . and clever. We needed better skills.

On the civilian side, in the four years after 9/11, we were able to hire about five hundred new linguists. We raised their pay too. A lot. Several times.

Some of the new hires were native-born in target languages and, since they were young, pretty tech savvy too. Others were older, desperate to serve, but they made it quite clear that they would never master the technical intricacies of the SIGINT system. They did make superb quality controllers on our translations.

There were special emotional strains in this line of work. Language analysts stay on a target for a long time and sometimes know their target better than they know their own families. They become part of the virtual life of the target. It can be a real emotional roller coaster. When a target has been designated for direct action and his death needs to be confirmed, it is often the same phone that is targeted, but now the communications comprise sobbing, grieving family members.

Some analysts have had real issues with confirming the identity of a communicant prior to direct action. Some just can't do it. This is conscientious objection to killing or at least to being a direct part of the killing, not a political view on the cause or conduct of a war. One senior recounted to me one of his linguists spontaneously beginning to cry as she was in the car with him. He asked what was wrong. She said, "Something at work," and when they got to the office, she explained the emotional stress of targeted killings.

Special people. And rare. One day I was returning from a meeting at Langley and my security detail looked a little impatient, as they had to wait for a stream of pedestrian traffic flowing outward from the NSA headquarters building. As they inched the SUV forward, I only half in jest cautioned, "Be careful. They could be linguists."

Before the Iraq war started, I wanted to talk to the entire workforce. The congressional vote on authorizing the invasion promised to be close, and I had every reason to believe that the workforce split along similar lines. I usually gave an important briefing once in the agency's Friedman Auditorium and then had it repeated and beamed electronically to workstations at Fort Meade and beyond.

Not this time. Too important. I wanted a personal touch. I gave the briefing to multiple audiences (clearly not to all 35,000 military and civilian workers, but you get the point) at Fort Meade and up near the Baltimore-Washington airport, where we had a large annex. Because we had folks working with Central Command in Tampa and in the combat theater, we knew CENTCOM commander Tommy Franks's concept of operations—"shock and awe"—and the broad outline of his war plan.

I walked the workforce through our responsibilities, how our emphasis would shift as the assault force went through its phases:

Phase 1.   Deployment.
Phase 2.   Shaping the battle space.
Phase 3.   Major force-on-force action.
Phase 4.   Post-conflict stability operations.

Knowing the political divisions in this country and the upcoming Senate debate, I acknowledged that there were surely some in the audience who opposed the coming conflict. So I reminded them of our duties as professionals, that if the republic authorized war, we would fight it savagely, limited only by the laws of armed conflict. I then added, "We could all agree that it would be a bad thing indeed if countries around the world got the idea that it was OK to be an enemy of the United States of America."

I was asked in several meetings how long all this was going to take. Don Rumsfeld had gotten the same question while visiting the US air base at Aviano, Italy. He said, "It is unknowable how long that conflict will last. It could last six days, six weeks. I doubt six months."

I had a little different answer. I said that the part that the American people would call war, phase 3, would be measured in weeks, not months. I then added that phase 4, post-conflict stability operations, would not be measured in months either. I got the WMD wrong, but I certainly nailed that one.

Even before Franks ordered his forces to cross the line of departure, NSA was already deeply in the fight, so some at the agency were surprised at my reaction to the traditional signs that NSA used at moments like this: "We support the warfighter."

"Don't say that," I said. "We're not support. We're part of the fight. We're responsible for final outcomes, not just our inputs."

I had concluded that we had to go forward with combat formations. When you are there, you are in the fight. When you are not, you are in the in-box, and no one reads their in-box when they are in a fight.

The major muscle movement before us was transitioning from being a SIGINT production factory to an intelligence consultancy. We couldn't just mail it in and merely sustain the old transactional relationship of delivering SIGINT products. We needed a living, breathing operational intimacy with people we used to call customers. We had to ramp up the forward deployment of our knowledge, skills, and abilities. One senior summarized it as sending our carbon units rather than our silicon units into the fray.

I thought that we were doing well enough until, after the war was under way, our chief of research, the one from Walt Disney Imagineering, took an extended trip through the theater. He reported that the new approach was working, to a point. "They love us at MNF-I [Multi-National

Force–Iraq] and corps headquarters. We're OK at division level, but below that they barely know who we are." As director of the *National* Security Agency, doctrinally I was charged with supporting the national leadership and Department of Defense echelons down to about the corps level. But doctrine wasn't working. Lower-echelon units weren't feeling the love (or getting and acting on valuable SIGINT).

We reached further down-echelon and embedded five-person NSA teams at the division level and linked regiments (in the Marine Corps) and brigades (in the army) to the highly classified NSANet. Once we trained them and cleared them for very sensitive information, low-echelon GIs were getting access to precious national databases, all the while being advised by high-end NSA professionals.

In one telling vignette, an NSA analyst at Fort Meade reported that he had "received a secure call from a master gunnery sergeant in the front line. He needed to know what kind of switching equipment was used in An Nasiriyah's central switch. Seems they were planning an operation against it and were interested in exploiting the switch, if they could get control of it. Fortunately, NSA had that information—it was an Alcatel E-10. I had a mental image of him sitting in the back of an armored vehicle, using a laptop to link into NSANet."

When we really got going, front-line SIGINT soldiers and marines were tuning orbiting satellites to home in on targets to their immediate front, while folks under my direct control at Fort Meade and Fort Gordon in Georgia were tuning antennas on tactical vehicles in the forward line of march.

To keep all of this synchronized, we held routine videoconferences every other day for all the relevant SIGINT units inside and outside the theater. My conference room screen would have a dozen or more locations beamed in as we shared information, assigned tasks, and de-conflicted operations. The playbook was "coherent centralized planning [with] decentralized execution; a networked information sharing enterprise; [leveraging] an unprecedented level of collaboration."

To be clear, we weren't trying to play Tom Sawyer in order to get a lot of other people to whitewash our fence. In fact, it was more the opposite. We welcomed more help but had to be careful whom we trusted with a brush.

Even though making SIGINT is hard work, a lot of people think they can do it. When customers think they're not getting enough of NSA's attention—or when they are, but the reporting is not what they want to hear—the agency sometimes gets a request for the "raw data." The request usually betrays a real lack of understanding of how this works.

"How raw do you want it? Before we process it, when it's still unintelligible beeps and squeaks?"

"No. No. After processing."

"Sure."

"But this is all in Urdu or Pashto or something."

"Yes, I know."

"But I need it in English."

"We don't translate and store everything in English. Just the important stuff."

"Yeah. Give me that stuff."

"But that's what you have been getting. We call it reporting."

On the rare occasion when we turned a raw SIGINT pipeline on, we usually received a request within hours to turn it off. Too much stuff.

We were being theologically correct (and consistent with our charter) to keep what we called the SIGINT production chain under our control. But we were truly dealing with a ton of material, and we could never be totally sure that we completely (or currently) understood our teammates' requirements. And frankly, people everywhere were now participating in processes that had always served them, but from which they had previously been personally barred, from teller machines to booking airline tickets to publishing books.

We needed to square this circle, and we hit upon the concept of the SIGINT production stream, our routine reporting at the mouth of our waterway and raw unprocessed traffic at the headwaters. We would allow people and organizations previously known as customers to swim upstream as long as they could protect the data they encountered and as long as they could add value to it. Those two caveats weeded out the casual request and the ill-considered demand.

The further upstream someone wanted to go, the heavier the requirement. "Protecting the data" meant secure spaces, secure communications, and secure people (read polygraphed). That was quite an investment. "Add value" meant that their efforts wouldn't simply result in more noise in the system. What they were doing had to be worthwhile. That required training (like protecting US privacy) and skills (like language).

We weren't going to provide a SIGINT peep show, but I also made clear to the NSA folks that the value added by these customer-producers didn't have to match the value we thought we could add. If they thought it worth their effort, we would not stand in the way. We had plenty of work to do, anyway.

Overall, we didn't do badly. A few days into the Iraq conflict we could report that the Iraqis were having trouble communicating and had evacuated several facilities; power outages were affecting some units and SAM sites had been damaged.

But we weren't getting the flood of signals we had anticipated. Chinese firms had put down extensive fiber-optic cable after the first Gulf War, and it was clear that the Iraqis were riding those lines now. We stepped up pressure on CENTCOM planners to put cable heads on the target list and to hit them hard even though some were in or near populated areas. The idea was to herd signals into the air, where we could intercept them.

It worked; kinetic operations were enabling intelligence collection. A week into the conflict, signals spiked to such a degree that linguists had to be called in off break to handle the increased volume. That greatly facilitated locating Iraqi units for destruction. Two weeks later we reported that the SIGINT targets we had been following in southern Iraq and Baghdad had "largely ceased to exist."

The early bombing campaign had been bedeviled by GPS jammers that the Iraqis were using to spoof the guidance on American smart bombs. The SIGINT system managed to locate these elusive devices, and they were added to the target list as well. We also intercepted the communications of technicians servicing the system and cleared our reports to support State Department démarches to the supplier country.

We had less luck keeping "Baghdad Bob," Saddam's irritating English-speaking spokesman, off the air. He was using the same kind of rugged, miniaturized satellite kit that embedded American reporters were using to file stories on the war. It proved near impossible to geolocate his short and unpredictable broadcasts in time to do much about them. We tried, but it was hard to make Baghdad TV stay dead for very long. It wasn't long, though, before his preposterous claims were given the lie by American armor doing gun runs through Baghdad.

The Geocell (chapter 3), launched shortly after 9/11, really came into its own in Iraq. Geocell developed its intelligence in dialogue with those who would use it. Procedures were crafted to match the rules of engagement of each client they served, since different forces have different needs with regard to the method and timeliness of their intelligence reporting.

In one instance, a product, built at the customer's request, was designed to be ripped off a printer and brought to a helicopter as the mission lifted off.

In another instance, the Geocell was in live chat with an AC-130 gunship on-station, allowing those on board to fuse SIGINT with what they were seeing and with their local Predator UAV feed.

By early 2006, four thousand military members had been trained by the Geocell and given access to its products and databases. Sailors with the Fifth Fleet in the Persian Gulf, for example, could access the database to determine which of the hundreds of small dhows transiting the Gulf might have a terrorist-related communications device on board.

During the main combat operations in Iraq I also amped up the production of what we called SIGINT assessments. SIGINT products are usually confined to a summary of a communication or a group of closely related communications. Anything more was traditionally done by all-source analysts at CIA or DIA. But I thought we were leaving a lot of SIGINT-derived insight on the floor, so I challenged our analysts to step back and write broad appreciations on what they were seeing and hearing. Two titles during this period stand out: "The Mood in Baghdad" and "Iraqi Irregulars Likely to Be a Long Term Problem." Turned out to be very long term.

We also knew that there were going to be losses. I think I caught my largely civilian staff off guard when, at a planning meeting before the invasion started, I simply asked, "So what are our casualty notification procedures?" The silence that followed was more than a silent bureaucratic "I don't know." There was a sobering message sinking in.

NSA has lost twenty-three cryptologists since I asked my question. Not a new phenomenon. The first US soldier killed in Vietnam was a SIGINTer, Specialist 4 James T. Davis, a DF (direction finding) specialist in the army's obscurely named Third Radio Research Unit.

As a DOD organization, NSA was pretty well prepared to sustain and support the military people we sent forward. We were far less prepared to support their families, and most of this was an entirely new experience for NSA civilians. My wife, Jeanine, had already been working on family issues in the summer of 2001, and now she took under her care a program we called Family Battle Rhythms. We talked to family members about services that were available to them, techniques to cope with stress, and opportunities to get acquainted with people in similar circumstances.

And this didn't just apply to the families of folks who were physically deployed. NSA had a large population of people we called "deployed in place"—folks who perhaps slept in Maryland or Georgia but who worked twelve hours a day in Iraq and Afghanistan because that's where their headsets took them. It was a new kind of stress: life-and-death circumstances at work, and a continuing responsibility to drive the soccer carpool that evening. We did what we could.

People had to take care of themselves, me included. After I showed up in an Iraqi deck of cards identifying American targets, I got a security escort every time I left base. I wasn't entitled to a car and driver, but we did get a chase vehicle. No spontaneous trips after that, but the security guys were friendly and professional.

And there were a few times I was glad they were there. In September of 2004 I attended a Steelers game in Baltimore with my family. Baltimore is a friendly city, unless of course you are decked out in Steelers black and gold on game day. Ravens fans were frisky, too, having won that day. As we were trying to leave the stadium parking lot, some rowdy fans gathered around our car slapping their faces to the windows. Until the loudspeaker in the SUV behind us bellowed out, "Slowly move away from the vehicle!" No problems after that.

I tried to keep my own battle rhythm manageable. I brought tons of work home but avoided the office on weekends. If I went in, a whole ecosystem would have accompanied me.

I kept to my running and even ran the Pittsburgh Marathon in May 2003. More credit to Pete, my security guard, though, who trained with me and then ran the race armed with his weapon in a small satchel pack.

The Iraq war was tough—tougher and longer than even we anticipated. At the tactical level, though, SIGINT put in an impressive performance. In April 2005, as he was leaving command in Anbar Province, Lieutenant General John Sattler, First Marine Expeditionary Force commander, sent a message to NSA headquarters thanking the agency for its work. He noted three recent captures set up entirely by SIGINT and then praised NSA "willingness to partner with our organic SIGINT enterprise [and] most importantly your willingness to put SIGINT based reporting in the hands of operational commanders at the secret level."

Not bad. We had demonstrated to our enemies that if you radiated on an American battlefield, you were likely to die.

Less certain, though, was our ability to inform broad questions of policy, like the decision to invade Iraq in the first place.

And then there was still that prickly issue of finding terrorists already inside the American homeland.

FIVE

STELLARWIND

FORT MEADE, MD, 2001–2003

Two days after 9/11, I walked into the large director's conference room at NSA. The chairs around the semicircular conference table and the rows of stadium seats behind them were empty. In fact, the room was empty except for my public affairs officer, Judy Emmel, and a few technicians.

I was going to speak remotely to the entire workforce, my first chance to do that since the evacuation order two days earlier.

Much of the speech was predictable. We are going to have to play defense for a while, I said. We'll have to characterize "what has happened" and "identify signs of what may happen."

I urged patience. "While we will always be alert for warning, our emphasis will shift over time. I think you all understand that the nation does not intend to play just defense forever." Predictable enough, I thought, although we had not yet received specific word on what the game plan might be.

I acknowledged that many of their loved ones might have been urging them not to come to work that morning, fearing for their personal safety.

I urged them to look on the bright side. "Right now, more than three hundred million Americans wish they had your job."

I ended with a thought that had been troubling me since the attacks: the preservation of American freedom. The people at NSA (including me) come from the same political culture that motivates all Americans (a reality often ignored by ideological purists in the periodic debates we have over security and liberty) and my liberal arts education had reinforced the idea that freedom was indeed a fragile thing.

I reminded our folks that "it's not just our safety but our character as a free people that is at stake here. Every nation is required to balance the needs of security with the needs of liberty. Thanks to James Madison and a bunch of his friends, we have planted our flag well on the side of liberty in that difficult question. But if a nation feels itself threatened, feels its children are at risk, it tends to move its banner closer to the requirements of security than those of liberty. That's what all of us feared when we told our families that we would wake up Wednesday to a different America. You and I have a role here. You and I can and will preserve American liberty and we will do it by making America feel safe again."

I often think of that speech, which I have kept, when I hear the harshest of our critics act as if we in the intelligence community somehow think less of American liberty than they do.

Right after 9/11, I did a lot of things that were within my own authorities. For example, almost immediately I shifted the standard for minimization of US identities in calls coming out of Afghanistan.

In covering foreign intelligence targets it is not uncommon to pick up communications to, from, or about an American. When that happens, NSA is allowed to continue to collect and indeed to report the information, but the US identity—unless it is critical to understanding the significance of the intelligence—is obscured, or what we call "minimized." The name of an individual, for example, becomes "US person number one."

If intelligence customers believe that the identity has to be unmasked to understand the intelligence, they can ask for reconsideration, and NSA has a regular bureaucratic process for making that judgment.

We had just seen a strategic assault on the homeland mounted from within the United States but planned in Afghanistan, and we had every reason to believe that more attacks would follow. So I directed our analysts to lower the threshold when it came to deciding what constituted "critical to understanding the significance of the intelligence." If potential al-Qaeda plotters were phoning in, we wanted the FBI to know as soon as possible whom terrorists were talking to and not to demand that the bureau formally request that information.*

Often we were not getting the content of calls but just the fact of connections between the United States and Afghanistan (the metadata). And to be sure, there were a lot of Afghans innocently in contact with family in America with each asking if everyone was all right. But with metadata alone, all we had was the fact of contact, and we passed many of these to the FBI.

"Anonymous sources" at the bureau later criticized NSA for sending them on what they derisively called "pizza runs," and I suppose we were. But we didn't intend these tips to be definitive, just data that could be mixed with other information in the service of analysis. That was our mistake. We thought the bureau did analysis in addition to kicking in doors.

I told George Tenet we were doing this, and he told the vice president and the president. They said, "Good. Can he do anything more?" Tenet called me with that question, and I replied, "Not within my current authority." He shot back, "That's not the question I asked." "I'll get back to you" was the best I could come up with at that moment.

Later the Joint Inquiry Commission (see chapter 3) would criticize NSA for failings prior to 9/11. The most telling of these had to do with terrorists inside the United States, specifically:

---

* Since this was a bit out of the ordinary, I informed the chair and ranking member of the intelligence oversight committees and offered to come down and brief the full committees. The House took me up on my offer, and I briefed them on October 1.

"NSA's cautious approach to any collection of intelligence relating to activities in the United States."

"There were also gaps in NSA's coverage of foreign communications and the FBI's coverage of domestic communications."

"NSA did not want to be perceived as targeting individuals in the United States."

"[In talking about one-end US conversations] there was insufficient focus on what many would have thought was among the most critically important kinds of terrorist related communications, at least in terms of protecting the homeland."

The JIC findings were published a lot later, of course, but frankly, we didn't need any help figuring out where our gaps in coverage were. I mention them here only to point out that what then followed, NSA's Stellarwind program, was a logical response to an agreed issue and not the product of demented cryptologic minds, as some would later suggest. By *Congress's* definition, what we had been doing had not been enough. What would they have us do if not a Stellarwind-like approach to fill the gaps they were so righteously identifying?

In any event, after George's call, I got my operations and legal team together and said, "All right, blank slate: What more can we do against this threat?" We came up with several courses of action, one of which was aggregating domestic metadata (the fact of calls to, from, and within the United States) and another that effectively allowed us to quickly intercept the content of international calls, one end of which might be in the United States, if we had reason to believe the call was related to al-Qaeda.

Neither of these would follow the procedures of the Foreign Intelligence Surveillance Act, or FISA (the law passed in 1978 after the last great NSA "scandal" and the Church Commission investigations), as the act was then understood and certainly as it was then implemented. FISA would have required detailed, individualized warrants, each approved by the court. To do what we were proposing, the law would have to be amended or we would have to rely on some other authority.

George invited me to see the president and the vice president at his morning briefing in the Oval Office, and there I laid out the operational advantages these steps would give us. Basically, by being able to query the metadata for possible connections to known terrorist numbers and then quickly go up on suspect numbers, we would increase the odds that we would catch the one thing that most eluded us before 9/11: terrorist-related calls, one end of which were in the United States. I sensed that things were going to move pretty quickly after this session.

George called and told me as much and then invited me back to the Oval. Besides being my boss, George was a good friend. I once blurted out on C-SPAN that I loved him like a brother. So I reminded him that since the ugliness of the Church Commission, NSA had acted like it had had a permanent one ball–two strike count on it. "We don't take many close pitches," I reminded him. "We need to be careful about this."

George clearly passed that on to the president, who no doubt got the baseball metaphor. As I walked into the Oval the next day, the president was offering me reassurances about the welfare of the agency before I had even sat down. He understood my concerns, he said, but we had to do what was right.

After the session, as I was being driven up the Baltimore-Washington Parkway toward Fort Meade, I alerted my office that I wanted to see Bob Deitz, my senior lawyer, as soon as I returned.

"The president is going to do this on his own hook," I told Bob as he came into my office. "Raw Article 2, commander-in-chief stuff. No new legislation. Probably would take too much time, as well as tipping off al-Qaeda. Justice is going to approve it but I need *your* views. Can he do it? Does he have the authority? Are we going to be OK here?

"By the way, the access control officer on this is the president of the United States. I'm authorized to read you in. No one else from your staff."

Tough challenge. Bob told me he would get back to me the next day. He spent a sleepless night thinking a lot about the Constitution and the

Fourth Amendment. Next morning he told me that it was a hard case, but that he had developed a more-than-plausible theory about its lawfulness:

> The Fourth Amendment posed no problem because, as he interpreted what the president was authorizing, we needed probable cause to believe that one end was foreign <u>and</u> one of the parties was a terrorist before we intercepted a communication;
>
> with regard to metadata, the Supreme Court had already held 5–3 in a 1979 case [*Smith v. Maryland*] that such information was not constitutionally protected;
>
> with respect to the Foreign Intelligence Surveillance Act [FISA, which *did* protect metadata], the statute did not allow us the speed or the agility to respond to this threat;
>
> and, finally, there must be an implicit exception to FISA in an emergency or, to that extent, the statute was unconstitutional.

We talked a bit about the legal theory. When I asked him what the Supreme Court would do, Bob refused to predict an outcome, but stressed that his theory was sound and the argument forceful. Bob knew a little bit about the turf; he had clerked at the court for Justices Stewart, Douglas, and White. Later he confided to me that he thought we would win it, 6–3.

Bob had his own questions for me. Just to make sure that we were on the same page, he asked what I would do when (and it was always a question of when) the program leaked and I was called to the Hill. His concern was that we would never lie to Congress. I assured him that I wouldn't. He also encouraged me to seek authority to brief the Hill or at least the senior leadership and the FISA Court. I strongly agreed.

Bob was comfortable with his opinion, but there was a lot of legal firepower at NSA that he couldn't access because of the president's restrictions. He obliquely raised my question with the agency's top operational lawyer and a real hard-liner on NSA's limits. Bob spoke abstractly and hypothetically, of course, but his comfort level increased when the lawyer endorsed Bob's legal theory. Within a week or so we were able to get other lawyers read into the program. There was no way we could play this close to the edge without a lot of legal oversight. The additional lawyers were quite comfortable with our legal position, by the way.

Even as he was content with his own reasoning, Bob wanted to understand the legal theory used by the Department of Justice's Office of Legal Counsel about why it thought the program was lawful and to compare it to his own. He called the vice president's lawyer, David Addington, within a couple of weeks on the secure phone asking to see the legal opinion. Addington refused, but he did read some of the operative paragraphs over the phone. Bob thought that John Yoo's approach actually proved too much and was unnecessarily broad, a kind of "Article 2 *über alles*," whatever the president thinks is necessary to preserve the nation, he may do. Deitz said his training at Harvard was in the common law tradition, which relies heavily on facts to achieve a case-by-case development of the law. Yoo's broader theory was typical of Yale, he told me. No rivalry there.

When the Department of Justice opinion on this program became public, it was clear that it had expanded its justification beyond the president's Article 2 powers as commander in chief to include the congressional Authorization for the Use of Military Force (AUMF) against those responsible for 9/11. That argument was contentious, since the law didn't specifically talk about intercepting communications, and the administration had not specifically requested that authority. In the complex 2004 Hamdi decision, however, the Supreme Court did seem to uphold the legality of detention—even the detention of a US citizen—as a legitimate incident of war even though it, too, was never mentioned in the AUMF. If you could detain an enemy without trial, intercepting his communications seemed a lighter legal lift.

My guys seemed to split the difference between unrestricted executive power and narrow reliance on the implied intent of a single statute. They believed and so advised me that the president as commander in chief had the authority to do *this,* and any congressional limitations to the contrary were unconstitutional attempts to limit the executive's power. It's all still contentious and the subject of much debate, but twice the FISA appellate court has held that "we take as a given that the president has inherent constitutional authority to conduct electronic surveillance without a warrant *for foreign intelligence purposes.*" I think my lawyers got it right.

I had one more requirement to fill in on my checklist. The afternoon I came back from the White House knowing that we were going forward (the same day I huddled with Bob Deitz), I left work early and invited my wife, Jeanine, on a walk through a patch of Fort Meade's largely sylvan campus. While on the walk I pointed out that we were fixing to do something controversial, that I was comfortable with doing it because it was right, but that at some point there was going to be high political and reputational risk, and I couldn't rule out legal risk either.

She listened intently and simply asked if I thought it was the right thing to do. I repeated that I did and she then said that, of course, I had to do it.

Gutsy call on her part, because the implicit understanding between us was that I was really asking her to volunteer herself, our grown children, and our grandchildren for what could be a very rocky ride at some point in the future. That she assented said a lot about her—and military spouses in general—especially since she had no idea what it was we would actually be doing.

After my session in the Oval, the vice president had turned to David Addington to draft an order that would eventually be approved by the attorney general, authorized by the president, and signed by the secretary of defense, directing us to carry out what we had already described as technologically possible and operationally relevant. It was John Yoo at Justice who insisted that this should flow through the secretary of defense and the chain of command as an element of war making. The

DOD fingerprints proved useful when Stellarwind became public and some in DOD wanted to dismiss it as "the White House program."

The complex approval process was also designed to make it absolutely clear that this was being done with the knowledge and support and under the direction of the president. That was also true with CIA's rendition, detention, and interrogation (RDI) program (see chapters 12 and 20), but there the paper trail was frustratingly thin, as I later learned.

On October 3, the vice president, Addington, and White House Counsel Al Gonzales took draft order number one to the president in the White House residence. As they entered the room, the president asked, "All ready?" He was familiar with what he was signing, but couldn't resist a question: "Well, David?" A bit at a loss for words, Addington simply pointed out the obvious: "No question that one day we will be publicly accountable." It was a great choice of phrase. Either way, there would be a reckoning on what the president did (or didn't do) that Wednesday evening with this order.

Addington then had to take the signed document to CIA to append to it the threat estimate and DCI recommendations that legitimized such dramatic action. Then to Justice for the attorney general to aver to its lawfulness, to Defense to direct its implementation, and then to me at Fort Meade to carry it out. David did it personally—no couriers, no pouches, no electronic signatures. Secrecy was paramount. No wonder he lobbied for (and won) forty-five-day cycles between each renewal rather than thirty.

David has a bit of a reputation as a snarly watchdog, but in setting up this meticulous process, he had my best interests at heart, as well as those of NSA, the president, and the country. He wasn't (always) the unrelenting ideologue that some portray him as, either. Speaking after the end of the first authorization, he reminded me that—as written—the order allowed the intercept of domestic-to-domestic communications if I thought they were al-Qaeda related. I reminded him that we were a *foreign* intelligence organization, that I wouldn't do that without a warrant, and besides, we didn't even have the plumbing to do that. The alleged architect of the "unitary executive" theory simply nodded, swung around in his chair, and amended the order that was on his screen so that it reflected exactly and only what it was we intended to do.

On Thursday, October 4, the day that the first authorization was official, I held a small meeting in my office for key people and asked, "Who should be in the room when I announce this more generally? We need to keep this tight."

As it turned out, there were sixty-six handpicked people in the director's conference room when I walked in there Saturday morning.

I began by demanding their undivided attention. I then outlined the events of the past weeks, how we had gotten here, and what the president wanted us to do. Bob Deitz was with me because, contrary to some uninformed views, NSA professionals are *very* conservative when it comes to the privacy of US persons and are so legally attuned that they recognized immediately that what we were going to do sidestepped FISA. Without visible, unqualified support from me, my deputy, and the legal folks (the ones who had been telling them the "thou shalt nots" for years), they wouldn't have done this. Deitz would reprise this session down the road at two town hall meetings to assure analysts of the lawfulness of the program and to explain why it was legal.

I left the operators in the conference room with their leadership for detailed briefings, but before I departed, I added that what we were about to do was unprecedented, but it was also lawful. I then said, "We are going to do what the president has authorized us to do but not one photon or one electron more."

When they were done they went downstairs to build a room and the connectivity they needed. By Sunday, work shifts had started. We had launched what would easily be the agency's edgiest undertaking in its history. We eventually called it Stellarwind, not because that meant anything, but because it didn't.

When I asked what the reaction was after I left the room, I was told that it was all business and dedication. People were excited that they would be able to do what they knew needed to be done. There was also a bit of an air of "This is a significant event. Don't screw it up."

One of the first things we needed was more computing power; this was going to be really big data. I contacted the CEO of a computer manufacturer that I had visited earlier. They found a shipment of about a hundred servers that met our needs and was already out the door, but not yet delivered to their customer. It was diverted to us, and we met it at a rest stop on Interstate 95 near Fort Meade, led the driver to our loading ramp, and assembled the components ourselves in the new Stellarwind offices.

Within about a month of launching, Stellarwind had several hundred people either committed to it full-time or otherwise cleared to support the program.

Of course, those numbers grew. By the time the *New York Times* revealed its existence in December 2005, well over a thousand people had been formally read into Stellarwind throughout the government, the majority of them at NSA, of course, but with significant pockets at FBI and CIA. Not all were active, but once read in, they were always knowledgeable.

Still, by government standards, for a four-year program, that's pretty tightly compartmented. After the program was disclosed, I received a true professional nod from David Pepper, the head of Britain's GCHQ. Entering my DNI office on a courtesy call, David simply smiled, and said, "Michael, my compliments. We had no idea."

When we were fully set up, just because of the way the telecommunications network functions, we had the theoretical ability to access a significant percentage of the calls entering or leaving the United States. Of course, we would access and collect a call only when the agency already had probable cause that it was affiliated with al-Qaeda.

NSA uses what it calls "selectors" when deciding to target a call; for telephone calls a selector could be the actual al-Qaeda associated number that is dialing or being dialed. Under Stellarwind, an overwhelming majority of the selectors were actually foreign numbers, and that proportion actually grew as the program matured.

From 2001 to 2005 there were hundreds of sole-source SIGINT reports, the kind derived from the content of communications, based on Stellarwind reporting. These reports covered terrorist planning, finances, logistics, training, travel, and contacts with people in the United States.

Because of the nature of modern communications, most of the content reports were actually from foreign-to-foreign calls that were merely transiting the United States. In 2006 alone there were nearly a hundred transit (i.e., both ends foreign) reports in which Stellarwind was the sole source and another thousand-plus in which Stellarwind accesses contributed to the final SIGINT product.*

Once disseminated, Stellarwind reporting was indistinguishable from the normal SIGINT production stream. Since one or both ends were always foreign, there was nothing that made their content stand out. What made them unique was how and where we acquired them.

We also gathered large volumes of metadata. In the first six months of the program we built up a bank of billions of domestic call events in addition to an even larger number of foreign ones. We used contact chaining from known or suspect "dirty numbers" to see if there were connections that suggested terrorist ties to the United States. These generated tippers that we would forward to CIA and FBI for further analysis (or action).

One agency wanted extensive three-hop metadata reports. A known dirty, that is, a terrorist-associated or "seed" number, calls A (hop 1), who calls B (hop 2), who calls C (hop 3). Admittedly that last hop to C is pretty attenuated from the original seed number. In most instances it only proves that everyone has a dentist or orders pizza. Things get interesting, though, when the last hop in one chain shows up in other chains from other seed numbers. We classified our tippers as high, medium, or low confidence based on the frequency, recency, and directness of con-

* Many SIGINT reports are composed of multiple intercepts.

tacts with the original dirty number. By December we were cranking out about ten potential leads per day, about one in ten of them high confidence.

The FBI had a policy to investigate every number sent. That approach really increased their workload.

Still, this all worked pretty much as we had anticipated. We traced threatening calls, showed suspicious contacts, uncovered illicit financing networks, detected suspect travel, discovered ties to aviation schools, linked transportation employees to associates of terrorists, drew connections to the illicit purchase of arms, tied US persons to Khalid Sheikh Mohammed, and discovered a suspect terrorist on the no-fly list who was already in the United States.

No one expected Stellarwind to stay secret forever. Nothing does. And we all knew that when it went public, the size of the storm would be in proportion to the success of Stellarwind and other counterterrorism programs. Specifically, if Stellarwind and other mutually reinforcing programs worked and the homeland remained safe, we would inevitably be accused of overreaching, of sacrificing liberty for security, and we would be treated to a whole bunch of misquotes of Benjamin Franklin, who actually said, "Those who can give up *essential* liberty to obtain a *little temporary* safety deserve neither liberty nor safety" (emphasis mine on the all-important qualifiers *he* inserted).

Most American intelligence professionals are well acquainted with the broad cultural rhythm connecting American espionage practitioners and American political elites: the latter group gets to criticize the former for not doing enough when it feels in danger, while reserving the right to criticize it for doing too much as soon as it has been made to feel safe again.

When the story broke in December 2005, it pretty much played out according to that script. Knowing that it would be no other way, we did our best from the beginning to cushion the inevitable shock wave.

One element was to make sure that we were doing this right. Because it was so tightly held, early oversight of the program was confined to our operations folks and our general counsel. By August 2002, though, we had expanded oversight to our inspector general's office. The core group here was composed of professional auditors and the inspector general himself, Joel Brenner, who was a skeptical outsider.

They put Stellarwind under a regime of routine reviews. One of their most important contributions was to take a program that had been rapidly established and make it more accountable through thoroughly documented procedures.

They found the kind of human errors one expects to find in any such undertaking: transposed numbers, for example. But, most significantly, they reported that, based on a statistically significant sample, they had determined that Stellarwind was adhering to the terms of the authorization and that tasking was appropriately reviewed, duly recorded, and correctly linked to authorized targets.

Joel was pretty much on record that any president who failed to collect the intelligence authorized by this program would have been derelict in his duty. He was equally passionate that we should move as much of this program as possible under the FISA Court and a broader (i.e., legislated) legal structure. We did, but not until years later.

Early on, we pressed the White House to allow us to at least brief the Hill. There is an air force adage: "If you want people to be there at the crash, you have to put them on the manifest." We had some pushback, not some kind of permanent prohibition, but more along the lines of "not now" and "we'll tell you when."

US law is pretty clear about keeping Congress "fully and currently informed" about significant intelligence activities, and Stellarwind certainly met that description. The executive has discretion, though, in limiting how many members actually get briefed.

A few weeks after we started the program, we got the OK to brief Congress.

On the morning of October 25 we met with the chairmen and ranking members of the two intelligence committees in the vice president's cramped office in the West Wing. I did the briefing after the vice president gave a solemn-toned introduction about the necessity of the program.

George Tenet was there to emphasize how serious the threat was. The order under which we operated was renewed by the president every forty-five days and was always accompanied by a DCI memo highlighting the dangers we were facing from al-Qaeda, including an ultimate threat to the continuity of government. With what had just happened in Washington and New York and Shanksville, we certainly didn't view that as an exaggeration, but over time the DCI's document was irreverently dubbed "the scary memo" by those of us read into the program. At this meeting George gave an excellent (if oral) "scary memo."

I had about two dozen paper slides outlining what we were doing; I also had numbers showing the scale of the work we were undertaking. When we met at NSA to prepare these briefings, I told the staff that we had to be totally open here, that the members had to see that this was "bigger than a breadbasket" (as I frequently put it), and that no one would get to say, when all of this was over and a national debate was engaged, "Well, I got some kind of briefing, but . . ."

It was all polite and professional in those briefings in the vice president's office, but we were blunt and explicit about how aggressive we were being and how different this was. I told the members how many US numbers had been tasked (targeted), the number of voice cuts (conversations) we had collected, and how many products (including reporting on US persons) we had created from this. We listed specific incidents where the program made a difference. We catalogued the raw volume of collection, both metadata and content. All in all, by the time the *New York Times* unilaterally "declassified"* elements of Stellarwind, we had had over a dozen meetings with members of Congress and all told had briefed fifteen members.

---

* Of course, the *Times* has no authority to declassify. What they did was to simply reveal the information.

At this first meeting, National Security Advisor Condi Rice sat near Congresswoman Nancy Pelosi, the senior Democrat on the House Intelligence Committee; Condi thought that Pelosi might need some extra convincing, as she had come to know the future Speaker, whose district was just up the interstate from Stanford, where Condi was recently provost. Neither Pelosi nor any of the other attendees (Porter Goss, Bob Graham, Richard Shelby) objected during the hour-long session, although Pelosi wanted additional reassurance immediately afterward. Standing under the awning on West Executive Avenue waiting for our cars, she turned and asked me, "Are you OK with all of this?" I had hoped that the briefing would have left her a little more confident but took the opportunity to reassure her that I was.

Actually, I wasn't aware of any stated objections from any of the members we briefed. I learned later that at some point Senator Jay Rockefeller (who became ranking member on the Senate Intelligence Committee and was "briefed in" in January 2003) wrote a letter to the vice president expressing his concern following another briefing in July. He complained about not being a lawyer, not being able to tell staff, and having nowhere to turn with concerns or objections. In truth, I suppose he could have demanded to see the attorney general (who was cleared and who we were saying had approved this), but he did not. The senator apparently kept a copy of the letter for himself, but when the program was made public, he couldn't find it and had to ask the White House for another copy.

The members were in an admittedly tight spot. They weren't being asked to *approve* the program; they were being *informed*. They couldn't talk to staff about it or even discuss it with other members. That said, I always viewed Rockefeller's letter as a kind of political insurance policy. If the program blew up politically, he could produce a record of his opposition. On the other hand, if something actually blew up in another terrorist attack, he could always claim that he was supporting all necessary measures to keep the country safe.

I took another of his later objections more personally. After elements of the program were outed, Rockefeller claimed that the briefings he received on it (all of them from me) were somehow shallow or incomplete; flipping through a bunch of slides was how he put it. I'm not sure how much more he wanted or could absorb, but so much for our strategy to be "full Monty" with our overseers.

Another senior Democrat later briefed on Stellarwind, Congress-woman Jane Harman, had some of the same political issues as Senator Rockefeller. Her path off that particular *X* was to claim that she had never been told that what we were doing was beyond the bounds of the FISA statute. So, were we having periodic, small-group, secret meetings in the vice president's office just to inform a very select group of Congress members and senators that nothing much had changed and we were doing this stuff just the way it had been done before 9/11?

No wonder, then, that Pat Roberts, later chairman of the Senate over-sight committee, rattled a pill bottle on one of those Sunday talk shows and declared that he was going to prescribe these "memory pills" for his colleagues.

In truth, though, we mishandled congressional notification—not con-stitutionally, but politically. We kept the circle small for noble reasons: to keep the secrets. But politically it was a mistake and strategically it led to a loss of political and, more important, popular support for what we were doing.

By keeping the circle so small we created a dilemma for the Democrats we had briefed; they would have to exhibit uncharacteristic heroism to resist their own political base when the program was revealed. Jane Har-man did so for a while when the *New York Times* published its account in December 2005. Most didn't.

And we actually motivated those who had not been briefed to oppose us simply on the grounds of process (or, in their view, lack of process).

A better course would have been to brief the entire House and Senate Intelligence Committees along with a limited number of staff on the whole program, effectively daring them to take action to stop *any* of it. That would have turned their natural political caution to our advantage rather than putting it on the other side of the issue.

I came to crudely put it that we should have made more people pregnant so that when this became public, no one could doubt who was already with child.

We informed the third branch of government, the judiciary, in early 2002, not because anyone thought that the president doing this under his Article 2 authorities needed the court's permission, but rather because Justice was understandably concerned that Stellarwind-derived data could work its way into applications for routine FISA warrants. Fearful of misleading the court if it was opaque regarding the sources in its applications, DOJ wanted at least the chief judge of the court to know the origins of such information (and confine applications burdened in this way to the presiding judge).

On one of those cold, overcast January days that seem so normal in Washington, my security detail escorted me from the Chevrolet Suburban up to Attorney General John Ashcroft's office to meet Judge Royce Lamberth, the presiding judge of the FISA Court. In the AG's anteroom I lashed up with John Yoo, who had written the DOJ opinion on which the White House based the legal justification of Stellarwind.

It was the first time that Yoo and I had met. This meeting would also be the first time that he would hear a detailed description of the program's technical operation, although he had seen Addington's order and Tenet's threat memo.

Yoo knew Lamberth pretty well from his time clerking for the DC circuit appeals court and the Supreme Court and as general counsel for the Senate Judiciary Committee. Lamberth came without staff and was his usual gregarious self. Yoo, Lamberth, and I settled into a circle of leather chairs as the attorney general sat at his desk. Ashcroft began the discussion with a broad treatment of the threat situation and a fairly nondescriptive overview of what we were doing, and then cued me to brief the judge.

This time, without paper slides, I walked the judge through what was essentially the congressional briefing except that as a judge on the FISA Court since 1995, Lamberth had a deep understanding of the law and a pretty good handle on the technology too.

Satisfied he understood what we were doing, he then turned to Yoo, and I got to sit back and watch the legal seminar as they went back and forth about the extent and the limits of executive power. Yoo admitted that when the president exercised his authority consistent with the intent of Congress described in statute (like the Foreign Intelligence Surveillance Act), he was operating from a very strong constitutional and political safe harbor. But he added that the president did not need such a haven when he was exercising his legitimate constitutional authorities as commander in chief, as he was in this case. Yoo noted that the Supreme Court had reserved this question. In other words, in previous opinions on surveillance it had clearly limited its reading on the Fourth Amendment's warrant requirement so as not to extend it to the collection of foreign intelligence.

The conversation was spirited, but not confrontational. Yoo was a little surprised, since the judge had been hell on DOJ the previous summer over mounting administrative errors in FISA applications. Lamberth wasn't leading the witness, but his questions suggested that he agreed with the argument grounding this in the president's commander-in-chief authority.

Others apparently did too. Only months later the FISA Court of Appeals, in its first ruling ever, unanimously cited earlier case law that "we take for granted that the president does have . . . inherent authority to conduct warrantless searches to obtain foreign intelligence information."

As we were closing, Yoo offered to give Lamberth a copy of his opinion, but the judge declined, saying that he understood the commander-in-chief-authority argument. The two also allowed themselves to speculate what might become of this issue were it ever to end up in front of the Supreme Court. Betting was in the 6–3 to 7–2 range.

Later, when Stellarwind became public, many commentators quickly labeled it unconstitutional on its face. Admittedly the Supreme Court dealt executive authority a series of body blows in the Hamdan and Hamdi cases (on Guantánamo detainees), but the arguments backstopping this program had strong history and precedent behind them. (And, if anything, the FISA Court endorsed the expansion of government surveillance in subsequent years.)

For our part, though, over the next two years, the Stellarwind program continued apace. We had growing confidence in its value, and I would periodically update the president and the congressional leadership on its success.

As I was walking through some slides one morning in the Oval Office, the president interrupted me and said, "So what you're telling me, Mike, is that this is working."

"Hold that thought, Mr. President," I responded. "Just three more slides."

We were able to brief real connections between overseas terrorists and people in the United States. We intercepted the content of communications as suspected terrorist-related calls exited or entered the United States. All this pointed to plotting in places like the northeastern and midwestern United States.

Was any of it decisive? I think so, but it's hard to prove definitively, since *good* intelligence is usually the product of multiple streams of information, and it's usually fruitless to try to untangle the streams to assign relative merit. But it is clear that Stellarwind covered a quadrant where we had no other tools.

What could be wrong with that?

THE FIRST WHEELS began to fly off entirely within the executive branch. Jim Comey had become deputy attorney general in December 2003, and early in his tenure I visited him in his office to acquaint him with Stellarwind. There was no way this program was *not* going to involve him, so we were anxious to give him the details.

I thought the briefing was unexceptional, friendly enough, but in retrospect it looks like Comey had other views. There have been several public accounts of the meeting from what has to be Comey's perspective, since I didn't talk to any of the authors.

One account says that I jokingly began with something along the lines of being happy to bring someone else into the circle, since sooner or later we were all going to have to raise our right hands when this became public. I was not intending any legal judgment, but certainly felt confident that politically that was where all this would inevitably end.*

Comey clearly wanted his own legal judgment, since he soon sent Patrick Philbin, a very conscientious lawyer whom we knew and liked from the Office of Legal Counsel, to do a thorough scrub of Stellarwind. Patrick routinely had complete access to both our legal and operational staffs. We didn't view this so much as an inspection but rather as one of those periodic checks you always wanted to have on a program like this. But it wasn't long before the NSA folks sensed that the legal consensus on which we were relying might not be as stable as we had thought.

At one point in early 2004 I crossed paths with Patrick in the hallway outside my office. We knew each other well enough that I could be candid with him. "Patrick," I said, "do I need to stop doing anything?"

"No," he replied, but ultimately what Patrick really meant was, "No, not yet."

A storm was brewing over certain aspects of the Stellarwind program, but decidedly not about all (or even most) of it. An aspect that was now in question (the details of which remain classified) involved collection that swept up some US person data. That is permissible—but only within limits—and now some in Justice thought that our current art and science weren't discriminating enough. Too much incidental collection of US person stuff. We obviously disagreed.

A lot of the legal Sturm und Drang played out in Justice beyond our view, but the thunder and the rain were visible enough when the Stellarwind authorization came up for renewal in early March 2004. Attorney General Ashcroft was in the hospital with acute pancreatitis, and Comey, as acting attorney general, would not aver to the lawfulness of the president's reauthorization. He was supported by Jack Goldsmith, the talented

---

* Given all my opportunities to testify in 2006, I was right.

new head of the Office of Legal Counsel (Philbin's boss), and FBI director Bob Mueller.

The storm hit, at least for us, on Sunday, March 7. I called an emergency meeting for about noon for my Stellarwind and counterterrorism experts to prepare me for a White House huddle later that day with the vice president, DCI Tenet, David Addington, Al Gonzales, and Andy Card. There we decided that Tenet would contact Bob Mueller directly; George later told me that Mueller had a high regard for Comey: "He's a serious guy. He shows up and his lead lawyers say they can't do it." George and I stayed closely connected and were on the phone a lot. But it was a hectic time. Calls were flying. I once hung up on the DCI to take a call from the vice president.

I was directed to prepare NSA technicians and CIA analysts for another briefing to Comey. We briefed Comey at the White House on Tuesday, March 9. It was the Sunday crowd, with John McLaughlin sitting in for Tenet, plus Comey and Mueller and others from Justice. Comey was a tough audience. He thought that this was the most aggressive assertion of presidential power in history (really?) and dismissed John Yoo's legal opinion out of hand. He angered my analysts by seeming to reject their claims and crediting traditional FBI approaches for what we believed were Stellarwind successes. We made no progress. It was a tense session, so Comey surprised me when he seemed to go out of his way to shake my hand as we adjourned.

We explored the possibility of legislative relief. On Thursday afternoon, March 10, the White House Situation Room was filled with eight senior congressional leaders.* They had been summoned there, from both chambers and from both parties, by an emergency phone call from the White House. Several had previously been briefed on Stellarwind; others had not.

The vice president began the meeting by outlining Stellarwind and

---

* Senators Frist, Daschle, Roberts, and Rockefeller plus Congress members Hastert, Pelosi, Goss, and Harman.

defending its utility, but also candidly describing the legal crisis we were now in over some aspects of the program. He then cued me to fill in the details on what we had been doing and particularly the details on what was now in dispute. Mine was an operational discussion, not a legal one. I brought two technical experts with me from the fort, and at one point, they laid out on the Situation Room table a complex (but nonetheless impressive) "spider chart" showing how Stellarwind could be used to identify and track a target. Two CIA analysts showed how this data could be folded into a larger analytical picture, using a then-current case as an example. That effort actually led to a number of arrests.

Senator Rockefeller, who was familiar with this from previous sessions, asked about due diligence, adherence to authorities, and positive controls. The vice president had us offer up the detailed Stellarwind checklist we used. I could also have added, as anecdotal evidence, that we couldn't target *all* terrorists under this program (only those connected to 9/11) and any expansion of targets required that the president specifically amend his direction to us. This had been carefully focused.

Small sidebar discussions developed as the explanation deepened. In one, Porter Goss, who as House Intelligence chair was very familiar with this, seemed to be explaining aspects to Senator Tom Frist.

It was a tough briefing, not because of any pushback, but because it was technical and wide ranging and it also had to be short. The Situation Room is small, and that day it was cramped and quite hot. Several members fought the urge to fall asleep.

I turned the floor back to the vice president and sat down in one of the chairs against the outside wall. A remarkable discussion followed.

When the vice president repeated that there were now significant headwinds from DOJ lawyers, one Republican wit acidly advised, "Then get some new lawyers!"

Another member raised the question of legislative relief, but this was ultimately rejected. Even if it were possible, it would take too long, and in any event, it was thought that congressional action would unmask too much of the program. (This was the course of action that my IG, Joel

Brenner, had been advocating. Interestingly, when the law was actually changed in 2008, the debate was indeed extraordinarily long, but the inner workings of the program were *not* exposed.)*

All in all, as I sat there with little to do but observe, I gradually grew more impressed with the members' inherent seriousness and patriotism. No one was celebrating the administration's legal or impending political dilemma, and there was no evidence that anyone in the room wanted this program to stop. On the contrary, they wanted this to work (within the law). One leading Democrat congratulated the administration on having such a meeting. As the session was closing, the vice president asserted that what he was hearing was that we should continue with the activity in question. No one disputed his statement.

Energized by the political consensus in the Sit Room that this needed to go forward while a permanent fix (still not in sight) was engineered, Chief of Staff Andy Card and White House Counsel Al Gonzales made one more try to get Ashcroft's signature on the renewal of the authorization. Their nighttime trip to George Washington hospital has been documented (and disputed) elsewhere. No one at NSA knew of the visit in advance, and we were given the briefest description of it afterward (David Addington mentioned it in passing to me during a phone call the next morning).

But now we had to make a decision, and I was asked Friday morning point-blank by the White House (in the person of Addington) whether I would agree to carry out the Stellarwind program if the White House counsel rather than the acting attorney general averred to its overall lawfulness.

After a short reflection, I said, "Yes, I would," thereby giving us another forty-five days to sort this out, get out of crisis mode, and more calmly (and collectively) agree on a way ahead.

I didn't regret the decision then and I don't regret it now. NSA lawyers, expert in this field, were still comfortable with what we were doing.

---

* Which, of course, became its own source of contention after Edward Snowden's revelations in 2013 (chapter 21). Sometimes you just can't win.

I was also heartened by the bipartisan political support I had sensed in the Situation Room the afternoon before. And—often missed in public accounts of the controversy—there's the fact that its lawfulness had been averred to about a dozen times, and even at this low point there was *no* DOJ opinion that it was unlawful, just a refusal to currently commit to its lawfulness. Let me repeat that. No one even now was telling us that we had been doing anything illegal, and when asked if they were preparing to do that, Justice said no. We were even later allowed to retain all the data we had previously collected under the program, a very problematic step if any unlawful acquisition had been so clear.

And I had one additional consideration. A few hours after Andy Card and Al Gonzales had left John Ashcroft on his sickbed at George Washington hospital, a series of backpack bombs began exploding on crowded commuter trains during the morning rush hour in Madrid, Spain. A total of 191 Spaniards were killed and nearly ten times that number were injured. With the morning's TV images from Europe fresh in my mind, I was not anxious to cut back on *any* intelligence collection.

Real-world events were imposing themselves. Operationally we were going crazy trying to keep pace with things like Madrid while also working an extraordinary number of hours supporting our general counsel and the Department of Justice. One of my best counterterrorism analysts told me that on his first day off in weeks, he was interrupted by phone calls at home from various offices in DOJ wanting clarification on the point papers he had submitted to them.

Andy Card informed the congressional leadership that we were going forward based on the White House counsel's and the president's view that this was legal. He emphasized the Madrid bombings in his rationale.

But that decision didn't hold. That Friday morning Comey and Mueller told the president that they would have to resign if the program continued unchanged. I got a call from Al Gonzales asking me what kind of operational effect discontinuing the contentious aspects of Stellarwind would have. He needed a sense of scale. Without much science behind me, I offered that we would lose about 20 percent of our overall Stellarwind effectiveness, but would keep 80 percent. I also had to tell the White House that it would take about a week to shut down those aspects completely and that I would need guidance on what to do with the troves of data already collected.

The president had told his team to find an approach that made Bob Mueller happy; the president could live with some objectors, but not with Mueller, for whom he had a very high regard.

The next day, Saturday, I received a phone call at home from Mueller. He just wanted to tell me that he still had the highest regard for me and for NSA, that the issue was never about my or NSA's respect for the law. It was a legal question, pure and simple. He knew we were trying to do the right thing. It was a kind gesture, but not really necessary. I never thought that the episode threatened our personal relationship, and I thought that *our* respect for law needed no defending.

The following Wednesday, March 17, my fifty-ninth birthday, Al Gonzales called to tell me that the president had decided to modify the Stellarwind program. We needed and were given until late March to complete the required changes, which we did.

All aspects of Stellarwind had previously been authorized by the president, in our view under his Article 2 authorities, in DOJ's view derived from the Authorization for the Use of Military Force against al-Qaeda. We knew all along that it would be more stable and less contentious the more we tucked it under the FISA Court. We now accelerated that process.

The White House gave us a target of May 6, the expiration date of the current authorization, to get the court's blessing on aspects of the program.

There was a flurry of meetings and phone calls over the next two weeks among ourselves, the White House, Justice, and the DCI about how to approach the court. The president was giving us plenty of running room. Al Gonzales called me at home to tell me that the president was very open to our having a very candid sit-down with the chief judge.

Jack Goldsmith and Patrick Philbin (who had raised the original concerns at Justice) now worked with us to move aspects of Stellarwind to the kind of broad legal footing more appropriate to a program that was now long-lived and not simply an emergency measure.

While our Justice colleagues were working legal theories, our task was to brief operational and technical details of Stellarwind to the presiding judge of the FISA Court, now Colleen Kollar-Kotelly. Our briefing included the disputed aspects of the program, since our lawyers still believed that they met the reasonableness standard of the Constitution, and we wanted to resume them.

Over two successive weekend days in mid-May 2004, NSA experts and lawyers, joined by senior Justice Department officials and the White House counsel, crowded into the top secret vault of the FISA Court. We explained what we had been doing, why, and to what effect. We also showed how we might tighten our effort in the disputed portions—potentially giving up some collection—so that we could decrease the proportion of US person information we had been ingesting.

In July, Kollar-Kotelly authorized NSA to collect, in bulk, certain e-mail metadata. Clearly this aspect was now under the court's authorization rather than the president's.* On the core issues, including the incidental collection of US data, the court had broadly gone with the White House's (and Justice's pre-March) view.

So, despite later published accounts of high drama and breathless runs up the stairs at George Washington hospital, given a little time the administration found an acceptable equilibrium for the Stellarwind program. Objections at Justice were quieted. In fact, Deputy Attorney

---

* Over time the court authorized the remaining aspects of Stellarwind and legislative underpinnings were created in the Protect America Act (2007), the FISA Amendments Act (2008), and the inclusion of some activities under Section 215 of the Patriot Act. By then, though, I was at CIA and largely out of the picture.

General Comey's signature was on several of the forty-five-day authorizations that were later issued.

As the summer of 2004 was drawing to a close, Stellarwind was still operationally sound, carefully run, and seemingly back on sound political and legal ground.

We felt pretty good. For a while.

SIX

GOING PUBLIC . . .
WILLINGLY
AND OTHERWISE

FORT MEADE, MD, AND
WASHINGTON, DC, 2004–2008

In early October 2004 the *New York Times* had a story, or at least part of a story, about surveillance of Americans without a warrant. One of the reporters on it was James Risen, an aggressive intelligence-beat veteran who had coauthored a book on Cold War espionage with CIA case officer Milt Bearden. His partner now was Eric Lichtblau, the *Times*'s Justice Department correspondent.

There's a rhythm to how stories about the intelligence community get written. Reporters usually circle the topic from the outside in, calling folks who they think know *something* about a topic, even if formally they may not know much. That way, when they get to more fully informed officials, they can began with, "I'm hearing that . . ." and thereby hope to force comment. Risen and Lichtblau's circles were tightening based on what we were hearing.

That set off multiple conversations between the White House, CIA,

Justice, and NSA. National Security Advisor Condi Rice was keeping the president informed about this, even though he was mostly on the road. We were just weeks out from an election, after all.

After the election, when the president asked me to speculate on who might be the source of the leaks on which this story was based, I suggested that—since the story the *Times* had was incomplete—the leaks likely came from people not actually read into the program. I said, "It sounds like watercooler talk, and a lot of the watercoolers seem to be in the Department of Justice."

I was at least partially right. In December 2008 Thomas Tamm, a career DOJ lawyer, outed himself in a *Newsweek* cover story as one of Risen and Lichtblau's key sources. Tamm was *not* read into the program, and since Justice did not pursue the investigation into the leak, whatever other sources Risen and Lichtblau might have had remain unknown.

Risen's tightening circles were getting close to me at NSA. He had already e-mailed the White House and had talked to Mark Mansfield in the Public Affairs shop at CIA. We put him off for about a week and then in mid-October I accepted Risen's call.

He began by asking me if we could talk in person about *this*.

"That would all depend on what *this* is."

He outlined his story: The president had authorized access to US telecommunications switches without benefit of court or new law. Some were questioning its legality. Could I help him better understand *this*?

I declined, saying that I couldn't discuss operational matters, but did say that everything we were doing was lawful, effective, and appropriate. I underscored the *effective* part to suggest that disclosures could put the nation more at risk.

Risen then went through a detailed description of his story: radical shift in policy; highly guarded secrets; access to large volumes of US communications; response to terrorist threats; backdoor arrangements with American telecoms; shaky legal opinions.

I thought that he had part of the story here. Some garble, though, and I was in no mood or position to correct him. He had some sense of the content collection we were doing under Stellarwind, although it seemed much exaggerated. He showed no knowledge of any acquisition of metadata.

I again declined to comment other than my "lawful, effective, and appropriate" mantra, which I repeated.

Risen then suggested that we talk about *this* off the record.

"Why would I do that?"

He said that he wanted to get it right, that he wanted to be "fair and balanced," inadvertently citing the famous Fox News line that prompted a chuckle from both of us as soon as he said it. He again pressed for a private meeting.

I told him that it would be hard for me to say anything more. I then added that, off the record, within US law I was duty bound to be as aggressive as possible. "Otherwise the taxpayers would be wasting their money on a lot of antennas out here."

Risen then doubled down on his carrots and his sticks. He said that I had done a great public service presenting NSA to the world and trying to clear up misperceptions. So it would behoove me to sit down and talk, since he had been following intelligence for a long time and this was the most serious story he had ever had.

It wasn't quite, "You're going down," but I think something like that was being messaged.

I pressed for a publication date (he said, "Only when it is ready") and thanked him for the call and the information.

I don't recall talking much to Risen after that. I *did* talk a lot to the *Times*'s Washington bureau chief, Phil Taubman. Taubman was a veteran, steeped in defense and intelligence issues, formerly Moscow bureau chief. He had spent a lifetime balancing the needs of transparency and security, so from our point of view, we could hardly have had a better interlocutor. (In 2008 Phil returned to his alma mater, Stanford, to teach about the tensions between a free press and national security. Both Condi and I have been guest presenters in his class using the *Times*'s Stellarwind saga as a case study.)

Condi arranged a meeting between John McLaughlin, the acting DCI, and Taubman and Risen. We held a secure videoconference with John before the meeting and set on the theme: "If you go with this story, you will set in motion a chain of events that, in a short time, will take away the most effective tool in our arsenal to defend America here and abroad against terrorism."

On an overcast October day, John McLaughlin, his chief of staff John Moseman, Taubman, and Risen met in the DCI's comfortable office in the Old Executive Office Building across from the West Wing. John remembers arranging the chairs in a semicircle in front of his large desk to make this an informal discussion rather than a lecture.

John had to be careful. He couldn't confirm anything. "If there were such an operation as this, it would be handled under strict protocols such as . . ." He continually emphasized its lawfulness and appropriateness even if never quite describing or confirming *it*. With questions and comments, it lasted the better part of an hour. Taubman seemed to be thoughtful and reflective throughout. Risen was described as obnoxious, argumentative, and combative, commenting only to rebut with a constant theme of the public's "right to know."

Contemporaneous notes indicated that Taubman understood the seriousness of the question, while "Risen doesn't give a shit, frankly."

I have always thought that a good rule when talking to a *responsible* journalist is to tell him more rather than less, even (especially) if your purpose is to prevent the publication of something you believe would harm national security. Taubman seemed to have a balance to his thinking and the more he knew, we reasoned, the more he would be inclined to protect what we believed to be properly classified information. The president seemed to agree. "Tell him whatever you need to tell him" was the guidance relayed to us.

So we became pretty forthcoming—with Taubman. The *Times* story was anchored on the actual content collection we were doing of phone calls. We stayed focused on that, as well. No moral, ethical, or legal requirement to bring up other activities of which they were, as of yet, unaware.

I emphasized that when we listened to a phone call, we already had probable cause that one or both ends of the call were al-Qaeda related. We made the case that FISA, as then constructed and then implemented (lengthy individualized warrants for any number on which you wanted to collect), denied us the agility we needed to keep up with the target.

The big meeting was in Condi's West Wing office one evening in late October. We gathered in couches and chairs around her coffee table. I believe (notes and memories have proved sketchy) that Bill Keller, executive editor of the *Times* and the ultimate authority on the go/no-go publication decision, was there. So was Taubman. On the White House side were Condi, Al Gonzales, and me. We approached the session with the same ground rules we had already been using: protect information by sharing more of it.

It wasn't a harsh or confrontational meeting. Not even impolite. On the coffee table between us I laid out an "analyst's notebook" graph that showed a variety of different nodes of the al-Qaeda network. Although it was an accurate and current chart, it didn't quite *prove* anything in the current discussion (which was about intercepting content). But it did show how things were interconnected, how individual pieces were important, and at least strongly *implied* that there was real risk if someone (like you, Mr. Keller) caused us to lose access to some of the pieces.

We never even thought of suggesting something as crude as "blood will be on your hands," but looking back, it's probably fair to say we were dropping more than hints that—barely three years after 9/11—none of us should start feeling lucky.

It was also important that the overwhelming majority of the calls we were *actually* intercepting under the president's authority were *foreign-to-foreign* (a reality that subsequent press accounts and even US government evaluations seemed to have trouble digesting or appreciating).

The peculiarities of FISA actually required us to get an individual warrant to fully cover each and any of the targeted numbers, an unintended consequence of a law drafted for a communications environment far different from the one with which we were dealing. If these international calls had been still bouncing into and out of the United States through the air—as they did in the 1970s when satellites were the long-haul system of choice—NSA would have been free to intercept them by targeting the foreign number. That's because the 1979 FISA law established a carve-out for collecting international satellite communications from US soil. But the subsequent telecommunications revolution now had these communications moving on a cable. To grab them from a cable on US soil generally required a warrant—a warrant on the targeted terrorist number—and that would have required literally thousands of individualized warrants against *foreign* numbers, which changed by the hundreds daily, a nearly impossible administrative task. There were targeted US terrorist-related numbers in the Stellarwind system, to be sure, but by far most of them weren't.

The 2004 presidential election came and went without the *Times* publishing, but what the *Times* would ultimately do was still unresolved after the election. We knew that Taubman's greatest concern was American privacy. I needed to send the message that we didn't take that lightly, that we were still respectful of US privacy, that this was being done by serious people. In mid-November I invited Phil to my eighth-floor office at Fort Meade, and I had him sit on the sofa as I introduced him to Bob Deitz, the general counsel, and two of our senior analysts, one of whom had been with me in the dramatic White House Situation Room briefing the previous March (chapter 5).

I walked Taubman through the importance of the program once again and then pointed out that US privacy was still a priority. Hanging from the ceiling in the room where this was done was a large black-and-gold sign headed by the question "What Constitutes a US Person?" Below the question was a description of the four categories that got an individual or a group into that protected status. Despite the aggressive collection, US person identities would be "minimized" (masked) unless that identity was absolutely essential to understanding the intelligence we were reporting.

I then stood up and, much to the surprise of my two analysts and Phil, announced, "Phil, you probably have specific questions you want to ask these guys. Let me leave you alone for a few minutes."

Walking toward the door, I turned to my officers and told them, "Just answer his questions."

Spontaneous as this was, it wasn't really very daring. These guys were smart and really believed in what they were doing.

One of the analysts later told me that after this session he had rushed from my office to the general counsel, much like an errant Catholic rushing to confession, to ask how he could possibly pass his next polygraph, since he had just told a journalist some of America's deepest secrets. "It was authorized," Deitz responded. "Don't worry about it." Apparently he didn't. He passed his next poly.

I returned to my office after a decent interval to say goodbye to Taubman. As he was leaving, I said, "Do you realize you've gone where no one in your profession has gone before?"

He quipped back, "Yeah, and I expect to get bumped off in the parking lot."

We still had one more card to play. We put Taubman in touch with Jane Harman, who was willing, in broad terms, to express her comfort with what we were doing.

On December 8, Condi called me to relay the news that the *Times* had decided not to publish. Taubman called me with the same message, with the usual caveat that we would let him know if someone else was smelling around about the story. I agreed, and added that we had gotten "a small burp" from the *Washington Post,* but that had gone away.

Editor Bill Keller later had to defend the *Times*'s decision not to publish in late 2004. I'd like to think our national security argument swayed him, and although we have never talked about it, I think Taubman was a genuine voice of caution within the *Times*.

The presidential elections may have been a factor too. It would have been hard to publish a story that could have had a powerful, perhaps decisive (if unpredictable), impact on the presidential election. That's a pretty heavy lift for a newspaper, even one that claims to be the nation's newspaper of record. And publishing such a story right after the election would have been running against a president who had just received a national mandate based, in part, on his counterterrorism policies.

THERE WERE NO PRESIDENTIAL ELECTIONS pending the following November (2005) when Phil Taubman called me personally to tell me that the *Times* was reconsidering its position. He added, "Other people have come forward with concerns."

More of Lichtblau's sources in Justice, I silently mused.

Phil didn't mention it then, but it soon became clear that Risen was holding his own newspaper hostage. He had already sent a final draft of his upcoming book, *State of War*, to his publisher, and the Stellarwind story was going to be one of its flagship chapters. Essentially the *Times* was faced with a "use it or lose it" dilemma. And they really wanted to use it.

Although Taubman called *me*, I was gone from NSA and was serving as principal deputy director of National Intelligence under John Negroponte (chapter 9). I had to catch up and so began a series of secure videoconferences with NSA over the next week or so. I was still corporate memory, though, since Al Gonzales was now attorney general with Harriet Miers in his place as White House counsel. Condi's deputy, Steve Hadley, had fleeted up to the national security advisor position. I alerted the new players to the pending crisis and promised I would talk with Phil.

Taubman was as evenhanded as ever, but he was pressing hard on the "others have come forward" theme, and that, he said, showed that there was tension within the administration over the program. I assured him that there was no contention over what we were doing, which was true as far as it went. I wasn't at liberty to discuss the crisis of March 2004, which, after all, had been settled (satisfactorily from our point of view) and in any event involved an aspect of the program that was not part of the *Times*'s story.

Phil persisted and pushed for access to members of Congress in order to personally gauge whether or not they were on board. That was going to be tricky. It was one thing for me (for the administration) to show more leg, but quite another to get politically cautious members of Congress to do the same thing. "I'll look into it," I told Phil.

We reprised the 2004 meeting in the office of the national security advisor in late November 2005. Hadley hosted, joined by Condi (now at State), Harriet Miers, John Negroponte, and me. Keller and Taubman were there from the *Times,* and this time they were joined by Eric Lichtblau, one of the reporters. This session was edgier in tone than the previous one—it seemed less a discussion about whether or not to publish and more a last chance for the administration to prevent it.

The *Times* kept returning to the theme of internal dissent, and their natural inclination to publish was reinforced by Risen's imminent book. After all, this *was* going to become public, one way or another. The only question for them was whether or not they were going to get credit for it.

I also suspect that the *Times* shared, reflected, and was trying to lead a changing mood in the country. After four-plus years of both public and elite opinion clamoring for us to do "whatever it takes," the burden of proof was now clearly on us to show that what we were doing was both lawful *and* unarguably essential. We weren't going to win any close calls.

We had a program that was an aggressive use of executive power, but one made known to the other two branches (more broadly known than many covert actions). It was carefully run, there was no evidence of abuse, and we believed it was contributing to making the nation safer.

Now the *Times* (and other outlets once the story broke) was ready to descend with a fury if we couldn't prove that all of those claims were airtight. Congressional notification looked flawed: too few members; too few details; no staff. How could we claim there was a consensus within the executive branch when their reporters kept getting those phone calls? We said there had been no abuses. How could they possibly confirm that?

It was the effectiveness metric that was most difficult to show. Good intelligence is like a tapestry with multiple threads woven into a beautiful whole. And here we were being asked to show when and where *this* strand did it all (not unlike a later debate over the effectiveness of CIA interrogations). Besides, almost all of the concrete cases we had were still part of current operations, active investigations, or open court cases. Openness has its limits.

What they were looking for, and I couldn't provide, was a case where a Stellarwind intercept had led to our tackling a sniper on a roof just as he was chambering a round. Anything short of that was unconvincing.

We were still losing. We took it to the Oval.

There the government cast was the president, Chief of Staff Andy Card, Harriet Miers, and me. The *Times* contingent comprised Taubman, Keller, and Arthur Sulzberger Jr., the publisher. The president sat in his usual chair in front of the fireplace. The vice president's chair to his right was empty. After a very brief greeting the president motioned the visitors to sit on the sofa to his left, where the national security advisor and chief of staff usually sat for the morning PDB.

Sulzberger tried to break the ice by jokingly pointing out that both he and the president were now working in their fathers' offices. No ice was broken.

Sulzberger then attempted to lay out the *Times*'s position on the matter at hand. No go there, either. The president cut him short and said this conversation was about his telling the paper why going with the story was wrong.

The president said that if another attack was successful, he expected the *Times*'s leadership to be up on the Hill, right hands in the air along with the leadership of the intelligence community, explaining to Congress how they permitted it to happen.

The president cued me for my regular presentation on the program. It could have gone better. I was physically too far away from the target audience, two of whom had heard this before and one of whom seemed to think this was a pretty pro forma step.

As the meeting inconclusively adjourned, the *Times* contingent renewed their request to meet with members of Congress to gauge whether they believed that the program should remain secret. They also promised *not* to go with the story without giving the White House a chance to comment.

We stayed behind in the Oval. I suggested to the president, who had done an eye roll when the idea of letting the *Times* talk to Congress was raised, that we had to take that step. I would arrange it exclusively for Taubman, whom, I said, "we could trust."

I worked through Pat Roberts, chairman of the Senate Intelligence Committee, to set up the session. One night in mid-December, Taubman met with Roberts and his Democrat counterpart, Jay Rockefeller, along with Pete Hoekstra and Jane Harman from the House side. I consciously absented myself. Some may have seen risk in that, but I believed that the presence of *any* administration official at the meeting would cause even supportive views from the members to be discounted.

Afterward I talked to the folks who were in the meeting. All of them were very forceful that the story should *not* go forward. "We disagree on some things," one member offered, "but not on this program." Another referred to the effort as the "crown jewels" to explain why only a small group had been briefed. Taubman was told that "people have a right to privacy, but they also have a right to live." One member colorfully reported to me afterward that "the Four Horsemen stood firm."

It didn't matter. Early in the evening of December 15, the *New York Times* Web site posted a screaming headline: "Bush Lets US Spy on Callers Without Courts." The timing may also have been related to the renewal of the Patriot Act, which had been pulled forward on the legislative calendar and was now being debated. The *Times*'s bombshell delayed passage until the following March. There were also reports that the *Times* feared prior restraint—the administration going to the courts to prevent publication.

The night the story hit, my wife, Jeanine, and I were hosting Pete Hoekstra and Jane Harman for a small dinner at our house at Bolling Air Force Base along the Potomac. The chair and ranking member of the House Intelligence Committee really weren't getting along, so I can't claim that everyone's cell phone going off ruined what had been to that point a thoroughly relaxing evening.

But go off they did. After four years of Stellarwind, the public was being given a necessarily incomplete and often flawed account of what its government had been doing to protect it. The *Times* had *a* story, but not really *the* story, at least from our point of view. The questions for us now were what we were going to do to defend ourselves and in that process how much of the program we could make public.

President Bush drew the battle line the next morning, Friday, when he directed that his regular Saturday radio address, which he had already recorded, be scrapped. He would go live on Saturday morning, defend the program, condemn the leak, and promise to keep on doing what he was doing.

The president began, "To fight the war on terror, I'm using authority vested in me by Congress . . . [and] I am also using constitutional author- ity vested in me as commander in chief."

After emphasizing that this involved international calls, that at least one end was always outside the United States, and that any intercept was always based on the belief that the call was affiliated with al-Qaeda, the president condemned the unauthorized disclosure of this information and then said that he had "reauthorized this program more than thirty times . . . and I intend to do so for as long as our nation faces a continu- ing threat from al-Qaeda and related groups."

In the intel community, when someone runs a story that threatens to win a Pulitzer Prize (Risen and Lichtblau did indeed win one, although the Pulitzer Committee had to do some creative categorizing that year to honor both them and Dana Priest's exposé of CIA black sites), everyone holds their breath to see if the political leadership that told you to do this in the first place is going to man up and back you. President Bush manned up that Saturday morning. (And after the holidays he went to Fort Meade to support the NSA workforce and personally thank the Stellarwind crew for their work.) We could exhale.

On that same Saturday my wife and I were trying to squeeze in some Christmas shopping at the Annapolis Mall. My cell phone rang. It was Jane Harman, senior Democrat on the HPSCI, knowledgeable about the program and, up to that point, supportive. She wanted me to brief all the members of the House Intelligence Committee on Stellarwind. She said that it was the right thing to do, and although she didn't say it, I knew that it would give her some badly needed and well-deserved political top cover.*

Andy Card was supportive, so I prepared to close down the shopping trip and head downtown. I shouldn't have bothered. Before I could leave the mall, the project had been nixed. I was never told by whom.

If Harman was trying to help, others were looking for cover. As the press stories piled up, I got a phone call from Congresswoman Nancy Pelosi, House minority leader, who had been briefed five times on Stellarwind at that point.

As she was ranking Democrat on the intelligence committee, I had also briefed her shortly after 9/11 on a separate issue: the instructions I had given with regard to communications between the United States and Afghanistan, essentially directing that analysts should interpret "intelligence value" rather liberally when deciding whether US person information should be included in reporting (chapter 5). After all, three thousand of our countrymen were dead in an attack organized in and directed from that country. We didn't want to miss or delay anything. Following *that*

---

* In air combat, top cover refers to fighter aircraft flying at high altitude to protect more vulnerable forces below. We owed Harman something like that since she wanted to be supportive, but it would be at great cost within her party.

briefing (which was given before Stellarwind existed), Congresswoman Pelosi sent a letter to NSA expressing some generalized concerns about US privacy, which we dutifully answered.

Now the congresswoman wanted me to expedite declassification of that October 2001 letter. I said that I would, but added that her letter—although its language was general enough to allow it to be construed to be about the subject of the *Times* story—was decidedly *not* about that program.

"Ma'am," I argued, "this is apples and oranges."

"It's all fruit," she replied.

The Sunday after the *Times* story broke, Al Gonzales and I were in the Senate Intelligence Committee chamber, where Pat Roberts, the chairman, had invited the chair and ranking members of the Senate Judiciary Committee. It was scheduled late to accommodate the senators returning to Washington. The ranking member, Senator Leahy, was a no show. He certainly proved to have a view on all this, but he never got our description of exactly what we were doing.

So it was the three of us and Senator Arlen Specter, then Republican (later Democrat) of Pennsylvania and a former district attorney in Philadelphia. Judge Gonzales gave a broad overview and then turned to me for a detailed lay-down.

It was slow going. As a former prosecutor, Specter had a law enforcement view of surveillance, so intelligence rules (even pre-Stellarwind intelligence rules) constituted new ground for him. At one point, he simply asked, "But how do you protect privacy?" I began to outline all the US person privacy protections, minimization of US identities and the like, when he interrupted again to add, "No, everyone's privacy. Foreigners' privacy."

I hadn't expected that one. My instinct was to say something about the Fourth Amendment not being an international treaty, an instinct I wisely suppressed, and probably muttered something about confining ourselves to things that were operationally relevant.

That should have been a lesson. This was going to be harder to explain than I thought, since so many people lacked a basic understanding of what NSA did. Stellarwind was a departure from normal, to be sure; a legitimate question was how many sigmas, how many deviations from the mean. Without an understanding of the baseline, everyone was free to imagine the worst.

Early next morning (Monday) I walked the short distance to the White House from the New Executive Office Building, where the ODNI's temporary offices were. It was less than a week from Christmas, decorations were out, and the air was crisp and clear. Lovely morning for a walk through Lafayette Park.

There had been broad suggestions over the weekend of a press availability that morning. Good thing I went over to check. A few minutes after I arrived, I was ushered into a packed White House pressroom with Al Gonzales to do a backgrounder on what the White House now called the Terrorist Surveillance Program (i.e., that part of Stellarwind revealed by the *New York Times*).

Judge Gonzales began by explaining the program. International calls only. Related to al-Qaeda. Justified by the president's constitutional authority as well as being "incident" to war as declared by the Authorization for the Use of Military Force even though surveillance (and detention) were not specifically mentioned.

I pointed out that "there are probably no communications more important to what it is we're trying to do to defend the nation; no communication is more important for that purpose than those communications that involve al-Qaeda, and one end of which is inside the homeland, one end of which is inside the United States."

When challenged why we could not do this under FISA, I responded,

FISA is very important, we make full use of FISA. But if you picture what FISA was designed to do, FISA is designed to handle the needs of the nation in two broad categories: there's a law enforcement aspect of it; and the other aspect is the continued collection of foreign intelligence. I don't think anyone could claim that FISA was envisaged as a tool to cover armed enemy combatants in preparation for attacks inside the United States.

The whole key here is agility. . . . FISA was built for persistence. FISA was built for long-term coverage against known agents of an enemy power. And the purpose involved in each of those—in those cases was either for a long-term law enforcement purpose or a long-term intelligence purpose.

This program isn't for that. This is to detect and prevent. And here the key is not so much persistence as it is agility. It's a quicker trigger. It's a subtly softer trigger. And the intrusion into privacy—the intrusion into privacy is significantly less. It's only international calls. The period of time in which we do this is, in most cases, far less than that which would be gained by getting a court order. And our purpose here, our sole purpose, is to detect and prevent.

It is not designed to collect reams of intelligence . . . [and if] this particular line of logic, this reasoning that took us to this place proves to be inaccurate, we move off it right away. We can't waste resources on targets that simply don't provide valuable information . . . and in this program, the standards, in terms of reevaluating whether or not this coverage is worthwhile at all, are measured in days and weeks.

That's about as clear an exposition of the program as I have ever given. It didn't matter. The place was a snake pit. Helen Thomas kept up a mumbled growl at me from her front-row seat with sounds that may have contained a question.

Others chimed in. "I wanted to ask you a question. Do you think the government has the right to break the law?" Followed by, "You have stretched this resolution for war into giving you carte blanche to do anything you want to do." We were then told, "You're never supposed to spy on Americans." Followed by the accusation that we were "into wiretapping everybody."

I was challenged about what was really compromised by the *Times* story. "General . . . don't you assume that the other side thinks we're listening to them? I mean, come on."

I responded that the program's success was a prima facie case against that assumption but that "the more we discuss it, the more we put it in the face of those who would do us harm, the more they will respond to this and protect their communications and make it more difficult for us to defend the nation."

When I said that decisions on whose communications to target were made by intelligence professionals, I got hit with, "So a shift supervisor is now making decisions that a FISA judge would normally make? I just want to make sure I understand. Is that what you're saying?" I said that it was. And I was saying it "to remove any question in your mind that this is in any way politically influenced."

Near the end, I was actually asked a fair and important question: "Can you assure us that all of these intercepts had an international component and that at no time were any of the intercepts purely domestic?"

I could. "I can assure you, by the physics of the intercept, by how we actually conduct our activities, that one end of these communications is always outside the United States of America."

It was a long thirty-two minutes. We didn't have much success in advancing either human knowledge or national understanding of what we were trying to do.

We kept at it. We spent Christmastime 2005 answering the phones and initiating calls to folks in the press we had talked to in the past. It was a hard sell. Some reacted viscerally. As good a reporter as John Diamond of *USA Today* was furious at us for what he viewed as our betrayal of his trust in earlier stories. We didn't see it that way, but it hardly mattered.

We also spent Christmas week trying to get our hands on Risen's book, *State of War*. A junior ODNI officer finally tracked down a copy before they went up on the shelves of a local bookstore, brought it back to the office, and proceeded to xerox multiple copies for us. We pretty much knew what the Stellarwind content would be, but were willing to risk a minor copyright violation to see what other state secrets were going to be revealed. I must admit that it also felt good not to pay for it.

After the holidays, we were tapped to brief the entire FISA Court on the Stellarwind program. Since I had set the program up, I was to be the lead briefer. I spent two long days at Fort Meade preparing.

On January 9 we briefed the chief FISA judge, Colleen Kollar-Kotelly, and eight of her associate judges. It was a long session: four hours without a break. Attorney General Gonzales was there at the beginning to thank the court for the opportunity to brief and to introduce me—as Colonel Hayden, a misstep that provoked some laughter and actually seemed to break the ice a bit. We laid it all out. Lots of questions, many mixed with skepticism. One FISA judge, James Robertson, had already resigned in protest, stepping down a few days after the original *Times* story, although it appears he acted based on the news accounts rather than any fuller description. At this session, though, after about two hours the center of gravity of the discussion seemed to shift in the direction of how the FISA regime could be made more relevant to twenty-first-century threats and technology.

When I got back to my security detail after this session, I had a note to call my sister Debby in Steubenville. My arrival at the FISA Court had apparently been reported in the media, and in our old neighborhood in Pittsburgh showing up in front of a judge was hardly ever good news. I assured her that I wasn't appearing before that kind of court. Not yet, anyway.

In late January, I had another shot at a public presentation at the National Press Club. I reminded folks that this was targeted and focused, "the hot pursuit of communications entering or leaving America involving someone we believe is associated with al-Qaeda. . . . It is not a drift net over Dearborn or Lackawanna or Fremont grabbing conversations that we then sort out by these alleged key-word searches or data-mining tools or other devices that so-called experts keep talking about.

"This is not about intercepting conversations between people in the

United States. When you're talking to your daughter at state college, this program *cannot* intercept your conversations. And when she takes a semester abroad to complete her Arabic studies, this program *will not* intercept your communications."

Since we were at the press club, I decided a modest lecture to the press itself would be in order. "I know how hard it is to write a headline that's accurate and short and grabbing," I conceded. "But we really should shoot for all three—*accurate*, short, and grabbing. I don't think domestic spying makes it. One end of any call targeted under this program is always outside the United States. . . . I've taken literally hundreds of domestic flights. I have never boarded a *domestic* flight in the United States of America and landed in Waziristan. In the same way . . . if NSA had intercepted al-Qaeda ops chief Khalid Sheikh Mohammed in Karachi talking to Mohamed Atta in Laurel, Maryland, in say, July of 2001—if NSA had done that, and the results had been made public, I'm convinced that the crawler on all the 7 by 24 news networks would not have been 'NSA domestic spying.'"

That was the only example that I used that day, but there were more available. Accusations are always simple; truth is often complicated. And as the quotation etched into the wall of the CIA lobby suggests, it is truth—not simplicity—that will make you free.

Then at the press club I said something I believed to be true then and I continue to believe to be true now. "Had this program been in effect prior to 9/11, it is my professional judgment that we would have detected some of the 9/11 al-Qaeda operatives in the United States, and we would have identified them as such."

It was a long speech, but it was the clearest and most comprehensive public exposition of what NSA was doing and why that we had ever made. Of course, it was limited to that part of the Stellarwind program that the president had confirmed, intercepting the content of one-end US international phone calls. I didn't announce that there were other activities that I couldn't talk about, but I did caution that "this is a little hard to do while protecting our country's intelligence sources and methods.

And, frankly, people in my line of work generally don't like to talk about what they've done until it becomes a subject on the History Channel."

Nonetheless, I continued: "I much prefer being here with you today telling you about the things we have done when there hasn't been an attack on the homeland. This is a far easier presentation to make than the ones I had to give four years ago telling audiences like you what we hadn't done in the days and months leading up to the tragic events of September 11."

I took questions, a measure of modest courage, since the press club definition of "press" is rather broad and C-SPAN was streaming all this live. It wasn't quite the bar scene on Tatooine in the first *Star Wars* movie, but it had its moments. Some questions were based on genuine efforts to understand a complex topic (like the details of an emergency FISA warrant). Others were unarguably combative ("Are you asserting inherent so-called constitutional powers . . . to violate the law when [the president] deems fit?"). Still others were thinly veiled infomercials for specific groups (like something called The World Can't Wait!: The Call to Drive Out the Bush Regime).

As near as we could tell, the session did not create any change in the tone (or from our view, the accuracy) of the press coverage.

Two weeks later Jeanine and I were in Detroit to see our Steelers play the Seahawks in Super Bowl XL as guests of my Catholic junior high football coach, Dan Rooney, the owner of the team. I think Dan was taking a little pity on me, what with all the publicity. In any event it was great to see a win from the owner's box even if I had to do two Sunday talk shows that morning. Near the end of the game, with the Steelers up 21–10, Dan apologized that he had to leave the box early to go down to the field to accept the Lombardi Trophy.

"Dan," I assured him, "this is a good thing."

There had been so many Steelers fans at the game that there was a long backup at the tollgate between the Ohio and Pennsylvania turnpikes the next morning. No one seemed to complain, though.

I flew back to Washington that Monday morning, too, and basically reattached myself to my deputy DNI job. We had made our case as best we could. No need to keep feeding the media beast.

We just held the line like the president said we were going to. We kept on doing what we were doing on the grounds that it was proportional, lawful, effective, targeted, had not been abused, and was consistent with the US Constitution.

When the public debate subsided (a little), the White House and Justice continued to press for legislation to backstop what the president had authorized to create a political and legal safe harbor for the executive. It took time, but they got their way. In a series of steps from 2006 through 2008—renewal of the Patriot Act, the Protect America Act, the FISA Amendment Act—almost all that President Bush had authorized via Stellarwind was codified in law. And—despite the earlier journalistic outrage—a lot more to boot. Go figure.

SEVEN

THE PUBLIC'S RIGHT
TO KNOW . . . AND BE SAFE

FORT MEADE, MD, AND LANGLEY, VA, 1999–2009

The Stellarwind story was symptomatic. It was but one example of growing administration-press tensions, or more accurately, it was an expression of the continuous tension between transparency and secrecy in a free society.

I was accustomed to my public affairs officer running into my office at either CIA or NSA and suggesting or requesting or demanding that I call an editor or publisher to scotch a particularly egregious story. When I agreed to do that, I would invariably begin the conversation with, "Thanks for taking my call. I know that we both have a job to do protecting American security and American liberty. But I'm afraid that how you are about to do yours is going to make it more difficult for me to do mine."

To be fair, those calls I made to slow, scotch, or amend a pending story were worth making. Many on the other end of the line were open to reasonable arguments. In one case a writer willingly changed a reference that had read "based on intercepts" to "based on intelligence reports," somewhat amazed that this change made much of a difference. (It did.)

Another reporter, quite experienced, casually and quite responsibly volunteered to my press office, "I know this is SIGINT, but I don't need that for my story."

The *Washington Post*'s Dana Priest, not one with high favorables at Langley, did not publish the locations of alleged CIA detention sites in her Pulitzer-winning series in late 2005. The agency argued that such a revelation would put the citizens of these countries at increased risk from terrorists. She agreed.

But sensitivity to the national welfare was not a universal condition, and I wasn't alone in this assessment. In January 2008 twelve senior leaders of the intelligence community (including me) signed a letter to the leadership of the Senate opposing a pending journalist shield law, which would have put even more procedural steps in the process we had to follow to track down and prosecute leakers. We said that it would "undermine our ability to protect intelligence sources and methods."

None of us were insensitive to the principles of the First Amendment, to the role of the press in our democracy, or to the delicate balance and inherent tension between security and openness. We just thought that some things were legitimate secrets. I laid out that case at an informal, off-the-record gathering of journalists in October 2006. I was admittedly a little pissy after several sensitive NSA and CIA programs had become press fodder.

I began with the premise that there exist in the world things that are legitimate secrets: this is true for the family, the PTA, the Lions Club, and the press. Society understands and recognizes this need and has established rules for when secrets will be recognized and afforded a privilege and when they will not. We recognize the marital, the attorney-client, and the priest-penitent privilege, and rules have been developed for when these privileges are overcome because of the greater community need.

Like other communal entities, governments, too, need secrets. Within the federal government, all three branches claim this right. The deliberations of the courts are secret. Congressional markup sessions are done in private. The Federal Reserve keeps secret its discussions about the overnight discount rate so as not to affect markets. Crop support levels are kept secret until a certain date and time set by the Department of Agriculture.

The position is actually unassailable. In November 2008 *New York Times* correspondent David Rohde was kidnapped by the Taliban in Afghanistan and taken by the Haqqani network to Pakistan. *Everybody* knew. But none of this appeared in the press until Rohde escaped. None of this: not the fact that he had been kidnapped, not what the *Times* was doing, not what I was doing diverting CIA-controlled resources to look for him (a fact about which I quietly informed the *Times*). The *Times* thought that Rohde's plight was a legitimate secret. So they exist! Even the press seems to concede that there are necessary secrets (including especially its own sources, of course).

But that wasn't always the rhetoric, so I was challenging a public talking point of the press people gathered with me in 2006 when I said, "So let me set up a contrary position to what the press speaks of as the 'public's right to know.'"

The "right to know" is far from an absolute. In fact, in some ways the public has already decided what it does and does not want to know. The president and other members of the executive branch have been authorized by legislation to classify information whose release, in their collective judgment, would damage national security. The Supreme Court has repeatedly recognized this authority.

The press kind of recognizes this right. According to David Broder of the *Washington Post*, "It's the government's responsibility to keep its secrets." But then he goes on to say, "And it's our responsibility to ferret out information so the public is aware of the actions being taken in its name." In other words, the government, under the authority of the public's lawfully elected representatives, has the right to keep secrets, but they should remain secret only unless and until someone leaks them to the press. You don't have to drive the premise to the extreme before this begins to border on the incoherent.

Of course, the counterpoint is that the press would never divulge legitimate secrets, and (an important corollary) the press has to be the final arbiter of what is and is not a legitimate secret. Even assuming goodwill and setting aside the question of legal authority, there remains the issue of competency. David Ignatius, no apologist for intelligence community secrecy, summarizes it nicely: "We journalists usually try to argue that we have carefully weighed the pros and cons and believe that the public benefit of disclosure outweighs any potential harm. The problem is that we aren't fully qualified to make those judgments."

I laid into the journalists at my 2006 off-the-record gathering with a catalogue of specific harm done by leaked secrets. I had leaned hard on my own ops folks to get my talking points cleared for the discussion.

I told the journalists that one recent spate of stories cost us five promising counterterrorism and counterproliferation assets, who feared we couldn't guarantee their security, and most of them weren't even reporting on the same subject as the stories. In August 2002 a sensitive clandestine source actually saw his reporting disclosed on TV during a meeting with his case officer. When a covert CIA presence in a denied area was revealed in the media, two assets in the area were detained and executed. Our officers there wrote: "Regret that we cannot address this loss of life with the person who decided to leak our mission to the newspapers."

Another leak, on weapons of mass destruction, led to one of our assets being arrested by a foreign government on suspicion of espionage; details in a follow-up story convinced the government that they had the right man and he was convicted and sentenced; a third story caused his family's property to be seized, and we had to move them out of the country to protect them.

I concluded by pointing out that several years prior to the 9/11 attacks, one chief of station reported that a press leak of liaison intelligence had "put us out of the bin Laden reporting business" locally. The service ceased counterterrorism cooperation for two years.

I wasn't done. Beyond possible (I was being kind) errors in judgment, there was a question of journalistic slant. Everyone seemed anxious to double down on the prevailing story line. Brian Ross (whom I have since gotten to know and respect) led off the ABC nightly news during the

Stellarwind surveillance kerfuffle, waving an NSA memo at the camera and claiming that "whistle-blower" Russ Tice had been warned not to talk to the House Intelligence Committee about some activities because the committee was not cleared for the material. Having so much trouble containing his outrage, Ross was apparently unable to discover that Tice—who was cleared for and talking about DOD rather than NSA special access programs—needed to talk to the Armed Services Committees, rather than the intelligence committees, about his allegations.

I then asked the assembled journalists some rhetorical questions. Did any of you report that Tice did indeed finally appear before congressional staff? How did that go? Did you report the results of those sessions? Any congressional outrage to tell us about? (None that I know of.) Maybe a good question to ask would have been how long Tice had been at NSA (not long; DIA kind of dumped him on us) and then follow up with how long he was at NSA *and* cleared (even shorter; he spent most of his time on the loading dock). Actually kind of important stuff, but what the country got was Ross and Tice ominously walking out of the shadows (literally) on prime-time news.

The *New York Times* reprised this genre of drama-above-all reportage in an only slightly different format in June 2006, when Eric Lichtblau and James Risen (coauthors of the NSA stories) reported that the US government had access to the financial transaction database of SWIFT (Society for Worldwide Interbank Financial Telecommunication). The government and the intelligence community fought against the disclosure, since we knew it would harm our counterterrorism activities. Following the money was an incredibly useful tool.

The *Times* later argued that its story was protected by the First Amendment (unarguably true) and provided "information the public needs to make things right again" (a very arguable point). The *Times* trotted out the old saw that terrorists obviously knew that this was going on, and then vouched for their own patriotism by claiming that this bore "no resemblance to security breaches, like disclosure of locations, that would clearly compromise the immediate safety of specific individuals."

Lichtblau's personal defense was that this was "above all else an interesting yarn about the administration's extraordinary efforts since 9/11 to stop another attack." Interesting yarn?

In October 2006—months after the original article—the public editor of the *Times* reversed his earlier position. He said that it still was a close call but now declared that, in his view, the story should not have been published. Wow! That was a relief.

Years later, in December 2009, the *Times* editorial board bitched and moaned that nine years after 9/11, "there is still a seemingly limitless stream of cash flowing to terrorist groups." Its editorial was titled "Follow the Money." Thanks for the suggestion. Talk about hypocrisy.

I brought up the SWIFT story to Bill Keller and Jill Abramson during a visit to the *Times* in New York while I was at CIA. I conceded that even I understood that there was a civil liberties quotient in the Stellarwind story. "But why did you go with the SWIFT story?" I asked. "Every justification you gave for going with Stellarwind—it wasn't done under a warrant, there was no outside oversight, congressional staff had not been included, an insufficient number of congressional members had been told—all of those conditions were met in the SWIFT program."

Keller hesitated only a second, and then responded, "The president was a lot weaker by then."

I didn't respond in the meeting, but when we got back to LaGuardia and the government jet that had taken us to New York, I turned to other members of my party and simply asked, "Did he say what I thought he said?"

"Yep."

Journalists correctly argue that an informed public is the lifeblood of democracy. And I readily concede that people like me can be prone to keep too much hidden. Many say that the US government overclassifies things. They're right. For years I debated whether or not I could actually say CNA—computer network attack—to public audiences. Even today government spokesmen (and even retirees like me) have to bend themselves into linguistic pretzels of passive voice and oblique generalizations for fear of uttering which arm of the US government may or may not conduct targeted killings from UAVs.

Even when there are genuine reasons to classify or compartmentalize, there is a price to be paid. Doing an autopsy of one of CIA's darkest hours, the Bay of Pigs, Harold Wilensky observed that "the more secrecy, the smaller the intelligent audience, the less systematic the distribution and indexing of research, the greater the anonymity of authorship and the more intolerant the attitude toward deviant views."

Intelligence people need to talk more, to engage more, to dialogue with press and public even when the IC isn't being accused of something. I did my share of public speeches. When I was at CIA in 2007 we decided to commemorate 9/11 with a major address at the Council on Foreign Relations in New York.

I was unapologetic, but before I detailed the what and the why of renditions, detentions, and interrogations, I explained why I was there. "There are things that should be said. . . . Our agency, CIA, operates only within the space given to us by the American people." So I was going to outline a rough approximation of that space, along with our belief that "the American people expect CIA to use every inch we're given to protect her fellow citizens."

In the spring of 2008 I became the first agency director to appear on a Sunday talk show, sitting down with Tim Russert on *Meet the Press*. Russert's questions pretty much covered the waterfront: stability in Iraq, Nouri al-Maliki, Iraqi WMD, Iranian WMD, the fate of al-Qaeda, CIA analysts, CIA interrogations, the future of Pakistan, and CIA liability insurance policies.

At one point Russert played a tape of the vice president five days after 9/11 predicting that we would be "spend[ing] time in the shadows."

I answered, "This is a special and unique role that is performed by the good men and women [of CIA], law-abiding men and women, your friends and neighbors, but operating somewhat in that space that the vice president described.

"On the dark side, in the shadows."

"In the shadows."

Russert gave the interview a lot of time. We were delighted with it. He was too. He sent me a personal note just days before his tragic and untimely death thanking me and pointing out that ratings had spiked during the interview. And no one had even come close to spilling any secrets.

I had informed Steve Hadley about the *Meet the Press* invitation. He was fully supportive. I wasn't quite asking for Steve's permission, but I wanted to hear if there was any compelling downside. There wasn't. Leon Panetta's 2014 book, *Worthy Fights,* suggests that he chafed under the Obama White House's restrictions on doing similar things. I appreciated and used the running room given me by the Bush White House.

About a year into my tenure at CIA, I spoke to a conference of the Society for Historians of American Foreign Relations. We were using the occasion to publicly roll out something called the *Family Jewels.* Compiled in 1973 in response to Director Jim Schlesinger's edict to catalogue the agency's sins, the *Family Jewels* comprised nearly seven hundred pages of very unflattering commentary on CIA's past.

Schlesinger didn't stay on long enough to deal with what was under agency rocks. That fell to William Colby, whose candor and near-preternatural calm in front of the Congress angered the White House he was serving and ultimately cost him his job.

Our point now in 2007 was that we had kept these ugly things secret because they were legitimately secret, not because they were ugly. With the passage of time, they were no longer secret and we were making them public (well, most of them; one was still too sensitive) even though they were all deeply embarrassing.

I told the gathered historians that CIA had a social contract with the American people, and as part of that contract, we had to balance "two crucial obligations: our need to protect information that helps us protect Americans and our need to inform the public—as best we can—about the work we do on their behalf." Secrecy in a democracy was "not a grant of power, but a grant of trust."

I argued that this was more than an obligation. It was in our own self-interest, since it helped the public, Congress, and the executive branch appreciate the courage and integrity of CIA officers. It also helped people understand the limits of our craft.

The speech actually got some pretty wide press coverage. Maybe a little too wide. The next day I was before the House Intelligence Committee in closed session on an unrelated matter when several members brought it up. "What do you mean by social contract with the American people?" The question was actually phrased in a tone that I would not call friendly. It seems that some members didn't want us talking directly to the American people. Just to them.

We had never thought that steps like this could be viewed as undercutting congressional oversight. That certainly wasn't our intent. I tried to explain, but sometimes it's hard to explain the merit of something that you think should be intuitively obvious.

We held our ground there, and outside the committee room as well. Early in my tenure at CIA I had told the PRB (the Publications Review Board, which has to approve any writings by current or former CIA officers) that we needed to draw hard lines to protect what was truly secret, but warned them that if we were drawing them on the margins, we were doing ourselves a disservice. If we were unwilling or unable to tell our story (within limits), how could we condemn the inaccuracies in others' accounts of us?

Part of our problem was structural. Manuscripts were shopped among various offices of interest by the PRB. Each had the authority to give a thumbs-up or a thumbs-down to various passages or entire documents. It made for inconsistent and opaque decision making and for unproductive and lengthy disputes. The packages were rarely important enough to float to the top of an in-box, and no one would ever be held to account for saying no to a release. There was no risk in that. Saying yes was another matter.

I decided to centralize declassification review at the corporate level. Various offices could be used as subject matter experts, but the final arbiter would be the PRB. I never thought of it this way, but in later years this was dubbed the "Hayden Doctrine" in some agency channels. I learned that when one of my successors was called to the Hill to explain books like Jose Rodriguez's *Hard Measures* and Hank Crumpton's *The Art of Intelligence,* books whose contents had survived PRB winnowing enough to tell richly detailed stories about what the agency really did and why. Working to deflect congressional criticism, my successor apparently fingered me.

That was the only guidance I ever gave the PRB, though. I certainly didn't want myself or any of the leadership to get involved in the process of approving or disapproving text. My response to former director Tenet's struggles to get part of his memoir, *At the Center of the Storm,* through the PRB was a heartfelt "Noted."

The same with Valerie Plame's book, *Fair Game.* Plame was the CIA officer outed in the press when her husband, retired ambassador Joe Wilson, was sent to Niger by the agency to follow up on allegations that Iraq had pursued the purchase of yellowcake (a uranium source) there. It became a very ugly affair. Wilson accused the administration of lying. The agency filed a crimes report to protest the disclosure of Plame's status. Scooter Libby, the vice president's chief of staff, was indicted for perjury. Plame resigned from the agency.

And then she wrote a book, which the PRB had to review.

The core issue was what she could or could not say about her life in the agency. There was no precedent to clear the kind of information she wanted to clear, and the PRB stuck to its guns.

I stayed out of it, even when senators and their offices started to call to protest what they called the agency's politically motivated stonewalling of Ms. Plame's efforts. Senator Kennedy's staff took my explanation politely and without comment. Senator Feinstein personally charged that this was all the work of the vice president, even though I said that it was our doing and that I was fairly confident that the vice president didn't even know that the manuscript existed.

I should add that we weren't indifferent to what others might say about us or about our people. In June 2008 Scott Shane of the *New York Times* was finishing a piece highlighting a CIA analyst turned interrogator who had great success with Khalid Sheikh Mohammed. It was an interesting story, but the *Times* was insisting on using the true name of the officer. He wasn't undercover, but we believed that the use of his name would invade his privacy and might jeopardize his safety. Besides, he had refused to be interviewed for the story, so this looked like one of those "we can talk with you or we can talk about you" episodes.

Two days before publication Defense Secretary Bob Gates retired me from the air force after thirty-nine years of service, and I was entertaining the Hayden clan—who had arrived from Pittsburgh, Chicago, and other points—under a large tent in my backyard at Bolling Air Force Base. I broke away from the party to call Bill Keller. DC *über*lawyer Bob Bennett, who had been hired by the officer, was making similar calls.

"Shane's a good enough writer that he can create this persona without naming names," I told Keller. "You don't need to do this." I guess I didn't show enough fire. Keller later described my effort as "doing it out of respect for [the officer's] and his family's concerns more than a concern the CIA had."

Probably true, but hardly disqualifying. Later the *Times*'s public editor said that putting the officer's name out there did not put him into any greater danger than that experienced by the scores of others involved in counterterrorism who had been identified. Let me rephrase that in an unkind way: we do this all the time. What's one more, one way or another?

Sometimes we pushed back after a story had come out. We certainly weren't above condemning the inaccuracies in books about us. In 2007 Tim Weiner pushed out *Legacy of Ashes*, his self-described definitive history of the CIA. We thought it so bad that we allowed a CIA historian to review it on the agency Web site, an unprecedented step.

With regard to being definitive history, our reviewer wrote, "[T]he thing about scholarship is that one must use sources honestly, and one doesn't get a pass on this even if he is a Pulitzer Prize–winning journalist for the *New York Times*. Starting with the title that is based on a gross distortion of events, the book is a 600-page op-ed piece masquerading as serious history; it is the advocacy of a particularly dark point of view under the guise of scholarship. Weiner has allowed his agenda to drive his research and writing, which is, of course, exactly backward. . . . Weiner is not honest about context, he is dismissive of motivations, his expectations for intelligence are almost cartoonish, and his book too often is factually unreliable." And that's in the first 225 words of a 6,000-word review.

Even if we were going to be more willing to toss material out there, there were still going to be issues attached to who was catching it. Some writers were hopelessly agenda-driven (Weiner, Jane Mayer, and later Glenn Greenwald and Laura Poitras come to mind). Others were not so much agenda-driven as simply allowing their writing to follow the general trend in coverage of American espionage, which is to say walking the story to the darkest corner of the room. And there always seems to be a quotable official from an NGO, the ACLU, or even a disgruntled agency former officer eager to show the way.

Then there's the choice of terms. Routinely labeling activities or documents as "torture" flights or "torture" memos buries the very point of contention in a casually used and conclusive adjective. The same could be said of "domestic surveillance" or "assassinations." They are useful catch-phrases, but they are not always accurate and often oversimplify complex issues. They are also conclusions masquerading as narrative.

I would also argue that some of what claims to be journalism isn't about keeping the public informed, but rather is about keeping the public titillated—espionage porn, if you will.

When intelligence officials see unarguably classified information in the press—when someone has obviously and without authorization leaked classified material—we are required to file what is called a crimes report. In ten years of working at the highest levels of the intelligence community, I probably directed, participated in, or at least was aware of scores of such reports. In all that time I saw one case make it to a courtroom—the leak of Valerie Plame's identity as a CIA officer—and that was about perjury rather than unauthorized disclosure.

Since I left government, prosecutions have become more robust. So robust, in fact, that even I have been uncomfortable about some of them. It's not that real secrets haven't been revealed. They have. Sources have been compromised, and journalists, of all people, should understand the need to protect sources and relationships.

But the investigations have been very aggressive, and the acquisition of journalists' communications records has been broad, invasive, secret, and—one suspects—unnecessary.

A quick survey of former Bush administration colleagues confirmed my belief that a proposal to sweep up AP phone records or a Fox reporter's e-mails—as done by the current administration—would have had a half-life under them of about thirty seconds.

They would have judged the target (leaks and leakers) to be legitimate, but the collateral damage (squeezing the First Amendment and chilling legitimate press activity) to be prohibitive.

The government may also want to adjust its approach to enforcement. The current tsunami of leak prosecutions is based largely on the Espionage Act, a blunt World War I statute designed to punish aiding the enemy. It's sometimes a tough fit. The leak case against former NSA employee Thomas Drake (chapter 2) collapsed of its own overreach in 2011. Drake eventually pleaded to one misdemeanor count of exceeding the authorized use of a government computer and was sentenced to community service.

Later, former CIA case officer Jeffrey Sterling was accused of leaking details of CIA covert action against Iran's nuclear program. I was long out of government when the jury rendered a guilty verdict, but earlier, while I was CIA director, Justice had asked me, "How much classified information are you prepared to reveal at trial to get a conviction of Sterling?"

By then unauthorized leaks had become so routine that I decided to break with tradition (which was to be cautious) and simply told DOJ, "Whatever it takes. Just tell us what you need." The cumulative effect of previous, cautious, and individually correct decisions to guard against further disclosures at trial had fostered a climate of impunity. There was no claim to whistle-blower status here either. Failed, clumsy, or even stupid covert actions aren't a crime. Sterling was eventually convicted of violating the Espionage Act and sentenced to three and a half years in prison.

As this case was still being contested in 2015, I was interviewed by *60 Minutes* as Jim Risen, the *New York Times* reporter who had written the story, seemed to be facing jail time if he did not expose Sterling as his source. I still had strong feelings about the case. As national security advisor, Condi Rice had convinced the *Times* to scotch the story, but Risen put it in his 2006 book, *State of War,* anyway.

So I wasn't sympathetic at all to what Risen had done or what he had written. It was irresponsible and caused real harm to the safety of the nation, and I said so. But I also said that redressing this particular harm by compelling Risen to reveal his source might cause even greater damage to American freedoms if it chilled a free press. If I had to choose, I was willing to sacrifice secrets, but not the First Amendment.

That remains sacred, even when it is being abused.

Which leaves me conflicted, and resigned that this legitimate free press–legitimate government secrets thing is a condition we will have to manage, not a problem that we will solve.

EIGHT

LIFE IN THE CYBER DOMAIN

SAN ANTONIO, TX—FORT MEADE, MD— LANGLEY, VA, 1996–2010

I was certainly NOT a cyber pioneer. I'm not even a technologist. I still hand the TV remotes to the grandkids when they're around.

"Daniel, make the TV remember this show."

Decades earlier—when computers meant punch cards, raised floors, and cold, windowless rooms—I had intentionally blown a test in air force tech school to avoid that line of work.

But now, in 1996, I was thrust into dealing with and understanding the cyber domain when I took command of the Air Intelligence Agency (AIA) in San Antonio, Texas.

Immediately prior to that, I had been chief of intelligence (J-2) for all US forces in Europe (EUCOM), and at that time we were deeply involved in supporting UN peacekeeping units in the third Balkan war of the twentieth century. I had been an attaché to a Balkan country and spoke a Balkan language (Bulgarian), so I had some understanding of the historic depth of that conflict.

Winston Churchill once wisely observed that "the Balkans produces more history than it can consume." That certainly matched my experience.

When I left EUCOM and headed to Texas, I was leaving behind knowledge of, and responsibility for, a conflict medieval in its origins and Byzantine (almost literally) in its complexities, to take command of a unit on the cutting edge of a whole new type and domain of warfare.

Thank God I had a great staff in Texas. They began to educate the new guy with the fervor of those attempting a conversion.

And the first article of faith at AIA was simply that cyber was a "domain."

"You know, General. Land, sea, air, space, *cyber*."

Actually, when you convince a GI that something is a domain, a lot of things click. He doesn't clutter his mind with extraneous concepts like networks, bandwidth, and the like. It's a domain, an operational environment, and—just like all the other domains—it has its own characteristics. This one is characterized by great speed and great maneuverability, so it favors the offense. It is inherently global. It is inherently strategic.

And, my new staff added, we need to treat it like we treat the other domains. America expects us to operate there. Just like the other domains—air, for example—we're going to use it for our purposes when we want to and deny its use to others when we choose to.

At least that's going to be our mission. The language of air dominance and air superiority, which easily tripped off our tongues as airmen, quickly became information dominance and information superiority in our new lexicon.

AIA worked to make this more than just words. The first audience we had to convince was the air force itself. In September 1997 we had the chance to demonstrate what we wanted to do to a gathering of air force three- and four-stars. The chief of staff, General Ron Fogleman, invited me to Scott Air Force Base in Illinois for his semiannual meeting, called Corona Top, to give a presentation about new technologies, new weapons, and new modes of warfare. Fogleman gave us an unprecedented two hours on the agenda.

I would be onstage to give the background to our approach and a touch of the doctrine we were debating, but I would also be connected by video link to my headquarters and operations center in San Antonio. We were going to demonstrate live some of the tools then under development.

We almost met with disaster when a south Texas thunderstorm hit my headquarters on Security Hill just before we were about to begin. Through heroic efforts we came back online just in time, and all the technology worked as briefed. In one example, we remotely disabled some workstations, and in another I demonstrated how we could spoof a radarscope to show one thing while the actual aircraft it was following was doing another.

Not bad. Senior leadership was impressed. No one volunteered any money from his fighter or bomber programs, but they were impressed. At least we had planted a few seeds.

Back in San Antonio we had already retooled our traditional operations center into an Information Operations (IO) Center. There I was routinely briefed on broad indicators of action in the cyber domain, the status of air force networks, the character of attacks against us. We also regularly deployed information warfare support teams to air force tactical units to better prepare them (and to spread the gospel).

These thoughts and actions in San Antonio ultimately had outsize influence. Not much more than a decade later Bob Butler—the talented young lieutenant colonel who headed up my IO center—was now the deputy assistant secretary of defense for cyber policy, and those nascent concepts from San Antonio had pretty much become American military doctrine. Butler worked for Bill Lynn, the deputy secretary of defense, who wrote a seminal piece in *Foreign Affairs* in the fall of 2010 that brought the concept of the cyber domain and cyber dominance into full public view.

"As a doctrinal matter," he declared, "the Pentagon has formally recognized cyberspace as a new domain of warfare. Although cyberspace is a man-made domain, it has become just as critical to military operations as land, sea, air, and space. As such, the military must be able to defend and operate within it." It was as if he had copied our notes from Texas in 1996.

Our ideas had stuck, but in retrospect we had admittedly been living within a unique culture and underappreciated that an entire generation was growing up outside our fence-line thinking of this domain as a global commons, a pristine playground, not a zone of potential conflict where powerful nation-states would want to work their will.

American doctrine doesn't militarize this domain more than many other nations around the world have, but we certainly have thrown a lot of resources into our efforts, and our natural transparency and casual use of language expose us to charges that we have.

Go back to Lynn's article. The most telling line in the whole piece was the one at the bottom of the first page: *William J. Lynn III is U.S. Deputy Secretary of Defense.* The seminal American thought piece on cyber wasn't written by the deputy attorney general or deputy secretary of state or deputy secretary of commerce or even by the president's science advisor. It was written by the deputy secretary of defense. People outside this country notice things like that.

So do people inside this country. There was little coordination of Lynn's 2010 article in the interagency process in Washington. There were a few discussions with cybersecurity czar Howard Schmidt at the White House, but not much beyond that. The Department of Homeland Security, up on Nebraska Avenue, and the Department of State, over on C Street, were as much surprised by the article as some foreign audiences.

They pushed back. Within six months of Lynn's article, Jane Holl Lute, the deputy secretary of Homeland Security, coauthored a piece in *Wired* that proclaimed, "Cyberspace is not a war zone." Rather, she wrote, "cyberspace is fundamentally a civilian space—a neighborhood, a library, a marketplace, a schoolyard, a workshop—and a new, exciting age in human experience, exploration and development."

Michele Markoff, the deputy coordinator for cyber issues at the Department of State, would tell anyone who would listen that our emphasis on a new domain that was (allegedly) severable from the physical realities that comprised it (servers, for example, had to be somewhere in physical space) was making her work very difficult.

Markoff was tirelessly trying to create international norms for cyber behavior. DOD's construct of a separate domain tended to mute the traditional principles and responsibilities of sovereignty, and it wasn't helping. From Markoff's point of view, DOD was actually focusing on a physical object, say a server in Malaysia, not on some abstract node in a near-mythical new universe.

Audiences also had to notice a section in Lynn's piece entitled "Leveraging Dominance," as well as his wonderfully alliterative and somewhat ominous description of something he called active defense: "part sensor, part sentry, part sharpshooter." You can imagine how that last word was read in many foreign capitals.

The debate continues today. Not long ago, I was sitting in front of a Skype screen in Colorado arguing via video link with author Jim Bamford, who has made a living writing unauthorized books about NSA. One of my distant NSA predecessors, Linc Faurer, wanted to have him arrested over his first opus, *The Puzzle Palace*, when it hit the streets in 1982.

I tried to more productively cultivate Bamford two decades later when I was director, even inviting him to dinner and allowing him to have a book signing in NSA's National Cryptologic Museum. It didn't work. When the Terrorist Surveillance Program was made public in late 2005 (see chapter 5), he joined an ACLU lawsuit against NSA.*

The Skype debate was for a TV trade audience in Beverly Hills on behalf of PBS hyping an upcoming *NOVA* special on NSA. Bamford was a coproducer and was arguing that America had tragically militarized the cyber domain through actions like Stuxnet, which he described as an American cyber attack on the Iranian nuclear facility at Natanz. America's intemperate behavior, he claimed, had legitimized Iranian responses against the giant oil company Saudi Aramco and against American banks. The Internet was now a free-fire zone, and it was our fault.

---

* The suit was later dismissed since neither Bamford nor the other plaintiffs had standing. They could not show that they had been the target of anything.

I responded by defaulting to my "land, sea, air, space, cyber" construct. "The cyber domain wasn't the only global commons on the list," I said. "The maritime domain had been such for eons. And no one objected to the existence of navies. In fact, a good case could be made that navies were essential to keeping that commons common."

I could have added that the cyber domain has never been a digital Eden. It was always Mogadishu. The president of Estonia, Toomas Hendrik Ilves, knows something about this. His country's Internet collapsed in 2007 under attack by "patriotic Russian hackers" (read criminal gangs repaying a debt to the Russian state for the freedom of action they enjoy there) after Tallinn tried to move a Red Army memorial from downtown to the suburbs.

President Ilves has a wonderful way of capturing all this. He says that, lacking a Lockean social contract in the cyber domain, what we have is an almost purely Hobbesian universe, a universe where Hobbes's description of ungoverned life as "poor, nasty, brutish and short" really applies. There is simply no rule of law there.

I have often compared the current evolution of cyberspace to the last great age of globalization, the centuries of European discovery. That era, for all its accomplishments, jammed together the good and the bad and the weak and the strong in ways that had never been experienced before. What the Europeans got out of it was land, wealth, tobacco, and syphilis. Much of the rest of the world got exploitation of entire populations, global piracy, and the global slave trade. We are in a somewhat analogous condition now except that today's connectivity isn't at ten knots with a favoring wind. It's at 186,000 miles per second. It didn't take Stuxnet to make the cyber domain a very dangerous place.

THESE DEBATES were all in the future when I arrived at NSA in March 1999. I had had only eighteen months in San Antonio, but the people there were cutting edge and the education they gave me was invaluable when I got to Fort Meade.

And it was invaluable right from the beginning. Keep in mind the purpose of the National Security Agency. NSA's job was all about communications. Historically that was electronic data in motion: global high-frequency communications, shorter-range microwave signals, photons and electrons moving along a cable.

Agencies like CIA handled other materials—human sources, purloined documents, pilfered codes—more or less physical data sitting at rest.

The division of labor was clear. Electronic data in motion—NSA. Physical data at rest—CIA. But the new digital domain had created a different state of nature: electronic data at rest.

It's easy to forget how novel this really was. Since Marconi we had been turning physical data into an electronic form only to move it. I still remember my days at a fighter wing in Korea as recently as the 1980s where, to send a message, we would type it out with something called an OCR (optical character recognition) typewriter and walk it across the street to the communications center, where it would be scanned, turned into electrons, and transmitted to Washington. Once it arrived there, the electrons would be converted back to a printed page that was thrown into a pigeonhole, where it awaited a clerk to come pick it up.

That now sounds archaic, and it is inexplicable to our children. By the late 1990s we were all moving data routinely (like e-mails) that would never exist as anything but electrons, and we were all storing data in electronic form, much of which—documents, spreadsheets, files, notes—would never be electronically transmitted.

The former was clearly a communication (electronic data in motion) but the latter, well, that was something new. To NSA it was electronic and hence fair game. To CIA it wasn't moving and hence was equally fair game.

This bureaucratic issue didn't end up in a death match across the Potomac between the two agencies. President Bush settled it in a memorandum after 9/11 declaring it fair game for both agencies, with NSA treating it in accordance with SIGINT rules and CIA handling it like HUMINT.

But the fact that it was an issue at all says a little about American intelligence bureaucracy and a lot more about how disruptive the digital age was for American intelligence.

At NSA we had to develop a whole new language. We were moving to *active* SIGINT, commuting to the target and extracting information from it, rather than hoping for a transmission we could intercept in traditional *passive* SIGINT. This was all about going to the *end point*, the targeted network, rather than trying to work the *midpoint* of a communication with a well-placed antenna or cable access.

We also knew that if we did this even half well, it would be the golden age of signals intelligence, since mankind was storing and moving more and more data in digital form with each passing day.

That was the good news, and at the turn of the century we were all-in trying to retool our infrastructure for the new era. But that was going to be difficult. Money was tight.

I tried to disinvest about $200 million a year from ongoing collection to invest in what we needed to work the end point, and I heard about it from all over Washington. No one was willing to surrender any current take for future capability. Someone went to the mat about degrading coverage of Nigerian organized crime, for God's sake.

We did what we could. In the last days of 2000, as we were rewiring the entire agency's organizational chart (see chapter 2), we set up an enterprise called TAO, Tailored Access Operations, in the newly formed SIGINT Directorate (SID). We had toyed with some boutique end-point efforts before, but this was different. This was going to be industrial strength. We actually divided up SID into end-point and midpoint boxes, the better to measure and meter the growth of the former, even if it had to be at the expense of the latter.

As it turned out, it didn't. The terrorist attack less than nine months later ensured a steady stream of additional human and material resources across the agency. And, even in a period of generalized growth, TAO became the fastest-growing part of NSA post-9/11, bar none.

TAO's growth also benefited from the bursting of the dot-com bubble and the massive surge of patriotism after the 9/11 terrorist attacks. Talk about the best and the brightest: we got an incredible cohort of young, technically talented, innovative, and adventurous new SIGINTers. We hired several thousand people in the four years after 9/11; their average age was thirty-one, well below the agency average at that time. It wasn't lost on any of the new recruits that we were offering them the opportunity to legally do stuff that would be felonies in any other venue. We effected a generational change in our workforce in a matter of a few years.

Our new cohort had one hell of an attitude. One veteran confided to me that they had a "no target impossible to penetrate" mentality and, from the beginning, bypassed low-hanging fruit to attack the hardest targets.

Some of these took years to penetrate. Grant's capture of Vicksburg is still cited at the war colleges as the classic example of the indirect approach; unable to take the city from the Mississippi River side, Grant mounted a months-long campaign from the landward side before the Gibraltar of the Confederacy fell. When the war colleges are allowed to teach how TAO gained some accesses, TAO's efforts will parallel the strategic lessons of Grant—patience, indirection, and persistence—in the curriculum.

Other nations' security services were trying to work the end point, but none of them were embedded in a SIGINT system as global as NSA's. Traditional passive SIGINT often holds the key to active SIGINT's success—mapping networks, communications paths, and in general providing the kind of detailed information that is essential to success.

We also had a great supporter in DCI George Tenet, who repeated, mantra-like, "SIGINT enabling HUMINT, HUMINT enabling SIGINT." Some targets thought that they were permanently isolated from the World Wide Web. That wasn't always true, thanks to HUMINT enabling.

Of course, we also worked to create our own *remote* accesses, using a variety of techniques, like tempting targets to click on a link in an innocent-looking e-mail. At home we were all complaining about the emergence of spam on our networks. At work, we willingly hid in the growing global flow as we targeted specific networks.

It was a good thing that we were getting our game on. Turns out that we had underestimated how much al-Qaeda was using the Web. Pre-TAO, we hadn't seen much al-Qaeda activity there and so assumed that there wasn't much. There was. As US forces rolled up hard drives in Afghanistan and as we inspected pocket litter (the generic term for stuff found on or near a detainee) from al-Qaeda takedowns globally, we began to harvest Internet addresses and identities that allowed us to eventually turn al-Qaeda's use of the Web into one of our best counterterrorism tools.

TAO was becoming a gateway to great intelligence. And to other things too.

My predecessor at NSA was Ken Minihan. Ken had also been one of my predecessors in Texas, and a lot of what I had learned there was actually started and nurtured by him. I had been proselytized and converted by his disciples.

Although Ken and I were career intelligence officers and pushed endpoint collection hard, neither of us was limiting his thinking to just espionage. We saw cyber as a domain of real conflict and believed that NSA could add a lot to American power there, beyond just spying, but the agency was constrained. It could legally manipulate a target only to cover its tracks or break the target's encryption. Anything beyond that wasn't in the mission or charter, a flaw we worked to correct.

US law is pretty clear about the distinction between espionage and war fighting. Spying is controlled by Title 50 of the US Code and overseen by Congress's intelligence committees. Warfare falls under Title 10 and the Armed Services Committees. The distinction works pretty well in the physical domains, but even there, things get a little muddled with CIA covert action and paramilitary activities.

The distinctions break down entirely in the cyber domain. Take reconnaissance. In physical space it always happens (or should) before someone attempts a kinetic operation. Robert E. Lee sought Jeb Stuart's counsel. A patrol in today's army will launch a handheld drone to report on the reverse slope of a ridge before crossing it.

In physical space the reconnaissance is almost always easier than the operation. Learning where the Army of the Potomac might be was hard and dangerous work, but not as hard and dangerous as defeating it. The same with defeating an entrenched enemy squad on the backside of the ridge that your drone just imaged.

Reconnaissance should come first in the cyber domain too. How else would you know what to hit, how, when—without collateral damage?

But here's the difference. In the cyber domain the reconnaissance is usually a more difficult task than the follow-on operation. It is tougher to penetrate a network and live on it undetected while extracting large volumes of data from it than it is to, digitally speaking, kick in the front door and fry a circuit or two.

Let me go further. An attack on a network to degrade it or destroy information on it is generally a lesser included case of the technology and operational art needed to spy on that same network.

About a year before I got to NSA, Minihan hit upon an ingenious approach to squaring this circle. He launched an enterprise called the Information Operations Technology Center, the IOTC. It was located within the NSA headquarters building, originally lived off NSA dollars and talent, but was officially not part of the agency. It was a joint DOD and Intelligence Community undertaking.

The label Information Operations was broad and gave the center the license to touch on all the IO things you might ever want to do against an adversary: spy on him, corrupt his network or his information, or capture his computers to use them to create physical destruction. NSA could legally only do the first, but since this was a technology rather than an operations center, it was free to develop tools that could be used by others with different authorities. It was an elegant solution that got the toolbox for all kinds of cyber operations filled quickly.

Minihan had gotten a real boost the year before from a DOD exercise called Eligible Receiver. The exercise had been sponsored by General Jack Sheehan, a tough Boston Irish marine who was commander of Atlantic

Command in Norfolk. Sheehan had enlisted NSA as his red team for a cyber assault against Department of Defense networks. The results were embarrassingly awful. The red team, without any special information or special tools, penetrated wherever it targeted.

Minihan was eager to lead the remediation, but the military services were pushing back hard against a more powerful role for a defense agency. Their experience was that defense agency growth was usually at the expense of their budget top line. John Hamre, the deputy secretary of defense, finally enlisted DCI George Tenet's support and then just plain overruled the reflexive service objections to the enterprise.

When I arrived in 1999, the head of IOTC was Bill Marshall, a professorial-looking and exceptionally competent NSA veteran.

By all accounts his most difficult partner wasn't any of the military services. It was the leadership of the National Security Agency below the eighth floor (where the director's office was housed). A lot of folks just wanted to do the traditional SIGINT mission; this exotic IO stuff was a costly distraction from an already tough job, and there was fear that IOTC tools in the hands of others would compromise NSA's fragile endpoint operations.

Bill Black, who later became my deputy (chapter 2), was an unabashed advocate for IO being housed at NSA as a natural extension of the SIGINT mission. Bill volunteered himself to Minihan to be his assistant director for information operations. Since the agency couldn't actually carry out most of what could be called IO, it could fairly be described as an advocacy post, and Black was tireless in his advocacy. The internal NSA opposition to the concept was so strong that Black later retired in disgust.

Disillusioned and frustrated, Black warned Marshall that one way or another, he was bound to fail. If he actually succeeded operationally, NSA seniors would hate him. On the other hand, if he simply failed, he would just be viewed as incompetent.

When Minihan hired Marshall, he told him that everyone believed that the IOTC was only PowerPoint deep in substance. He challenged Marshall to produce real results, to build coalitions across DOD and the IC, and to get the resources he needed to do the job. In return, Minihan promised him top cover against those who would oppose him and try to starve the project.

Marshall was internally very intense and focused, but he moderated that outwardly with a collaborative and communicative spirit. Over time he wore down resistance. He started with a few dozen people, but over three years had grown the IOTC to several hundred. His expanding team doggedly developed, gathered, evaluated, modified, catalogued, and stored tools that might prove useful to defend networks or to spy on an adversary or to deny, degrade, disrupt, or destroy an adversary's network or information.

As his stack of tools grew, Marshall forced a whole series of legal and doctrinal and organizational questions. You can't stockpile tools and weapons without compelling DOD lawyers and national policy makers to give you some guidance. And that engendered debate and controversy and forward-leaning thinking. In retrospect, Marshall chalks that up as the center's most lasting achievement.

The IOTC became the cyber-gathering place where cyber concepts could be defined, discussed, challenged, debated, and tested. Even more important than his growing tool kit, Marshall and his center kept the doctrinal fire (and controversy) of cyber operations alive.

FORT MEADE IS about forty minutes from downtown Washington, on a good day (like a Sunday). The relative isolation is nice. It puts you just outside the circle of the capital's politically charged everyday routine.

The distance also means that you do not routinely get the casual visitor. People coming up the Baltimore-Washington Parkway do it with purpose or not at all.

We worked hard to get as many thought leaders to Fort Meade as we could. We wanted to fill their heads with our thoughts and actions and ambitions in this new domain.

To clarify the discussion, we started talking about something called computer network operations (CNO) and said that you could divide it into three bins: computer network defense (CND), keeping your own networks safe; computer network exploitation (CNE), stealing other people's data; and computer network attack (CNA), destroying data, networks, or physical objects.*

We then usually dove into computer network defense, or CND, since it was least threatening, least novel, and therefore least controversial.

NSA had had a charter to secure American government communications since almost forever. The old secure phone, the STU-3, was an NSA product. There's a picture of President Bush on one of them in that Florida classroom on the morning of 9/11.

So CND was a fairly easy role to slip into, at least bureaucratically. About a fifth of NSA's budget and manpower was already committed to defense. The challenge here was more technical and operational: How do you defend in a domain that we were finding pretty easy to exploit when we played offense?

It was hard. A few weeks before I left NSA in 2005, at the strong insistence of Bill Black (now my deputy), we launched NTOC, the NSA Threat Operations Center. If we were going to be throwing cyber rocks, we had better start protecting our glass house. I called on Bill Marshall again to head it. He began with ten people, no dedicated work space, and no budget. Three years later the center was a thriving concern with almost a thousand folks in place.

If it hadn't been at NSA, the NTOC would have been just another CIRT, a Computer Incident Response Team, combining information as-

---

* At NSA my predecessor and I were air force officers who had also commanded the Air Intelligence Agency. Our categorization had an eerie resemblance to the way that American airpower is organized and explained: reconnaissance (CNE), bombers (CNA), and fighters (CND).

surance technology, network sensors, and internal communications data to map what was happening on a network.

But NTOC was at NSA, so it was hot-wired into a vast global SIGINT system that could send digital scouts out beyond the perimeter to identify activity and threats long before they hit the local firewall. NTOC's 24/7 operations center monitored the heartbeat of the entire cyber domain and provided early warning to US national security networks.

It was the Information Operations Center I had in San Antonio on a massive regimen of steroids. Predictably, its unique combination of SIGINT and information-security authorities, expertise, and resources aroused bureaucratic suspicion around Washington, so NTOC had to prove itself during skeptical reviews by officials in DOD, the Congress, and the Office of Management and Budget. It passed them all.

More still needs to be done, as there are other unresolved challenges for cyber defense. NSA's charter is to defend American government secrets. It does not extend to other, unclassified government networks or to the private sector, where an awful lot of American intellectual property, trade information, and critical infrastructure reside. To this day, these networks are not adequately defended. Witness the theft of credit card data from Target and Home Depot or F-35 designs from US government contractors.

The second activity under the broad rubric of computer network operations was what we called computer network exploitation, or CNE. That was the end-point, active-SIGINT, Tailored Access Operations–centered activity already described, and we pretty much had all we needed to thrive, at least in terms of law and policy.

Actually, little noticed (or appreciated) at the time was how easily we transferred our system of governance from the old world to the new. With little debate, we went from a world of letting radio waves serendipitously hit our antennas to what became a digital form of breaking and entering. We were penetrating foreign networks and were saying it was the same thing as scooping up signals from the ether and that the same rules applied. To us it was, and they did, but in retrospect it was a remarkable transition, one that appeared to some to be less innocent and less inevitable when it became the subject of intense public debate in 2013 (chapter 21).

The final category of action under computer network operations was computer network attack, or CNA. This was action designed to disrupt an adversary's network or, in its most extreme form, take over the network in order to use it to create some level of physical destruction. NSA still had no authority to do that; it was limited to defending American information and stealing other people's. But we knew that defense, exploitation, and attack were technologically and operationally indistinguishable even though they were separated in legal authority, funding streams, and congressional oversight—all the result of putting new (digital) wine into old (eighteenth-century, actually) bottles. To us, that made as much sense as America having three air forces—one for reconnaissance, another for fighters, and a third for bombers—when it was really *all* about control of the air.

One of our regular visitors to Fort Meade was General Jim Cartwright, a free-thinking marine aviator who had taken charge of Strategic Command in Omaha in 2004. STRATCOM had been given a dog's breakfast of additional tasks, with its charter mission of nuclear deterrence declining in importance. Cartwright had to organize the command to deal with global reconnaissance, missile defense, counterproliferation, and space as well as the traditional global strike role.

He also had responsibility for offensive cyber operations, the CNA function that Fort Meade could perform but didn't have the legal authority to do.

There was no way a single headquarters could master all of STRATCOM's diverse missions, so Cartwright hit upon the scheme of enlisting the big defense agencies to his cause. Most were already designated "combat support agencies" and most were headed by military officers, so it would be a fairly simple matter to subordinate them to him for specific functions.

Cartwright and I talked and met often. We agreed that he could devolve his authority and responsibility for cyber attack to Fort Meade and dual-hat me as his action arm under the unwieldy title of commander, Joint Functional Component Command–Network Warfare (JFCC-NW).

We were essentially going to expand the IOTC, rebrand it, and give it operational authority through Cartwright's position as a combatant commander. The combined team at Fort Meade would access and conduct reconnaissance of a target based on my authorities as DIRNSA and then, on order, could manipulate or destroy the target based on Cartwright's exercising his combat authority through me.

We were running downhill as we undertook this. Cyber warfare was a hot topic, and there was consensus that we needed to better organize to fight in the domain.

Cartwright wasn't quite pushing on an open door to get the Joint Chiefs on board, but he was essentially offering NSA's resources to enhance DOD cyber-combat power at little cost to the services. Unlike their opposition to the IOTC in 1997–1998, this time around they were open to the idea.

The chairman of the Joint Chiefs, air force general Dick Myers, was supportive but wanted some personal assurances. I had known him for several years. Our paths had often crossed, especially when he headed all USAF units in the Pacific and then US Space Command, so it was easy to have a personal session with him to explain what we were up to.

It was a typical military tabletop briefing, a few charts and slides with just the two of us in his office in the E-ring of the Pentagon. When I finished, he simply asked, "Mike, is this going to fix this?"

"Not a chance," I replied. I assured him that this was the right thing to do now, but added, "We'll be back again in a couple years. And by then we'll be screwing this up at a much higher level."

The irreverence was intended to put down a marker that JFCC-NW was a way station en route to a full-up cyber command.

Our plan did not require congressional approval; it was already within the authority of the secretary of defense to implement. Secretary Rumsfeld bought in, and Cartwright got the president's OK after a session at the Texas ranch over the Christmas holidays in 2004.

Even without needing legislation, Cartwright and I still briefed Congress. We weren't dumb, and this wasn't our first rodeo. We didn't need to prompt any opposition out of pique.

Our technique was to bring the members into our confidence and our "ask" was to give this unusual relationship of Title 10 (war making) and Title 50 (espionage) authorities a little space and time to mature before we had to explain all the fine print (a lot of which didn't exactly exist yet).

What we were doing did not fit nicely into the congressional oversight structure. It blended activities, some of which were traditionally overseen by the intelligence committees and some of which were overseen by the Armed Services Committees—and nothing is as jealously guarded on the Hill as jurisdiction.

In fact, what made it attractive to the Joint Chiefs—living off a lot of NSA resources to backstop what were unarguably combat rather than intelligence activities—could potentially torpedo the whole idea with the House and Senate intelligence panels. Congressional committees are as protective of their funding streams as they are of their jurisdiction.

That's why we took pains to explain ourselves. We appeared together in an informal session before the Senate overseers. Cartwright handled the House side on his own, but made the same arguments.

We did well enough. Congress imposed no roadblocks, and Joint Functional Component Command–Network Warfare (i.e., the nation's computer network attack force) stood up in January 2005.

I was the first commander, but I didn't stay very long. A month later the president announced my nomination as the first principal deputy director of National Intelligence, and I was confirmed by the Senate for that job in late April.

But we now had a structure to go along with our vision: a defensive center in the NSA Threat Operations Center (NTOC), an offensive arm in Joint Functional Component Command–Network Warfare (JFCC-NW), and an ongoing espionage enterprise in Tailored Access Operations (TAO).

All were big, thriving enterprises set up in about a decade—the speed of light by Washington standards.

We also had a vote of confidence from the Joint Chiefs and enough promise that Congress swallowed an unusual command relationship.

ALL WE NEEDED NOW were some real weapons.

Despite the cyber domain's tilt toward the offense, this is still hard work (harder than we sometimes advertised in our enthusiasm). To attack a target, you first have to penetrate it. Access bought with months, if not years, of effort can be lost with a casual upgrade of the targeted system, not even one designed to improve defenses, but merely an administrative upgrade from something 2.0 to something 3.0.

Once in, you need a tailored tool to create the desired effects. Very often this has to be a handcrafted tool for the specific target. It is not the same as cranking out five-hundred-pound bombs and putting them on the shelf with their laser guidance kits.

A lot of the weapons in the IOTC's toolbox were harvested in the wild from the Web. Tools with a Web history would make attribution an even more difficult challenge if they were ever used. But some of those exploits could be pretty ugly, so they had to be modified to meet our operational and legal requirements.

What we wanted were weapons that met the standards of the laws of armed conflict, weapons that reflected the enduring principles of necessity, distinction, and proportionality. To a first order they had to produce an effect that was predictable and responding to a genuine military need (necessity). Disabling an air defense system (which the Israelis were alleged to have done in 2008 while destroying a Syrian nuclear reactor) comes to mind. Pounding the Web sites of important banks with massive distributed denial of service attacks so that they cannot be accessed by normal citizens (which the Iranians did to US banks in 2012) does not.

And even when the effects were predictable and legitimate, policy makers wanted to know if you could limit them to the intended target (distinction) and, to the degree you could not, if the desired effect justified the collateral damage (proportionality).

These are time-honored, universal principles for any war maker with a conscience, but in physical space there was often a century or more of experience to fall back on. "A high-explosive warhead of this size hitting at this angle against this type of target will create an area of lethality of this size and shape," for example. We have even developed an irreverent shorthand for the uneven splotches of red (dead), yellow (maybe), green (safe) in the visual display of such formulas: bug splats.

Now, what does a bug splat look like for a cyber weapon that has never been used in anger and against a unique network that is well, but not perfectly, understood?

In concrete terms, the dialogue in the Situation Room begins with the national security advisor saying something like this:

"So, you're saying that you can disrupt the power supply to this key military facility."

"Yes, sir, and through persistent attacks keep it down."

"Good. Now what else is on that net?"

"Well, sir, we think we can keep the effects confined to a pretty small physical area."

"How small?"

"Probably thirty to forty square miles."

"Worst case, how many hospitals in that area?"

"Worst case, four. Maybe five."

"Do they all have UPS [uninterruptible power supply]?"

"We're working on that now."

The national security advisor pauses, seems to reflect, and then moves on by saying, "OK. Get back to me. We'll take this up again next time."

And the next time, and the next time, and the next time.

And this meeting is invariably in the Situation Room, not in the Pentagon or at Langley or at some combatant command headquarters. From their inception, cyber weapons have been viewed as "special weapons," not unlike nuclear devices of an earlier time.

But these weapons are not well understood by the kind of people who get to sit in on meetings in the West Wing, and as of yet there has not been a Herman Kahn (of *On Thermonuclear War* fame) to explain it to them.

To a first order, there is the technical challenge. After a few sentences, the cyber briefer often sounds vaguely like Rain Man to many of the seniors in the room. With a few more sentences, most are convinced that he is.

I recall one cyber op, while I was in government, that went awry—at least from my point of view. In the after-action review it was clear that no two seniors at the final approval session had left the Situation Room thinking they had approved the same operation.

Beyond complexity, developing policy for cyber ops is hampered by excessive secrecy (so says this *intelligence* veteran!). Look at the bloodline. I can think of no other family of weapons so anchored in the espionage services for their development (except perhaps armed drones). And the habitual secrecy of the intelligence services has bled over into cyber ops in a way that has retarded the development—or at least the policy integration—of digital combat power. It is difficult to develop consensus views on things that are largely unknown or compartmented or only rarely discussed by a select few.

I was on a panel at Georgetown University with several prominent cyber experts after I left government. Without any prior coordination, we all commented that cyber secrecy had retarded the development of cyber policy and doctrine. One panelist, Siobhan Gorman, who had covered the NSA beat for the *Baltimore Sun* before moving on to the *Wall Street Journal*, volunteered that counterterrorism data was easier to pry from the government than any form of cyber information.

Technical challenges and policy ambiguities did little to dim the spirit of cyber enthusiasts, though. We truly were like airpower enthusiasts before World War II: "The bomber will always get through!" Like them, however, for a long time we were long on theory and short on practical success.

In 2004 and 2005 I would candidly admit that, to date, we had largely been spray painting virtual graffiti on digital subway cars. We could harass, but we weren't decisive. An effort right before the invasion of Iraq to e-mail Iraqi officials warning them of their fate and suggesting alternative courses of action seems to have done little more than just annoy them. In another operation, we made Slobodan Milošević's phone ring incessantly, but there is no evidence that it shortened any aspect of the Balkan conflict.

The dramatic event in the annals of airpower was the sinking of a captured German battleship, the *Ostfriesland*, off Hampton Roads in 1921. The ship was undefended and not under way, but with multiple waves of attacks over two days she was sent to the bottom by land-based bombers. It was not even close to an operational test, but airmen hailed it as the dawn of a new age.

I reminded our cyber warriors that as staged as the *Ostfriesland* event had been for Billy Mitchell's biplanes, we were even less convincing. We hadn't yet come close to sinking the *Ostfriesland*.

America's cyber warriors kept trying, though, perhaps at times a little too hard.

With wars under way in Iraq and Afghanistan and globally against terrorist networks, the Joint Chiefs had issued a standing execute order (EXORD) authorizing action to counter adversary use of the Internet. It went by the unwieldy acronym CAUI (pronounced "cow-ee"). On the surface it appeared like broad authority, but it was actually quite limited, since it required specific, senior-level permission to undertake any operation that wasn't merely tactical in its conduct and very local in its effects.

In the run-up to one of the 9/11 anniversaries, it was proposed that broad CAUI authorities be used to block a video that Osama bin Laden had prepared to mark the occasion. His purpose was to taunt us and demonstrate that we couldn't dilute his propaganda. Ours was to visibly frustrate his timetable to get his message online in time for the anniversary. That wasn't really a strategic effect, but it was attractive enough to be approved at a Deputies Committee meeting.

The plan called for denying al-Qaeda access to Web sites that it intended to use for distribution. Some could be controlled cooperatively. Others had to be taken down.

Among the latter was a site controlled by a counterterrorism partner in the Middle East. It was a pretty vile site, the better to attract genuine jihadists to it, and the debate over taking it down reflected a perennial question for us. Did we want to take jihadists on in the cyber domain, or was it better to just monitor them there to better attack them in physical space? The traditional answer was the latter; in this case we were going with the former.

The attack was quite successful. The site went down hard. The 9/11 anniversary passed without a bin Laden release, but before there were any celebrations, my own regional experts were all over me complaining about the impact on our CT partner. The partner knew they were being attacked and were sure they knew who was doing it. And every time they rebuilt their site, down it would go again.

No one thought we could keep the video off the Web forever. There were just too many sites that could be used. It was time to stop this.

Over our objections, though, the attack persisted, so I called Jim Cartwright, now vice chairman of the Joint Chiefs of Staff. Jim seemed to understand the dilemma: we had achieved a tactical success, but now were threatening an important strategic relationship.

Cartwright approved my calling my counterpart and promising that the attacks would stop within twenty-four hours. I did so on a Saturday morning, confident that this would end by Sunday.

It didn't. I still can't explain why. Billy Mitchell had broken some pre-arranged ground rules to demonstrate his point with the *Ostfriesland*. That really angered the navy. Now it seemed that we were doing the same thing here except that this time we were disappointing, angering, and almost betraying a partner, one who put great stock in personal relationships and trust. I broke ranks and confessed to the partner that we did not support the continued action, but were powerless to stop it.

Later, at my request, Jim Cartwright also apologized personally to our ally in my office.

For my part I requested some private time with Steve Hadley, the national security advisor. "Steve," I began, "there is no need for CIA to attend future meetings on proposed cyber operations. Until we get a governance structure that is more sophisticated and sensitive than this last 'fire and forget' drill, we'll just mail it in. Put us down as opposed."

Steve was taken aback. The anger was a little out of character for me, he said. And he was probably remembering that I was JFCC-NW's first commander. Just shows how mad we were.

To be clear, it wasn't that we at CIA were ideologically opposed to cyber ops. Quite the opposite. We even had our own cyber force, the Information Operations Center (IOC), chartered to conduct full-spectrum cyber operations, sharpen cyber tradecraft, protect agency systems, and enhance CIA's cyber analysis. George Tenet had launched the IOC, and it grew steadily under him, Porter Goss, and me.

CIA didn't try to replicate or try to compete with NSA or JFCC-NW. When asked about it, I explained that the IOC was a lot like Marine Corps aviation, while NSA was an awful lot like America's air force.

Marine Corps aviation is an integral part of the marines' air-ground team. It doesn't try to match the US Air Force; it simply provides airpower to support the marines' historic missions. The IOC develops cyber power so that the agency can perform its traditional missions too.

In aviation, it is important that both the marines and the air force are on the same air-tasking order. Otherwise, you could have fratricide.

The same is true for the IOC and NSA in the cyber domain. Each has to be aware of the other's actions, and those actions have to be deconflicted. That actually works pretty well. There is plenty of work to go around.

I LEFT GOVERNMENT in February 2009. A few months later the secretary of defense directed STRATCOM to plan for a new cyber command. In May 2010 JFCC-NW went the way of IOTC, and US Cyber Command stood up at Fort Meade, just the way Minihan and I and scores of others had envisioned more than a decade before. Keith Alexander, the DIRNSA, got a fourth star and became the new commander.

Keith eventually stayed at NSA for a total of eight years. Combined with my six, that was nearly a decade and a half of fairly consistent vision. That is a very unusual phenomenon within the federal government.

Alexander continued the tradition of aggressively proselytizing the cyber mission. From the outside it looked from time to time like he had overachieved and was getting out in front of the administration's more cautious cyber headlights. There were reports of his going downtown for meetings with Howard Schmidt, the cyber czar, and even being taken to the woodshed by John Brennan, the president's homeland security advisor.

By mid-2010, though, a little more than a year after I left government, there was little doubt that cyber weapons had come of age. Someone, almost certainly a nation-state (since this was something too hard to do from your garage) used a cyber weapon that was popularly labeled Stuxnet to disable about a thousand centrifuges at the Iranian nuclear facility at Natanz.

For someone of my background, that was almost an unalloyed good. It set the Iranian program back some six to twelve months, according to estimates.

But let me describe that achievement in just a slightly different way.

Someone had just used a weapon composed of ones and zeros, during a time of peace, to destroy what another nation could only describe as critical infrastructure.

When the fact of the attack became public, I commented that—although this did not compare in any way in destructive power—it felt to me a little bit like August 1945. Mankind had unsheathed a new kind of weapon. Someone had crossed the Rubicon. A legion was now permanently on the other side of the river.

We were in a new military age. What had been concept and anticipation only two decades earlier in Texas was now reality.

I had been a part of it. Probably pushed some of it along. Certainly got a chance to be present at some important milestones and decisions.

And now I knew that we would all have to live with the consequences.

NINE

IS THIS REALLY NECESSARY?

THE ODNI, 2005–2006 AND BEYOND

The modern American intelligence community traces its roots to Pearl Harbor. Everything since that attack has been designed to prevent strategic surprise. We were surprised on September 11. People wanted to know why.

Everyone had a view, including a commission headed by former Indiana congressman Lee Hamilton and former New Jersey governor Tom Kean. They launched their work with a congressional mandate in November 2002 and were clever enough not to drop their report or its recommendations until July 2004, as the presidential campaign was getting into full swing.

The recommendations amounted to a major restructuring of American intelligence even as, that summer, the intelligence community was waging a relentless and largely successful global war against al-Qaeda; the intelligence community's analysis that post-invasion Iraq would be inherently unstable was proving spot-on; and a CIA officer, Steve Kappes, was running back-channel communications that would eventually convince the Libyans to abandon their nuclear and chemical weapons programs.

There were few in the intelligence community at the time who thought that restructuring was a good idea. I certainly did not. Operational tempo was extremely high, and we all knew that this would be a time and energy sink. But we also knew that we had not prevented the horror of 9/11. The American people had forgiven us for getting some things wrong, but they and their representatives in Congress wanted to see some *visible* change.

Candidate John Kerry endorsed the findings of the 9/11 Commission within hours of their release, certainly before he had read them. President Bush waited a decent interval and then followed a few days later.

Following the elections, Congress returned to Washington and to the question of intelligence reform with rare energy.

For many of us in the business it seemed that the Hill had sprouted 535 intelligence experts, practically overnight. John McLaughlin, acting DCI while the law was being debated, used to liken discussions at both ends of Pennsylvania Avenue to being on a hospital gurney, with a lot of people in white smocks poking at you, with nary a medical degree in sight.

It's hard for Congress to legislate better analysis or more aggressive collection or more foolproof covert operations. Choices are limited. Congress can move money (it had already given us a lot), it can add people (we were recruiting at record rates), and it can restructure organizational charts and strengthen authorities.

In adopting many of the Kean-Hamilton recommendations in the Intelligence Reform and Terrorism Prevention Act of 2004, Congress decided to restructure the intelligence community and strengthen authorities. Once you cut through the empty and emotionally charged criticisms of "Cold War mentalities," "stovepipes,"* and "bureaucratic turf," it was clear that the Hill was trying to recalibrate the critical balance that any complex organization has to manage—the balance between freedom of action for the parts and unity of effort for the whole. Too little autonomy for the parts leads to inaction, inflexibility, hesitation, and lost

---

* An accusation that information, like smoke, moves vertically in an organization but not horizontally between organizations.

opportunities. Too little unity of effort means that individual agency achievement is not synchronized, harmonized, exploited, or leveraged.

They were going to strengthen the center of the community and create more centripetal forces at the expense of centrifugal ones. They were also going to relocate and rename the center. The director of Central Intelligence (DCI) would become the director of National Intelligence (DNI), and whatever else he might be, he would *not* be the head of CIA. He would not even be allowed to have his offices at Langley.

The diagnosis that we needed more "glue" was only partly right. When it came to integration and synchronization, we got plenty of criticism, usually about as sophisticated as "You guys are all screwed up." But a line I *never* heard following that one was "So you need to be more like the _____." Because there wasn't a country to fill in that blank that made the sentence true. Even if we might need more integration, and we did, on 9/10 the American IC was already the most integrated intelligence community on the planet.

DCI George Tenet was actually a powerful figure. As director of NSA, I was called and directed to act by George more than any combination of people in the Department of Defense or anywhere else in government, for that matter. George had the ear of the president, with whom he met six days a week. He had an outsize personality and a work ethic to match. He also headed up CIA, and that "C" still stood for *Central.*

When George called me, he would usually begin the conversation with, "Mike, my guys were just in here," and usually end it with "and here's what I want you to do." And the antecedent of George's "guys" in these conversations was not his relatively small Community Management Staff, but rather his operational, analytical, and technical folks from CIA proper. In other words, in terms of creating unity of effort and operational cohesion, the strongest "glue" we had was the fact that the head of the community (the DCI) also headed up its most operationally relevant agency (CIA).

And Tenet wasn't alone. Charlie Allen had nearly a half century of CIA experience and had touched all the agency's sensitive operations during that span. Based on my observations, he never slept. He was George's chief of collection for the entire intelligence community, and he conducted the collection orchestra like a maestro.

My standing orders to NSOC, my operations center at NSA, was simply to do what Charlie told them: "If he calls and says we have to move satellite collection in the Persian Gulf from Iraqi air defenses to Iranian test ranges because they are preparing a missile shot, just do it. And you can tell me in the morning. Unless someone else is going to call me and complain, you don't need to call me."

So the diagnosis that the DCI was not especially strong was wide of the mark. But there was a corollary that a source of his strength—that he was the head of CIA—brought with it inherent limitations, and that was closer to the truth.

When I became director of CIA (the first occupant of that suite not to have also been DCI) I would regularly tell the CIA workforce that one of the advantages of the new ODNI structure was that I could concentrate on just being director of CIA. Indeed, hardly a day passed that I did not wonder aloud how any of my predecessors could have done both tasks.

John Negroponte or Mike McConnell, the first two DNIs, would have to wake about 5:00 a.m. and begin their day by climbing into their armored SUV with their PDB briefer en route to the DNI's office in the Old Executive Office Building. There they would prep for the morning meeting with the president, reading cables and field reports, reviewing specific PDB articles, adding or cutting as required, demanding more information on this or that matter. The DNI and the president's briefer would cross West Executive Avenue and gather outside the Oval Office a few minutes before 8:00 a.m. The meeting with the president would last thirty to forty-five minutes and would often be followed by a formal or informal huddle with the national security advisor. And then the DNI would get back into the SUV for the drive to his office, arriving (on a good day) just before 9:30 a.m. At that point I would have been in my office, fully focused on CIA, for about three hours. How could someone with those demands run both CIA and the larger community?

A second limitation on the DCIA as head of the intelligence community was a little more subtle. There is an argument that any director of CIA would inevitably view the world through a CIA lens. Can the head of the nation's human intelligence (HUMINT) service be counted on to make wise resource trade-offs between HUMINT, which he directly controls, and, say, signals intelligence (SIGINT), which he does not? My experience with George Tenet says that he can, but the question is not an unfair one.

I often wondered what President Bush really thought of the move to the DNI. Politically he had no choice but to support it; to oppose the 9/11 Commission during the campaign would have been read as an endorsement of failure. And the president paid a lot of personal attention to implementing the new structure once the law was passed and the campaign was behind him.

But his father had been DCI, and based on my contact with Bush 41, he had loved the job. The agency reciprocated the feeling. During our sixtieth-anniversary celebrations in 2007, we had a Texas barbecue on the lawn in front of the Original Headquarters Building. As I emerged from the lobby with Bush 41, the applause was instantaneous, warm, and sustained.

We all knew that Bush 41 had advised Bush 43 to keep George Tenet on as DCI after the 2000 election. Bush 41 had been in the job less that a year under President Ford and he had wanted to stay. He didn't think that the job should be political. Incoming president Carter disappointed him and picked Stansfield Turner.

President Bush 43 was in my office at Langley with my family just before my ceremonial swearing-in in June 2006. He casually commented, "So, this was my dad's office."

My wife then asked, "Did you visit your dad while he was here?"

"No. I was considered too much of a security risk back then," the president deadpanned.

He then looked around at the empty bookshelves (I had not yet moved in) and added, "They say you can tell a lot about a man from his library."

Whatever the president or his father might have felt or exchanged in their personal conversations, in 2004 we all knew that the new law was going to take direct control of CIA away from the new head of the community. That meant that the legislation had to deal the new office a *very* powerful hand and had to do it formally and specifically. That's what I told Senators Collins and Lieberman, key architects of the law, when I met with them that summer. That's why Jim Clapper and I warned the House Intelligence Committee in late summer that a feckless DNI would actually make things worse.

Jim and I hit the same theme in front of a group of intelligence community seniors at the Wye River Plantation, on the Eastern Shore of Maryland. We were even less inhibited there, since this was within the family, in a classroom setting, and was totally off the record. *Right.*

Before we finished our meals and left for the Bay Bridge and the trip home, somebody in the class had called the under secretary of defense for intelligence, Steve Cambone, and delivered a Stasi-like* report on our views.

That quickly got us invited to a lunch with Secretary of Defense Rumsfeld that included his deputy, Paul Wolfowitz, General Pete Pace (vice chairman of the Joint Chiefs), and Cambone. Clapper and I were lined up across the table from the DOD leadership and were invited to make our case. The alignment reminded me a bit of the table at Panmunjom, where I used to negotiate with the North Koreans, except that we had Mexican food between us rather than miniature national flags.

Rumsfeld was more cold than angry during the meal. He had some justification. The sitting heads of two of his agencies (I was head of NSA, Jim of NGA) had been going around town trying to strengthen legislation that he and his department opposed. We should have let him know. We should have gone to him first.

We certainly knew where the secretary stood. Brent Scowcroft, the

---

* The East German intelligence service notorious for the voluminous files it kept on everyone, files created by citizens reporting on other citizens.

former national security advisor, had shopped an ODNI-like structure around town in 2002 when he was head of the president's intelligence advisory board. Rumsfeld had labeled it the dumbest idea ever.

Rumsfeld had also worked out a good relationship with George Tenet; even before he returned to government, he had made it clear that he thought CIA an essential partner of DOD. He and Tenet routinely settled their inevitable issues over Friday lunches. The last thing Rumsfeld wanted was another player in that mix or another bureaucracy to deal with. Besides, he reasoned, what would a DNI be able to do that a DCI could not do *if* the president really wanted something to happen?

That was correct, of course, but it really didn't matter. We were going to get a DNI, and there was real danger that Congress would create a leader of the IC who had less power than DCIs had actually wielded. We told Rumsfeld that this would be ruinous and argued for legislative language that would codify a robust role for the DNI even over those big national collection agencies (the National Security Agency, the National Geospatial-Intelligence Agency, the National Reconnaissance Office) inside DOD. Jim even suggested a future where those agencies would be outside DOD and directly under the DNI.

As lunch ended and the secretary and his team were leaving, certainly dissatisfied with our explanation, I plaintively commented that we could be headed for disaster unless DOD could find it in its heart to be "generous."

Secretary Rumsfeld understood the importance of intelligence. He made that clear to me very early on, well before 9/11. After his confirmation in the spring of 2001, he invited me to his office for a "get acquainted." It was just the two of us, he in his characteristic sweater vest at a small table. I had a few paper slides outlining NSA and its work, but I didn't get very far. "Who do you work for?" he quickly interrupted.

"You and George Tenet, Mr. Secretary."

"Which line is solid and which line is dotted?"

"They're both solid," I replied, "and I suppose that could present me with a problem if someone around here paid any attention to us."

I went on to explain that the "Good" in my "Good morning, Mr. Secretary" that day was the first syllable I had exchanged with a secretary of defense, even though I had been at NSA more than two years.

Rumsfeld fixed that condition. He paid attention.

By 2004 the nation had been at war for three years and it should come as no surprise that the defense character of NSA, NGA, and NRO had become more pronounced as the years of war rolled on, even though a significant portion of their mission remained national and their first initial remained "N."

Rumsfeld did not want to put that at risk, so he pushed back hard on legislation designed to strengthen the "center" and give the DNI more say over the current operations and future direction of the intelligence community.

The Armed Services Committees in Congress agreed and had already acted boldly on Rumsfeld's behalf in 2003 when they created the under secretary of defense for intelligence. The new post—effectively a senior DOD official *between* the nation's intelligence chief (then DCI, now DNI) and several of his big collection agencies—was reluctantly accepted by George Tenet but revealingly was inserted into the Defense Authorization Bill by the Armed Services Committees without the participation of either chamber's Intelligence Committee. George confided to me at the time that he thought that it was all about "control."

So it was no surprise that the 2004 intelligence reform act was gutted as it made its way through Congress. Duncan Hunter, chairman of the House Armed Services Committee, inserted language in Section 1018 of the bill that nothing therein would abrogate the prerogatives and authorities of cabinet secretaries. Read that to mean that the secretary of defense had the final word on four of the biggest organizations in the American intelligence world: NSA, NGA, NRO, and the Defense Intelligence Agency.

The way this was playing out, we were going to reorganize, but the guy at the center was probably going to be weaker than George Tenet was at the end of his term.

This guy better be a hell of a choice, I mused at the time. At a minimum, when the president finally walked out to introduce the new DNI, most of America couldn't be saying, "Who is that guy with George Bush?"

A lot of Americans should have recognized John Negroponte when President Bush introduced him in mid-February 2005. Negroponte was a respected career diplomat with recent stints in Iraq and at the United Nations. He didn't know much about intelligence except as a consumer, but he was politically savvy and bureaucratically smart. His quiet style and unassuming personality were exactly what was needed. He also brought a personal gravitas to the job. Reactions from intelligence professionals and from the Hill were universally positive.

The law gives the DNI a Senate-confirmed principal deputy—the PDDNI—and recommends that either the DNI or his deputy be someone with military experience. I fit the bill and was announced at the same press conference where Negroponte was introduced. The *New York Times* story on the event, in its one-sentence mention of me, said that my choice—after having been at NSA since 1999—underscored the "seriousness" with which President Bush viewed the new ODNI.

I was honored to have been selected. I had been at Fort Meade for six years, then the longest tenure in the agency's history. I was ready for a change. Porter Goss had floated the idea of my being his number two at CIA, but I wasn't anxious to swap out the director post at the country's largest intelligence agency for a deputy position elsewhere, even at CIA. The deputy DNI job was different. It meant a fourth star, but also a great challenge, since we were being dealt a tough hand trying to make a structure I considered badly flawed function effectively.

Prior to this, I had known Negroponte only by reputation. We hit it off. He was generous with me to a fault. We became good friends.

Good thing. Even without the responsibility of running CIA, the law gives the DNI two massive tasks: acting as senior intelligence advisor to the president and ensuring the smooth functioning of the whole intelligence community. Each is monumental. Together they are more than any one man can manage effectively. The morning briefing and other policy meetings downtown can easily consume the DNI, so it falls to the principal deputy to play Mr. Inside and routinely check the plumbing.

I enjoyed that. I'd walk around the new ODNI spaces, enter an office, and ask, "So what do you do around here?" I got some interesting answers. I could also hold confession and counsel various office chiefs as tensions with new and untried relationships surfaced.

Negroponte and I were blessed with a very strong senior staff. Good people were interested in the new enterprise. The chief of staff was David Shedd, a career intelligence officer who had shaped the administration's position on the intelligence reform legislation while at the NSC. David had been in Mexico with Negroponte; he later would become the deputy director and then the acting director of DIA. His deputy was Mike Leiter, a veteran of the commission that had looked into the Iraq NIE debacle and later head of the National Counterterrorism Center. Head of administration was Pat Kennedy, a career State Department officer who had held a similar post in Baghdad for Negroponte; Kennedy later became the under secretary of state for administration, a post he held under two administrations. The deputy for analysis was Tom Fingar, former head of the State Department's Bureau of Intelligence and Research. Major General Ron Burgess, later head of DIA, headed our customer-facing office. Head of collection was Mary Margaret Graham, a career CIA case officer.

That was a powerful group, and we all used our contacts to put other strong people in key posts for human resources, research, and the like.

Negroponte also pulled in a bunch of the young folks who had worked for him in Baghdad. Looking over this crew one day, I told Larry Pfeiffer, my talented chief of staff, "In addition to taking care of me, would you make sure these children don't break anything?" Turned out they were all quite talented, loyal, and incredibly hardworking.

But we made a mistake in filling out the rest of the staff. We were in too much of a hurry and transferred the entirety of the DCI's old Community Management Staff to the ODNI. That was the small staff George Tenet had used in his intelligence community governance role. It had pockets of real talent, but folks there had been habituated in the old structure to act as coordinators and even as supplicants to the big three-letter agencies around town. We weren't going to find many disruptive forces there. We imported a conservative culture at a time when we would have benefited from aggressively recruiting some new blood. An unforced error.

One more unforced personnel error: I was PDDNI for only thirteen months before moving on to CIA. The position was vacant for ten months after I left, and indeed, by the time Stephanie O'Sullivan, a career CIA officer, was confirmed in early 2011, the position had been vacant for half of the preceding six years.

Bad mistake. Even if he had had the time, John Negroponte did not have the background to take on many of the inside tasks that had devolved to the deputy position.

And there was so much to be done. We were essentially managing a start-up. We didn't even have an organizational chart, at least not until we started taping butcher paper to the walls of a temporary office in the Old Executive Office Building and marking up options. We had to spend time deciding the right shade of blue on the DNI shield and how many stars should be in the outer corona. More important was debating where we wanted the permanent ODNI to be and if we could tolerate a river between us and the White House.

Early on I created a list of some big things that we should try to accomplish in our first year. I wanted people to see that there was a new sheriff in town. Maybe I was thinking of Voltaire's rationale for killing an admiral from time to time: *"Pour encourager les autres."* My list included: 1) kill a program, somewhere, anywhere; 2) move some money from one account to another—it didn't have to be a lot; 3) question (but not necessarily reject) a Pentagon personnel choice. Those were certainly stretch goals as far as the language of the law was concerned, but I was trying to leverage the bow wave of support we had at our launch. Negroponte was forever the diplomat and in effect said, "I hear you, Mike, but I'm not here to pick fights."

We did manage in that first year to kill an element of a satellite program called FIA (Future Imagery Architecture). But this was little noticed; it was a troubled program anyway. We essentially shot the wounded and the stragglers.

There were other wins. One was creating the National Security Branch inside the FBI and getting the bureau to establish an intelligence discipline and intelligence branch. The events of 9/11 had shown the need, and Congress had mandated domestic intelligence in the 2004 legislation, but domestic intelligence has never sat easy in the United States. Indeed, other English-speaking democracies have domestic intelligence services—MI5 in Britain; CSIS in Canada; ASIS in Australia; NZSIS in New Zealand—but our culture is different, and none of our friends have put their intelligence service inside their federal police force.

This was difficult in 2005. It still is. We wanted FBI agents to gather information in the spaces between cases and develop data without a criminal predicate, but it took until the last months of the Bush administration to get the attorney general to issue guidance on exactly how to do this.

The handoff of the President's Daily Brief to the DNI was seamless. Negroponte was good at it, and we involved the community beyond CIA in its production. CIA still did the most, but others got some daylight.

This was progress, but CIA was a recurring problem, and it absorbed more and more of our time. Even with perfect goodwill, calibrating the new ODNI-CIA relationship would have been challenging. The law put the ODNI at the center of the American intelligence community. History and tradition and many current operations still put CIA there, and CIA's collective culture was *very* reluctant to admit otherwise.

Porter Goss had been DCI, the head of the community, for seven months before being "demoted." When he showed up on a videoconference I was having with several agency heads, I quietly called him afterward and asked him to send his deputy to future sessions. It made me genuinely uncomfortable, and there was no need to rub this in.

There were other issues. Some folks at the agency were directing a nasty rearguard action, denying the ODNI goods and services and transportation while trying to countermand DNI directives. A lot of it was pure petulance, like a four-year-old acting out. It made us wonder if anyone at Langley had read the law. Negroponte and Goss were Yale classmates, and they dealt with this as best they could.

I had to deal with the CIA staff and finally just asked to come to Langley to talk to the senior leadership. The meeting lasted more than an hour. I knew most of the people in the room. They were grumpy, tired, and a little beaten down.

I listened to their concerns and then gave the best explanation I knew of how we could make this work. Using military references, I suggested that CIA and the ODNI were on or near the same "grid reference." The only way for us to prevent fratricide was to separate in altitude. The ODNI would work at the higher altitudes: set policy, give overall direction, de-conflict. CIA should work the lower: coordinate, conduct, operate. That seemed to help. But they were still grumpy.

CIA was having its own internal problems. In September 2005, as we were all struggling with this major adjustment, the number two officer in CIA's Directorate of Operations very publicly and very suddenly resigned. Rob Richer was a tough, outspoken former marine who had served at the agency for thirty-five years, was a respected case officer, and wasn't shy about telling colleagues (who then spoke to the press) that he was leaving because he had lost confidence in the agency's leadership. And this was on top of the number one and number two officers in the DO leaving under similar circumstances less than a year before.

A lot of wheels were flying off in the midst of a global counterterrorism fight, two insurgencies, and us in the ODNI still getting settled.

When the Richer story hit, I immediately picked up the secure line and called Jose Rodriguez, the head of the National Clandestine Service and Richer's boss. Jose had stepped up to that post from head of CIA's Counterterrorism Center, where he had been a tough presence. He had been a career Latin America officer and put his experience dealing with corrupt regimes in murky legal environments to good use at CTC. A lot of our counterterrorism stars came from the Latin America or Africa divisions.

"Jose," I began, "you're not thinking of making any life decisions today, are you?" He assured me that he wasn't. Good, since we were already hemorrhaging talent.

CIA was a growing problem, but in truth, I was getting some of this wrong too. When I explained the American intelligence community to John Negroponte for the first time, I broke the sixteen agencies into three tiers. Those five in the bottom tier, the intelligence efforts of the military services and the Coast Guard, needed little attention, since they were largely departmental. Irreverently I told him, "Invite them to the Christmas party. They'll be happy enough."

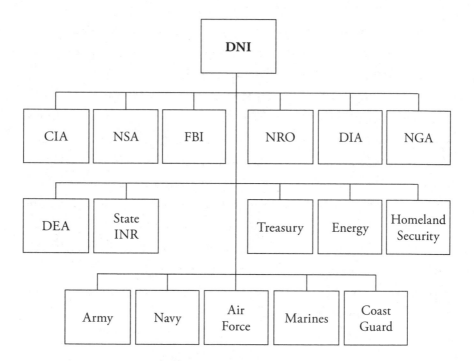

Here's the code for some of the obscure ones: Defense Intelligence Agency, National Reconnaissance Office, National Geospatial-Intelligence Agency, Drug Enforcement Administration, State Department's Bureau of Intelligence and Research.

The next tier was different. They were all small, but they did things for him that nobody else could do, like the deep, thoughtful analysis of State Department's Bureau of Intelligence and Research or the unrivaled nuclear expertise of the Department of Energy. The Drug Enforcement Administration's human intelligence skills were second to none, and there was a growing nexus between drugs and other intelligence targets. The Department of Homeland Security was still trying to define, let alone master, homeland security intelligence but was sitting on a trove of information from immigration, customs, border control, and other DHS elements that could have great intelligence value. Treasury's intelligence shop was the gateway to the precision-guided weapon of the twenty-first century: targeted sanctions.

"These won't demand too much of your time, but pay attention to them," I said.

I then told Negroponte that the top tier of agencies comprised six massive organizations that were defined by their intelligence-collection focus: CIA (human intelligence), NSA (signals intelligence), NRO (space-based collection), FBI (domestic intelligence), NGA (imagery), and DIA (military intelligence).

"Get those six right," I exhorted, "and everything will fall into place. Get them wrong, and nothing else will matter."

With the language of the new legislation, I assumed that CIA, shorn of its community duties, was on the same line as the other five. I was wrong. Within six months as PDDNI it was clear to me that CIA was unique, still special, still central.

Only CIA conducted covert action, and it ran the most sensitive human collection. It had the only stable of analysts not attached to the interests of a cabinet secretary. It also had the largest stable of all-source analysts in the government, by far. CIA's station chiefs were our face to every intelligence service in the world.

CIA's success or failure affected the whole more than any other organization's performance. Get CIA right, I began to think, and everything will be OK. Get it wrong and the rest won't matter. Too important to fail, I concluded.

And that was months before I had any inkling that my next stop would be Langley.

The law actually seemed to recognize that the most important relationship within the IC was the one between the DNI and the director of CIA. It was so important, in fact, that the law said that the DNI would nominate the DCIA to the president, the *only* agency head so identified.

But in the history of the DNI, a DCIA has been nominated by a sitting DNI only once. John Negroponte actually suggested me to President Bush, but then I served as CIA director under the ambassador for only about six months before he moved on to *his* dream job—deputy secretary of state. In 2008 DNI-designate Blair played no role in selecting Leon Panetta to be the new administration's DCIA. Dave Petraeus's appointment was a product of White House maneuverings. And John Brennan's personal relationship with the president ensured that he would be issued to Jim Clapper as Petraeus's replacement if Brennan wanted the job (which he did).

Implementing the ODNI structure was always going to be hard, but steps like this clearly made it harder than it should have been.

We weren't helped by external events, either. Folded into the first fourteen months of the new structure were three of the most controversial leaks in the history of US intelligence. In November 2005, Dana Priest began the Pulitzer parade with an exposé of CIA's detention and interrogation program, the notoriously labeled "black sites." Little more than a month later the *New York Times* hit the streets with another Pulitzer winner by Eric Lichtblau and James Risen on NSA's Stellarwind program. Then the following June three national dailies reported that American intelligence had been mining the international financial transaction database called SWIFT to identify terrorist movement of money.

These were all big stories, and they sucked a lot of energy and attention from the new DNI leadership even as the enterprise was being constructed. That was the bad news.

The good news was that the president was turning to the newly minted DNI to handle these crises. Negroponte was unarguably the point man for the administration's response, and he had full access to the president in crafting the way ahead. George Bush had read the legislation.

Still, there were unresolved questions over the DNI's authorities, and these were thrown into sharp relief in January 2008 when the NSC staff recommended that Executive Order 12333 be updated and amended to strengthen the DNI's hand. EO 12333 was a Reagan-era document that outlined the roles, responsibilities, authorities, and limitations of US intelligence. It in no way, of course, reflected the new legislation or even the existence of the DNI.

The White House was betting that friendship among the key players—Secretary of Defense Gates, DNI McConnell, Jim Clapper (who now headed up defense intelligence), and me—would cut through entrenched bureaucratic interests.

We tried. But sometimes goodwill isn't enough. There were lots of issues in redrafting the EO, but the key one was the virtual veto for the secretary of defense (and therefore for all cabinet officials with elements of the IC within their departments) created by Section 1018 of the 2004 intelligence reform act. The section itself seemed to give an opening to at least limit the provision's impact, since it specifically called on the president to issue implementing guidance. That had never been done, and the rewrite of EO 12333 was a perfect opportunity to remedy that. The original draft of the new EO that DNI McConnell proposed boldly proclaimed that the DNI, in carrying out his responsibilities under the EO or under the law, should be *presumed not* to be abrogating the authorities of the various department heads. That would have tilted tough issues in the direction of the DNI. Cabinet officials would have to be the ones appealing to the White House if the DNI decided to act boldly (and without consensus).

I argued strongly for the proposition, since it was consistent with the original intent of the statute: strengthen the leader of the community. As director of CIA, though, I wasn't wholly altruistic, since ours was the only agency not "protected" by a cabinet official's prerogatives, and absent that kind of presumption, the DNI and especially his staff would focus more and more on CIA for the worst of all reasons—because they could. And this under a law that was designed to weaken the DNI's direct supervision of Langley while strengthening it everywhere else.

I argued strongly, but (except for McConnell) mostly alone. After all, the room was filled with cabinet officials.

The final version of the EO sharpened some aspects of the DNI's writ, but not on this key issue. It pointedly directed that, in carrying out his responsibilities under the EO or under the law, the DNI *shall respect and not abrogate* the authorities of the various department heads. The impact of Section 1018 had not been softened; it had been hardened.

Well below the level of an EO, other issues continued to linger. One of these was beyond trivial. It was stupid. But sometimes in Washington, it is over just these kinds of questions that battle lines are formed.

Early on as Negroponte's deputy, I had the staff draft a message saying that CIA station chiefs around the world would also function as the DNI's personal representative to the local intelligence service. It seemed little more than a tracking change to align our foreign representation to our new structure (the station chief had been the DCI representative).

The first hiccup was CIA challenging our ability to even do that. Then the complaints began to roll in from other big agencies. What about us? Why can't our rep in a foreign capital where our relationship is particularly strong be the DNI representative?

Frankly, there weren't many places where that would be true, and even then the CIA station chief would always remain the senior intelligence advisor to the ambassador. Why confuse ourselves *and* our allies?

Besides, the very law that created the DNI specifically carved out foreign intelligence relationships as the province of CIA. Acting DCI McLaughlin, when the law was being debated, managed to have the Hill recognize that the director of CIA (not the DNI) would "coordinate the relationships between elements of the intelligence community and the intelligence or security services of foreign governments."

Henry Kissinger routinely gets credit for observing, "Academic politics are so vicious precisely because the stakes are so small." Ditto this one for the intelligence community, as the DNI rep question became a manhood issue for many, and especially for CIA.

This is the kind of thing that never needs to be written down. In the abstract, who could question the right of the DNI to name his own representatives, even if a few were not from CIA? Negroponte and I didn't do it that way, but not because we lacked the power to do it.

For the reasons stated above I thought it would always be a bad idea *in practice*, but the number of circumstances where the contrary view was even arguable were *so* few that if they ever became a question, the issue could be handled as a one-off in quiet phone discussions with affected ambassadors and agency heads.

Formally codifying the right would rouse a lot of ghosts, especially at a CIA that felt its traditional position threatened by just about every aspect of the intelligence reform act. Even Steve Kappes, my deputy who was thoroughly CIA but also thoroughly thoughtful, once described this as a "nuclear red line" at a ODNI session.

When I got to CIA, my senior staff urged me to take the issue out of the intelligence family to someone in the West Wing. They didn't say it, but they wanted me to trade on my relationship with Steve Hadley or Josh Bolten, the chief of staff. I was quick to point out that if the issue got to that level, we would lose. There was no way that the White House could *not* back the DNI on such a question. Whatever the merits of our underlying arguments, I predicted that they would pale in comparison to the overarching issue of DNI authority.

Privately, I had told the new DNI, Mike McConnell, that I had to fight him tooth and nail on this one. But I added that I knew that the final decision was his. I said that if it came to it, I would die like a man for my cause. He smiled. He knew the position I was in, and he understood what I was telling him.

This was almost resolved at a meeting of what the DNI called his EXCOM, the heads of all the intelligence agencies. We rotated venues, and this one was being held at Fort Meade around the NSA director's

massive conference table, which looks like it was ripped off the set of
Dr. Strangelove.

I had just about made up my mind to concede the issue, contingent on
the understanding that what we were talking about here was the DNI's
abstract powers. I was sitting near the center of the U-shaped table and
McConnell began at the far right. Keith Alexander, the head of NSA, was
the first to speak. He made a strong case that he actually wanted to fill
some of these positions with NSA officers and do it now. Bob Murrett, a
navy admiral who was head of NGA, made a similar argument.

It was suddenly clear to me that we were not talking about a theoretical matter. If I agreed to the proposition, we would have begun discussions as to which posts would go to other agencies. As I said, I thought
this was a bad idea. And I certainly didn't want to spend the next months
arguing about specific positions. By the time McConnell got to me, I was
recommitted to opposing the proposition and argued that—based on the
law—foreign intelligence relationships were under my purview as the
DCIA. Period.

McConnell snapped back that the law also said I would do that under
his direction, but then he let the matter drop.

That was as close as we ever got to resolving this. We (I) should have
done better. Mike McConnell and I had known each other for years,
were friends, and between us had nearly three-quarters of a century of
intelligence experience. We should have buried this. We didn't.

Although the issue remained unresolved, McConnell did not force it.
We were like two kids throwing a baseball back and forth for the rest of
our terms. As long as we didn't let the ball hit the ground, this would not
cause any damage. We kept the ball in the air until January 2009 and
passed this on to our successors.

I know that this all sounds trivial. I've already said that it was. But it
ultimately led to the first forced dismissal of a DNI in history.

President Bush, taking a page from his father, recommended to the
incoming president that both McConnell and I stay on for a while. We
weren't asked to.

Denny Blair, President Obama's choice for DNI, came to the job with energy, commitment, and some clear ideas of what he wanted to do. He selflessly picked a deputy, Dave Gompert, with deep policy experience to cover many of the high-profile meetings downtown so that he could carve out more of his own time for the lower-profile, tedious, and often thankless task of running the intelligence community.

But even Blair's best-motivated steps had him digging out of a political hole. His selection of Chas Freeman—an iconoclastic career diplomat with controversial views on just about everything, especially Israel, China, and Saudi Arabia—to be the head of the National Intelligence Council was designed to stir up the analytic community. It succeeded only in stirring up several lobbying groups and ultimately the White House.

Another public tempest was created by Blair's quite accurate memo to the intelligence community that, whatever his personal discomfort with enhanced interrogation techniques (EITs), the use of those techniques on several al-Qaeda leaders had led to valuable intelligence. And his testimony to the Hill that the "High Value Detainee Interrogation Group" should have questioned the December 2009 Detroit underwear bomber forced the president's press team to hurriedly explain that the administration had not actually gotten around to setting up that group yet.

Blair's distance from the president and his team was the product of more than just his being periodically off message (which, by the way, is not a vice for an intelligence official). The president and Blair did not know each other and did not meet frequently during the transition. I mentioned to someone close to the administration that there seemed to be a real gap in the administration between the "campaign guys" and those (like Blair) who came later. My contact corrected me. "Not the campaign guys," he said. "The pre-Iowa guys." Blair would never be in that group.

In the news more than he wanted or needed to be, not having a close relationship with the president or his close staff, Blair now had to establish a working relationship with his most important agency head—the director of CIA. And Leon Panetta was politically deft—a former congressman—and personally close to Rahm Emanuel, the White House chief of staff, who had been with Panetta in the Clinton White House.

In his confirmation hearing in front of the Senate Intelligence Committee, director-designate Panetta was asked how he viewed his relationship with the DNI. Tough question, actually, since the intelligence reform act says that the DCIA "reports" to the DNI but carefully avoids words like "authority," "direction," and "control." Concluding his responses to a series of questions, Panetta summarized, much to the satisfaction of the committee, "The DNI is my boss."

It must not have seemed that way to Blair a year later when Panetta told his station chiefs to ignore a directive they had received only days earlier from the DNI on the still touchy subject of DNI representatives. Like McConnell, Blair wanted the right to choose someone other than the CIA station chief for some of these positions. Except Blair just announced the right by fiat and without much warning.

The ensuing very public spat between the nation's two most senior intelligence officials (neither of whom were career intelligence officers) had to be solved by the White House. The issue I said should never go there because CIA would lose did indeed go there, and I was wrong. This administration sided with the DCIA. The DNI lost and lost publicly.

If White House backing for Blair seemed weak on this issue, it all but disappeared in the aftermath of the attempted bombing of a Northwest airliner on Christmas Day 2009. There was the usual finger-pointing, and some genuine shortcomings were uncovered.

The striking issue was not that there was faultfinding, but rather who was doing it. It was not being done by the DNI, the putative head of the intelligence community, but by John Brennan, a retired CIA officer, who was the president's homeland security advisor. The DNI and affected agency heads were informed of Brennan's findings only shortly before the president was going to go public with them, and the announcement was delayed as they furiously (apparently in all meanings of that word) pushed back against some of the conclusions. Brennan became the public intelligence face of the administration in the days and weeks that followed.

Although he, too, commissioned a thorough review of the intelligence leading up to the Detroit incident, the DNI was little to be seen.

It seemed only a matter of time before Blair would be asked to step down. It was an open secret that the president's Intelligence Advisory Board had already been poking at the status of the DNI. Chuck Hagel was chairman and asked me to come chat. When asked what to do, I recommended that they have the White House photographer take a picture and widely circulate it: Denny Blair and the president, the only two visible in the frame, huddled closely, poring over a map or document; the president and his intelligence advisor sharing secrets and sharing views. It was only that image—backed, of course, by a corresponding reality—that could give Blair what he needed to truly function.

It never happened.

Blair's release was particularly graceless, with little advance notice before the press was alerted and little more than boilerplate gratitude for the work he had done.

The DNI rep issue really contributed to this. Having failed to spare Blair that particular problem and finish this issue with Mike McConnell, the best I could do was to remind my CIA friends who were quite upbeat after winning this battle about the last scene in the film version of Herman Wouk's *The Caine Mutiny*. That's the scene where a drunken José Ferrer (who was the crew's defense counsel during the court-martial) reminds the celebrating ship's officers that their job was not to defeat the captain, but to help him succeed.

Jim Clapper was nominated to join the line of talented men— Negroponte, McConnell, Blair—who had been tapped to be DNI. But as the administration moved to swap out DNIs in the spring of 2010, they were also swapping out definitions of the job. In his remarks nominating Clapper, President Obama noted that Clapper, as chief of Pentagon intelligence, had "successfully overseen the military and civilian intelligence personnel and budgets that make up the bulk of our sixteen-agency intelligence community." That's those big intelligence agencies in DOD; the clear implication was that he would *not* be doing that in his next job.

The next day's *Washington Post* carried a feature story clearly sourced to White House officials describing the president's "invaluable go-to person" on many intelligence questions. Except they weren't writing about the new DNI nominee; they were writing about John Brennan. Although officials denied that Brennan was a de facto DNI, there is no denying that Brennan used his vast knowledge of the intelligence community to direct or question specific offices and shops without always informing the agency head, let alone the DNI.

The 9/11 Commission had actually toyed with the idea of the DNI being housed in the White House. Ultimately, that was rejected. But Brennan was trusted and hardworking enough that he came dangerously close to that status even while serving in an unconfirmed position, beyond congressional oversight, and commingling in the West Wing with colleagues responsible for policy and political decisions.

Finally, on the same Sunday as the *Post* article, Defense Secretary Gates (who had pushed for Clapper) gave reporters a thoughtful and seemingly well-prepared analysis of what the DNI job really was. He punctuated his remarks with multiple references to "temperament," "positive chemistry," "getting along," and bringing people along by "accommodating their interests" and getting them to "voluntarily work together." He suggested that the position of DNI was closer to that of a "powerful congressional committee chair than it is to a CEO."

As a career CIA officer and former DCI, Gates knew his subject. He had been offered the DNI job by President Bush, but turned it down because he thought that the position lacked adequate power. He had written an op-ed during the debate over the 2004 law expressing support for an empowered intelligence chief. Now his call for Clapper to lead what amounted to a coalition of the willing suggested that he had concluded that this was the best that could be hoped for.

There is no doubt that the law and the DNI have created some good stuff. The DNI's National Counterterrorism Center, for example, is an unqualified success.* Foreign and domestic data, intelligence and law enforcement information, and multi-agency inputs are fused together there every day. That could never have taken place under the old DCI structure. America's political culture could never have accepted such a robust commingling of domestic law-enforcement information with raw foreign intelligence in a structure directly under a community leader who was also the head of the nation's foreign espionage service.

Mike McConnell also used the DNI position to effect change that would otherwise have been impossible. He bore the brunt of savage personal attacks from some members, doggedly persevered, and almost single-handedly got Congress to amend the FISA Act in 2008, something that neither Keith Alexander nor I could have done as directors of NSA. He also sold President Bush on the immediacy of the cyber threat and convinced him to launch the Comprehensive National Cybersecurity Initiative, a program rebranded but fundamentally endorsed under President Obama.

With some strong CIA support and participation, McConnell also launched powerful initiatives on information sharing and joint duty that will bring great benefits over the long term.

Jim Clapper focused on fusing the community's multiple IT systems into a whole. He also set up mission managers to coordinate collection, analysis, and counterintelligence by target or topic rather than collection discipline or organization. There is now consolidated budget guidance for the national and military intelligence programs.

These steps rarely make the papers, but over time they create the better integration that the law intended.

This kind of long-term, consensus-driven change may be the best that can be hoped for. And that may be good enough and the most anyone should realistically expect. For one thing, there really are no permanent

---

* The NCTC, not to be confused with CIA's Counterterrorism Center (CTC). Both organizations persist, undoubtedly with some overlap and duplication, but with NCTC broadly focused on threats and CTC broadly concerned with taking the fight to the enemy.

solutions to the original dilemma that animated all of this: balancing autonomy of action with unity of effort.

Certainly, no one in the business of intelligence really wants Congress to lift the hood and start pulling out carburetor wires again for another major overhaul. In retrospect, most of us involved with this suspect that we may have dodged a bullet with the 2004 statute. It could have been a lot worse.

This structure can work. It will just depend on people and relationships rather than on formal structures or statute.

First is the president. In this structure no one else can have the DNI's back. Rumsfeld was right. Like the DCI, there is practically nothing the DNI cannot do *if* the president wants it. Things are better when the president takes a personal interest in the health of the community and not just its products. President Bush personally presided over Negroponte's and my swearing-in ceremony. Steve Hadley pulled the DNI in weekly to talk about intelligence community matters and I got to join every other week.

Next is the character of the DNI. He, by definition, must be incredibly and peculiarly talented, since he will govern via the skills of a community organizer more than those of a combat commander. He will also need a close relationship with the president, either before being named or quickly developed on the job.

Then the DNI also has to be tight with the director of the Central Intelligence Agency. He owes the DCIA a fair amount of running room; in return, he deserves a lot of transparency into the agency's operations. That requires a lot of *personal* trust, well beyond what the institutions will ever be willing to give one another.

Good people overcome imperfect structures. That's usually not the formula for success recommended by management treatises, but in the real world of complex and important enterprises, it is sometimes the best we can do.

TEN

"I WANT YOU TO TAKE OVER CIA"

WASHINGTON, DC, MAY–SEPTEMBER 2006

M ike, the president is going to want to talk to you tomorrow."
John Negroponte, my boss, the director of National Intelligence, was calling from New York. "He's going to want to make some changes at CIA." It was early May 2006.

Ambassador Negroponte had already told me that he thought I would make a good CIA director. The moment, it seemed, had arrived, a lot sooner that either of us had expected. The CIA, deeply engaged in multiple wars, was suffering from a kind of battered child syndrome.

And in a few days, the agency's number three official, Kyle Dustin "Dusty" Foggo, would be implicated in a bribery scandal, his office cordoned off by yellow crime-scene tape.

Powerful people in America were accusing CIA of felonies that went far beyond Foggo's corrupt contracting. The *Washington Post* had already alleged the existence of agency secret prisons, and the media was reporting extensively on waterboarding and other aggressive interrogation techniques agency officers had used against detainees at those sites.

And CIA's misjudgments about weapons of mass destruction in Iraq had become part of its history.

Morale was bad and the agency was starting to bleed real talent. Later, I was told by people who were there, and really starkly by people who were no longer there, that this was about the existence and future of the institution.

Some of them even thanked me for saving CIA. I doubt that it would have come flying apart, but the immediate crisis reflected a variety of anxieties, not least of which was the office I had found myself working for, the Office of the Director of National Intelligence. CIA had lost much of its primacy in the American intelligence community.

I could have been viewed as part of the problem, since I had been Negroponte's principal deputy, but fortunately, I was a fairly known quantity at Langley, a four-star air force general and a career intelligence officer. During my six years at NSA, I was out at Langley three or four times a month. We did things at NSA they were happy with. I knew the people, and many of them knew me. But the poison in the cup was that I was coming from the ODNI, at the time an institution less in vogue at Langley than Russia's FSB or old KGB.

It didn't take a genius to figure any of this out. When I'd taken over NSA in 1999, it needed to be shaken up. Now that I would be leading CIA, I knew it needed to be settled down. After Negroponte's call, I let my chief of staff, Larry Pfeiffer, know what was in the works and stepped into my outer office at Bolling Air Force Base, overlooking the Potomac River. It was staffed by two women, Mary Jane Scheidt and Mary Elfman, who had been exiled from CIA by Goss's immediate staff, unfortunately known by all at Langley as the Gosslings.

"Find Steve Kappes," I said. Mary Jane and Mary looked at me, they looked at each other, they looked back at me, they looked at each other, and a little smile broke out on both their faces. Kappes had been the highly regarded director of operations until he quit a year earlier after running afoul of the Gosslings for refusing to fire a subordinate. We found him within minutes on the platform at Waterloo station in London, where he was working in financial services. He answered his cell phone.

"Steve, this is Mike Hayden."

"Mike, how are you?"

"I'm OK."

"How can I help you?"

"Have you ever thought of being deputy director of the Central Intelligence Agency?"

"No."

"Well, would you?"

"Mike, that would depend an awful lot on who the director was."

"Steve, I'm not at liberty to get into this, but I am the one making this call."

"I'll get back to you."

Two hours later, he called back. He had talked to his wife, Kathleen.

"If you're the director, I'll be the deputy," he said.

I was really intent, as my name surfaced as the new director, that it be part of a team, Hayden-Kappes. Otherwise, my appointment would be seen as a hostile takeover on behalf of the DNI, the military, or something, putting both me and the CIA at risk. The president agreed. He knew Steve from his negotiations with the Libyans, talking them back from their WMD program. So that's the way the administration rolled it out: Hayden-Kappes. That was important.

The next morning, I went to see President Bush in the Oval Office. He knew me well enough. We had seen each other in the Oval and in the Situation Room on and off over the past year, and our relationship had earlier been cemented by my work at NSA on Stellarwind in the immediate aftermath of 9/11.

But that was seeing me as head of a SIGINT agency. CIA was different. It did HUMINT. And covert action. Somewhere between the president's confidence in me and his lack of other alternatives, he had decided to offer me the job. He said he wanted me to take over CIA and straighten things out at Langley. I was reticent, well aware of the enormity of the challenge. "Actually, Mr. President, I'm really happy where I am," I said.

"Mike, I want you to take over CIA," he simply repeated.

That was all the convincing I was going to get. He was out of options, and, I think, saddened by the state of affairs at Langley. He personally liked and depended on the agency. Word from the alumni association was that his father, a former DCI, had also been hearing things and weighing in. The president had asked Goss, himself a former case officer, to give up his seat and his chairmanship of the House Permanent Select Committee on Intelligence to run CIA.

Porter, one of my first friends in Washington when I became director of NSA, dutifully accepted, but some of the aides he brought over with him from the House kept him isolated from the workforce, a remarkable feat given Porter's dedication, personal warmth, and good intentions. And then to have his executive director caught up in a bribery scandal left President Bush little choice but to make a change. There seemed to be a political inevitability to his decision.

When I finally got to Langley, Porter—ever the gentleman—had left a note in the center drawer of an otherwise empty desk. "Good luck," it said. (I got only one other note during this period, from the Australian ambassador, who had formerly headed up ASIO, Australia's internal intelligence service. "It's not as bad as it looks" was his cheery summary.)

I was the selection—and reasonably confident that I would be confirmed. But with a weakened Republican president and the Democrats expected to win both houses of Congress in November, the president could have nominated St. Francis of Assisi and had problems.

I made the usual rounds of the Senate in the competent hands of Michael Allen from the White House legislative office. I had never really had to do this before. Confirmation for the PDDNI position (and my fourth star) was more like a victory parade, since everyone wanted to be associated with the new IC architecture that had been declared by Congress. In that round, Senator Biden broke off from a small group he was addressing in order to come over and shake my hand and wish me well as I was merely passing by outside a Senate office building.

Now I could not move in any of the Senate office buildings without suffering a paparazzi assault. This was going to be tougher, and each private session had its own character. Senator Levin, who would be my smartest and toughest questioner, warned me that he would ask me about the infamous Bybee memo on CIA interrogations and then offered me some genuinely helpful pointers on how I should answer him.

I was warned that several senators I would see were part of the black-helicopter crowd (i.e., they trended toward a conspiratorial view of the world). They weren't really that bad, but they did have tough questions, one of them issuing challenges in a remarkable rapid-fire format.

I met Senator Patrick Leahy in a social setting at the residence of the Australian ambassador. I had once been one of his constituents, having lived in Vermont four years as an ROTC instructor. He was actually a graduate of the college where I taught, and he had sent his children to the same Catholic elementary school where we had sent ours. We had a passing, respectful relationship. Leahy grabbed a private moment at the reception, and simply warned me not to lose my humanity. He was obviously sincere, but it wasn't a very comforting thought.

One senior Democrat said some very kind things about me in a well-covered photo op outside his office. As we were walking away, he asked where my next stop might be. I told him I was en route to Senator Wyden's office. "Speak slowly," he advised me. Good advice.

Wyden entertained me with his feet ostentatiously on the coffee table between us, not so subtly messaging that he was relaxed, but that I shouldn't be, as he made it clear that he was going to make this a tough hearing.

There indeed were issues. First, there was the optic of my being announced within a breath of Porter's sudden departure, thus eliminating even the illusion that the Hill had been consulted on the choice. Even Republicans felt compelled to push back.

Some objected to a military officer becoming CIA director, arguing that I would be a creature of the Pentagon. Pete Hoekstra, chairman of the House Intelligence Committee, was the most adamant: "I do believe he's the wrong person, [at] the wrong place, at the wrong time. We should not have a military person leading a civilian agency at this time." Of course, he was on the House side, so he wouldn't get to vote on my appointment.

Besides, anyone who knew me and my relationship with Don Rumsfeld, which was respectful but hardly warm, knew that I wasn't a creature of the Pentagon.

It may have been a phony issue, but it was one I had to deal with. The president even raised it with me prior to my confirmation hearing. "Mike, you may have to retire from the air force," he said. "We're getting some pushback on that." As it played out, I didn't have to.

The more problematic issue was my role in the Terrorist Surveillance Program. I had done this, so it was personal—it was about *me*. I was going to sink or swim on what people thought of me, knowing full well I had done that.

At a minimum the Senate would leverage my nomination to pry more information about the program out of the administration. It worked. While Michael Allen and I sat in SSCI chairman Pat Roberts's office, the vice president called to tell Roberts that the president had decided that the full committee should be briefed on Stellarwind. Roberts drafted a press release while Allen informed the House intelligence chairman of the news.

My closed confirmation hearing with the SSCI was pretty much about Stellarwind.

After confirmation, I closed out the Stellarwind account (for me, at least) by also appearing before the HPSCI.

During my public confirmation hearing in the Senate, critics—led by Wyden, the Oregon Democrat—repeated the charge that I had never been fully forthcoming about the program. I had provided more than a dozen classified briefings to lawmakers since the program had begun, and none had ever objected or suggested a change to me. "What's to say that if you're confirmed to head the CIA, we won't go through exactly this kind of drill with you over there?" Wyden asked at one point.

Wyden also made a run at me about NSA's Trailblazer program (chapter 2). He quoted from my testimony the year before, saying that I had claimed that NSA had "overachieved" in the program. I remembered my use of the word. In describing our disappointment with Trailblazer, I said that our concept was going to the private sector for solutions. We had "overachieved" in that regard, since the private sector did not seem to be much better than we were when breaking new ground. I had actually been criticizing our approach, but the senator would have none of the clarification.

This was getting to be pointless bantering. I impatiently closed the briefing book in front of me, signaling that from my end, at least, this conversation was over. "Well, Senator," I concluded, "you're just going to have to make a judgment on my character."

I was up in Boston for the wedding of the son of one of my security officers at NSA when I got word that I had been confirmed by the Senate. Everyone who voted against me was a Democrat: Barack Obama, Hillary Clinton, Ted Kennedy, Evan Bayh, and just about anyone else who might be thinking of a run for president.

After the rehearsal for the wedding, the priest recognized me on my way out of the church and put a small crucifix in my hand, which I still have, and offered me his prayers. After I climbed into my SUV with my security detail, I got a phone call from Senator Bayh.

"General, you know how I voted?"

"Yes, sir, I do," I said.

"Well, you're going to be a great director. And I am going to give you my full support. You are a wonderful choice."

Senator Bayh and I have stayed close, but I've never spoken to him about the phone call again. I just find it heartening that he thought enough to call me up and say, pay no attention to the final tally. In the end, I was confirmed by a vote of 79–15. I've still got the tally sheet in a frame in my office.

I was sworn in as CIA director on May 30, 2006, in the West Wing by the vice president. (The president later presided at Langley for a more formal ceremony.)

Immediately afterward, I drove up the George Washington Parkway for my first meeting with the workforce in "the Bubble," the CIA auditorium, which was packed. I tried to be reassuring. "Number one, nobody sent me up here to blow anything up," I said. "You people are the best in the world at what you do, so here's the thing. Blow into the paper bag, get your CO_2 levels back to normal, and go back to work. This stuff is over. You do what you do. I got the stuff beyond the fence line. That's *my* job. We're also going to be out of the news . . . as source or subject!"

Then I took questions. Near the end, a young employee in the back raised his hand. "What do we call you?" he asked. I hadn't thought of that one, standing there as I was in my dress blues with four stars on *each* shoulder. But I also knew that CIA functioned as a very egalitarian organization.

"Whatever makes you feel comfortable," I finally said. As it turns out, it was the most important forty-five seconds of the whole speech. More than a year later I learned that this one sentence was a pass-fail one for the workforce in sizing up the new guy.

I got another, even more subtle test, a few weeks later in a counterter-rorism update. The briefer, a member of the band of sisters that helped track down bin Laden, laid a complex spider chart out in front of me and proceeded to show the obscure connections that were driving her analy-sis. I actually knew something about this and began to ask a series of questions, causing a slight smile to form on her lips. Again, I later learned that I had been facing a roomful of skeptics, but had begun to change their minds. In their view, I was more substantive and more interactive than the average director. Everyone brings his own strengths to a job. This was one of mine.

At my first formal staff meeting on the seventh floor, I walked into the conference room, and nobody stood up. Interesting, I thought. This is a different culture.

I sat down and began: "I didn't hire any of you people, and if that's a problem for you, you've got forty-eight hours to tell me. Otherwise, I'm going to assume you're on my team." That was the senior-level version of "Nobody sent me up here to blow anything up." I had three people come and talk to me, but only one left (for personal reasons).

My offer did not apply to the Gosslings, that small group of advisors that Porter had brought with him from Congress. They had to go, but not because I was convinced they had done anything wrong. Frankly, I didn't care and I wasn't going to spend any time finding out. They had to go because CIA needed a fresh break between directors.

I directed that while they were still on the payroll, they would not report for work at CIA headquarters but at one of our outlying facilities. And then I told the general counsel and head of personnel to use my full authorities to build as platinum a parachute as we could for each one of them. They got great severance packages. There is a good reason that the director of CIA has extraordinary personnel authorities. You don't want people knowing big secrets leaving the agency with big grudges.

Of course, I had to identify exactly whom I meant. A lot of people worked for Porter. It was natural that many agency veterans would have been close to the director. I directed that those who had parachuted in with Director Goss had to go. Those who were here all along with the infantry would stay.

The best of the Gosslings was Mike Kostiw, whose earlier career with the agency was cut short two decades before over whether or not he intended to pay for a pound of bacon he had grabbed at a local supermarket. Kostiw understood my current decision and later frequently dropped by for friendly and useful conversations.

Kostiw's longtime sponsor, Senator John McCain, wasn't nearly as understanding. He called me, and in a tirade, placed the entire blame for Kostiw's fate on Steve Kappes. It was all I could do to interrupt and note that it could not have been Kappes's fault, since he was not yet on board. "I did this, Senator." Click.

It didn't take very long to realize, as I began settling into the job, that the biggest immediate challenge would be dealing with what I came to think of as the elephant in the room—CIA's program for detaining and interrogating senior al-Qaeda members. We were still holding leaders of the terrorist organization in a network of secret prisons, which Dana Priest of the *Washington Post* had written about the previous fall. Predictable outrage ensued, at home and abroad. Shortly after the *Post* articles, the *New York Times* reported that CIA's inspector general had issued a classified report suggesting that interrogation techniques used in those secret prisons, including waterboarding, might violate the international Convention Against Torture. These issues—this black cloud—had to be dealt with, that was obvious.

To me it was clear that this could no longer continue as just George Bush's program or CIA's program. We had to build up a consensus to make it America's program by explaining and justifying whom we held, where, for how long, and what techniques we used when interrogating them. Presidents—any president—get to do one-offs based on raw executive authority, but long-term programs, like this one had become, needed broad political support. I quickly realized that I had to be willing to pull back on some things and perhaps be less aggressive if that was needed to build up such a consensus.

In one sense, inside the administration, I was pushing on an open Oval Office door. Although he never specifically said this to me, the president was already working to make the programs on which he was relying available to his successors. That meant building political consensus and political support.

We were going to continue seizing people, and some would be transferred to a third party through a process known as rendition—the apprehension and extrajudicial transfer of an individual from one country to another—but we would still want to keep some ourselves and we would still need some place to hold them. And we needed legal clarity on which of those thirteen previously authorized interrogation techniques—including waterboarding, slapping, nudity, sleep deprivation, and food rationing—we wanted to continue using. Porter wisely had put all of them on hold after the Detainee Treatment Act changed the legal landscape in late 2005. I knew some would be taken off the table, but I wanted to preserve others for our interrogators.

The Department of Defense was in the process of rewriting the Army Field Manual on interrogations, trying to get right with the American people after genuine abuses by army guards at Abu Ghraib prison outside

Baghdad, where Iraqi detainees were led on leashes and physically and sexually abused. We knew the military would produce an extremely conservative document—too conservative, perhaps, for a war against the most dangerous and violent terrorist organization on the planet.

At my office at Langley I had access to several three-ring binders, each four or five inches thick, that were pretty much the *encyclopedia detainus*—they had everything in them, from legal opinions, to what interrogation techniques we used against which people, how many reports we got from each detainee, everything. I would take them home on weekends and thoroughly read and master them.

I also had interrogators come in and talk to me about their experiences. There was one I gained a great deal of respect for. He had interrogated Khalid Sheikh Mohammed, the al-Qaeda mastermind of the September 11 terrorist attacks. He had built up a personal relationship with KSM, who was born in Kuwait of Pakistani and Bosnian descent and was captured in Pakistan in 2003. The officer is still undercover, so I can't use his name. KSM referred to him as Amir, a term of respect for the man who had waterboarded him and made him feel, over and over again, as though he were drowning. The interrogation techniques—in KSM's case, especially sleep deprivation—had pushed him into what the interrogators called a zone of cooperation from his previous zone of defiance and after that, KSM's questioning resembled more an interview than an interrogation. The information we got from him and others was incredibly valuable.

As I dove deeper into this program as a new director, I could see that all of this had been done out of a sense of duty, not enthusiasm, and no one was defending using waterboarding and the other aggressive techniques against all enemies in all circumstances. We were not trying to make a universal case. The techniques were for this one time for this one enemy—fanatically religiously motivated—who had flown jet airliners into the World Trade Center and the Pentagon, killing thousands, and would do so again and again if they had the chance.

Abu Zubaida, a Saudi national and al-Qaeda leader who was arrested in Pakistan in 2002, was the first terrorist waterboarded by CIA. When he was all done, he actually said that we owed this to all the "brothers" who would come into the interrogation program. Cooperating with us was a sin, he said, and he could go to hell. But Allah teaches that he will not send a burden that is more than we can bear, he told us, and we had done that. And therefore he could cooperate with us and still go to paradise.

By late July, I had spent the better part of two months taking all of this in. I had become a sponge, reading the binders, talking to people, weighing multiple points of view. I could have walked away from this and recommended to the president that we shut the program down. I had to make a choice. Was this right? Was this worth it?

I thought about the similar circumstances surrounding the beginnings of the Stellarwind program. Now, like then, I knew that pushing forward would bring its own risks and inevitable controversies.

I decided that the CIA program *as we were re-crafting it* would be worth the freight and that we could buy down the tariff if we aggressively briefed Congress and solicited some public support from it; if we briefed the American people in as open a way as possible; and if we quietly informed our allies more fully of the parameters and limits of what we were doing.

My first challenge would be within the executive branch. I remember sitting at my desk on the seventh floor of our headquarters in Langley overlooking the sylvan woods of northern Virginia, turning around to face my computer, and drafting a two-page memo on what we needed to do. It would become my talking points for a meeting I scheduled with Steve Hadley, the national security advisor, in early August.

I briefed Steve on five big points related to CIA's black sites. "Number one—really important—we're not the nation's jailers," I explained. "There's got to be an exit strategy." We still had a number of people in those prisons. "I don't claim the intelligence value of these guys is zero, but it's low enough now that other things are more important." In truth, detainee reporting had slowed down dramatically. There had been no new entrants for nearly a year, EITs had been suspended, and we judged that only a few of the residuals (like Abu Zubaida and Khalid Sheikh Mohammed) still retained significant intelligence value. In the first half of 2006, only about 5 percent of CT reporting had come from detainees.

There were some detainees whom we wanted to hand over to the Department of Defense prison at Guantánamo Bay, Cuba. And there were some we could send to other countries for continued detention. The dividing line, I told Hadley, was what we called an RTB—a Reason to Believe we could prosecute them. If we had an RTB, they went in the Gitmo column, and if we didn't, they were going to a country that had a legitimate interest in them.

"Number two, Steve, we still need to keep open our options for holding terrorists and interrogating them, especially with the Pentagon rewriting the Army Field Manual on interrogations in a way that took even such techniques as sleep management—pretty much what we do to our own military recruits—off the table at Guantánamo and other DOD prisons.

"Number three, as we capture terrorists in the future, we will think of holding them for only about sixty days at a time, and we won't put anybody in detention without an exit strategy." We could always decide to hold them for another sixty days, or another, if we thought they still possessed valuable information, but we would have to make an affirmative decision to do so. Absent this approach, detention for many would become open-ended, as it had for people we'd been holding for three and a half years. Besides, we found that immediate requirements had usually been met within thirty to sixty days following transfer to CIA custody, and tactical information more dated than that was of diminished value.

"The fourth element is that we still want to have lawful authority on interrogation techniques we feel we need," I said. My interrogators wanted to be able to use seven. Four were *de minimis*—two aggressive grasps, and two slaps. The fifth and sixth were diet and sleep manipulation to weaken resistance, as long as they didn't cause permanent damage to anyone. The seventh was nudity, which the interrogators really wanted since its "on-off switch" was so immediate.

None of this was particularly pleasant. I've been asked on television how I felt about the full set of thirteen techniques that had been approved earlier, including waterboarding. Would I have approved waterboarding someone? My answer was that I thanked God I didn't have to make that decision. And, in a very real sense, I didn't have to, because others did. Folks who have been spared that decision should keep that in mind before they jump to criticize.

Finally, I explained to Hadley, "I want to brief the full membership of the House and Senate Intelligence Committees on everything we have done and everything we have gained, except the locations of the sites, and tell them we want to go forward with the program under the strictures I just described."

Up to this point, we'd only been briefing the so-called gang of eight—the leadership of the House and Senate as well as the chair and ranking members of the two intelligence committees. But if we wanted more political support, we had to tell more politicians what we were doing. That was the plan.

The fulcrum point of this whole discussion was in a videoconference a short time later while I was down in Key West on vacation for the last days of August. We were staying in one of the town houses at a Defense Department facility called Truman Annex, and I walked over to a secure videoconference room in the office of a counterdrug task force to make pretty much the same case I had made to Steve Hadley to the president and the vice president. For the videoconference, I was dressed Florida vacation casual, while the president, vice president, and national security advisor were all in starched shirts, suits, and ties in the White House Situation Room.

I repeated some of the things I had told Steve about this needing to be America's program: operationally, I can't manage interrogation techniques and detention procedures with an on-off switch every two years based on the American election cycle. I need some stability. So I am willing to give up some things that are lawful—things we could do if we wanted to—in order to get consensus on what it is we will do.

I knew that the president wanted to publicly lay out the whole plan in a White House address—what we'd done, what we'd gained, and how we intended to go.

"Mr. President, we are right now at your moment of highest political leverage on this issue. We will have emptied the black sites right before your speech, and you will be able to set forth, without apology, everything we've done, and what we're going to continue to do, again, without apology."

The vice president was characteristically cautious and said he wasn't sure about pulling back on techniques that had worked to produce valuable intelligence. And he correctly predicted that going "full Monty" to the Hill wouldn't buy much cooperation. But the president had made up his mind. He concluded with words to the effect that "No, Mike is right. If he's happy operationally, he's right about the political leverage. This is as good as it's going to get."

With the president's speech scheduled for the Tuesday after Labor Day, we secretly transferred Khalid Sheikh Mohammed, Abu Zubaida, Ramzi bin al-Shibh, and eleven other terrorists from black sites to the military prison at Guantánamo Bay. We moved a number of others from the black sites to third countries.

In the writing, that seems like a simple task. It wasn't. It had to be done efficiently and secretly. And the world's population of "tail spotters," those dedicated to identifying real and imagined CIA-affiliated flights, was steadily increasing. The office responsible worked very hard—multiple aircraft, limited refueling stops—to keep covert things covert. I later went down to their spaces to thank them.

The remarks the president gave in the East Room of the White House on September 6, 2006, were magnificent. He laid out what we'd done since 9/11, and why. "Captured terrorists have unique knowledge about how terrorist networks operate," the president said. "They have knowledge of where the operatives are deployed and knowledge about what plots are under way. This intelligence—this is intelligence that cannot be found any other place, and our security depends on getting this kind of information. To win the war on terror, we must be able to detain, question, and when appropriate, prosecute terrorists captured here in America and on the battlefields around the world."

He explained that a number of suspected terrorists and terror leaders had been held and questioned in secret sites operated by the Central Intelligence Agency. He said that information they divulged during questioning had prevented attacks on the United States and across the world. And he said CIA used an "alternative set of procedures" during the interrogations that were safe and legal. "I want to be absolutely clear with our people and the world," he said. "The United States does not torture. It's against our laws, and it's against our values. I have not authorized it, and I will not authorize it."

The CIA prisons were now empty, the president said, though having a CIA program for detaining and questioning terrorists would continue to be crucial.

"We will also consult with congressional leaders," he said, "on how to ensure that the CIA program goes forward in a way that follows the law, that meets the national security needs of our country, and protects the brave men and women we ask to obtain information that will save innocent lives."

He spoke, reading from a text, for over an hour, and to sustained applause, and then took a few minutes after he had finished to shake hands with family members who had lost loved ones during the terrorist attacks.

I had spent all summer dealing with the issues that had produced so much agony for CIA and the Bush presidency. Now we had a way forward, as the president had explained with such confidence and conviction. It wasn't a sure thing. Congress would have its say. But this day, standing way in the back of that room, the emotions of the families were infectious. It was hard for me not to suppress a tear.

ELEVEN

THREE "EASY" PIECES

BAGHDAD, ISLAMABAD, KABUL, 2006

As we wrestled with what to do about CIA's black sites and the techniques we employed when interrogating terrorists, the agency remained on a war footing. In a big conference room right across from my office on the seventh floor, we convened an operational meeting three times a week at 5:30 p.m. with more than thirty people crowded around a long, rectangular table. Monday and Wednesday, we dealt with counterterrorism and reviewed, in detail, operations under way across the globe.

Friday was reserved for Iraq and Afghanistan, the nation's two post-9/11 land wars. In late July 2006, the situation in Iraq was particularly dire, a point two young women analysts had come to make one Friday in rather dramatic fashion. Both women, post-9/11 hires with five or so years' experience, had concluded in a paper that we call a "serial flier"—a *New Yorker*–length article—that Iraq had descended into civil war.

The Iraq analysts had been pondering this for some time, I later learned, ever since the destruction of the Golden Mosque in Samarra in February 2006. That attack on one of the holiest sites in Shia Islam had ignited an orgy of killings and attacks on other mosques and suggested a sea change in the character of the violence and the hardening of sectarian lines—both classic indicators of civil war.

These same analysts had fought earlier to label the fighting in Iraq an insurgency and not just the last gasp of dead-enders from the previous regime. That had been a tough and unwelcome message downtown, but Steve Hadley had congratulated them afterward for performing a real service to the president by giving him a better sense of the realities we faced.

The issue of civil war continued to be argued within the shop, and by August 2006 most (but not all) of the analysts felt that it was now the best descriptor of the conflict.

My antennae went up immediately when I heard the term and I thought to myself, There's a headline.

"You're the analysts," I said. "But let me ask you a question, because this has great import: What definition of civil war are you using?" They freely acknowledged that there were all sorts of academic definitions, and we talked about the complexities of the situation in Iraq.

The sectarian killing was so bad that academics and some officials were seriously considering plans for partitioning Iraq into Shiite, Sunni, and Kurdish sectors. Militias and death squads proliferated in Baghdad and other urban areas. Sunnis blamed the violence on the Shiite-dominated Ministry of Interior. Shiites said those complaints were a smoke screen to obscure the atrocities of Sunni death squads. It was all so bad that the UN reported that over a hundred civilians had been killed per day on average in June.

We debated how the label of civil war would help the president. "If we think it, isn't it our responsibility to say it?" they asked. Besides, the new description could lead to alternative courses of action. In fighting an insurgency, it was axiomatic that you would want to strengthen the Iraqi police. But if they were but one predatory element in a complex civil war, strengthening them might actually make things worse.

With a trip to Iraq already scheduled, I invited the analysts to come with me, talk to the station, and see things for themselves before finishing their paper. There were some hurt feelings. From the analysts' view, it was worrying that I seemed to be putting a higher premium on proximity to the problem than their expertise.

Still, they piled into a giant C-17 cargo jet alongside my security detail, my immediate staff, and all sorts of other agency people who needed to get to Iraq for one reason or another.

Once in-country, we had a very long meeting with all the analysts there in one of Saddam Hussein's palaces that we had taken over as our station in the Green Zone. We dug into the situation, and the assessment we heard in graphic detail was deeply troubling—and not too different from what the two headquarters analysts had concluded. They mostly listened to their Baghdad-based colleagues, nodding occasionally.

After the session, I went out and held a town hall meeting for the entire station beneath the palace dome. The stairs behind me were packed, as were the balconies around the second floor. I began with my customary introduction, telling everyone that I was the new director and was there to help. Then I almost blurted out, "What the hell is going on around here?" It was a long meeting. I asked a lot of questions.

Luckily, the station wanted to tell its story. I think some might have been a little skeptical that a new director and especially one in uniform would be willing or able to make an unbiased call when he got back home. But the station chief had told them that he was going to tell it no-holds-barred and had invited them to do the same. Everyone knew what was at stake. They didn't pass on the opportunity.

I posed the same questions (sort of) to the Iraqi political leadership— Shiite prime minister Nouri al-Maliki, Kurdish leader and Iraqi president Jalal Talabani, and Sunni vice president Tariq al-Hashimi.

The CIA view of Maliki was pretty dark. It proved correct. As a member of the Shia Dawa Party, Maliki had spent much of his adult life in exile in Syria and Iran, constantly in fear of Saddam's assassins. When I met with him in his Green Zone office, he was guarded by Shia militiamen rather than by government security guards, and not just any Shia—

these guys were Dawa. Maliki seemed to exude a fear that there was a Sunni Baathist behind every bush out to kill him. No doubt for much of his life, that had been arguably true. The station chief told me of a bizarre verbal tic the prime minister had. Every time we said "Salafist" or "terrorist," he would mutter "Baathist" under his breath. In my session with Maliki, he acknowledged the heightened violence in Iraq but oddly didn't try to characterize it, calling it "random."

The station chief's assessment wasn't so dark that he believed Maliki to be an Iranian agent (as some thought); he gave the prime minister credit for being tough, honest, and thoroughly Arab. Maliki even later made war on some fellow Shiites in Basra and in Baghdad's Sadr City slums.

But Maliki was a complicated man, possessing a strange and—at times—even a stunted personality. He rarely showed evidence of charm or humor. Our intelligence reporting suggested that the Iranians had as much trouble slogging through his dour personality as we did.

It was also pretty clear that we weren't pushing the Sunni neighbors hard enough to be inclusive and supportive of the Shia prime minister. The Jordanians were skeptical but at least made an effort, but others, like the Saudis and the Gulf States, were nowhere to be seen. The king of Saudi Arabia made it clear that he viewed Maliki with contempt. At times it must have seemed to Maliki that he had nowhere to turn in the region other than to Tehran. We should have done better.

Talabani, the Kurdish president, was as charming as Maliki was sour. We convoyed out of the Green Zone to have lunch at his compound along the Tigris and were joined by several members of the cabinet, mostly the power ministries—Defense, Interior, Foreign Affairs, and Finance—along with Talabani's security advisor Wafiq al-Samarrai and national security advisor Mowaffak al Rubaie. Talabani could deliver the powerful, at least for lunch.

We gathered around a single large table, before us an impressive spread, highlighted by a local fresh fish delicacy that, all the Americans hoped, had not just been pulled from the (obviously polluted) Tigris River.

Talabani, from our point of view, had his own "too close to the Iranians" issue. He once excused himself to me by saying that people got to choose their friends (us), but not their neighbors (Iran).

For the benefit of the two headquarters analysts in the party, I asked the president and the others for their assessment of the current situation. I began with a rather bleak appreciation of my own, highlighting the horrific levels of sectarian violence and terrorist attacks.

National security advisor Rubaie pushed back, rejecting the concept of a civil war and even discounting that this was really terrorism. In fact, he said, a lot of it was our fault. We had not hammered the Sunnis enough, and they were still strong enough to take their vengeance out on the Shia. The so-called Shia death squads were simply a natural and almost legitimate response to this and would stop as soon as we took care of the Sunnis and al-Qaeda. "You are treating the symptoms, not the cause," he concluded.

Others joined in to relate that Sunnis and Shias in Iraq had coexisted for centuries. Tribes and marriages were routinely mixed. Sustained civil war was just not possible in the Iraqi psyche. My entire lunch group seemed disconnected from, and somewhat cavalier about, the levels of violence.

Talabani's analysis was long and a little indirect, but far from apocalyptic. "If you think it's bad *now*, you should have seen it when the other guy [Saddam] was here" was something the Iraqi president never quite said, but was the summary forming in my head as I was buckling on my Kevlar and settling into the armored SUV for the ride back to the Green Zone.

Talabani was avuncular; on our many visits, he gifted me with so many rough-hewn Kurdish chess sets that I could outfit all of my older grandchildren with one.

The other senior Kurd in the Iraqi government, Barham Salih, the deputy prime minister, was equally approachable, but far more professorial. I once characterized him as the smartest man in Southwest Asia. He had fled Iraq as a young man after being persecuted by Saddam Hussein's regime and had been educated in the United Kingdom. He was an Iraqi official that I always had time for. On one visit I had a pleasant and informative dinner with Barham and his family on the lawn outside his house in the Green Zone.

I reciprocated at my house when he came to the United States. For such dinners I often had musicians from the air force band, trying to match up the music with the guests. We once had opera for the Italians, for example. The band knew little about Kurdish folk music, however, so—since Barham had gone to university at Cardiff in Wales—we defaulted to Celtic music for the evening.

Near the end, at my request, the group played "Ashokan Farewell," the haunting fiddle solo that forms the backdrop for Ken Burns's magnificent TV series about the American Civil War. I described that background to Barham and reminded him that during our Civil War the population in America was roughly equivalent to that of modern Iraq.

He then asked, "And how many died?"

"About six hundred thousand," I answered.

"Let us hope it doesn't come to that."

During that August 2006 visit, it looked as if it might. Working my way through the Iraqi leadership, I called on Tariq al-Hashimi, the vice president, who was less charming than Talabani, but not nearly as sour as Maliki. He wasn't nearly as wise as Salih, however, so it wasn't long before he began to catalogue the ills of Sunnis in the new Iraq. He was animated, very physical in his gestures. I remembered thinking that he looked every inch like a union organizer back home, Teamsters or perhaps dockworkers. He was the kind of guy who always seemed to have his fist clenched. There was no love lost between the prime minister and the vice president. Five years later, as the last US soldier was leaving Iraq, Maliki issued an arrest warrant for Hashimi. Maliki's government later tried and sentenced the vice president to death in absentia.

The noblest Iraqi I met on this first visit did not work or live in the

Green Zone. Mohammed Shahwani was head of INIS, the Iraqi National Intelligence Service, and I visited him at his headquarters in the al-Khark district. He had set up his home there along with a pet gazelle and a lovely dog he sardonically named Chalabi after the Iraqi exile turned politician that CIA loved to hate.

I had every reason to be solicitous. He was a friend, and we had worked with interim prime minister Ayad Allawi to put him in place when the Coalition Provisional Authority created the INIS in 2004. But Shahwani was an impressive man in his own right, an Iraqi war hero who ran special forces missions in the war against Iran. A champion pole-vaulter in his youth, he had carried the Iraqi national flag at the opening of the Rome Olympics in 1960.

Shahwani was clearly talented and courageous, too much so for his former boss, Saddam Hussein, who had cashiered him. Shahwani fled right before the first Gulf War and became part of the Iraqi opposition (and known to the agency) while he was in exile in Jordan. His three sons, all military officers, stayed behind and eventually were executed by Saddam in the mid-1990s for their opposition to the regime. In one of the rare displays of emotion that Prime Minister Maliki ever permitted himself, he told Shahwani at their first meeting, "I know your past. I know your sacrifice."

Following his sons' deaths, Shahwani relocated to the United States. His quiet suburban life in northern Virginia came to an end in 2002 when we again pulled him into our ranks to prepare for war in Iraq.

He was a great choice to head the INIS, and during my 2006 meetings with him, he wanted to talk, professional to professional, and I was more than happy to accommodate him. Characteristically, he brought his junior officers in to brief me on the work of his agency.

I visited the STU, INIS's Special Tactics Unit, at Al-Rashid Air Base across the Tigris. I got an impressive tactics demonstration from Shahwani's paramilitary strike force, but more impressive was the makeup of the unit (about fifty-fifty Sunni and Shia) and of their targets, distributed in the same way. The station chief estimated that the STU had to fire in anger in only about 5 percent of their strike missions, they were so well conceived and executed. There were few if any false hits, no grabbing of neighborhood mopes unlucky enough to have an AK-47. And, since INIS had no capture or arrest authority, all of their captures were preapproved to go into the Iraqi judicial system.

INIS paid a price for its excellence. Almost a hundred of its officers had been killed, and the families of seniors had to live in Amman, Jordan, for their own safety. On balance, it was probably the most professional, nonsectarian organization in the Iraqi government.

Except that the Iraqi prime minister did not consider the INIS to be a part of his government. We tried to impress on Maliki that this indeed was his service. Shahwani was his intelligence chief. "He serves at your pleasure," I told him. But Maliki would never bite on that. The station chief arranged one session with Shahwani briefing Maliki alongside Stan McChrystal (who was conducting missions similar to INIS on the US side), but it seemed to have no effect.

Maliki simply never trusted Shahwani. He was a Sunni, and a Turkoman to boot. He was hated by the Iranians (many of whose countrymen he had killed) and he was being pushed by CIA (with whom he was quite comfortable). But Maliki wouldn't move him out either, even when we invited him to do so. He just had little to do with him. The only time Maliki tasked Shahwani was to gather information on the prime minister's political rivals, which Shahwani refused to do.

In time the Shia-dominated government came after Shahwani. They accused him of a role in the improper sale of aircraft from the Baghdad Aero Club, an unfounded charge of petty corruption in a country whose capital city resembled one of Dante's circles of hell and whose political elites were skimming tens of millions of dollars in US aid. The police raided Shahwani's office and home while he was abroad, and we parked him in Amman while we ratcheted up pressure on the Iraqis to resolve the case. It took time, but we succeeded. On return to Baghdad via a CIA aircraft, Shahwani was ushered into the CIA station, where he took a welcome-home call from me. The station chief told me that the INIS boss was visibly moved by the consideration.

Shahwani was back, but we were working with a losing hand. Maliki set up a separate service, contrary to Iraqi law, just one part of an overall campaign to make sure that all security organs were Shia (rather than national), beholden to him (rather than the government writ large), and acceptable to Iran. The INIS was marginalized, purged, and slowly faded. Shahwani finally resigned in 2009.

A lot of that was still in the future in August 2006. The visit had been incredibly productive for me. I got to see the situation firsthand and to visit with a variety of Iraqi officials. I also got to appreciate the burdens under which the station was operating.

The station had a thermometer in front of its entrance. As I walked out onto the asphalt street, the dial on the thermometer was maxed out at 117 degrees. It simply couldn't read any higher.

You try to sustain normalcy, even in such circumstances. On Saturday evening a few of us walked over to the double-wide trailers that served as the Green Zone chapel. The Mass and the sacrament followed the global Catholic script, but everything else was different: like almost everyone else I was in desert camouflage, Kevlar, and armed throughout holy Mass. I was touched, though, as I went to communion and the lay Eucharistic minister, perhaps recognizing the name "Hayden" on my name tag, said, "*Michael*, the Body of Christ."

Sunday morning we helicoptered out to the Baghdad airport, surrounded by our security detail and Blackwater contract guards. That was easier than trying to drive the ten miles from the Green Zone, even though the station and American GIs had to move supplies and people along that route daily. The embassy's armored bus service always drew fire.

Iraq was a mess. It had been a sobering visit that left me troubled and worried about where the nation's most important foreign policy thrust was heading.

In Islamabad, Jose Rodriguez and I met with Ashfaq Parvez Kayani, head of Pakistan's Inter-Services Intelligence agency, the ISI. It was the first of many meetings I had with this thoroughly professional but soft-spoken, almost mumbling, chain-smoking former corps commander. Those last characteristics often had me leaning into the cloud of smoke that routinely enveloped the ISI chief in order to understand him.

Kayani later became the most powerful man in Pakistan as chief of army staff, and Admiral Mike Mullen, chairman of the US Joint Chiefs, burned up the air miles between Islamabad and Washington trying to cultivate him. As ISI chief in 2006, Kayani was important enough already. Musharraf would never have put anyone into the job whom he didn't totally trust.

Kayani commanded respect as a soldier's soldier, but working with Pakistan, and working with ISI in particular, was always very difficult. Pakistani and American interests in Afghanistan and in the region were not the same. That didn't evolve out of malice, but out of very different worldviews. In an effort to figure out why, I often asked myself, What constitutes Pakistan? Some nations (like Germany) put a lot of stock in blood; others (like us) wrap themselves around ideology. What about Pakistan?

I came up with two things. First, it was *not* India. And second, Islam. And it soon became clear to me that it didn't matter what specific issue I was raising with my ISI counterpart. Fundamentally, what I was asking my partner to do was to pay less attention to India (which he would never do) and cooperate with me in making war on a small and particularly virulent slice of Islam (which he would find very difficult to do).

ISI was a complex organization. We got along well enough with the counterterrorism branch, but we also knew that, all the while, other parts of the organization were sustaining Pakistani ties to Pashtun and other militants as a hedge against Indian encirclement. For us, Afghanistan was a war to be won against the Taliban and al-Qaeda. For Pakistan it constituted strategic depth in the primary struggle against India.

Mullen, even with expending so much effort cultivating Kayani, ended his time as chairman in September 2011 by accusing ISI of supporting the terrorist Haqqani network's attack on the US embassy in Kabul. "The Haqqani network acts as a veritable arm of Pakistan's Inter-Services Intelligence agency," he concluded.

Some uninformed observers have opined that the Abbottabad raid in May 2011 to kill bin Laden poisoned the relationship between the United States and Pakistan. It didn't. It merely tore the veil off.

Shortly before the Abbottabad raid, a Kayani successor, Ahmed Shuja Pasha (chapter 18), was named one of the world's hundred most influential people by *Time* magazine in 2011. The magazine asked me to draft a short write-up on Pasha. I agreed and then called current and former US government officials to get some advice on what to say, particularly something to say that might help the overall relationship. I asked for specific words to describe Pasha and ISI. One of the gentler ones suggested to me was "duplicitous."

That wasn't particularly useful, so I just observed that "changes in Pakistan—the growth of fundamentalism, nationalism and anti-Americanism—have squeezed the space in which any ISI chief can cooperate with the United States. Pasha, a Pakistani patriot and American partner, now must find these two roles even more difficult to reconcile—and at a time when much of US counterterrorism success depends on exactly that."

Pakistan had been a good enough partner in the period immediately after 9/11, when Musharraf had agreed to turn up the heat on Arab and Uzbek terrorists who were running free in Pakistan's settled areas. Indeed, CIA may have captured more terrorists with ISI cooperation than with any other service. While terrorists were in and around Pakistani cities, they were as much a threat to Pakistan as they were to us. When al-Qaeda settled in the distant tribal regions, the Pakistanis were less interested and, frankly, far less capable of helping us.

Then there was the threat of violent blowback. The Pakistanis always made it clear that if bin Laden or Zawahiri were ever located, for example, the potential blowback might prohibit a Pakistani response.

The 2006 visit with Kayani wasn't personally strained. We were just coming from different places, and in truth, we Americans bore part of the responsibility for the strategic estrangement. I was once with Kayani on a small aircraft preparing to land in the United States. As I looked at the increasingly visible landscape out the window, I turned to the general and said, "When I am on final approach in a foreign country, I try to let the landscape wash over me and tell me something about the country I am visiting. What do you think, General, when you look out this window?"

Kayani told me about his time at the army's Command and General Staff College in Kansas in the late 1980s. When he was there, he and his wife used to take weekend excursions. They would simply head in a cardinal direction for four or five hours to see what they could see. When they had driven far enough, he would pull off at an interchange, park the car, and go into one of those ubiquitous motels to see if they had a room for the night. Kayani turned and looked at me, and said approvingly, "In every one of those instances, it was clear to me that the motel clerk assumed that I was an American."

Kayani's was the last Pakistani cohort to attend American military schools. Such training opportunities were ended by the United States in 1990 because of Pakistan's ongoing nuclear program. Without such contacts, the Pakistani and American military and security communities were strangers to one another and remained so for more than a decade. Action in one sphere (counterproliferation) had impacts in another (counterterrorism).

I left Rodriguez in Islamabad and flew off to Kabul, Afghanistan. Things were so hectic that summer that a few days after my exit, the Pakistanis arrested Rashid Rauf, a British citizen of Pakistani descent who was thought to be the mastermind of an al-Qaeda plot to bomb multiple wide-body jets flying from London to the United States.

His arrest forced British authorities to round up some two dozen of his co-conspirators in London, whom they had under surveillance. The Brits were none too happy with the Pakistanis or us. They'd been hoping to have time to gather more evidence for a criminal case against the plotters. They ultimately charged some of them with conspiracy to commit murder and other offenses, but the trials—because of a lack of admissible evidence—were hard, lengthy, and often inconclusive.

The Pakistanis arrested Rauf because they had a fleeting chance while he was on the move and they knew what he was doing—and they didn't want to take the heat if any of those airliners actually went down.

But ISI did not want to move against Rauf without American support and cover. Jose tells the story that the Pakistanis knew that Rauf would be passing through one of their checkpoints. "Should we arrest him?" they asked. It came down to Jose having to make a decision while being driven by ISI to a dinner. He understood the Pakistanis' motivation. He said, "Yes," and as quickly as possible called Washington—where the US government had recently given London assurances that the United States would not push for the arrest of Rauf. All hell broke loose at my headquarters. I was glad to be in a war zone.

The next month Rodriguez and I were together heading to New York. The subject of Rashid Rauf came up. I sympathized with Jose. I saw no benefit in looking back. "You made the only call you could."

In any event, disrupting the plot was a great success. We had provided the British an awful lot of the background information that led to the arrests. It was a truly cooperative and remarkable achievement by British and American intelligence. This was the most serious plot since 9/11, and we owned it. The only issue we had was when we were going to arrest these guys. In the end, the Pakistanis made that call for us.

After the plot had been disrupted, a CIA officer asked to see me. He wanted to present me with a model of the United airliner that was used on Heathrow–East Coast runs. His brother was a pilot on that run and he wanted him to give this to me. "I don't know what you guys did. I just want to say thank you" was the message from the pilot.

Kabul was the third stop on the August 2006 trip, and there I got the chance to visit the CIA station. Like our other war zone station in Baghdad, it was very large and doing very important work.

I also had a pleasant dinner with Afghan president Hamid Karzai at the presidential palace. Karzai is a complex individual, and there is no doubt that history has put him in positions for which history did not prepare him. But this was before most of that was painfully obvious and before his real alienation from the United States. This night, Karzai was relaxed, conversational, and approachable. We ate family-style, and as I filled my plate with Afghan delicacies, the president of the Islamic Republic of Afghanistan warned me not to eat the salad. "Unless, of course," he said, "you want an extended stay in Kabul." You don't get that kind of warning from every head of state.

He was pleased that I seemed to like Afghan food and commented that there were many good Afghan restaurants in Washington. "But, Mr. President, the best ones are in Baltimore," I said. At which Karzai smiled, silently conceding that I had done my homework and was aware that his elder brother owned such an establishment.

On a more serious note, I found Karzai then and later easy to talk to and comfortable with us. Perhaps it was because we would always discuss things that neither of us intended to become public. Almost by definition I was working to not put him (or us) in an embarrassing position. When I was alone with him briefing him on proposed courses of action, he was universally serious and supportive. He continued to talk to CIA even after his public spats with Washington began.

Then-senator Biden famously threw his napkin down and declared, "This dinner is over," in February 2008 when Karzai denied there was corruption in Afghanistan. Biden was with two other senators, and from the press accounts, it sounds like one of the family-style dinners I had enjoyed with the president. I can think of no worse course of action than to humiliate Karzai this way.

I also spent time in Kabul with Amrullah Saleh, the head of NDS, the National Directorate of Security, Afghanistan's intelligence service. Amrullah was young, barely thirty-five, energetic, and self-taught. He had thoroughly mastered English, mostly through reading, and his occasional mispronunciation of obscure English words made his earnestness even more endearing.

Although he was serving a Pashtun president, Amrullah was a Tajik from the Panjshir Valley and a disciple of Northern Alliance chieftain Ahmad Shah Massoud, who was killed on 9/9 by al-Qaeda suicide bombers (chapter 3). Amrullah was a patriot, fanatically anti-Taliban, and most important for us, thoroughly honest. He was someone we could work with to professionalize the NDS, get it to respect basic human rights, and eliminate ghost officers from its payroll.

Amrullah was also thoroughly distrustful of Pakistan, which complicated our efforts to get any sort of cooperation across the Durand Line. Sir Mortimer Durand's 1893 line cuts through the Pashtun nation, with 29 million Pashtuns south of the line in Pakistan and 13 million north of it in Afghanistan. Of course, the 13 million north of the line constitute a much larger percentage of Afghanistan's population, more than 40 percent, making them the largest ethnic group there by far.

For Pakistan, Pashtuns provide a tool of influence in Afghanistan that they are loath to surrender, and they are not particularly sensitive about which Pashtuns' loyalty they buy. Hence the ISI's ties with the Taliban, the Haqqani network, and others. President Musharraf once described for me the division in the Pashtun nation as simply north and south of the line. He made no mention of militancy or the lack of it as a discriminator.

For Afghanistan, fundamentalist Pashtun networks north and south of the line constitute a profoundly destabilizing threat. President Karzai pointedly described the division in the Pashtun nation to me as between moderates and extremists, with no reference to geography.

So Amrullah had his issues with ISI, but sometimes personal relationships can trump institutional or even national animosity. We gave it a shot and invited Amrullah and Kayani to a bucolic site controlled by CIA in the United States. It was private, comfortable, and secure. Over two days, the three agencies—CIA, ISI, and NDS—compared views on the situation in South Asia. There were no real confrontations and we allowed plenty of sidebar time for casual meals and informal conversation.

In the end, it didn't really help. Amrullah believed what he believed. Kayani, for his part, struggled to mask his irritation toward someone a generation younger who had not gone through the rigorous life of a Pakistani military officer.

At least we all enjoyed the countryside. During our last session, Amrullah observed that the location seemed to meet the Koranic definition of paradise, except for the virgins, of course.

During the 2006 visit to Afghanistan, I also got to visit Khost, where seven CIA officers and contractors would be killed three years later. Khost was tucked up against the Pakistani border. It was a strategic location, and we were not the first to be there. The end of the runway was littered with the scattered hulks of Russian aircraft left over from their unhappy time in Afghanistan.

One of my hosts was the Khost Regional Force, a paramilitary unit fighting the Taliban in the area. I also got to meet an individual described to me as the "combat mullah," a local preacher with a very powerful voice attached to an even more powerful radio station. Hearts and minds. Local forces. Good intelligence. Seemed like the right plan.

In 2006 there were only twenty thousand American troops in Afghanistan. It was still the good war. Iraq was the real problem.

When I got back to Washington, I asked my chief of staff, "Whatever happened to those two Iraq analysts?" We had left them behind in Iraq when Jose and I flew on to Islamabad. He called them and reported back to me that they were surprised I still wanted their serial flier. So they finished it, graphically describing the circumstances on the ground. I said, "Good paper—I'll brief the president personally."

The CIA was no longer responsible for providing the PDB, or President's Daily Brief. That responsibility now fell to Negroponte even though the briefers he would accompany into the Oval Office came from the agency. The president devoted a lot of time to these sessions, and he was incredibly interactive with the briefers, and very knowledgeable. I remember during one briefing on Pakistan, he just yelled to the outer office, "Get me Musharraf!"

There were other days when we could hear the rotor blades from Marine One out on the White House lawn. The president was heading out, and everybody else on his staff was running to the helicopter, but the president wasn't budging until his briefing was over. President Obama stopped the practice of getting a personal briefing every day, but Bush was fanatical about it—he wanted a daily briefing, in person, six days out of seven.

I wasn't doing the PDB, but President Bush still insisted on a weekly update on covert actions and sensitive collection, so I got thirty minutes every Thursday morning immediately after the thirty-minute PDB.

I took advantage of that window to brief President Bush on my trip to Iraq. I didn't dwell on labels, but I did give him a really candid description based on the paper and my personal observations. "Mr. President, we can't even get out of the Green Zone to meet sources without a massive armed escort," I said. The situation there was very ugly, and I could tell I was triggering an emotional reaction from the president of the United States. He knew me, he had picked me to be his CIA director, he trusted me. And I'm telling him: your signature foreign policy thrust is going really, really badly. The hand we were playing wasn't winning.

This was probably not the first time the president had heard something like this directly, but it was the first time he heard it from me. He was quiet. There was no pushback. I don't remember a lot of the usual give-and-take. This was a very dark picture.

Back at the agency I had the Iraq analysts come to the office for a back brief. "So, is our conscience clear?" I asked. Then, motivated by a belief that all this was better discussed in the Oval than in the press, I added, "We delivered a hard message to the president this morning. Help me protect my ability to deliver hard messages."

I got to reprise this stark picture about two months later in the Roosevelt Room in the West Wing of the White House. The occasion was a
meeting of the Iraq Study Group, a hard look at the war commissioned
by Congress and led by two prominent Americans, former secretary of
state James Baker and former congressman Lee Hamilton. Other luminaries in the room were former Supreme Court justice Sandra Day
O'Connor, former deputy secretary of state Larry Eagleburger, former
secretary of defense Bill Perry, former senators Chuck Robb and Alan
Simpson, former attorney general Ed Meese, former congressman and
former White House chief of staff Leon Panetta, and civil rights leader
and Clinton confidant Vernon Jordan.

Bob Gates had been in the group until the week before. Nominated to
be secretary of defense, he had withdrawn. I later learned that my dark
picture broadly coincided with the one he had already developed.

I called Baghdad to check my notes with the station chief before I
headed downtown. We were in agreement. Security was degrading in
Baghdad, and there were no obvious inflection points in our future to
reverse the trend. It was not yet a time for despair, but we had our work
cut out for us.

I didn't pull any punches with the study group. "Our leaving Iraq
would make the situation worse. Our staying in Iraq may not make it
better" if we continued our current approach without modification.

We had created tactical successes, but without strategic effect. We had
sponsored a government that was democratically elected and ethnically
and religiously balanced, but could not function. "The levers of power [in
Baghdad] are not connected to anything." This all seemed irreversible, at
least in the short term.

I expressed amazement at what I had observed in August, that the
Iraqis seemed willing to accept incredibly high levels of violence. Drawing on my Balkans experience, I suggested that the parties might have to
fight themselves to exhaustion before our efforts at reconciliation could
bear fruit. Right now everyone was huddling in their own ethnic or sec-

tarian corner for protection, so our efforts at strengthening Iraqi security forces—often more sectarian than national—weren't an unalloyed good.

I used the Pittsburgh Marathon as a metaphor, telling the panel that at mile twenty-two in that race a runner got to a one-mile downhill stretch, and after that, the three miles remaining were no more than you would do before church on any given Sunday. "I can't see a twenty-two-mile marker that tells me that at some point this is going to get easier," I said.

Less than a week before this session, Secretary of Defense Rumsfeld had offered the president his resignation. It was clear that this was the signal for a major strategy review.

That review consumed most of my and Steve Kappes's time for the rest of the year and that of a large chunk of our workforce too. We met morning and afternoon most days under Steve Hadley's leadership in a large conference room in the Old Executive Office Building. The battle rhythm at Langley comprised a morning huddle with our analysts followed by me or Steve going downtown, a debrief to the same group after the session, and then a repeat of the pattern in the afternoon with Steve and me swapping roles.

These OEOB meetings were very candid sessions, and multiple options were explored. The role of intelligence was to set the left- and right-hand boundaries of logical discussion. We emphasized that many if not most of the security forces in Iraq were predatory in their behavior toward the population and that strengthening them without reform could actually make the situation worse.

As we debated what later became "the surge," we agreed that inserting five brigades of professional, nonsectarian combat power in and around Baghdad would push the violence down. Although that was a good effect, it wasn't a strategic one. We wanted to push the violence down to create time and space for the Maliki government to be what it claimed to be: a national, unity government. To that point it was 0 for 3 in those characteristics. It was neither national, nor unified, nor, for that matter, a real government.

And Maliki, we emphasized, was a low-probability shot at changing this situation. Given his character and personal history, he would have to "govern beyond his life experience" for this to have a chance to succeed.

Congress had its own interest in our assessments. Six powerful senators (all Democrats) had written the DNI in July and again in September asking for a new Iraq National Intelligence Estimate, including an assessment of whether the country was in or descending into a civil war. They also requested that the NIE's key judgments be made unclassified, confirming that great political use would be made of whatever we said.

DNI Negroponte consented, and community teams went to work. Not surprisingly, the civil war question consumed a lot of energy. There was little dispute over the facts on the ground, just the accuracy of the label and, frankly, its utility, since this was going to get real political real fast. (It did. The administration used the NIE to support "the surge," Senate Democrats to oppose it.)

State Department intelligence pushed against the civil war description, claiming that the situation wasn't clear enough to make that judgment. Defense, on behalf of CENTCOM, also pushed back, pointing out that DOD did not have an accepted definition of civil war.

I recalled that when I was in Iraq, the view from MNF-I (Multi-National Forces–Iraq) was that this was a lot more like the Congo than Beirut. People weren't fighting over control of the government, which didn't control much of anything. Smaller and smaller groups were competing for power in smaller and smaller environments, and a lot of the violence seemed more about rage than purpose.

But my guys were adamant. Civil war had to be in. I said so and said that I would be "uncomfortable" were it to be removed. Beyond my view, my analysts mounted a flank attack to support me. My Iraq office chief e-mailed the DNI's top analyst that even if the language was removed, his folks would have to testify differently if asked by Congress. And we all knew that Congress *would* ask.

In the end the NIE asserted that "the term civil war accurately describes key elements of the Iraqi conflict, including the hardening of ethno-sectarian identities, a sea change in the character of the violence, ethno-sectarian mobilization, and population displacements."

But it was worse than that, we added. We also had extensive Shia-on-Shia violence, an insurgency, al-Qaeda terrorism, and widespread criminality.

We were pessimistic about the future: "Iraqi leaders will be hard pressed to achieve sustained political reconciliation in the time frame of this estimate [twelve to eighteen months]."

We feared it could get worse. We identified events that could "shift Iraq's trajectory from gradual decline to rapid deterioration with grave humanitarian, political, and security consequences."

Finally, we added, we were the stopper in the bottle. "Coalition capabilities, including force levels, resources, and operations remain an essential stabilizing element in Iraq."

The NIE was published in early February 2007, after the "surge" decision had been announced, but Steve Hadley was quick to point out that intelligence had led policy and that the IC had been a full participant in the policy deliberations.

We had.

Our other message was heard as well, the one about Maliki. The president sent the five brigades, but he also scheduled routine personal videoconferences with the prime minister to urge, coach, and mentor him in a positive direction. It wasn't uncommon for the president near the end of NSC sessions to chase the rest of us out of the Situation Room as the appointed time for his private meeting drew near. President, prime minister, translators. No one else.

The president also conferred almost constantly with two incredibly talented and tireless ambassadors in Baghdad, Zalmay Khalilzad and Ryan Crocker. He invested his personal and political capital in securing a status of forces agreement, or SOFA, with the Iraqis that allowed us to keep troops there at least until 2011.

We made progress, perhaps more than I had expected, but the personal intervention of the American president ended in January 2009. And when the SOFA was not renegotiated and extended and the last American troops left at the end of 2011, Maliki reverted to type. Sadly, we had been right all along.

TWELVE

A UNIQUE VIEW

P resident Bush's East Room September 2006 speech didn't settle much. In fact, it drew sharp battle lines.

That meant that the policy and politics of renditions, detentions, and interrogations were going to suck a lot of air out of a lot of rooms at Langley for quite a while.

I ended up spending a lot of time talking about, explaining, and defending the agency's record and trying to craft a way ahead.

Some of that was self-justification, not for me personally, but for the agency generally. Even though much of this had happened before I came on board, I felt duty bound to defend good people who had acted in good faith. In the world as it was seen from Langley, folks there believed they had done the right things morally, legally, and operationally.

And then there was the historical record. No one with any knowledge of this program doubted that it had provided unique, actionable intelligence. And I was convinced that some version of it had to go forward.

That made it a little lonely at times, since CIA was serving a government with a definition of this conflict that far outstripped any other. Within that government the agency was serving an executive with a bolder view on how to conduct the conflict than many in the legislature, and within the executive branch Langley was operating on the outer edges of executive prerogative more than any other arm of government.

This was going to be doubly hard, since the centerline of public discourse had also shifted. For several years after 9/11, CIA had to defend itself against criticism that it had been too cautious; from about 2006 onward, the more common accusation was that the agency was being too aggressive.

I drew attention to that dynamic. I told audiences that in our headquarters, in a counterterrorism office, there was a sign that had been up for years, but one that never blended into the woodwork. It simply read "Today's date is September 12, 2001." I usually added that, when I got into the car and left CIA's guarded campus, it was not long before it began to feel like September 10. My point was not that I believed that another attack was imminent. It was just that for the rest of the country the impact of 9/11 had begun to fade. That was actually a measure of our success, but it was not an attitude that the agency could afford to share.

There was already concern that as the political pendulum began to swing back, it would sweep up agency officers in its path. In a step that a theologian might call sacramental, since its intent was to be both sign and substance, I decided that the agency would subsidize professional liability insurance for any officer who wanted it. The move didn't bust our budget, since it wasn't all that expensive, but it did enlist private providers who would pay legal fees and damage claims if officers were hauled into court because of what they may have done performing their duties.

The substance part was clear: officers should not have to consider risking their children's college savings before deciding to follow a lawful order. With regard to the sign, we hoped that this would show that real people with real families were involved here—not Jack Bauer clones. Unfortunately, the move was barely noticed outside the fence line.

Everyone noticed our making more of CIA's past activities public. That was part of the broader effort to regularize (and, where appropriate, limit) the emergency measures that had been put in place after 9/11. Steve

Hadley had said as much in the backgrounder he and I gave right before the president's September 6, 2006, speech announcing the transfer of CIA's detainees to Guantánamo. "The president wants to put this questioning program and other tools in the war on terror on a sustainable long-term footing with congressional support and public understanding." If we didn't, we and the president knew that these tools would likely not be available to his successors.

As part of this, I made an unprecedented appearance for a CIA director before the Council on Foreign Relations in New York City. We billed it as a major speech on the fight against al-Qaeda and scheduled it a few days before the sixth anniversary of 9/11. We got a packed house of several hundred well-connected, sometimes skeptical, but always serious, foreign policy devotees.

I explained my presence: "There are things that should be said. And sometimes our citizens should hear them from the person who's running their Central Intelligence Agency." I then characterized our circumstance as being in a state of war. "It's a word we use commonly without ambiguity in the halls of the Pentagon and at Langley." The enemy remained determined, and I gave him high marks for regenerating in the tribal region of Pakistan and planning mass casualty attacks in the homeland. We were less certain about the last remaining element that al-Qaeda needed: "planting operatives in this country."

I candidly and unapologetically talked about renditions, detentions, and interrogations and attempted to give a sense of scale to our actions: fewer than a hundred high-value detainees and another group of about half that number subject to rendition. "These programs are targeted and they are selective. They were designed only for the most dangerous terrorists and those believed to have the most valuable information, such as knowledge of planned attacks."

I conceded that this raised important issues. I quoted Germany's interior minister, Wolfgang Schäuble, who had recently cast the situation in these stark terms: "The fact is that the old categories no longer apply. The fight against international terrorism cannot be mastered by the classic methods of the police. We have to clarify whether our constitutional state is sufficient for confronting the new threats."

We were also concerned with what we called "the deep battle: blunting the jihadists' appeal to disenchanted young Muslim men and, increasingly, young Muslim women as well. The deep fight requires discrediting and eliminating the jihadist ideology that motivates this hatred and violence. It requires winning what is essentially a war of ideas."

I conceded that "some of the actions required by the close fight can make fighting the deep fight even more complicated." There were always second- and third-order effects to any action, even lawful and necessary ones. "But it's actually very rare in life that doing nothing is a legitimate or a morally acceptable course of action. Responsibility demands action, and dealing with the immediate threat must naturally be a top priority."

It was a serious discussion and continued to be so even in the sharp Q&A that followed (once we got past some tired accusations of CIA guilt for overthrowing the Mossadegh regime in 1950s Iran). It was a trip worth making. And we quickly posted the transcript on our Web site.

I had made a similar speech at the German embassy in Washington in the spring of 2007 to the ambassadors to the United States from all the states of the European Union. The Germans were in the chair of the EU at the time, and Ambassador Scharioth was in the habit of gathering his Euro-colleagues for lunch and perhaps a guest speaker. I guess he thought I'd be interesting.

The CIA director has a great staff, and they write great speeches, but I took a personal hand in this one. Early on I turned my cards faceup to our European friends.

"Let me be very clear," I started. "My countrymen, my government, my agency, and I believe that we are a nation at war. We are in a state of armed conflict with al-Qaeda and its affiliates. We believe this conflict with al-Qaeda is global in its scope. We also believe that a precondition for our winning this conflict is to take the fight to this enemy wherever he may be."

We later learned that I got good marks for candor, but there wasn't another country at that lunch that agreed with any of those four sentences. They did not accept a single one for themselves *and* they rejected the legitimacy of all of them for us.

That made international cooperation tough. To be sure, every country in that room would accept threat intelligence from CIA no matter what the source. But they were really careful about the information they provided us. None of them could be seen as enabling American action—like killing a terrorist outside an internationally agreed theater of conflict—that was forbidden by their laws or policy.

Saleh Ali Saleh Nabhan was the head of operations for al-Shabab, the AQ affiliate in Somalia. According to press accounts, he was killed in a raid by US Navy SEALs in September 2009. There was no attempt to capture him, and the SEALs were on the ground only long enough to swab up enough DNA to confirm the kill. It was a successful mission and well fit America's legal and operational approach to the conflict. But there isn't an intelligence service in Europe, certainly Western Europe, that would have provided information that they thought could be used to enable that raid. Under their laws, it would have been abetting a felony. Most were glad he was dead, but that didn't matter.

That kind of stuff bollixed up relationships with even close friends. Binyam Mohamed was an Ethiopian who had trained with al-Qaeda. He ended up in Guantánamo, but claimed he had been held earlier by CIA in Afghanistan, then transferred to Morocco, and added that he had been tortured in both places. As a former UK resident he sued in British courts and in August 2008 won a judgment that the British government had to turn over intelligence documents (more specifically *American* intelligence documents) to his lawyers.*

We were livid and penned a screaming memo to our British counterpart, MI6, that the logical outcome of Her Majesty's Government not

---

* Mohamed later received a one-million-pound settlement from the British government, in part to spare the government more litigation and the need to release even more documents in its own defense.

being able to restrict distribution of American intelligence would be that Her Majesty's Government would get less American intelligence. It was a very hard message, so as I was approving the cable, I placed a call to John Scarlett, my counterpart and a dear friend and perhaps the best intelligence officer I have ever known. I told John about the message and then added, "John, you have to understand. We really mean it."

John had his own occasion to be disappointed. In February 2008 I flew to London to inform him that contrary to our previous assurances, two CIA rendition flights in 2002 with detainees likely on board had refueled on the UK-administered island of Diego Garcia in the Indian Ocean.

It was an honest mistake. We came across data during a routine review of our past records, and even then, there were conflicting accounts of whether or not detainees had actually been on the flights. The preponderance of evidence said that they were, so I flew to London to tell John. One of the detainees had been en route to Guantánamo, the other to his home country. Neither were part of CIA's high-value detainee (HVD) program.

John and I worked out a timetable for a coordinated public release, but John couldn't control British political dynamics. Foreign Secretary David Miliband and his Labour Party were politically vulnerable to charges of collusion with American renditions and interrogations. In good faith they had accepted our earlier assurances about our never using Diego Garcia for such flights, and had said so publicly. This new information was not going to get better for them with age. Miliband went to Parliament almost immediately with the news, but his speed and candor did little to dampen the inevitable accusations of complicity.

The whole incident highlighted the differences between us and even our best friends on these issues. Later at that German embassy lunch, Ambassador Scharioth tried to bridge the gulf when he highlighted Europe and America's common cultural heritage by reminding me that "we are all children of the Enlightenment." I agreed, but quickly added that while Europeans seemed to put a great deal of stock in Locke and the nobility of man in his natural state, we Americans tended to huddle around Hobbes and his darker formulation.

Discussions with Congress never reached that level of elegant philosophical abstraction, even after we had started to go "full Monty" to the Hill the morning of the president's East Room speech in September 2006. We followed that up with a series of other appearances. We provided a list of those who had been held in the HVD program, the techniques to which they had been subjected, and the number of intelligence reports we had gotten.

I told Congress that the HVD program had evolved out of the debacle early on when CIA officers made battlefield captures in places like Afghanistan with no training and even less guidance on how to interrogate. Abuses had been too common.

I *tried* to explain the history. Enhanced interrogation techniques had been used on about a third of the hundred or so HVDs that had been held. The techniques were *not* used to elicit information, but rather to move a detainee from defiance to cooperation by imposing on him a state of helplessness. When he got to the latter state (the duration varied, but on average a week or so), interrogations resembled debriefings or conversations. I estimated that about half of what the agency knew about al-Qaeda at that time had come from detainees of one type or another.

Clearly we thought the techniques were important, but we freely admitted that they were not the agency's most important tool. That was our knowledge: knowledge of terrorism, knowledge of the terrorists, and knowledge of the philosophy that was motivating them. In that September press backgrounder with Steve Hadley I stressed that "CIA subject matter experts with years of experience studying and tracking al-Qaeda are the ones who participate in these questionings."

I later spoke with one of those experts, a young woman whom the agency hastily deployed to help with the interrogation of Abu Zubaida. Within twenty-four hours of the decision to send her, she was standing face-to-face with Zubaida at a black site. She later described it to me as her most surreal experience ever and confessed that "no one wanted to be there."

But she also added that, with a second wave of attacks thought imminent, "how could we in conscience have outsourced this interrogation to a third party and trust that they would ask the right questions or give us truthful answers." For some prisoners, perhaps, but not for the likes of Zubaida or, later, Khalid Sheikh Mohammed.

She knew al-Qaeda cold, but like everyone else in this new enterprise, she was feeling her way. She asked Zubaida questions to explore his knowledge and his truthfulness. At team meetings she had to give her assessment. She told me that she was struck by the degree of certainty that the interrogators demanded of her that Zubaida was lying or withholding before they would agree to continue with the enhanced techniques.

They did, of course, until Zubaida became compliant, and then he became a torrent of information. She described him in some sessions as chatting "like an adolescent girl at a slumber party." Even here, though, knowledge was still power. She would entice Zubaida to share his views with questions reflecting CIA knowledge of al-Qaeda well beyond his expectations. He confirmed some data points, challenged some, and filled in the blanks between others. She would even sometimes prompt him with recently acquired sensitive intelligence (no problem telling him—he wasn't going anywhere). A lot of the data he (and other detainees) revealed looked on the surface like trivia—what kind of car, who else was at the meeting, casual relationships, an e-mail address—but it built up the storehouse of granular information that would be used to build threads to ultimately kill and capture terrorists and disrupt plots.

Speaking in 2015, she observed that even then, a week didn't go by that she didn't want to check a data point or follow up an issue with one or another of the detainees. (She couldn't, of course.) She spoke almost longingly of the days when the agency could keep going back to detainees to check details, challenge them with newly acquired data, or play one detainee off against another.

She reminded me that one of the key clues in the pursuit of bin Laden was that KSM and Abu Faraj obviously lied when confronted with new information about bin Laden's courier. That was just another thread in a complex and slowly woven fabric.

As I've said, historically the agency had had thirteen approved techniques, including waterboarding, cramped confinement, stress positions, and water dousing. In 2006–2007 we were proposing to cut the authorized techniques in half, eliminating all of the above, while retaining a grasp of the lapels and of the chin, two slaps (a backhanded belly slap and an insult slap to the face), and the authority to manipulate diet and sleep. Enforced nudity was sometimes on and sometimes off our amended list. I have said that the interrogators wanted it, since it could quickly be turned on and off, but Secretary of State Rice and Steve Hadley had concerns.

I think it was the image. I know that Steve regretted not better understanding the history of waterboarding and the association of a technique by the same name with Japanese war criminals and the Philippine insurrection. This time we talked it through. I took nudity off the list. I had a high regard for their views, and besides, this was about creating consensus. Still, we were edging close to the line about which the vice president often cautioned me: Will these be effective enough?

None of this, by the way, was to pass judgment on the past use of nudity or any other technique. I was always careful to emphasize that. George Tenet and Porter Goss had their circumstances; I had mine. And in late 2006 we had more knowledge of al-Qaeda, deeper penetrations of its network, and better understanding of its threats than we had had in 2002 or 2004. I could afford to give up some things, especially if that led to the kind of political consensus we were seeking.

I wanted Congress to be part of that consensus. That required a serious discussion with them. That discussion never happened. The members were too busy yelling at us and at one another.

The House Intelligence Committee was especially contentious, particularly after the November midterms put the committee into Democrat hands. The new chairman, Silvestre Reyes, was a Vietnam veteran, a former border patrol officer, and perhaps the most decent man in Congress. I had once flown to his hometown of El Paso to give a speech at the local university, and he made sure that our military jet home was stocked with tortillas from his favorite local restaurant. He had been trashed shortly before taking over the committee by Jeff Stein, then the *Congressional Quarterly*'s national security editor, when Reyes failed to distinguish al-Qaeda as a Sunni organization. We didn't care. It had been an ambush. Stein was tough and knowledgeable, but he specialized in snark. We were more impressed by Reyes's honesty. We'd fill him in on the rest.

The new Speaker of the House, Nancy Pelosi, had picked Reyes because of her personal feud with the obvious choice, senior intelligence Democrat and fellow Californian Jane Harman. Harman was just too centrist on security issues and too soft on Bush. Pelosi then packed the committee with loyalists. Anna Eshoo (CA), Rush Holt (NJ), Jan Schakowsky (IL), and John Tierney (MA) had impeccable liberal credentials and were, well, tough to brief.

Hearings often became shouting matches. In one session I was asked if I would waterboard my daughter. Then (in lieu of a question) I was accused of looking bored during a lengthy lecture on the American political system and how this chamber was "the people's house." One member candidly admitted that he was just opposed to *all* covert action. There were moments (a lot of them, actually) when I was convinced that several members were opposed not just to some of the agency's actions, but to its existence.

One agency senior left such a session, commenting, "I had no idea people treated other people that way."

Republicans had their issues too. Pete Hoekstra (MI) was jealously protective of congressional prerogatives and routinely and angrily complained to us about the limited flow of information from the executive branch.

We were kind of on his side. After all, CIA had pushed for extending the briefing on black sites to all members of the intelligence committee and to staff. We also pushed to brief the leadership of our appropriations committee, Jack Murtha (D-PA) and Bill Young (R-FL).

That session didn't go well. Murtha was a friend, a western Pennsylvanian, and a Steelers fan like me, who had actually introduced me in my PDDNI confirmation hearing. I had lent him my cassette tapes of Shelby Foote reading his magnificent history of the Battle of Gettysburg to listen to on his drives between Washington and Johnstown. So I was surprised when Murtha jumped all over me when I entered the briefing room. His ostensible reason was my tardiness (less than five minutes because of traffic), but it was so uncharacteristic that I suspected that there had to be more. That was confirmed when Murtha excused himself rather than being briefed on the details of interrogation techniques. He didn't want to know, and he didn't want to be there.

The Senate Intelligence Committee was marginally more civilized than its House counterpart, but the dialogue there was no more productive. In one case Senator Feinstein had been publicly excoriating the agency for slamming the heads of prisoners into walls, like ramming skulls into turnbuckles during a World Wrestling Federation death match.

I dutifully got on the senator's calendar and briefed her and her staff director on the now eliminated technique of "walling": pushing the shoulders of a detainee whose neck had been braced into a false plywood wall that gave off a loud bang. She took notes while staring at me solemnly and then proceeded to publicly repeat the same accusation a few days later.

Senator Jay Rockefeller (D-WV), a veteran member of the intelligence committee, became its chair in 2007. I had briefed him multiple times, and although we were never close, I think there was some mutual respect (even though we did routinely spar over Pitt and West Virginia football). The relationship, such as it was, steadily deteriorated. At one private session with just his staff director and my legislative affairs chief with us, he abruptly interrupted the flow of conversation to challenge me: "You don't believe in oversight, do you?" I still don't know what prompted it, since I was briefing him on a sensitive activity at the meeting. Over time the senator was increasingly reluctant to accept briefings on material that wasn't cleared for release to the whole committee. "Why are you telling me this?" he once asked.

I testified on detentions and interrogations to the full oversight committees of both houses in September and November 2006 and again in April 2007. The April 2007 session with the SSCI was typical. Fourteen senators attended all or part of the hearing along with twenty-one staff. Those are big numbers for a sensitive covert action.

Besides the usual coterie of backbenchers, I brought John Rizzo, the general counsel, Steve Bradbury from Justice, and one of Khalid Sheikh Mohammed's principal interrogators, someone KSM took to calling Amir, to testify with me. I often deferred to them for details.

We also brought documentation. We handed each senator a matrix with thirty or so names down the left side and the thirteen formerly authorized techniques across the top. The Xs in the boxes that were formed showed which detainee had undergone which techniques. We also discussed another important metric, the intelligence derived from the detainees, some eight thousand reports.

Intelligence is sometimes described as putting the pieces of a jigsaw puzzle together, except that we hardly ever get to see the picture on the top of the puzzle box. The individuals that CIA detained gave us many new puzzle pieces, but most important, given their positions in al-Qaeda, oftentimes they had seen the picture on the top of the box too.

The National Intelligence Council published an estimate on the threat to the homeland in the summer of 2007. The NIE's judgments were shaped by the intelligence we obtained from our detention program. More than 70 percent of the human intelligence reporting used in that estimate was based on information from detainees.

I tried to show Congress the care with which the program was now being run. The average age of those interrogating detainees was forty-three. Once they were selected, they had to complete more than 250 hours of specialized training before they were allowed to come face-to-face with a terrorist. And we required additional fieldwork under the direct supervision of an experienced officer before a new interrogator could direct an interrogation.

I was committed to making Congress a partner in all this. My Congressional Affairs chief, Chris Walker, was an experienced Hill hand. He had worked for Speaker Denny Hastert before coming to us. Chris dutifully responded to my direction to keep the committees "fully and currently" informed about *all* agency activities. We set indoor records for CNs (Congressional Notifications), formal hearings, and briefings.

Over one twelve-month period CIA officers testified at fifty-seven congressional hearings and completed twenty-nine congressionally legislated reports. We answered 1,140 QFRs—that's Questions for the Record—as well as 254 other letters, queries, and requests.

CIA experts gave more than five hundred briefings to members of Congress and their staffs. (The 110th Congress was in legislative session for 349 days, so we were providing more than one briefing per legislative day.)

I personally briefed the Hill nine times just on RDI (rendition, detention, and interrogation).

The oversight committees were exhaustive in their demands for ever more detailed information, like how many lumens of light and decibels of sound detainees were subjected to while in CIA custody. One congressman wanted to know whether or not CIA complied with "buy America" legal requirements for construction materials used in black sites overseas.

We answered the questions, but the times were tough: we were talking about controversial things on behalf of a weakened president with the opposition in control of both chambers and a lot of people positioning themselves for a run for president. Not good circumstances. Briefings on Iraq became so caustic that I told Chris that analysts were empowered to simply leave if the abuse became excessive.

And it wasn't just CIA. In March 2008 DNI Mike McConnell had arranged a two-day off-site at a CIA location in Virginia for members of the House Intelligence Committee. We were to have a short introductory session followed by drinks and dinner Sunday night and then a good day of work Monday before returning to the capital.

Of course, most of the IC leadership was in the comm center before sunrise on Monday checking their cable traffic and the press clips. One story caught our eye. Siobhan Gorman, a smart reporter formerly of the *Baltimore Sun* but now at the *Wall Street Journal*, had filed a long, page-one story that screamed exposé on ominous-sounding data-collection programs at NSA. Except that three NSA directors—me, McConnell, and the current DIRNSA, Keith Alexander—couldn't quite figure out what it was about. That's unusual. When a story appears in the press, even when incomplete or inaccurate, you can usually discern the actual activity behind the headline. Not this time.

So DNI McConnell decided to go off-script (with our enthusiastic support) and directed that copies of the article be made and put at everyone's place for the morning session. He invited everyone to read the piece and then began the discussion with a plea to the members that only they had the credibility to defend the IC when such stories appeared. We were an open book to them, so they were well positioned to scotch such rumors. Sounded reasonable to me.

Not so much to them. The first member to speak baldly stated that he would not do that, since he "did not know that story was untrue." And things went downhill from there. One member flatly accused Keith Alexander of lying to him. Another, out of the blue, attacked the director of the National Reconnaissance Office for secretly putting "weapons in space," a charge so outrageous that we expected harboring space aliens would be the next allegation. A third member shifted the topic only slightly by observing that the real problem was their being forced to rely on a bunch of white guys and that racial and gender diversity would markedly improve American intelligence. We finally got back on the original agenda, but the damage had been done; the whole thing left a gaping hole below the waterline.

The same with the intended dialogue on RDI. In the end, the Con-

gress of the United States had *no* impact on the shape of the CIA interrogation program going forward. Congress lacked the courage or the
consensus to stop it, endorse it, or amend it. We finally simply informed
them that we would seek legal authority from Justice to use six techniques; that we would not put anyone into CIA custody without an "exit
plan" (Guantánamo or a third country); that we would keep detainees for
a short, fixed period (about two months); that it would require a positive
decision to extend that period; and we would contemporaneously inform
the committees of every detainee and how they were treated.

Ironically, we had more productive discussions on this stuff with the
International Committee of the Red Cross than we did with Congress.
The White House wasn't particularly enthusiastic about that, but it didn't
get in the way either. ICRC officials became frequent visitors to Langley.
The ICRC has a passion for secrecy that rivals the agency's—its access,
like much of ours, depends on it—so at least in one sense we were kin-
dred spirits.

The agency also quietly gave the ICRC a heads-up before transferring
some of the later detainees to Guantánamo, and we offered what information we could to help keep ICRC people safe around the world.

But it was difficult to find middle ground on our core issue. We felt
we were most effective gaining intelligence when we held prisoners secretly with no outside contact; the Red Cross was all about notification
and visitation. We believed that Geneva didn't require that because of the
unlawful combatant status of our detainees, but the Red Cross disagreed
based on common international practice. We were exploring an approach
to notification (informing the ICRC that we had *somebody*) when the
2008 election mooted all of our discussions.

Even when we failed to find mutual understanding with the ICRC,
however, we did develop some mutual respect. In one meeting, I was
struck by their observation that "CIA often refuses to answer our questions, but when it does, we know the answers are true." At least somebody
believed us.

The ICRC, of course, got access to the fourteen detainees we had moved to Guantánamo in September 2006 and prepared a report based on those interviews that it gave to CIA as the former detaining authority. The report was predictably harsh in its charges of torture and cruel and degrading treatment. We shared the report, in strictest confidence based on ICRC requirements, with the oversight committees and a very few executive branch offices. We reminded them that the document was based *solely* on detainee claims. When the Senate put on its public calendar that it was going to have a closed hearing on the report, the ICRC was understandably upset that the very existence of the report had been made public. We intervened and got the committee to take the posting off its Web site.

Then in April 2009 the entire report was published in the *New York Review of Books* by Mark Danner, a UC Berkeley professor of journalism and frequent critic of US conduct in the war on terror. The ICRC expressed regret that "information attributed to the ICRC report was made public in this manner." Danner would only say that "the document came into my hands from parties that thought it should be made public."

The leak was exquisitely timed to support (and justify) the administration's decision to declassify DOJ memos on interrogations a few weeks later (chapter 20). What a coincidence!

THERE ARE DAYS when a director of CIA is inclined to think that he is running a large public affairs, legal, and legislative liaison enterprise attached to small operational and analytic elements. Of course, it is (or should be) the other way around. That meant that there was no sense arguing about detainees if we weren't going to capture any. If continuing this was going to be politically painful, we had better be getting something out of it.

That meant action, and that put a heavy moral and legal burden on the agency in general and me in particular. We were denying people their freedom, likely forever, in a program of extrajudicial detention.

Some people found that objectionable under any circumstances; anyone would find it objectionable if you were doing it to the wrong people. There were occasional mistakes: plain mistaken identity, or correct identity but miscalculating the detainee's knowledge of impending evil and thus eligibility for such an extraordinary program. But we couldn't hold ourselves to a court-of-law standard of beyond reasonable doubt either. Courts deal with crimes already committed and are usually not driven by impending future events. Intelligence is all about the future and is designed to enable action in the face of continuing doubt. Still, you had to be careful.

Abdul Hadi al Iraqi, a veteran al-Qaeda commander, was captured in late 2006 as he was traveling back to his homeland. He had a tough-guy reputation within al-Qaeda—cold-blooded, hard-charging, no-nonsense. He had also developed, largely through news accounts, an incredibly cartoonish idea of what we did and how we did it. When he arrived at the black site, we informed him who we were and also told him who he was, cutting through the cloud of aliases he was using.

He cooperated almost immediately, offering a string of rationalizations. "You know everything about us, we know everything about you. It won't matter in the end. It will just be a waste of time, because we are going to prevail regardless of how much you know about us." It was going to be a long conflict, anyway. "You fight a ten-year war, while we are prepared to battle for a hundred years if that's what it takes, so what I say here won't matter."

Our interrogators welcomed his rationalizations, agreeing with him where they could, and respectfully disagreeing where they couldn't. They consented to the debriefings going forward in a standard manner, but warned that at his first verifiable lie, they would change the tenor of the questioning.

CIA subject-matter experts tested him with a number of knowns, which he answered credibly, and then moved on to unknowns, which they all agreed he answered credibly as well. Hadi told his interviewers that he was impressed with their questions and their knowledge. He said it was like they were there. For their part, the analysts on-site and at headquarters were happy with his participation.

Abdul Hadi's interrogators briefed me on all of this in early 2007, and I invited them to come back to my office the next day to meet with Senator Feinstein, who was already on my calendar. It was all part of making Congress a partner.

The interrogators pretty much repeated their account for the senator, who then asked if they were aware of any attacks that had been thwarted based on their previous work with detainees. They deflected that as a question better asked of analysts. Their job was to condition detainees to respond credibly to questioning, and while they were aware of a number of occasions where attack information was revealed and reported, they didn't have a box score on it.

After the interrogators explained how Abdul Hadi's inaccurate version of what we did led to his cooperation and our decision to proceed with a standard debriefing, the senator asked if this was how we were going to conduct interrogations "from now on." They told her that this was the way that interrogations had always been conducted. Start with an interview to determine the willingness to participate voluntarily and credibly and stick with that if it's producing an appropriate level of information. At the first sign of fabrication, though, they were prepared to request approval for enhanced techniques.

The senator then turned to me and asked what I knew about Russian poisonings in London (Alexander Litvinenko's polonium poisoning was two months earlier). We were done talking about interrogations.

Muhammad Rahim al-Afghani was captured in the summer of 2007. Rahim was a tough, seasoned jihadist who had prepared Tora Bora as a hideout for bin Laden in December 2001. He was not cooperative and didn't seem frightened by the prospect of interrogation. He was definitely a candidate for EITs, but before we did that, we needed a final Justice Department opinion on the six surviving techniques. And before that could happen, we needed an executive order clarifying Common Article 3 of the Geneva Convention.

It was complicated. First, a little history. With the Hamdan decision in June 2006, the Supreme Court had extended the protection of Common Article 3 of Geneva to the unlawful combatants of al-Qaeda. I'm not a lawyer, but I was frankly surprised by the decision, since Common Article 3 refers to conflicts not of an international character. The traditional reading of that had been intranational (i.e., civil wars). But the court (5–3) extended Common Article 3 to include the current conflict, since al-Qaeda was not a nation, even though the conflict was unarguably global.

So we needed legislative help. Our problem was not that we wanted Congress to approve or disapprove any techniques. Our problem was that we didn't know what Common Article 3 meant in the context of American law. When the Senate had ratified other portions of international humanitarian treaties like the Geneva Conventions, the legislative history or specific statements of the Senate sometimes clarified the meaning of the treaty in terms of American law. For example, in ratifying the Convention Against Torture, the Senate was careful to define the international commitment against cruel, inhuman, and degrading treatment or punishment by referring to our domestic law against cruel and inhumane treatment or punishment as found in the Fifth, Eighth, and Fourteenth Amendments to the Constitution. There is a body of precedent that gives meaning to that.

Congress had delivered no such clarifying language with regard to Common Article 3 (perhaps expecting, like me, that it would never apply to us). The language of Common Article 3 is firm but vague, like its prohibition of "humiliating and degrading treatment." It would be very hard for me to confidently direct an agency officer to do some things with such vague language. I was looking for some definition.

One of the "solutions" that was proposed was that the Military Commissions Act then being considered would expressly criminalize a small set of heinous activities, and as long as CIA officers didn't do them, they wouldn't be prosecuted. Everything else would remain undefined.

The administration, the agency, and I rejected that solution, since it would put us in the position of turning to an agency officer and saying, "I would like you to do this with regard to this detainee; neither I nor Justice have any idea whether or not it violates the Geneva Convention, because we really don't know what parts of the convention mean. But I'm pretty sure you'll never have to go to court for it (or, at least not to an American court), so would you go do that for us?"

This whole issue was largely an argument with the Republicans, and it was largely fought out in the Senate.

In one large session I raised my concern about tasking an action without knowing its lawfulness and called it about the worst locker-room speech I could imagine giving to an agency officer.

Later a senator heckled me for allegedly just "wanting to give a speech." I interrupted him and said that what I wanted to give was an order that I was confident was lawful.

Senator McCain had another approach that just cut out Congress. In a ticking-time-bomb or similar scenario, he said, the president should just do what he had to do. Legality be damned; it came with the job. Steve Hadley told him that the president wouldn't do that. He was the chief law enforcement officer in the country, after all. And even if he did order it, he reasoned, in those circumstances he would likely have to do it himself.

In the end, Congress wasn't going to make any tough calls, so it decided instead to reinforce already existing presidential authority to define the meaning of treaties for the United States. For anything beyond the grave breaches enumerated in the new law and the previous requirements of the Detainee Treatment Act, it would be up to the president to define the requirements of Common Article 3 for the United States and publish such decisions in the *Federal Register*.

Which is what President Bush did at our request in July 2007, which in turn enabled the Department of Justice to confirm the lawfulness of six interrogation techniques beyond those contained in the Army Field

Manual on the subject. I don't know of anyone who has looked at the manual who could make the claim that what's contained there exhausts the universe of lawful interrogations consistent with the Geneva Conventions. The Army Field Manual was crafted to allow America's army to train large numbers of young men and women to debrief and interrogate, for tactical purposes, transient prisoners on a fast-moving battlefield. Those were not CIA's circumstances.

I authorized EITs on Rahim, eventually including a liquid diet and extended sleep deprivation. I remember staring down at the page, pen in hand, hesitating to take that step.

As the interrogator who questioned Abu Zubaida pointed out, no one wants to be in these circumstances. I never came close to her situation of standing face-to-face with a defiant terrorist, but I had visited Camp 7 at Guantánamo after we delivered the fourteen HVDs to DOD custody there in September 2006. It was hard to catch even a glimpse of the men in their solitary cells, but I could observe each of them via TV monitors in the control room. Some were sleeping, some praying, some pacing, others fingering prayer beads.

The facilities were clean and bright, there was an exercise room, and detainees could talk to adjacent prisoners from each cell's porchlike extension. Contact was all tightly controlled (and electronically monitored), of course.

Detainees could also draw on a library and a collection of music and videos (although some complained that the offerings were less robust than at their black site). Turns out that Harry Potter books were immensely popular.

It was a civilized confinement, but there was no getting around the fact that these people were going to be in these circumstances forever.

As I was about to leave, the camp staff showed me the empty Styrofoam container that had been used to deliver Abu Zubaida's lunch that day. He had etched on it in pencil the kind of stylized lightning bolts and complex designs one is accustomed to seeing on a high schooler's notebook. I was told he did that routinely.

There was something a little poignant about Zubaida's adolescent art-work. It reminded me that although I took professional satisfaction in his and the others' confinement, it offered little personal joy. You can only dehumanize an enemy from a distance.

With that never far from mind, I signed the authorization to begin EITs on Muhammad Rahim.

He proved one tough Afghan. (One of my CT veterans said Afghans were routinely tougher than Arabs.) Rahim wasn't telling us anything of real value. He was fanatically loyal to bin Laden.*

I extended the EIT authorization and we tried a variety of approaches, but we made little progress. At one point Rahim said that he was having hallucinations and suicidal thoughts. The on-site psychologist stopped the interrogation, and sleep deprivation was halted to give him adequate time to recover.

The question was now how long we were going to do this and whether or not we could ever get him into a zone of compliance. Using even legal, authorized techniques borders on abuse if there is little prospect of success.

The Counterterrorism Center prepared a package for the use of EITs one more time. When it got to me, Jose Rodriguez, head of the National Clandestine Service and former head of the CTC, had not signed off. Since Jose had pretty much run the EIT program and fought for its con-tinuation, that got my attention. I called him at home over the weekend on a secure line. He was not optimistic that the currently authorized techniques would make Rahim talk. He had concluded that Rahim had figured out how far we would go with the techniques and that he was prepared to withstand them. He didn't object to trying and would sup-port the decision either way. He just wanted me to know his views.

During the summer of 2006 there had been a rough consensus that

---

* Apparently, loyalty continued to be a big thing with him. He later wrote a letter from Guan-tánamo to his Ohio-based lawyer trashing Akron native LeBron James as a "very bad man" for leaving the Cleveland Cavaliers.

the new suite of techniques *would* work in most cases. I wasn't ready to throw that judgment overboard now. As Thomas Edison once said, "Many of life's failures are people who did not realize how close they were to success when they gave up."

We knew that Rahim had been a fixer and facilitator, and we had good reporting that senior al-Qaeda folks along the Afghanistan-Pakistan border had started to relocate when he was captured. *They* apparently thought he knew something. So there were no easy choices. Cut bait and perhaps lose a real chance to get important intelligence. Press on and embrace the moral dilemma that it might lead to naught. I decided that we would try one more time.

It didn't work. Despite our best efforts at coercion and kindness (we tried both), Rahim told us little before we transferred him to Guantánamo in early 2008. Our lack of success with him was an important data point, but I wasn't prepared to declare it a trend line. We kept the program in place for the remainder of 2008, but since we had no more detainees, we weren't able to harvest any additional data points. The interrogators on-site concurred with our decision to stop with Rahim; in fact, we did it based on their recommendation. One later confided to me, though, that he was fully confident they would have made Rahim compliant if they could have used the full set of previous techniques.

We gave Congress detailed updates on Abdul Hadi and Rahim and even made the captures public when each was shipped to Guantánamo. The reports to Congress were received largely without comment (or objection), but there was no sign that they ever helped our relationship with them much.

By late 2007, things were so bad that it was hard to imagine how we could make things with the Hill any worse. Unfortunately, we found a way.

In November, Mark Mazzetti of the *New York Times* was circling like a bird of prey over what he considered a blockbuster story. Our network began to light up as CIA alumni called in with reports that Mazzetti was chasing after the destruction of videotapes that had been made of some early interrogations. He was obviously closing in on that final pro forma phone call to the agency for comment before hitting the send button.

Two years earlier Jose Rodriguez had ordered the destruction of about a hundred tapes of the interrogations of Abu Zubaida and Abd al-Rahim al-Nashiri, the first two HVDs. Most of the tapes showed the detainees sitting around in their cells, but they also contained some graphic images of interrogation techniques being applied.

Jose said he did it to protect his officers who were visible on the tapes. He'll be forever remembered at the agency as a hero for it, but he did it through a narrow legal window (they weren't respondent to any internal, legislative, or judicial inquiries) and over the objections and without the approval of Director Goss, DNI Negroponte, and the White House legal advisor—all of whom were furious with him.

The tapes were neither created nor destroyed on my watch (as my talented public affairs chief, Mark Mansfield, kindly pointed out in his backgrounders), but I was in the chair as the story was about to break. I personally informed the president of the saga and told him that the White House should deflect all questions upriver to Langley. This was our mess. The president confirmed that he had never been briefed on the existence or the destruction of the tapes and that he would be more than happy to have his staff state that fact as they redirected inquiries to us.

Back at Langley I decided to preempt Mazzetti and send an unclassified letter to the workforce (designed to be released publicly) describing the history of the tapes. I wanted first shot at shaping the story line. Besides, even though Mazzetti was a professional, he had kept us in the dark on this one, so we didn't owe him a damn thing.

Mansfield called Mazzetti to let him know we had a statement on the tapes that we would release based on our own timetable. Mansfield then shot a copy to Pam Hess, the intelligence reporter for the Associated Press. Giving our story to a wire service would give it maximum exposure. And the Associated Press wasn't the *New York Times*.

In the letter I pointed out that in 2003 the leadership of the two intelligence committees had been briefed that the tapes existed and that the agency intended to destroy them. I also said that the tapes had been reviewed by the inspector general, who found them consistent with the reporting cables from the black site. We had no further use for the tapes, which had been made to help write and verify reporting cables. Actually, they hadn't been very useful in the first place.

Once the story broke (on the day of our Christmas party, unfortunately, but we had to hurry to preempt the *Times*), all hell broke loose. Senator Kennedy recalled Watergate from the Senate floor. "We haven't seen anything like this since the eighteen-and-a-half-minute gap in the tapes of President Richard Nixon," he thundered in a blistering speech. The intel committees held multiple hearings and vented their anger that more members had not personally been informed about the tapes and their destruction. Rush Holt, a consistent agency critic, took control of the investigation in the House. Commentators had a field day, alleging that evidence of heinous crimes had been destroyed. Amid the furor, the attorney general commissioned federal prosecutor John Durham to see if any laws had been broken.

At the height of all this handwringing, in February 2008, during an open session of the Senate Intelligence Committee with C-SPAN cameras rolling, I tried to rein in the wildest speculation.

"CIA has waterboarded three people," I casually noted. "Zubaida, Nashiri, and Khalid Sheikh Mohammed. The last waterboarding was in March 2003." The names of those waterboarded had never been made public before, nor had the last date that the technique had been used. It was a modest backfire against a raging inferno of speculation and accusations.

While the members were taking a moment to figure out how to respond to what I had just said (we had not given any forewarning), I added that the use of the technique reflected the circumstances of the time, the fear of further catastrophic attacks, and our lack of knowledge of al-Qaeda. Two days later in front of the House, again in open session, I refused to speculate on whether waterboarding would still be legal with both circumstances and law having changed. We weren't asking for it and it hadn't been used for almost five years. Period.

Things died down a bit after that as John Durham's criminal investigation effectively dampened any congressional enthusiasm for further inquiries. Besides, as the presidential campaign heated up, it was clear that any real determination on a way ahead awaited the outcome in November.

That outcome sealed the fate of CIA detentions and interrogations despite agency arguments to the contrary (chapter 19). And then, over the next several years, the new administration and congressional Democrats pulled the agency through a series of wringers for its past behavior (chapter 20).

Outside of overt combat operations on battlefields in Iraq and Afghanistan, America (not just CIA) was largely out of the detention and interrogation business. We had finally succeeded in making it so legally difficult and so politically dangerous to grab and hold someone that we would simply default to the kill switch to take terrorists off the battlefield.

THIRTEEN

GOING HOME

PITTSBURGH, PA, 1945–2014

In the 1997 hit film *Grosse Pointe Blank*, John Cusack plays an assassin back in town for his high school's ten-year reunion. Searching for his boyhood home, he discovers that the site is now a convenience store. "You can never go home again," he phones his psychiatrist, "but I guess you can shop there."

In my case, I guess I can buy Steelers gear there. My boyhood home was on the site of Three Rivers Stadium and later Heinz Field on the Northside (now called the North Shore) of Pittsburgh. The house was actually torn down to facilitate the construction of the first stadium.

The neighborhood was great, tucked between the main line of the Pennsylvania Railroad and the north bank of the Allegheny River. It could fairly be called industrial, with some light manufacturing (including Clark Candy), lots of truck parks, and a good number of bars.

The place was typically ethnic—Irish, Italian, one square block African American—and old-country identities were still strong. When I jumped onto a board with a nail in it in the second grade, one Irish neighbor stuck the offending metal into a potato to speed my recovery.

The neighborhood was also largely Catholic. You could see most everybody at Sunday Mass at St. Peter's, and most of the kids—and there were a lot of them—attended the church grade school run by the Sisters of Mercy.

Sports were everyone's outlet. Throw a ball out, and it would draw a crowd, no matter the season. Not that there were any proper fields. There was nothing anywhere near us that could be called a lawn. There was one small concrete playground, an unpaved parking lot or two, and then there was always the street. "Go deep. Hook at the Buick. I'll hit you there."

There was one legitimate field, Monument Hill, that was on top of a four-hundred-foot-high humpbacked hill just north of the neighborhood. The name came from a Civil War memorial that had been moved to, and later removed from, its eastern edge years before. It was nothing fancy. Well cared for with permanent stands, but a skin, heavily oiled field (that means no grass—ever—for those not lucky enough to have experienced it). For us, though, it was the best. Most of my weekend days and week-day nights from May through August were spent there. I got good enough at baseball there to earn a letter and hit .316 as a senior in high school.

There was always enthusiasm for local sports teams or heroes. You could collect enough "pop" bottles around the neighborhood on a week-day summer morning to make enough money for streetcar fare and a $1.50 general admission ticket to sit behind Roberto Clemente in right at Forbes Field. That Clemente was the city's greatest pro athlete—ever— might be suggested by the precise height of the right-field wall in Pitts-burgh's newest ballpark, PNC Park. The wall is twenty-four feet high to commemorate Clemente's number as a Pirate.

And then there were the Steelers. Another St. Peter's parish family was named Rooney. They owned the football club. Oldest son Dan—later president of the team and still later ambassador to Ireland for Barack Obama—coached the grade school football team, and I was his quarter-back in the eighth grade. "The only kid who could remember the plays" was his explanation. I later worked at Steelers training camps to help pay for college, and when I was in graduate school and Dan's schedule with the team got too demanding, I took over his grade school coaching duties and actually brought home the city championship my last year.

We were attached to the Steelers. As a young man, my grandfather Mike Murray used to run with Art Rooney, the scion of the family. My aunt Pat, my mom's younger sister, was a contemporary and classmate of several of the Rooney boys. We all went to the same church. No surprise, then, that I listened with near tears in my eyes to the Steelers' first Super Bowl win on Armed Forces Radio at a B-52 base on Guam in 1975. (Things got better. I was in the owner's box for Super Bowl wins five and six in 2006 and 2009.)

We lived in my grandfather Mike Murray's home, a row-house rental except that the rest of the row had been torn down, with my mom (Sadie), dad (Harry), and siblings Debby and Harry III. We had twin sisters who had died shortly after birth when I was about ten. I've prayed for their souls at Mass every Sunday for more than half a century.

Dad was a welder at Allis-Chalmers, not far from the house, but he retired early when the Pittsburgh plant closed. Mom filled in where she could. Years later, when I was a senior officer in the air force, she and a few friends formed the cleaning staff for a local office building.

My granddad was one of the most generous men I have ever known. He took me fishing and camping. Because of him, our house was the neighborhood gathering place for pinochle, BBQ ribs on Saturday night, or just sitting on the stoop to listen to the Pirates on the radio. He supplemented his meager income in the shipping room of a printing company by running football pools and numbers. Where I grew up, that was as natural as going to church on Sunday. When I was an altar boy and served early Mass on weekdays and ran home for a quick breakfast before school, my mom would clear Granddad's "paperwork" off the kitchen table for me.

Mom and Dad took great care of us, limited only by their resources. Supper was always a family event. Although it was the usual basic Irish immigrant fare—well-cooked meat, potatoes, vegetables—Sadie's baked beans were a requested dish at every family and neighborhood picnic, wake, wedding, and christening for fifty years.

Mom and Dad emphasized our education, since theirs had been limited by economic demands during the Depression. Mom finished tenth grade. I still remember her reading *Treasure Island* aloud to me, complete with pirate accents, as a bedtime story every night over several weeks.

Dad finished eighth grade. He had been a promising athlete before economics, war, and bad knees intervened. He taught me a lot. I bat left, throw right because of him. Despite his best efforts, though, I wasn't going to get any athletic scholarships.

So the education my folks imposed on me was as important as it was good, first with the Sisters of Mercy at St. Peter's. I thought at the time that the order was badly misnamed, and years later during debates over CIA's enhanced interrogation techniques, I took pains to remind my audience that I had experienced four of the techniques (two grasps and two slaps) in diocesan grade school. Still, the education was first-rate and basic. No frills.

Same at the regional Catholic high school, North Catholic. Classic parochial fare. Discipline. Required curriculum. Theology. Latin. Classics. History. The whole liberal arts tradition. That was supplemented by one of those neighborhood libraries that robber baron/philanthropist Andrew Carnegie dotted throughout his adopted city. I was a regular at the Northside branch. Pretty much worked my way through the history stacks.

A local school, Duquesne University, was the natural choice for college: Catholic, affordable, and near home. I was on active duty with America's air force before I ever sat in a classroom that didn't have a crucifix in it. I was also in the air force before I needed a car to get to school. Grade school, high school, and college were all within walking distance, and public transportation was there in bad weather. I have sometimes wondered if my later, more global, lifestyle was a reaction to those early years.

There was a war on in Vietnam while I was at Duquesne. In my neighborhood, universal military service actually meant *universal*—everyone served—so I opted for ROTC so that I could at least go as an officer. We didn't have any kind of strong military tradition at home. Dad served in North Africa and France in the Signal Corps in World War II, and my uncle, my mom's younger brother, lied about his age to join the marines, cruised around the Mediterranean for a while, and then ended up surrounded by tens of thousands of Chinese "volunteers" during the marines' icy retreat from the Chosin Reservoir in Korea. One of my first memories of TV was my grandfather staring worriedly at the newscasts during that time.

The air force let me stay on at Duquesne to get a master's degree in history before I entered active duty in the summer of 1969. Service life didn't come a moment too soon. I had married a Duquesne classmate, Jeanine Carrier from Chicago, still the best decision of my life. We had an infant, Margaret, and our second, Michael, was on the way. The prospect of steady pay and dependable medical care never looked better.

Although we would visit family and go to occasional Steelers and Pirates games and my elongated vowels in words like *out* or *down* or *fire* would occasionally prompt a question about my being from Pittsburgh, we would never go back there to live. Little exceptional in that. The city exported college graduates and others for more than two decades as the mills that had been the city's lifeblood shut down. Good people. Good town. No work.

The city would eventually revive based on education and health care and sustaining a variety of corporate headquarters. It became a white-collar town, but kept its blue-collar attitude. All three rivers are now clean enough to fish, but the city population is about half its former size.

Uninformed NFL analysts are prone to say that the Steelers travel well when black-and-gold-clad fans waving the team's trademark Terrible Towels show up for Steelers road games. In November 2008, I was at FedEx Field to watch the Steelers and the Redskins play on a Monday night. Because of crowd noise, the Redskins (the home team) had to go to a silent snap count. One Redskin, asked after the game why that had happened, angrily pointed out, "Because we couldn't hear the f—ing QB." But that crowd noise was less about the Steelers traveling well and more about a great diaspora of Pittsburghers in the 1970s and 1980s for whom the team remained their strongest link to home.

Every Christmas season the director and deputy director of CIA stand in the lobby for photos and shake hands and exchange holiday greetings with whoever is willing. It lasts for hours. An amazing number of folks at such events identified themselves to me as being from western Pennsylvania.

I also had a fair number of Pittsburghers in my security detail at CIA. Jeanine and I had Steelers season tickets and made every game we could. For me, watching the action between those white lines from 1:00 p.m. to 4:00 p.m. on Sundays was a complete break with the rest of the world. Apparently, security didn't mind the four-plus-hour drive each way to Heinz Field. Steelers security treated us well: total access passes for all of us to ease entry and exit. Everyone could see the game. CIA security never wanted for volunteers for the trip.

What I and others took from Pittsburgh was the blue-collar ethic of the region, an ethic well captured in the words of World War II combat journalist Ernie Pyle during a 1937 visit to the city: "People here just work." For years a yellowed copy of that article has been affixed to a bulletin board at the topside station of the Monongahela Incline, one of the hillside funiculars that still service the city.

An ad campaign for the Pirates in the mid-1990s, when talent-wise they were simply awful, captured the ethic perfectly. A bare picture of home plate; a black lunch pail is dropped on it, and a voice intones, "Come out and watch a ball club that works as hard as you do." Hard to picture the Dodgers or the Yankees with a similar theme.

I've run in several Pittsburgh Marathons since 2002. They are always great events, and running through your hometown streets to the cheers of supportive crowds is something special. But only in Pittsburgh would the crowds be offering runners a pierogie and think they were doing a good thing.

A recent book called *Singing the City,* an anthem to living in Pittsburgh, cited one observer who noted how blast furnaces used to turn the night sky yellow and how he pitied the poor kids in the Midwest who never saw such a sight.

Pyle summed up a similar thought nicely in 1937: "A dirty shirt collar here means prosperity."

And the "just work" meme is the industrial equivalent of Woody Allen's adage that 80 percent of success is just showing up. My dad's edgier corollary, delivered after I had come home complaining after a fight, was simply, "Quit whining. Act like a man and defend yourself."

A second lesson was a little more personal, and it came from my more immediate environment. It was a hardscrabble neighborhood. Some of my friends and relatives ended up as cops or criminals; a couple were both. My parents imposed a high (practically guilt-inducing) moral standard on us, but insisted on a great degree of tolerance for others: "Judge not, lest . . . We are all God's children."

Good life lesson overall. *Really* important if life sets you across the table from Ratko Mladić, the Bosnian Serb war criminal, at Lukavitsa barracks on the outskirts of Sarajevo in 1994. Or if you host at your CIA office Moussa Koussa, the head of Libyan intelligence, while wondering how involved he was in the death of 270 innocents in the Pan Am Flight 103 tragedy over Lockerbie, Scotland.

But all that was years in the future. Jeanine and I and baby Margaret left Pittsburgh in the summer of 1969 to begin life in the air force at a tech school for intelligence officers in Denver. Michael was born there before we headed to Omaha and then eventually to Guam, where our youngest, Liam, was born. We stayed close as a family, doing things together like donning ponchos and toting lawn chairs to the always rain-threatened outdoor theaters at the base on Guam. There I usually worked the 0300–1200 shift, so I had plenty of time with the young children in the afternoon and Jeanine would feed us and put all of us to bed at seven in the evening.

Jeanine and I never really decided to make the air force a career. We took it one job at a time from North America, to Asia, to Europe, and back to North America again. We and our children saw things we never expected to be able to see. It was a great experience. At some point I suppose we became committed, but we never really sat down and formally delivered that verdict.

The kids were out of college and starting families of their own by the time I got to NSA in 1999. When I arrived at CIA in 2006, we already had three grandchildren and family time was a little harder to come by because of their schedules and mine. We squeezed in a couple of beach weeks on the Outer Banks of North Carolina over Thanksgiving or Christmas, what our oldest grandchild called going to "the cold beach."

We also managed to take three grandchildren (then ages ten, eight, and seven), without their parents, for a long Labor Day weekend to a wonderful beach house at Patrick Air Force Base in Florida in 2008. Lots of time in the surf, but work was never far away. On each of the three nights my security detail pounded on the door between 2:00 a.m. and 4:00 a.m. for me to walk up the beach to my communications team and make a decision.

I got to talk about this blend of family, roots, and work at Duquesne University's graduation ceremony in May 2007. I was honored that they had invited me. Apparently it wasn't quite a unanimous decision. I was told that some faculty members had concerns.

I didn't learn about that until *after* we had arrived in Pittsburgh. The last several drafts of the speech had smoothed off the rough edges on some hard issues. That afternoon, unwilling to miss an opportunity or concede a point, I put some of the splinters back in.

I never learned the exact character or extent of any objections, but several years later a Duquesne English professor went on record opposing the city of Pittsburgh's recognition of me. At issue was an honorary street sign, General Michael V. Hayden Boulevard, that had been put up in 2008 adjacent to Heinz Field and about six hundred feet from my boyhood home.

Mayor Luke Ravenstahl had ordered up the sign after spending an evening with my brother, Harry. Harry is sixteen years younger than me and would have been a great case officer: smart, sociable (he knows everybody), and skilled at eliciting both information and behavior. It probably didn't hurt that the mayor was young (twenty-eight at the time) and a fellow Northsider and North Catholic graduate.

When Harry informed me of the mayor's decision, my only response was to ask whether or not I could park there on game days.

Two years later the Duquesne professor saw the sign as he and his family were visiting the Carnegie Science Center across the street, and was offended. "General Hayden has done a great deal of service to the country, but I don't think, given his role in the Bush administration's policy of torture, the city should be honoring him with a public plaque," he said.

He gathered a few dozen signatures petitioning the city for the sign's removal, and the council put it on its public docket. He and several supporters made their case while my brother and a half dozen others made counterarguments. Harry pointed out a factual error: "The people here to protest the sign accused General Hayden of waterboarding detainees, so they really don't know ANYTHING about General Hayden. The last act of waterboarding took place in 2003, and Mike became the director of the agency in 2006." He went on to note that CIA actually took it off the table after I arrived. He then testily added something about there being no standing requirement to run national security decisions by the Duquesne University English department. (Nice touch, I thought.)

Team Hayden was buttressed by a dozen or so veterans and American Legion and VFW representatives who attended. They also had in hand a letter of support from my grade school football coach, ambassador to Ireland and Steelers owner Dan Rooney. The mayor's office stood its ground on leaving the sign up. My contribution was to ask my brother to inquire if I could buy the sign if indeed it were to be removed.

Pittsburgh is a Democrat city, so the council members didn't mind a little Bush bashing. My brother claims he lost circulation in one leg as a friend squeezed his thigh hard to prevent him from jumping up to protest. Finally, a friend on the other side of Harry leaped to his feet and screamed, "Bullshit!" after a particularly egregious accusation, an intervention that prompted a lot of supportive yelling from the veterans present.

In the end, the council was wise enough to recognize that a lot of the people who supported the sign actually vote in municipal elections and that the council really had no expertise when it came to judging American intelligence policy. The council was also clever enough to realize that since it had no hand in putting the sign up, it really shouldn't have to decide whether it should come down. The issue pretty much just went away.

I suppose similar concerns prompted the alleged objections to my May 2007 graduation appearance. Although the school administration was anxious, there was nary a protest, gesture, or unkind word. Good thing. It was a combined commencement for Duquesne's many schools—the first time they had done that in years—so graduates and families filled the university's spacious Palumbo Center.

My message to the graduates was pretty straightforward. First, the kind of education they got at Duquesne would help them deal with a tough and turbulent world. They would be able to make connections that others might not see.

I told them about a trip to Israel and a flight on an Israeli military helicopter passing "over Bethlehem and then Jerusalem, with the Wailing Wall and the Al-Aqsa Mosque clearly in sight. A few minutes more flight time and I could see . . . the Sea of Galilee."

Holy ground for three great monotheisms, but at that moment the "second intifada had been churning for nearly a year [and] Israelis and Palestinians were dying in the streets." It took a broad (and historical) view to recognize that despite the chaos, "what connects us runs deeper than what divides us."

Then I conceded that they weren't walking off campus with all the answers, and I assured them that I hadn't either. None of my professors had ever put his arm around me after class and said, "Mike, here's a good reading list that will come in handy when you're doing National Security Strategy for Bush 41," and my Western Civ class's wonderful treatment of the Austro-Hungarian Empire didn't describe what to do when Yugoslavia imploded and I was standing in Sarajevo in 1994 looking up at Serb artillery in the surrounding hills.

But, I continued, "I actually *was* prepared to deal with these situations, not in detail, because they were not predictable, but in general because I got as close to a classical education as is possible in modern America, and so have you."

My other major point dealt with values. I told the graduates that in dealing with tough questions over the years, "something became obvious to me: the more senior I get, the older I get, the more basic, the more fundamental the problems and issues seem to be. And the more that happens, the less I rely on any kind of professional expertise that I've picked up along the way and the more I count on the basic values that I learned here in Pittsburgh, at my mom or dad's knee, at North Catholic, at St. Peter's grade school just across the river, and at Duquesne."

I described "the challenging philosophy and theology courses [I had at Duquesne as] wonderful gifts . . . gifts that keep on giving. They give me an anchor in what is often a turbulent sea. They give me a compass when the way ahead is far from clear. *They give me a beam of light when I have to work in the shadows.*"

I concluded by reminding the graduates that "life will soon bring you increased responsibilities, and it is rare that you will have a legitimate choice to do nothing. [That was one of the splinters I put back in.] Responsibility usually demands action. My responsibility has to do with the defense of the republic, and my conscience, formed here at Duquesne University, compels me to act. [That was another.]"

I thanked the graduates and their families, turned, and walked to my seat onstage. As I bent down to put the binder, from which I had been reading, on the floor next to my chair, the priest beside me whispered that I needed to go back to the podium. The graduates were applauding, and many of their parents were standing and clapping.

I walked back and waved a heartfelt thank-you to the hometown crowd.

FOURTEEN

"NO CORE. NO WAR."

AL-KIBAR, SYRIA, 2007–2008

W e had a lot of friends among the intelligence services of the Middle East. In April 2007, the tough, tireless head of one of them came into my office at Langley. This man was without pretense, all business—but with a tough-love kind of human touch.

That day he was bringing big news. He carried with him photos of a nearly complete nuclear reactor in the eastern Syrian desert near a town called al-Kibar. We had picked up on the facility as it was being completed through satellite imagery, but its false walls and roofs made it difficult to identify. NGA (the National Geospatial-Intelligence Agency) had started to more regularly image it in 2006 and had labeled it "enigmatic." That essentially meant that it looked important, but we couldn't exactly tell what it was.

We had shared a decade's worth of sporadic evidence of North Korean–Syrian nuclear cooperation with our liaison partner and had even pointed to the eastern desert and the cooling waters of the Euphrates River as likely candidates for a site. As resources were available we tasked our own satellite imagery to search the region for suspicious construction, but Syria was on the same overhead orbital path as Iraq and the needs of the war there consumed a lot of that resource. In the end, we got the facility in our sights, but long after its appearance had been altered and its use obscured.

Our evidence had given us a kind of strategic warning that something was up. But now we had nearly a hundred handheld photos of the site while it was still under construction. You could see the false walls being erected over a shape eerily similar to North Korea's Yongbyon nuclear reactor. To the side, under a tent, you could see reactor components. An interior shot showed rebar and concrete being used to create a floor into which uranium rods could be inserted. This was high-quality *tactical* warning.

Espionage protocol discouraged us from asking our friend how his service had acquired the images. The fact that our friend was sharing them with us at all was remarkable, given the absolute need for secrecy and the US government's less than stellar record in keeping secrets. (I suspect our friend needed us to flesh out the North Korean connection.) Our best guess was that the photos had been downloaded from the computer of a sloppy Syrian scientist, but it didn't really matter. It was pretty convincing stuff, *if* we could be confident that the pictures hadn't been altered.

Once alone in my office, I tasked exactly that. Over time our experts reported that the photos were genuine and undoctored except for one where some writing on the side of a pickup truck had been pixelated out. Our folks were even able to take the handheld photos and our own overheads to create a three-dimensional model of the building, and each image fit perfectly. They were genuine photos of the same facility.

The morning after my colleague's visit we briefed the president on what we had. Since my colleague had been part of a delegation to the White House the day before to talk to the vice president and Steve Hadley, this wasn't going to be a total surprise. As we were getting settled in the Oval, I leaned toward Vice President Cheney, who had long been convinced of a Syrian nuclear program, and confessed, "You were right, Mr. Vice President."

I laid out the photos and our own background. The last thing the president needed on his plate was this: an action that couldn't stand, in a part of the world where any move could precipitate a war . . . with an ally who could and would act on its own.

Given the intelligence debacle on the Iraqi nuclear program, the president's first demand was, not surprisingly, that we be sure, absolutely sure. He also demanded that this stay a secret to maximize his freedom of action.

Certainty and absolute secrecy. Individually these were tough tasks; together they approached being mutually exclusive. To get to certainty, you wanted to collect more information, to get some eyes on the ground. You would also want to bring in more experts to evaluate the information you already had. Expand the circle, as it were. But those kinds of steps increased the odds that the information would leak and the Syrians would be on to us. And as soon as that happened, we only half-jokingly concluded, Assad would announce that the site was housing a day-care center.

The facility itself was oddly hiding in plain sight. We could see no obvious security, but the site had been carefully selected in a wadi off a road that paralleled the Euphrates River, and a berm had been constructed to completely hide it from the highway. It was in the middle of nowhere, so much so that anyone detected snooping around on the ground would have had a cover story that ranged from very thin to nonexistent.

We cranked up national technical collection and dug into the archives to see if there were any clues there. The record of individuals affiliated with Korea's nuclear program visiting Syria was pretty extensive. There was also sporadic evidence of mysterious shipments between the two countries. The new information gave meaning and importance to scattered data points we had on a North Korean and Syrian nuclear relationship that went back to at least 2001.

In early June we could see in imagery that the Syrians were gouging out a cooling-water intake along the banks of the river and were digging two trenches up the wadi for pipes to bring cold water to the facility and discharge hot water back to the river. The building still looked like a

Walmart warehouse from above, but there was *nothing* other than a nuclear reactor that would create enough heat to warrant that kind of cooling. And the fact that the Syrians opted for the low-profile underground pipes and cooling system rather than large cooling towers fit the clandestine nature of the facility.

But the president said we had to be sure, so we took other steps. First, we carefully briefed all of our data to an outside expert and asked his opinion. "It has to be a nuclear reactor," he reported.

Then we gave the data to a red team, dedicated contrarians, and directed they come up with an alternative explanation. Build an alternative case as to why it's not a nuclear reactor; why it's not intended to produce plutonium for a weapon; why North Korea is not involved. They racked and stacked what we knew against other possibilities. "If it isn't a nuclear reactor," they concluded, "then it has to be a fake nuclear reactor."

So it was a reactor. But that was just the start. We searched for the other things that Syria would need if it were to have its own viable nuclear weapons program. We knew of other suspicious facilities, but there were key components still missing. We could not, for example, identify work on an actual warhead. There was also no reprocessing facility we could locate, but not for want of trying.

Good intelligence was also going to be critical to deciding on a policy way ahead. The reactor at al-Kibar had to go, but not in a way that generated another Middle East conflict. The analytic staff at the agency knew the challenge and had developed a nice shorthand summary of the president's policy objectives: No core. No war.

Intense policy discussions on a short menu of options followed. A purely diplomatic approach never got much traction. Naming and shaming wouldn't be effective, nor would condemnatory language out of the UN (assuming we could get it). Assad could stonewall inspectors until the facility went hot and any démarche would tip our hand that we knew of the facility without being decisive. We could end up looking pathetic.

We took a hard look at special operations. A small team could enter, approach the site, destroy critical equipment, and then depart. There was no obvious guard force, and the reactor was in isolated desert pretty far from towns or military facilities. Destroying the reactor this way would be low-key and somewhat anonymous and might not prompt Damascus to respond militarily. The issue was whether or not a small team could carry enough with it to effect sufficient destruction on steel, rebar, and concrete. An alternative branch of this planning called for destroying the pump house at the water intake in the Euphrates. That was more easily accomplished, but would slow the Syrians down more than stop them. It would also tip our hand. And for either scenario there was always the danger of detection.

Then there was an air strike. We knew the precise location of the facility and its specific makeup. Selecting aim points and weapons would be easy enough. Stealthy B-2s from the States could do the job, as could land-based air in the region or carrier-based air from the Mediterranean or the Gulf. Air defenses were respectable, but not prohibitive, and there was absolutely no evidence that they had been beefed up in the area. All good—and doable—but such a raid would reinforce a regional image of a United States facilely opting yet again for preemptive war.

The more we talked, the more we discussed what we called a hybrid option: publicize the existence of the facility and demand that Assad prove us wrong via inspections, all against a timeline and an ultimatum that left no doubt of eventual action. That showed restraint and respect for international institutions, but had the weakness of giving Assad time to prepare his defenses and, with seven thousand US citizens in Syria, time to take hostages too.

A lot of this depended on our assessment of Syrian president Bashar al-Assad. We knew that he was never meant for this job. His older brother Bassel had been the heir apparent to Hafez, the ruthless but savvy father. Hafez had fought his way to power from humble beginnings in an Alawite village near Latakia to become president in 1971. He brought Syria stability by ruling with an iron hand for the next three decades.

Bassel followed in his father's footsteps. He had a military background, headed up the Presidential Guard, and seems to have been highly regarded. He also had a love of fast cars that proved his undoing, as he died in 1994 racing at eighty miles an hour on a foggy night to the airport.

Bashar had never been close to his father or much associated with governance. He completed medical school in Syria and then did postgraduate work in ophthalmology in London. Now, with Bassel in the grave, his father began a crash course grooming Bashar for the presidency.

The dynamics of the Assad family often reminded me of Mario Puzo's fictitious American mobster clan, the Corleones. Certainly the Assads and the closely affiliated Makhloufs, families linked by marriage, seemed to be partners in crime and ruthlessness as much as governance. And, like the Corleones, whose obvious heir Sonny was killed, the Assads unexpectedly lost their chosen, Bassel, as well. Don Corleone had the good fortune to have the far more talented Michael to fall back on. In many ways, Hafez had to settle for Fredo. One wonders if the elder Assad launched the al-Kibar project before his death in 2000 precisely because he recognized his son's weaknesses.

Our view of Bashar was pretty dismal; we had tried to work with him to stem the flow of foreign fighters into Iraq, without much success. The Syrians seemed to be turning a blind eye to it while doing just enough to keep us at bay. Then again, a lot of the movement could be attributed to local corruption, lack of control, policy differences within the leadership, and flat-out government weakness. Not really a recipe for solid decision making now.

We had long described Bashar as a "serial miscalculator." In the crisis we were about to create, we feared he would refuse any off-ramp we might offer him no matter how logical it was or how much we sweetened it. He wasn't a confident or firm decision maker, and when pushed into a corner, he often became unpredictable. He feared humiliation, so he would likely want to look tough, and there wouldn't be many in his inner circle calling for calm. When he considered his own survival, he knew that he was most threatened when he looked weak. After his embarrassing withdrawal under pressure from Lebanon in 2005, another such display might be fatal for him—literally.

A lot of our analysts judged that he would not—could not—let the destruction of al-Kibar pass without responding. At a minimum they warned of "spontaneous" demonstrations that could threaten the embassy and individual Americans; calls to patriotism would likely elicit a positive response, as we speculated that many Syrians would feel pride at the attempt to go nuclear. Assad could also make life more difficult and dangerous for US troops in Iraq. He might even up the ante with the Israelis on the occupied Golan Heights, since he was mistakenly reading the 2006 Israeli-Hezbollah conflict as exposing Israeli weakness.

The analysts added that the Iranians could see the destruction of al-Kibar as a test of their resolve as well, the first step in a theater-wide rollback of nuclear ambitions, and they would try to steel the spine of their Syrian client.

Our decisive policy meeting took place in June at the White House, but not in the West Wing. We met on the second floor of the residence in the Yellow Oval Room to keep the session off the president's public schedule. All the members of the national security team were there: secretary of defense, secretary of state, chairman of the Joint Chiefs, national security advisor, director of National Intelligence, and more.

We settled into the overstuffed chairs and couches as White House waiters topped off our ice tea and exited. The president turned it over to Steve Hadley, who asked for the latest intelligence.

"Mr. President," I began, "we've got four key findings for you. One, that's a nuclear reactor. Two, it's clear that the North Koreans and Syrians have been cooperating on nuclear questions for about a decade. Three, the North Koreans built this thing. And four, this is part of a nuclear weapons program."

Before anyone could react, I cautioned them to wait. The national estimate on the Iraqi nuclear program had been wrong, but beyond wrong it had also given a false sense of confidence. We had since learned to share not just what we believed, but also our doubts.

I resumed: "It's a nuclear reactor. High confidence. Can't be anything else. Take it to the bank.

"The Syrians and Koreans have been cooperating on nuclear developments for a long time. Lots of travel, back and forth. We know the people. High confidence.

"The North Koreans built this. Of course they did. It's a copy of Yongbyon, and the Koreans are the only ones who have built this kind of reactor since the British gave up on the design in the 1960s. But we haven't had eyes on. We haven't seen Koreans there except one group in one of the handheld photos. So we're giving this to you with medium confidence.

"This is part of a Syrian weapons program. Of course it is. There are no other obvious uses for it and a weapons program is the only thing that would justify such a high-stakes gamble.

"But Mr. President, I can't find the other parts of a weapons program. No reprocessing facility. No weaponization effort that we can see. So I can only give this to you with low confidence."

In the silence that followed, Condi said something about wishing she had had some qualifying caveats like this a few years earlier.

Then the president observed that his preemption policy demanded a threat be imminent before we would act. Our estimate of low confidence in a weapons program made that very difficult to justify, and therefore, the president declared, "We will *not* strike the facility."

Intelligence usually sets the right- and left-hand boundaries of policy discussion; it defines the limits of options. It is rarely as determinative as it was that day. It was like intelligence and policy were connected by a 1:1 gear ratio.

We stayed there quite a while discussing the point. Only the vice president offered a dissenting view. He believed that we needed to send a strong message not only to Syria and North Korea, but also to Iran. An

American strike would do just that and would be relatively easy to accomplish, since al-Kibar was isolated and distant from any civilian centers. But I sensed that there was little appetite in the room to suddenly bomb a country without warning or announced justification and feed regional fears of a permanent America bent toward preemptive war.

In the end, the president decided our approach would be to go public about the reactor as part of an overall package to unsettle Assad and make a series of demands on him. We preserved the option of force, but in the president's mind the real issue was Assad and overall Syrian policy, not just the reactor. Handled well, the coming crisis could give us unexpected leverage on a host of issues: Syrian support to Hamas and Hezbollah; the foreign fighter pipeline into Iraq; Damascus's continued meddling in Lebanon; Syria's alignment with Iran.

Syria had been a regular theme in White House policy discussions, largely along the lines of peeling the Syrians off from their Iranian sponsors or, as Steve Hadley often put it, "flipping Assad." In geopolitical theory it made some sense, since Damascus was by far the weaker partner to Tehran. But real progress was something else. Assad acted like he thought that this was all about *him*—regime change, in other words— and he even allowed his intelligence chief and brother-in-law, Assef Shawkat (with whom we were trying to cooperate on the foreign fighter flow to Iraq), to pass a message to us that what Damascus saw from the United States was pressure, unrelenting pressure and only pressure. Not a formula to entice a defection.

We really weren't trying to overthrow Assad, but CIA was expected to analyze what would likely follow him. In any orderly succession (read internal power struggle), we expected the follow-on regime to remain Alawite-dominated with a strong security service and military flavor, perhaps even with Bashar staying on as some sort of figurehead. We also judged that a botched attempt against Alawite rule could quickly descend into chaos. That path would strengthen the hand of the Muslim Brotherhood and Kurdish separatists, since they were the best-organized opposition in the country. The only way that the weak and divided liberal opponents to the regime would play a role required a slow demise of the government, giving them time to get their act together.

I have since wondered how much of that analysis saw the light of day when Syria began its descent into hell in March 2011, when regime security forces arrested about a dozen youths in Daraa for painting anti-Assad graffiti.

In 2007, though, our problem was a nuclear reactor, and the first steps in the president's plan—going public about al-Kibar and then waiting for IAEA inspectors to verify its nature—could not be done without the concurrence of the country with whom we had first discovered it. After all, a lot of this was based on their data. It didn't take long for them to make it clear that they could not wait for a long-term diplomatic gambit, even one sponsored by the United States and one that seemed to promise eventual American action. They would not agree.

And so we waited. While we did, if we weren't going to strike, we had to be careful to not even encourage anyone else to do so. We had to step back a little. The uninformed often think that intelligence agencies are lawless. Some are, but those in mature democracies, especially this one, are not. And we cannot enable someone to do something (even in their own national interest) that we are not authorized to do ourselves. We had no authority to bomb. We couldn't help anyone else do it, either.

So we could continue intelligence cooperation to understand the situation and gauge when the plant might go hot. But we wouldn't share anything that would directly contribute to targeting the facility—things like advice on weaponeering, or aim points or imagery so precise that it could help in what was called target mensuration—the precise calculations required to be sure that a weapon will create the desired effects. It was sometimes a fine line, but it was a real one.

But the clock was ticking. The facility was externally complete, the cooling system was being readied, and we had no idea when uranium would be introduced. A strike after activation was problematic; if that happened, the attacker would be blamed for every thyroid problem in the Middle East for the next half century.

On the night of September 6 the reactor at al-Kibar was destroyed. Later, when quizzed about any American role, Steve Hadley accurately noted, "No green light was asked for. No green light was given."

The strike force had no apparent problems with Syrian air defenses and, based on post-strike imagery, pretty much had their way with the target. The false walls and roof were blown away, revealing the damage done by delayed-fuse weapons on the steel and concrete sarcophagus that would have held the core. It was a nuclear reactor, all right.

Now the trick was keeping a lid on any Syrian (over)reaction. I talked often by phone with that tough, tireless liaison chief who originally brought the pictures into my office in April. He and his staff were inclined to think that a successful strike could be pulled off *without* a Syrian response if everyone would just keep quiet about it and not attempt to humiliate Assad. Not many Syrians, not even high-ranking officials, would have known about the site, they reasoned. Bashar may want to let this one pass without issue rather than putting himself on the *X* again as he did during the 2005 withdrawal from Lebanon. We needed to give him space to "climb back off the ledge."

I wasn't as optimistic, but certainly agreed that there was no upside to thumping our chest about this, so we were as secretive after the strike as we were before.

Press stories began to emerge almost immediately, but reporters were finding it hard to describe exactly what had happened and why. I experienced more than a little schadenfreude on the seventh floor at Langley as the press struggled to connect the dots. "Not as easy as it looks, is it?" I said one morning to no one in particular as I surveyed my daily press clips.

The Syrians certainly weren't filling in any blank spaces for journalists with their misleading talk of repulsing a strike on some nondescript desert garrison. They also quietly destroyed what was left of the reactor hall, paved it over, and topped the location with what looked like a metal warehouse.

Of course, keeping this under wraps before, during, and after the strike had a congressional component to it. The law requires Congress be kept fully and currently informed of all "significant intelligence activities," and this certainly fit that description.

But we kept the Hill group small—just the leadership of the two intelligence committees. To avoid curious Hill staff we had our first session that spring in the DNI spaces at Bolling Air Force Base, just across the Anacostia River from Congress's own secure facilities. It was all pretty straightforward. We weren't asking them to do or approve anything.

But as fall 2007 rolled toward winter, the four members who had been briefed were getting pretty impatient. *They* knew what the facility was and that it had been destroyed, and congressional leadership always has a hard time explaining to other members why they acquiesced in limiting who got briefed when things finally go public. With the recent furor over limited briefings on surveillance and detention and with a presidential election in the offing, there was little residual tolerance on the Hill. Pete Hoekstra, the ranking Republican on the House side, was often livid (and vocal) about the limitations.

Over time, after the strike, the agency began to slide to the congressional side on this one. Bashar had pretty much crawled back in off the ledge and was very unlikely to strike back now. Besides, as part of the permanent government, CIA saw little upside in alienating the leaders of its oversight committees. We were going to be here a lot longer than the administration.

But there was another, powerfully compelling reason. The administration was in the final stretch of negotiating a nuclear deal with the North Koreans. Ambassador Chris Hill was using his deep experience with the Koreans to get something on paper before the end of the administration. I had negotiated with the North Koreans at Panmunjom and in Geneva; they were maddening. I can only imagine how difficult Chris's work must have been.

But he was now negotiating a deal with a country that had just been caught red-handed in the single greatest act of nuclear proliferation in history. And they hadn't been called on it!

The president had committed to keeping this secret at the request of our ally, but by our reckoning we were well past the time when we had to do that to keep Assad in the box. We were now in a period where we needed to make it more public to avoid a North Korean nuclear deal being sold to a Congress and a public ignorant of this very pertinent and very recent episode.

We pressed hard at deputies and principals meetings of the NSC to brief multiple committees on the Hill—Intelligence, Defense, Foreign Affairs—while also recommending simultaneously rolling out a lot of the story publicly. That was a natural complement to briefing Congress. The story would be out after briefing so many committees no matter what we did, so it made sense for the administration to get it out there unfiltered.

It was the right thing to do. And we were hardly opposed to putting an intelligence *success* story—even a limited one—out there for a change. Agency veterans well remembered George Tenet sitting behind Colin Powell at the United Nations during the secretary of state's 2003 speech condemning Iraq for its weapons of mass destruction. Some were discomfited by the very image of the nation's intelligence chief in such a high-profile, politically charged image. Now, however, most were happy enough to publicly put one in the win column.

Steve Hadley finally took our side, but he had a condition. He wanted a movie. "Only with a movie," he reasoned, "can we show that we got this one right."

So we took the unusual step of crafting a video showing both the handheld photos and our own satellite shots. We added references to other sources of intelligence and laid out the logic trail that got us to "high confidence" that this was a reactor.

The movie didn't threaten for best documentary or best special effects that year, but one CIA analyst correctly observed, "I don't know how you could have more effectively conveyed the story in eleven minutes. . . . It took the life out of intel failure accusations."

In late April, a year after this all started, we briefed six Hill committees and then backgrounded the press at Langley. It had taken so long to get to Congress that we got little credit for the belated transparency. Pete Hoekstra, the senior Republican on the Intelligence Committee in the House, was so angry that he threatened to crash the press briefing scheduled for later that afternoon. My office told his staff that his entry onto the campus wasn't guaranteed, since he had not been invited to the press backgrounder. Thankfully, he stayed away.

New York Times chief Washington correspondent David Sanger was at the backgrounder. No slouch at these kinds of things, he later commented that it was "a remarkable briefing." Following the video, Steve Hadley, Mike McConnell, and I were leaning pretty far forward describing both the intelligence we had and the sequence of events.

So we chalked this one up as an intelligence success, after a fashion. Lord knows we were just in time and, even then, had needed help from our friends. Our analysis that it was a reactor proved correct, but our analysis of likely Syrian actions was not. And this certainly wasn't a HUMINT success. In fact, human intelligence had been sorely lacking.

Part of that could be chalked up to the reality that only a very small circle of Syrian officials had been witting, making the pool of potential HUMINT sources pretty shallow.* Still, American HUMINT had not tipped us off.

The whole episode also put into stark relief the problem of thinking about the unthinkable or, as one top analyst put it, "How do you chase down the weird stuff?" especially when you can't afford to chase all the weird stuff. The Assads, father and son, took this incredibly high risk, and it didn't even get them close to a nuclear weapon. Their gamble went beyond our understanding of them, perhaps fed by their pervasive sense of insecurity or a determination to get strategic parity with Israel or a desire to be the preeminent Arab state.

---

* Which also probably made it easier for Assad to let the eventual air strike pass without an outward response. More would have learned about the embarrassment if he had reacted.

Interestingly, Korean engineers paid a return visit to the al-Kibar site after it had been destroyed. That raised speculation that this could have been a Korean facility in Syria with plutonium being shipped back to Pyongyang, perhaps in return for a weapon later. Probably not, but since it did show that Pyongyang had few, if any, redlines, we began to scour the globe for places where they might try to reprise the al-Kibar gamble.

And what if the Iranians had been involved in this in some sort of trilateral nuclear arrangement? After all, North Korea was already helping both Iran and Syria develop missiles, and Syria was Iran's best (only) friend in the Arab world.

Like we said, it was weird. And there was still a lot of stuff we didn't know.

We had managed to keep this secret long enough to enable somebody to act. But even then, there was a cost. We successfully compartmented access, but if the destruction of al-Kibar had provoked a war, there would have been hell to pay for it. Policy makers and members of Congress (and surely some intelligence analysts) around town who had been kept out of the loop would have been livid that their counsel had not been sought. We had described the Middle East as "very dry timber" in 2007, but despite that, I cleared more of my weapons experts (was this really a nuclear reactor?) than my regional experts (and then what happens?) to be let in on the secret. That was ill-advised and risky.

Still, many agency folks rightly felt good about this. Four months later President Bush was eating lunch in the CIA cafeteria as part of an agency visit. A young analyst approached him as he was chowing down on his hamburger and fries. She offered him the coin that the al-Kibar team had minted to memorialize its efforts. On one side was the CIA shield. On the other a map of Syria with the location of al-Kibar marked with a star. Below that the simple words "No core. No war."

I took a coin, too, but was less comfortable pocketing a win. We had gotten it right, but it had been a near-run thing and we had been dependent on outside help (especially the late-arriving handheld photos). We marshaled the evidence well enough, but hadn't collected a lot ourselves. That's why less than a decade later I was skeptical of claims that American espionage was well positioned to track what the Iranians were doing. Visions of Syria, Iraq, India, and Pakistan filled my mind. If we were now suddenly better, we had made a hell of a step forward in the intervening years.

FIFTEEN

ESPIONAGE, BUREAUCRACY, AND FAMILY LIFE

LANGLEY, VA, 2006–2009

In the middle of side three of Bob Dylan's 1966 classic double album *Blonde on Blonde,* one hears his lament on disloyalty, "Absolutely Sweet Marie." And in the middle of that song is his insightful lyric: "to live outside the law, you must be honest."

CIA most assuredly does not live outside the law, or at least not outside American law, but its margin for legal or ethical misstep is often quite thin. CIA is asked to do things that no one else is asked to do, indeed things that no one else is allowed to do. I know of no other federal bureaucracy, for example, that has an office dedicated to disguises or another one called "flaps and seals" (the latter to access materials without leaving a trace).

The iconic image of CIA is the sweeping panorama of the marble entry concourse: CIA shield on the floor, stars of the anonymous fallen to the right, a quotation from St. John to the left: "And ye shall know the truth and the truth shall make you free."

A modern management consultant would label that line of scripture the agency's vision statement, a description of a desired end state. But if you walk through the concourse, ascend the marble stairs, and look to the left toward the agency museum, you see another quotation atop a stylized mural of Lady Liberty: "We are the Nation's first line of defense. We accomplish what others cannot accomplish and go where others cannot go." That, the same consultant would assure you, would be the agency's mission statement—the defining uniqueness of the institution.

It creates a heavy moral burden. I reminded newly minted case officers of that in my graduation speeches to them at the Farm, CIA's training facility. "You may be the only face of America that the people you recruit will ever see. And when you have recruited them, they are placing their fate and their family's fate in your hands. Don't ever forget that."

Analysts have a similarly heavy burden, not just to be honest in their analysis but to be courageous in its presentation. Very often they are the bearers of unwelcome news.

And everyone has a burden of secrecy that often leaves unexplained to loved ones long hours, somber moods, cancelled vacations, sudden trips, and stranded soccer carpools. In 2008 Angelina Jolie was preparing for her role as a CIA case officer in the upcoming film *Salt* and was talking by videoconference to several CIA women. I joined late to thank her for trying to learn more about our folks, but in the short ensuing conversation I also talked about work burdens at the agency and, if the screenplay permitted it, how beneficial it would be if some agency character in the film, late in a workday, would proclaim willingness to work all night but needed ninety minutes right now to pick up the kids and their teammates.

They didn't put that in, of course. Wrong genre. Too many chase and assassination scenes. But the soccer mom (or dad) would have been closer to reality.

I was at the agency for nearly three years. In all that time I never met Jack Bauer or even Jack Ryan, not even in the agency's most forward and isolated bases. In fact, the men and women of the agency were so centerline American that I took to describing them to outside audiences as "like your friends and neighbors . . . and if you live in northern Virginia, they probably are." CIA is composed of ordinary Americans. Ordinary Americans placed in extraordinary circumstances and expected to do extraordinary things.

The agency holds a family day every September, when its forested and secluded campus takes on the air of a county fair for most of a Saturday, as more than twenty thousand officers and family members descend on the headquarters. Kids crawl over the armored SUVs or visit with the canine officers and their charges. The disguise shop is standing room only for the youngest visitors, while parents drag teenagers to the polygraph booths for free "samples." Jeanine and I, after a brief welcoming ceremony, would plant ourselves outside the cafeteria (which takes on the air of a *very* large church picnic) to say hi. An impromptu receiving line invariably formed, and we got to talk to folks for hours.

Two distinct groups stood out. The first was composed of the twenty-something agency officers with Mom and Dad in tow. Mom and Dad just flew in from Albany or Phoenix or drove up from Raleigh, and, bursting with pride for their child, were obviously having an out-of-body experience.

The second group was smaller. These were the forty-somethings, accompanied by a teenager or two. On more than one occasion, the officer would introduce "Junior" to me and Jeanine and announce that today was the day Junior had learned where Mom or Dad (or both) worked—just a family outing through northern Virginia that took an unscheduled hard turn off the George Washington Parkway and brought the *whole* family for the first time into a new world. Jeanine asked one teenage girl how the day's discovery made her feel. "My mom's a spy," she replied. "That's really cool."

We have been fortunate that such people from across America want to serve. The agency has had the luxury of choice. My last full year as director (2008) there were 160,000 applicants. Not hits on the Web site, mind you—full-up, lengthy, privacy-invading applications. We could accept only about 1 percent or so. The average entering age for that new cohort was twenty-nine, and their most distinguishing characteristics were prior life experience (about a quarter had been GIs) and second language (the more exotic the better).

Jeanine and I tried to meet new folks in a series of new-hire socials that we initiated. We held one every quarter until we had worked through the backlog of the previous few years and then did it as necessary to meet fresh cohorts.

We invited the new hires and their significant others, and I directed senior agency leadership to attend as well. The event was scheduled to run from six until eight in the evening, but it was rare that Jeanine and I got out before nine-thirty.

A typical group of new hires ranged in age from about twenty to sixty. They were engineers, scientists, finance officers, HR administrators, security officers, special assistants, open source officers, linguists, analysts, core collectors, and more. Many spoke Arabic, Chinese, Persian, Korean, or Russian.

It was a special evening. We would talk to small groups and ask questions about their impressions of the agency. We especially asked the covert officers about the question of cover. Who knows you work here? How did you decide whom to tell?

One young woman said she told her mom and her dad, but was a little regretful that she told her father. He was so proud of her, she said, that he really had trouble keeping the secret.

Cover is such an important consideration for the agency that we had to decide whether or not we would "integrate" new-hire socials, that is, whether or not we would include covered and uncovered officers and their significant others at the same time.

In the end, we decided to mix it up and invite both groups to the same event. That allowed me, in my prepared remarks, to emphasize that our ability to protect the American people depended upon our family members in some very important ways.

"Even tonight's event presents opportunities *and* responsibilities," I said. "There are officers here whose affiliation with CIA is not acknowledged outside this building. As part of our family, we ask you to protect that information and we hope everyone can enjoy this unique chance to socialize with colleagues from every part of the organization." The unspoken but clear message was, "Welcome to the CIA (we really mean it)."

There were other opportunities to connect. I often ate lunch in the cafeteria, and I made a point to run in the annual OMS (Office of Medical Services) 5K. I liked to run—it reinforced a message for folks to take care of themselves, and you can learn a lot dripping sweat, sitting on the steps of OHB (the Original Headquarters Building—the one with the shield on the lobby floor) with fellow runners on a hot summer day.

As a GI, I considered PT (physical training) an accepted (almost required) part of any workday. At the Pentagon, not being at your desk because you were at the POAC (the Pentagon Officers Athletic Club) was about as solid an excuse as being at a family funeral. Not for folks at CIA. I had been there a year when my executive assistant told me that one office had finally screwed up enough courage to ask her the meaning of the PT entry on my daily calendar. I couldn't direct a bunch of civilians to exercise, but I did tell their supervisors that they could count up to three hours a week of PT as work time. I also limited the number of annual leave hours that could be carried forward into the next fiscal year. I wasn't trying to deprive people of leave. I was trying to force them to use it.

Five years after 9/11, this was a tired crew. It needed to take better care of itself.

We also hacked our way through a federal bureaucratic thicket to get some chaplains cleared for the headquarters. Again, second nature for the US military. Not so much for CIA.

Jeanine did tireless work helping families. She supported a proposal to make it easier for a "trailing" agency spouse to find agency work at an overseas station. She was instrumental in setting up a Saturday morning class in "Living and Managing Cover" for spouses. She often attended the beginning of the class in order to welcome the spouses. And at case officer graduations at the Farm she got up and told our officers that although this was likely the first graduation in their lives where their parents were *not* present, she was there to stand in their stead and say how proud they were.

She went above and beyond. She traveled well outside Washington alone (so as not to attract attention) and in alias to meet with a group of spouses of officers so deeply covered that the session could not be held at Langley. The point of the meeting for the agency was to coach the spouses on what to do in extremis (hard to just call the mother ship), let them share some experiences, and also let them know that the agency cared, even if it could never call or write. Of course, the spouses could never even acknowledge one another if by chance their paths ever crossed again. To this day, Jeanine has difficulty describing the meeting without tearing up.

There was more. She willingly sat on a rocking chair on the porch of a central Virginia farmhouse helping me grieve with the parents of a young officer killed the day before in a traffic accident in Central Asia.

As a military family, we were accustomed to a pretty robust support structure during deployments. That kind of support didn't exist at CIA even though since 9/11 we had become almost as expeditionary as America's armed forces.

There were special challenges. Our people lived in civilian communities, not on a base, and in many instances neighbors didn't even know their true affiliation, although many were probably the subject of "spot the spook" speculation, a common pastime in northern Virginia.

Jeanine worked with agency offices to build as much support as we could for the families of the many officers we had at austere locations in the middle of war zones.

When we left Langley, the agency gave her the Agency Seal Medal for her strong contributions to CIA, "its employees and their families."

LIKE THE REST of the federal bureaucracy, CIA has a legal requirement to look like America. But the agency has an operational requirement to look like the world, including America's adversaries. Tough challenge, but made easier by our still being a nation of immigrants.

CIA aggressively recruits from what it euphemistically calls heritage communities: first- and second-generation Americans. Aggressively re-cruits, but carefully. Any foreign intelligence service with resources and wit could see what we are doing and work to exploit it. Indeed, while I was director, there was evidence that some were. The very things that would make a recruit attractive to us—extensive travel, study or work abroad, near-native language proficiency nurtured by still close ties to a region—all these opened up counterintelligence challenges.

In the summer of 2010 a young Michigan man, Glenn Shriver, was arrested and charged with making false statements to the US government and conspiring to pass intelligence to China. He had lived, studied, and worked in China off and on for several years, spoke Mandarin exception-ally well, and had been paid by the Chinese Ministry of State Security (MSS) to enter the CIA recruiting pipeline in 2007.

Shriver was detected by traditional counterintelligence means rather than by any guaranteed fail-safe point in our application process. And it was no surprise that the Chinese would be among those making a run at us. Then and now I stand in awe (as a professional) at the depth, breadth, and persistence of MSS's efforts against the United States. China's cyber espionage has gotten well-deserved headlines, but its efforts are not lim-ited to the digital domain.

And, of course, China is not the only counterintelligence challenge.

That's why we poured as much effort into our Counterintelligence Center (CIC) as we did into recruiting and other activities. The CIC was paid to be distrustful, and they were very good at it. They didn't care that we were emphasizing heritage recruiting. They were suspicious of every-one without regard to race, creed, or place of origin.

The center had traditionally attracted high-end talent; my deputy, Steve Kappes, had once been its chief. My time at the agency was no ex-ception, and top-notch CIA people were joined by high-quality FBI de-tailees.

A CIA director ignores counterintelligence at great peril. One counter-intelligence head (James Jesus Angleton) had become so powerful and so destructively paranoid that he threatened the agency's very survival until summarily dismissed by William Colby in 1974. Jim Woolsey's tenure (1993–1995) was forever darkened by the Aldrich Ames case, even though that Russian spy was actually uncovered on his watch.

Bob Gates is fond of relating a conversation he had with former DCI Richard Helms in 1991. The revered Helms, the story goes, was invited to lunch in the director's dining room. As they were finishing, Helms turned to Gates and offered only one piece of advice: "Never go home at night without asking yourself, 'Where is the mole?'"

So I had a lot of time for the CIC and was updated by them regularly on their cases, leads, and suspicions. It was the most depressing ninety minutes on my calendar.

The case of Harold Nicholson is a good illustration. Nicholson was a veteran CIA case officer, former chief of station, instructor for new recruits at the Farm and, beginning in the mid-1990s, a Russian spy. He was tripped up by the agency's CI efforts, reenergized after the Ames debacle, when he indicated deception during a routine polygraph. Placed under surveillance by the FBI, he was arrested at Dulles trying to leave the country with classified information. In 1997 he was sentenced to more than twenty years in prison for espionage.

Case closed? Not quite. Throughout most of my time as director a decade later, the CIC routinely briefed me that Nicholson, during family visits in prison, was suborning his youngest son, Nathaniel, to pursue money he claimed the Russians still owed him. As directed, Nathaniel, who adored his father, pursued the Russians and his dad's back pay until he, too, was arrested in late 2008. (Harold got an additional eight years. Young Nathaniel turned state's evidence and got probation.)

I listened to the briefings with amazement bordering on disbelief. The CIC folks took it in stride.

Greed, dishonesty, folly. We can all lament the results of original sin. But this was something more than just human frailty. This was espionage. Intelligence services recruit human sources through money, ideology, compromise, and ego (abbreviated MICE in the trade). We were good at it. The work of the CIC was proof that we weren't immune from it.

Fortunately, during my time as director, there were no hostile penetrations of CIA (that have yet been detected, at least).

But there were plenty of other issues. Like when do you impose accountability when things go wrong? Working on the edge, with narrow margins, when should officers be judged culpable?

Some calls are easy. In one instance a small group of officers (actually highly regarded ones pursuing a legitimate objective) directed actions beyond their mandate. They were outside their lane, knew it, and covered their tracks both before and after the wheels started flying off the operation. Since they were less than forthcoming internally and we believed them, we weren't giving Congress the full story. When we finally learned the truth from outside sources, dismissal and referral to the Department of Justice was as swift as it was certain. *"To live outside the law, you must be honest."*

Then there was a completely different kind of case. In 2007 the CIA inspector general finished his review of the rendition and detention of Khalid el-Masri, a German citizen who had been detained by Macedonian authorities on New Year's Eve 2003 because his passport appeared suspect and his name matched a terrorist associated with the 9/11 Hamburg cell. A few weeks later he was turned over to CIA and taken to a black site for interrogation based on the analytic judgment of a senior in the AQ cell in the Counterterrorism Center.

El-Masri was the wrong man. He had a clouded past, but he was *not* the Khalid el-Masri we were pursuing. The passport checked out, and it wasn't long before interrogators knew that this was a dry hole intelligence-wise. He was released in late May.

There were lots of issues here. One was the time (weeks to months) it took to release el-Masri once CIA knew his true identity. Another was the manner of release: dropped on a road in the Balkans with no apology and little compensation. Finally, there was the public relations disaster (and later diplomatic storm) when el-Masri predictably went public with his story of confinement and claims of abuse.

But none of those formed the core issue in the inspector general's report. *The* issue there was the IG's recommendation that I form an accountability board (a kind of professional jury) to judge the behavior of the analyst who had launched the chain of events.

I declined, and that later became part of the SSCI Democrat narrative in their December 2014 report on detentions and interrogations that characterized us as a rogue and unaccountable agency.

Actually, it was a pretty easy call. The analyst was among the best al-Qaeda watchers we had. She had been doing this since well before 9/11 and her knowledge was encyclopedic. So I'm not sure whom I would have gotten to second-guess her judgment.

But there was a bigger question, and it had to do with the nature of intelligence and the near-absolute inappropriateness of applying law enforcement models to its conduct. We make much in American courts about our willingness to let the guilty go free to protect the innocent. Benjamin Franklin summarized it: "It is better a hundred guilty persons should escape than that one innocent person should suffer." But that is a process of assigning guilt and meting out punishment after an evil has been done, with time not a factor, and with the appropriate standard of proof being beyond reasonable doubt.

None of that applies to intelligence, where the evil is pending, time is always critical, and where the objective is to enable action even in the face of continued doubt. Absent clear malfeasance, if I had disciplined an analyst for a false positive (thinking someone was a terrorist when he wasn't), the system would have digested the lesson in the most perverse way: the most important thing is to avoid false positives (you'll be punished for those) even if it means a few true positives slip through (bad things might happen, but probably not to you).

What might be admirable for a court system is unconscionable for an intelligence agency. My goal was to create circumstances where we got more of both the positives and negatives right, not to incentivize one at the expense of the other. And one message I could not afford to send to our analysts was, "Take hard jobs, make tough choices, and if you f— up, we're coming after you." After all, we still wanted to get the *other* Khalid el-Masri.

I suppose I could have had that wrong. But it seems so clear to me—now as it did then.

El-Masri was out of CIA custody two years before I became director, but the discipline was mine to decide more than a year into my term. That's too long a time between flash and bang (and actually telling Congress about the mistake). But that was near instantaneous compared with my having to deal with an event from 2001 in 2008 as I was about to walk out the door.

On April 21, 2001, a Peruvian fighter jet participating in a counter-drug operation called the Air Bridge Denial Program fired into the fuse-lage of a small plane carrying an American missionary family from Michigan. The plane ditched in the Amazon, but not before the mother and infant daughter were dead. It was the fifteenth shoot-down in a program that began in 1994 and which, to that point, had been viewed as a success. CIA, operating under covert action authorities, energized the whole effort by helping the Peruvians identify and track potential drug-trafficking aircraft, but the authority to fire when a plane refused to land was always Peruvian.

The investigation into this tragedy was understandably disrupted by the 9/11 attacks, less than five months after the shoot-down. It wasn't until 2005 that the Department of Justice finally declined prosecution and returned the case to the agency for its own resolution. I became director five years after the shoot-down and began a routine of asking after the status of the IG investigation in my meetings with the inspector general.

The victims of the attack were from Congressman Pete Hoekstra's district in Michigan, and he viewed the delay as a cover-up. It wasn't, but I did agree with his charge that "justice delayed is justice denied." And not for just the Michigan family. One very hot Sunday morning I was sitting at a table in the mess hall of the CIA station in Baghdad when an officer sat beside me and simply recited a rather large sum of money she had spent over a rather large number of months. There, in a war zone, she was describing to me her personal legal expenses and the amount of time she had been left hanging after Peru. "Got it," I tersely replied.

The IG report got to my desk in August 2008. As recommended, I appointed an accountability board, six people in all, two from inside the agency, four from outside (including two who knew a lot about shooting down airplanes). They didn't report out until I was long gone. In 2010, Director Panetta sanctioned sixteen individuals, many of them retired from the agency, for "shortcomings in reporting and supervision." An accompanying agency press release emphasized that there was no evidence of a cover-up, that all the previous shoot-downs had met the legal criteria of "reasonable suspicion," and that no CIA officer had acted inappropriately even in the April 2001 event.

The *New York Times* was far more condemnatory than the final judgments of the accountability board or of Director Panetta and his press release. Based on the language of the original 2008 IG report, the *Times* alleged a "culture of negligence and deceit," and it said CIA officers "routinely violated agency procedures, tried to cover up their mistakes, and misled Congress immediately after a missionary plane was accidentally shot down in 2001."

So there was more than a little daylight between the IG's language and the agency's final resolution. More on the IG and its investigations shortly, but there was one comment from the IG report that I thought was spot-on. It said that a "failure to provide adequate oversight and report violations precluded a policy review and a possible change of course that could have prevented the shoot-down of April 2001."

The real issue with the Peru shoot-down was the validation of targets. The formal rules of engagement had been constructed to give policy makers in Washington comfort that almost nothing could go wrong. But in the field, it was difficult if not impossible to accomplish the complex, multistep, detailed validation process within realistic timelines.

But nobody said that, so the airborne interdiction program was on autopilot, could not be carried out consistent with its original guidance, and agency officers in the field just did the best they could to square an impossible circle.

Even the agency's later press release admitted that "procedures associated with this counter-narcotics initiative eroded over time." They had to if the effort was going to show any results. Turns out that April 21 was an event waiting to happen, since headquarters was unaware of the gap between promise and performance. That's more a Washington HQ than a Peruvian issue, and it dated back to the original mid-1990s finding that launched the program.

The whole mess shows why agency veterans are wary of covert actions. They counsel to underpromise and overdeliver. In my entire time at CIA the agency itself surfaced just one covert action new start. It was rejected.

Veterans also counsel to avoid temptation when, at the end of an inconclusive NSC meeting, all eyes are looking toward our end of the table for some sort of deus ex machina covert action relief. I frankly lost track of the number of meetings on the genocidal conflict in Darfur that ended that way.

And in those instances when a covert action is assigned and the agency must draft the directive that the president will sign to authorize action, the longest paragraph is invariably the one labeled "Risk."

Steve Kappes ran something called the CARG, the Covert Action Review Group, to keep us on the right side of issues. Monthly he deconstructed proposed and ongoing operations with a skeptic's, even a cynic's, eye. Tough sessions. No autopilots. *"To live outside the law, you must be honest."* Especially with yourself. All the time.

Steve had the right people in the room: all four deputy directors, the general counsel, lawyers from specific offices, public affairs, legislative affairs, and usually Michael Morell (the agency's number three). In addition to operators who had covert action successes, Steve always included some with covert action scars.

The group handled what we called the "authorities" and the "permissions." The "authorities" referred to the overarching approvals within which we functioned. They were usually expressed in documents called findings, because they began with the president's words "I find that . . ." The "permissions" referred to approvals for specific operations within a finding.

The Bush White House gave us a lot of room in which to operate. I would occasionally choose to call Steve Hadley when we had a unique circumstance, but those conversations usually began with my saying, "Steve, this is my decision and I will make it, but I wanted to alert you that . . ."

I was comfortable with that, since I had quality people helping me. In my first handoff briefing with Leon Panetta, I told him that he was getting the best staff in the federal government. I meant it.

My deputy, Steve Kappes, was one of the most highly regarded case officers in the history of the agency, even if he had kind of stumbled into applying while he was marine drill team commander at their DC barracks at Eighth and I Streets. Straightforward. No nonsense. Similar background to mine. Eastern Ohio to my western Pennsylvania. On more than one occasion, after the room had cleared and we had made a difficult decision, he would turn to me and ask, "Did you ever think two boys from Ohio and Pennsylvania would ever decide such things?" We were close enough that I had no problem, after making an operational decision, turning and simply asking, "You OK with this?" He almost always was.

Our number three was Mike Morell, also from Ohio. I pried Michael away from the National Counterterrorism Center when President Bush tapped me for DCIA. Since Michael had been President Bush's PDB briefer on Air Force One on 9/11, he strongly backed the move.

Michael's predecessor as executive director was about to be indicted for bribery, so Michael had some cleaning-up to do. He was up to it. I once described him to the workforce as having "insight, dedication, creativity, and sheer talent." Since he had been a career analyst, I made Michael the deputy director for intelligence, the head of our analytic work, in 2008. He said that it was like going home. Michael's replacement was Scott White, Naval Academy graduate, submariner, captain in the naval reserve, and agency veteran.

A very smart, really hardworking person I relied on to be my chief of staff was Larry Pfeiffer. He was career NSA on loan to the CIA front office when the intelligence reform act hit in 2005. With all the turmoil from the legislation, he was almost the IC equivalent of a stateless person when I grabbed him to be my ODNI chief of staff, and I happily kept him when I moved on to CIA. Smart move.

Another NSA veteran I enlisted was Bob Deitz, who had been my general counsel at Fort Meade. At Langley he was consigliere, a kind of gadfly in residence who stayed behind after a meeting to challenge everyone's thinking.

None of us had any grandiose schemes for reinventing CIA. There was a war on. We thought our job was to right the ship and keep it sailing. After the 2008 presidential election, Congressman Mike Rogers of the HPSCI told his old Hill friend and incoming White House chief of staff Rahm Emanuel that our crew had gotten the trains to run on time. We took it as a real compliment.

Early in our tenure, Kappes, Morell, Pfeiffer, and I did have one short off-site to set out some goals. We decided one area of emphasis would be agency culture.

Driving down Virginia Route 123 and looking through the fence line, CIA appears to be a singular noun to a casual observer. *The* CIA. It is not. On a *very* good day, CIA might be a collective noun. Most days, it is decidedly plural.

There are four big directorates in the agency, each with a culture of its own. The self-confident case officers in the National Clandestine Service reminded me of air force fighter pilots. Tenured faculty was the thought that came to mind when talking to some DI analysts. The folks in S&T (science and technology) were true heirs to James Bond's "Q." And the Directorate of Support housed the blue-collar, just-make-it-happen kind of folks I grew up with in Pittsburgh. They made the agency run—communications, logistics, security, and everything else we needed to operate.

All good. Each culture was geared to each directorate's specific task. In a Bubble session I explained that I wanted to strengthen everyone's CIA identity, but not at the expense of the directorates. I used my air force experience to elaborate. I told the audience, "America's air force spends the better part of most days trying to convince its fighter pilots that they are actually part of a larger institution. But at the end of the day, there is one thing they want them to remember. They really are fighter pilots."

And the agency wasn't nearly as internally fenced off as it had been in the past; at one point in the agency's history, case officers and analysts actually had separate cafeterias. Still, we thought that we could use a little more overarching "CIA-ness" in the mix.

One initiative was to set up a very small CIA subsidiary operation in Austin, Texas. Office space was cheap; Texas is on an independent power grid, so it reinforced continuity of operations; air service to DC was good enough; and there was a lot of great talent to recruit in the local area. The idea was—in the new location—to experiment with a structure that ignored the old directorate lines, a kind of small CIA-X where we could safely experiment with new approaches. We wanted to see what CIA would look like if we had a blank sheet and no legacy organizational structure, contractor base, IT system, or workforce. We never found out. Congress stopped us in our tracks. We were probably too late in the administration for them to countenance any new big ideas. But it also serves as something of a morality play when people complain about government inertia and inflexibility.

So we had to content ourselves with other steps. One technique was to communicate to everyone directly and simultaneously, the theory being that common knowledge would help build more common attitudes. My rate of e-mails to the workforce was comparable to the pace of DIR-GRAMs I had set at NSA, about two per week.

We set up a special account called "Ask the Director" so that questions and ideas (and gripes) could be aired internally, instead of being first heard from "anonymous sources" in the *Washington Post*. We got pretty heavy traffic for about ninety days, responded to all of it, and then saw the pace gradually taper off.

Many in the current workforce (and the press) often turn to former agency officers for their views, so we tried to rope in the alumni as well. We got pretty good crowds for alumni days in the Bubble, and although we couldn't clear them for classified briefings, Steve and I leaned pretty far forward telling them what we were trying to do.

We also tried things like lengthening the time in the on-boarding process where new arrivals got acculturated to the agency as a whole before heading off to their directorates.

We emphasized our common agency heritage and dotted most of 2007 with events marking CIA's sixtieth anniversary.

We also gradually pulled corporate activities like the ops center, information technology, finance, and HR out of the directorates and up to the agency level—the better to see, manage, and unify these important functions.

I think I surprised everyone my first summer by demanding to review how they were burning their money before the fast-approaching end of the fiscal year. We still didn't have auditable accounts (no one in the IC did) nor could we really tote up the real cost of manpower, but I at least made the point that I thought it was all *CIA* money, whereas in the past the wheelbarrow had dumped off funds to the directorates at the beginning of the fiscal year and that was the end of it.

We also took a bit of a run at contractors, the number of which had grown massively since 9/11. Unlike some, I wasn't mad at contractors. I considered them part of the workforce and managed them as such. I reminded folks that during my tenure, I put contractor stars on the wall. There was no doubt that our use of them made us more effective.

That last point was often contested by members of Congress, who accused us of using contractors to deflect accountability for our actions. Often, when I briefed them on an operation, they would ask whether it had been accomplished by a contractor or a government employee. I rarely knew and rarely went out of my way to find out. I usually took the question for the record, pointed out that the individuals involved were the best Americans available for the task, and then reminded them that I was as liable for contractor actions as I was for those of agency officers.

But if our use of contractors had been effective, no one could claim that it had been efficient. We often found that we were bidding against ourselves for contractor support, with different parts of the agency pursuing the same product or service from the same vendor. We were also a bit of a farm team for our contractors. Agency folks were leaving, with their experience and their clearances, for higher-paying contractor jobs.

I arbitrarily directed that we were going to reduce our reliance on contractors by 10 percent. There was no science behind that, but I knew there was at least that much slop in the system. When we met that goal in less than a year, I added an additional 5 percent cut.

I also said that CIA would not renew for one year the clearances of anyone who resigned from the agency to come back to work for us as a contractor. Retirees could—they had paid their dues—but not people who were just selling back to us what we had just taught them.

But that was on the dramatic end of my actions. I had promised the agency on my first day that no one had sent me up the parkway to blow anything up. I was true to my word. It was a way of telling people that I had confidence in them, that they weren't terminally screwed up, as some of their critics were claiming.

In that introductory conversation with Leon about the quality of the staff, I added, "If you give them half a chance, they won't let you fail, the way they wouldn't let me fail."

That actually applied to everyone at CIA, not just the senior staff, and Leon would learn soon enough why I was so confident in them.

Because my thirty minutes to brief President Bush on CIA's covert actions and sensitive collection were on Thursday mornings, you can imagine what the headquarters looked like on Wednesday afternoons, as items suggested by the staff began to flow into my office. I would do one review midafternoon and then another just before I left the office for the night. Then I would wake up very early on Thursday, spread the potential items out on my kitchen counter, and decide which were and were not ready for prime time. The important point is that easily 50 percent of the specific operational details I briefed on Thursday morning I learned about for the first time on Wednesday afternoon.

I felt fully in charge. Steve Kappes and I set the left- and right-hand boundaries of acceptable activities. We ensured that actions were purposeful and directed toward defined and legitimate objectives. But in the world in which we were operating, we had to depend a great deal on local autonomy and judgment. There was no other way. What we were asked to do couldn't be done with tight stick and rudder control from a seventh-floor suite in Langley, Virginia.

If we were a military organization, this would all have been called "mission type orders": broad direction and clear limits from headquarters. The rest is yours.

In a religious context, since we focused on removing impediments and enabling, we might have described ourselves as "servant-leaders."

At CIA we were director and deputy, charged to lead, decide, discipline, and (one hopes) inspire.

SIXTEEN

IRAN: BOMBING OR THE BOMB?

LANGLEY, VA, 2007–2009

During my time at CIA, the most discussed topic in the Oval Office was terrorism and the ongoing wars. Number two was Iran. It wasn't all that close, but we talked about Iran a lot. There really wasn't a number three. Sure, we addressed other topics, but we didn't aggregate around any of them enough that they actually earned third place.

When asked by public groups what our intelligence priorities were, I would respond with a bit of Washington alphabet soup: CT-CP-ROW. Counterterrorism, counterproliferation, the rest of the world.

So counterproliferation was a big deal, and during the transition when the president-elect asked me how much of our CP effort was focused on Iran, I answered without hesitation, "Eighty percent."

So *Iran* was a big deal, and President Bush was losing patience about it. He freely admitted the near impossibility of persistent penetration of a closed society like North Korea but wondered—with literally thousands of Iranian Americans able to routinely travel to their homeland, an economy that was largely integrated with the global economy, and an intelligentsia that was extensively Westernized—why we weren't doing better with Iran.

I didn't have a good answer. Iran was a tough target. Their counterintelligence services were numerous, large, and thorough. The MOIS (Ministry of Intelligence and Security) was the FBI's counterintelligence equivalent and a whole lot more. Nominally under the president, in practice it reported directly to the Supreme Leader. It was augmented by a shadowy arrangement with the IRGC (Iranian Revolutionary Guard Corps), formed by Ayatollah Khomeini after the 1979 revolution to guard the Islamic Republic against internal and external threats. Thought to number more than 100,000, the IRGC was the fanatically loyal, direct-action arm of the Supreme Leader. Domestically, the IRGC controlled the million-man Basij Resistance Force, an army of street thugs that delighted in cracking the heads of dissidents, especially the children of the privileged from cosmopolitan, impious North Tehran.

The IRGC's many external operations were under the control of the Quds Force and its dark, ruthless commander, Qasem Soleimani. And all of this was wrapped so powerfully into the rule of religious law (*velayat-e faqih*) rather than secular jurisprudence that it seemed that no action was off the table. Amazing what people will do when they think they're acting on the will of God.

We had some successes, increasing the number of what we called operational acts—the things you need to do to conduct espionage—inside Iran, but we were more than a brick shy of a load.

George Bush rarely showed anger toward me, but one day in the Oval after an unsatisfying discussion on Iran, he intercepted me as I was leaving, and with his right index finger pointing toward my chest, said, "Mike, I don't want to be left—I don't want any president to be left—with only two choices here."

The two choices were bombing or the bomb: going "kinetic" against the Iranian nuclear program or acquiescing in a nuclear-capable Iran.

The president was making a classic plea to his intelligence community. If knowledge is power, he seemed to be saying, work your magic to give me knowledge so I can develop options beyond being forced to accept the unacceptable.

Some very smart Americans have actually made it clear that *they* could accept one of the options. Brent Scowcroft and Zbigniew Brzezinski, both former national security advisors, believe that a nuclear Iran could be contained or at least that the alternative of bombing Iran would be worse. But that was not the policy of either President Bush or President Obama and, not that it mattered much, I agreed with the presidents. Now, what to do about it?

It was complicated.

On the margins of an NSC meeting late in the Bush administration, a senior official cornered me and asked what I thought Iranian nuclear doctrine might be. I replied, accurately enough, "I have no idea and I doubt that they do either."

My questioner persisted. "How many weapons might they get?"

"Probably just a few."

"And how many do *we* have?"

"Oh, all told, thousands."

"So why don't we just deter them?"

At which point the tumblers clicked, and I began to better understand the conversation. "Oh, this isn't about deterring them," I objected. "This is about deterring us. Look at their behavior—with Hamas, with Hezbollah, in Iraq, in Afghanistan. Hell, we judge that it is the policy of the Iranian government—approved at the highest levels of that government—to facilitate the killing of young Americans and other allies in Iraq. And this is before they have one of these things in the garage. Imagine what they might do with this as a trump card."

Iran was already an incredibly destabilizing force in the region, especially in Iraq. The Badr Corps, one of the most important Shia militias in Iraq, was an arm of Iranian policy. Tehran had also enlisted the aid of its Lebanese proxy Hezbollah and its murderous operations chief, Imad Mughniyah, to create a Hezbollah clone in Iraq, an effort supported by several training camps in Iran. The IRGC Quds Force was also aggressive on the ground. It helped plan a deadly raid—complete with faked identity cards and American-style uniforms—against a US checkpoint near Karbala in January 2007 that resulted in five soldiers killed (four of whom had been kidnapped).

The Quds Force was also manufacturing and shipping EFPs—explosively formed projectiles—to Shia militias. These were ingeniously designed shaped-charge devices that could penetrate even the thickest American armor. EFPs were the biggest killers of Americans in Iraq, and we knew, with high confidence, that this was the Iranian government's intent.

And they weren't bashful about any of this. Soleimani famously sent a text message to Iraqi president Talabani for the US commander: "General Petraeus, you should know that I, Qasem Soleimani, control policy for Iran with respect to Iraq, Lebanon, Gaza, and Afghanistan. The ambassador in Baghdad is a Quds Force member. The individual who's going to replace him is a Quds Force member." Such remarkable confidence, even a touch of messianic triumphalism, and this *without* a nuclear weapon.

But what to do? The first issue was to determine what *they* were doing. Acquiring a usable nuclear weapon requires three things: fissile material (i.e., the uranium or plutonium that creates the detonation); delivery systems, like ballistic missiles, that can get a weapon to a target; and finally, the warhead itself, sufficiently hardened and miniaturized that it can fit on a missile, survive reentry, and be detonated with confidence.

The toughest task of the three is manufacturing the fissile material, and blessedly that requires an industrial process complex and extensive enough that it's hard to keep completely hidden. So we followed it as best we could. How many centrifuges? How much enriched uranium? To what levels? On what timelines? At which sites?

We weren't bad at this. We were on to the unannounced uranium enrichment facility near the holy city of Qom well before it approached operational status and well before the Iranians knew that we knew. When the Iranians finally suspected that we were on to them, they sent a vaguely worded letter to the UN's nuclear inspectors in Vienna prompting President Obama and his British and French counterparts to out the illicit nuclear site during a September 2009 G20 summit in Pittsburgh.

The Qom facility was especially troubling. Built in secret, on an IRGC base, under a granite mountain, it could accommodate about three thousand centrifuges. That was too small to support the enrichment needed for a nuclear energy program. It was too big for some sort of pilot project. But it was just right for producing enough enriched uranium for a modest weapons effort.

With a boost from International Atomic Energy Agency (IAEA) reporting, we worked to get a good handle on the production of enriched uranium at Natanz, Iran's main facility. We needed to know how much had been enriched to 3 to 4 percent, the level needed for a civilian energy program, and how quickly that could be converted to 90 percent purity, the level needed for a weapon.

In 2010 the demand for information increased even more when Iran began to enrich to 20 percent, ostensibly for a research reactor in Tehran, still well short of the 90 percent needed for a weapon, but—because of the peculiar physics involved in enrichment—about nine-tenths of the way to weapons-grade material. We relied on technical intelligence to vet and supplement what they were learning on the ground.

There was a second set of questions. If we were going to influence Iranian decision making, we would have to have a pretty good idea of how they made decisions. President Bush was consistent on this theme. He wanted to know what buttons he could push, but Iranian decision making remained very opaque to us. I always preferred questions on the nuclear program itself.

Not having an embassy in Tehran didn't help. The Iranians would have labeled it a nest of spies, but I would have settled for some smart political officers able to openly absorb information as they walked through the bazaar. We were relegated to asking countries that did have legations in Tehran what their diplomats were hearing and seeing.

Late in the administration, Secretary Rice occasionally floated the concept of a US-staffed interest section in Tehran, much like we had in Havana. I always quickly seconded the motion even as the vice president just as quickly counseled against it as unnecessarily legitimating the regime.

The two strains—where are they in their program and how do they make decisions about it?—came to a head in a National Intelligence Estimate being prepared in the summer of 2007. It was meant to replace the previous estimate, which confidently assessed that "Iran currently is determined to develop nuclear weapons despite its international obligations and international pressure." A new draft had been prepared along similar lines, although the confidence level had eroded from high to medium, not because of any contrary evidence, but simply because the evidence we did have was aging off.

The original target for publication was spring, but we were unable to meet that as we re-scrubbed all our data, sources, assumptions, and judgments. We were also, at presidential direction, putting a lot more effort into collection, and that began to pay off. New data began to suggest that in 2003 Iran had suspended its work developing a weapon, perhaps in response to much of its nuclear program being outed the year before, or perhaps because there were two large American land armies to the east and west of Iran in Afghanistan and Iraq.

In any event, for whatever reason, the Iranians appeared to have stopped work on developing a warhead. They were still chugging away creating fissile material and developing missile delivery systems, but not the weapon itself. And this judgment was based not on the absence of evidence that such work was ongoing, but rather on evidence that it was not.

None of us thought that this ended our Iranian nuclear dilemma, but it did muddle the previous NIE's key judgment about Iranian intentions.

In the new intelligence structure, NIEs are the province of the DNI, not CIA. But the grunt work on this one was being done by CIA analysts, so my deputy, Steve Kappes, and I spent two afternoons grilling our analysts about their work. This was going to be a big deal. We had to be right.

We hit them from every direction we could think of. How many sources? What kind? Assumptions? Alternative explanations? They had mastered their facts and their brief. Like any analysts, they could have been wrong. But they clearly knew their stuff.

As one final check we threw their conclusions to the CIA Counterintelligence Center and asked if all of this could be Iranian deception. These people were paid to be suspicious. And they were. But the worst they could come up with, based largely on a generalized suspicion rather than on any specific facts, was a recommendation to give the judgment on halting weaponization no more than a medium confidence level. But that's not what the evidence said. We stuck with high confidence.

It was going to be tough to take this to the Oval. DNI Mike McConnell had prepped the battle space by giving the president and vice president a preview of what was coming. But this was a very unwelcome message, one bound to undercut the administration's efforts to build an international coalition to punish and isolate the Iranians for their nuclear ambitions.

To his credit, though, and at some political cost, the president directed that we declassify and publish as much of the key judgments from the NIE as we could. The administration had used the previous key conclusion, *Iran is determined to develop . . .*, as an anchor of its policy, so it felt duty-bound to publicly say that that judgment was now less certain. There was also the practical consideration that this was sure to leak anyway. It would be better to get ahead of the story.

It was a simple matter to redact the 15 percent or so of the key judgments that said too much about sources and methods. We let the other 85 percent stand as written. That was the right thing to do. Who could stand the story that the estimate was edited for reasons beyond classification before it was publicly released?

But we were releasing only two pages of key judgments from a 140-page NIE. A lot of important detail was going to be left on the floor. Nuclear issues are also especially complicated; they are difficult to summarize. And no NIEs are written for the general population or even intelligence-beat press reporters. They're written for a few hundred select government officials, cognoscenti who know and appreciate their arcane style, language, rhythm, context, and history. Now we were about to throw a much-truncated text out to the general public. All I could think of were bones being thrown before a circle of necromancers, with each free to make his own interpretation.

The administration belatedly figured this out. Mike McConnell was on a foreign trip, so as I was leaving the Shakespeare Theatre in downtown Washington on a rainy Friday night in late November, my security detail chief leaned into me and said, "Mr. Hadley wants to speak with you."

"He gets up early. It's late. I'll call him in the morning."

"No, sir. He wants to speak with you now."

"Get me the White House switch."

Steve wanted me to handle the public rollout of the NIE that was going to take place Monday morning. I was free to use the resources of the whole community to make it happen. (Oh, great. I get to play the old DCI for a very bad weekend, I thought.)

Steve added that I needed to develop a plan to inform the allies. They had not yet been brought in on what we were about to announce.

On Saturday we tiered our foreign friends based on our intimacy with them and on their interest in this particular question. We then prepared versions of a cable that varied in detail and sensitivity for each tier. Station chiefs were alerted to make sure liaison partners were briefed before this hit the press on Monday. They did. All this was far too haphazard, but it was good to have a responsive global network to fall back on.

We spent the rest of the weekend preparing for our own press release and backgrounder.

On Monday, after meeting with Steve Hadley, I huddled with my briefing partner, Don Kerr, former head of CIA's Science and Technology Division and the National Reconnaissance Office and now principal deputy DNI (my successor in the job, actually), and far more tech savvy than I'll ever be. We alerted the press and then sent some embargoed copies of the redacted key judgments to several key reporters.

We then set out for the K Street meeting location knowing that we had a heavy lift pushing against the easy (and, as it turned out, inevitable) headline: "Iran Halts Nuclear Program." After all, the NIE began with *"We judge with high confidence that in fall 2003, Tehran halted its nuclear weapons program."*

We pointed to the footnote (yes, the *footnote!*) where the analysts in this arcane art form actually identified what had stopped, namely efforts to construct an actual bomb and the Iranian military's clandestine enrichment program. We pointed in vain to the continuation of generalized enrichment, the increase in centrifuges at Natanz, and the continued development of long-range missiles that had little use without a nuclear warhead. Referring to a classic project management tool used to organize a complex task, I said, "If the Iranian nuclear program had a PERT chart, these would be the critical paths, not the weaponization effort."

Also lost in the shuffle was the formal judgment that we weren't out of the woods: "We also assess with moderate-to-high confidence that Tehran at a minimum is keeping open the option to develop nuclear weapons."

Or that they had had a weapons program and continued to lie about it: "We assess with high confidence that until fall 2003, Iranian military entities were working under government direction to develop nuclear weapons."

Or that the NIE, for all its controversy, was a validation of US policy toward Iran: "We judge with high confidence that the halt . . . was directed primarily in response to increasing international scrutiny and pressure resulting from exposure of Iran's previously undeclared nuclear work."

In other words, we were right to be worried about Iran trying to develop nuclear weapons, and although the risk continued, we had made some progress in trying to ensure that it didn't happen.

No matter. Once the NIE was released, many of our allies thought that the pressure was off and, here at home, the political right hammered us. Many concluded that the estimate was the intelligence community's revenge on the Bush administration for being forced to take the heat on the failed Iraq NIE. Within weeks, the Heritage Foundation published a primer, *A Complete Guide to What Is Wrong with the NIE*. The American Enterprise Institute's reliably hawkish John Bolton complained in the *Washington Post*, "All this shows that we not only have a problem interpreting what the mullahs in Tehran are up to, but also a more fundamental problem: Too much of the intelligence community is engaging in policy formulation rather than 'intelligence' analysis, and too many in Congress and the media are happy about it." I got a later dose of the same theme during a talk to the conservative Hudson Institute. It made for a nice, tight story, but it just wasn't true. The facts took us to our conclusions, not retribution or predisposition.

This estimate, by the way, despite some suspicious and troubling Iranian activity in the years since, has survived largely intact. That reality has been reflected in a variety of policy statements, like the one Secretary of Defense Panetta made in 2012 that if "we get intelligence that they're proceeding with developing a nuclear weapon, then we will take whatever steps are necessary to stop it." In other words, they have still not gone all out to develop a nuclear weapon.

The persistence of that American position later complicated the relationship between President Obama and Israeli prime minister Netanyahu. Reflecting on a meeting between the two in the Oval Office in March 2012, I suggested that even though both had announced that Iran's acquisition of a nuclear weapon was unacceptable, I suspected that the two men talked past each other.

I compared the session to high school math and being forced to solve algebraic equations, with Obama pointing out how hard we were working to solve for y, where y represented Iranian intentions. Unfortunately, in the prime minister's equation, y had already been defined as a constant. Israel believes that it knows where the Iranians are going. In its equation, the unknown is x, and x is what the United States intends to do about it.

The NIE clearly hurt the Bush administration's efforts in the short run, but over a longer perspective it's perhaps not been a bad thing that American intelligence has been more conservative than many on this question. No one can claim we were stampeding them.

DESPITE THE NIE, the press headlines, and the right's reaction, we still knew that the Iranian program was a dangerous thing. But how to stop it?

First, we had to up our intelligence game. Pointing to the successful example of the Counterterrorism Center in working al-Qaeda, CIA deputy director Steve Kappes recommended that we create an Iranian Operations Division (IOD) that put in one office under unified direction the operational, analytic, and technical talent working the Iranian nuclear problem. We launched it in midsummer 2007 as we were crafting the new Iranian NIE, and we assigned a veteran clandestine service officer, one very familiar with Iran, to head it.

He was a great choice. He began his inaugural briefing to me by saying, "The threat from Iran is lethal, strategic, and urgent." He has stayed with the topic, later leading the DNI's efforts and then becoming a constant presence supporting the Obama administration's nuclear negotiations with the Islamic Republic.

In 2007 we gave him license to raid talent from other CIA efforts and then backed him up when the predictable complaints came rolling in. He also created space in IOD for community partners, too, welcoming officers from DIA, NSA, and the FBI, and then he synchronized their HUMINT collection plans.

As we found with the CTC, the melding of ops and analysis and S&T enabled more focused collection, more relevant technology, *and* better analysis. With more centralized direction we could better prioritize requirements, craft collection plans, and ensure a stronger counterintelligence discipline against the tough Iranian services. We could also more comprehensively assess and synchronize what potential partners had to offer, and I traveled frequently to the region to extend their cooperation. The issue was of such importance that the sharing of very sensitive details with these partners was often unprecedented.

Of course, Israel was as seized with the issue as we were, so we routinely compared notes with them. This dialogue was incredibly useful, and we rarely disagreed about the facts on the ground, but in making assessments about future Iranian milestones, Mossad and Israeli Defense Intelligence tended to be more pessimistic than we were: more Iranian capabilities, sooner, in greater volume. Their estimates were always plausible, and with Tel Aviv less than a thousand miles from Tehran, I always understood the rationale for their math.

Steve and I demanded that IOD update us frequently on the seventh floor. They later told me that they sensed they were being held accountable. They also remembered my admonition (after a briefing showing markedly increased effort) that "activity wasn't the same thing as progress."

We also worked to up our policy game. Steve Hadley had begun informal twice-weekly sessions in his West Wing office, and the approach really took off in late 2007 and 2008. The sessions included Steve and his deputy—who was the note taker—the vice president, the secretaries of state and defense, the chairman of the JCS, the DNI, and me. On the grounds that middle-aged folks get cranky in the afternoon, Steve had the White House mess deliver nachos with cheese dip and taco sauce for the meetings.

There were no backups at these sessions, just principals. Agendas weren't announced in advance, so Steve got our views rather than those of our staffs. The vice president was a true participant and didn't use his office to unduly shape discussion. There was a lot of give-and-take, as we could confront one another without witnesses and without leaving bureaucratic scars. Any decisions made or directions set would launch a deputies committee meeting to put them into action through the formal NSC process.

We talked about Iran a lot during these sessions.

As always, good policy was a question of balance. With a complex problem, if you push too hard after one component, others fall off the rails. In this case we wanted to pressure the Iranians, but we didn't want to provoke a war with them. On the other hand, going too lightly could also provoke a war if states like Israel felt that their concerns were going unaddressed and they concluded that they had to act unilaterally. We were looking for a sweet spot between those extremes.

Some of us were especially concerned about the potential for Israeli action between the November 2008 election and Inauguration Day, reasoning that alienating an outgoing president but presenting an incoming one with a changed strategic reality might be attractive to them. As it turned out, such fears were unfounded.

One could conceive three broad approaches to the problem. The first was a given: make it as hard as possible for the Iranians to develop fissile material, a warhead, and delivery systems. In between the queso dip and taco sauce, we held up to the light every conceivable path we could think of to do just that: overt and covert; unilateral and cooperative; direct and indirect; virtual and physical; kinetic and nonkinetic.

We, of course, had a full menu of sanctions available to punish Iranian or supplier behavior *if* we could get international support (which admittedly became harder to do after the NIE was published). There was also the option of squeezing the supply chain of critical materials on which the Iranians depended. We could "name and shame" scientists affiliated with illicit activity.

Someone else took the brain-drain approach to a higher level. We weren't the only ones trying to slow the Iranians. Another actor was blowing stuff up and killing their scientists. We had our suspicions, but it was something I never raised with any of our partners, even on evenings like the one I spent at a partner's safe house in the region, thoroughly engrossed in what the Iranians were doing and what could be done to stop them. Not that we could help anyone if they were doing this. We couldn't even comment on whether or not we thought killing scientists was a good idea. (Operationally, yes. In terms of establishing international precedent, not so much.)

We did consider the prospect of a bombing campaign. The Pentagon plans for a variety of contingencies, and the plan for this one looked big. Lots of defense suppression before strikers began attacks against what was a large, dispersed, and hardened target. All of us—Gates, Rice, Hadley, Mullen, McConnell, and me—knew the risks of such a course, but the defense secretary may have had the darkest summary: "If we were to do this," he regularly reminded us, "we will guarantee that which we are trying to prevent: an Iran that will stop at nothing to, in secret, build a nuclear weapon."

And the results would be temporary, setting the Iranians back only a couple of years or so. In fact, we all knew that whatever our efforts, we were only slowing the Iranian program, not stopping it. If they wanted a weapon badly enough, they would get one, even after a strike, even after successful covert actions, even after a tough sanctions regime. We could slow and punish, but not stop, if they were willing to pay the price.

The second broad course available to us would address just that, their will. Could we change their minds? We doubted it, but this was too important to be left to just instinct. We were tasked to come up with a straw man. What would a plan to do that look like?

It was a hell of a homework assignment. Basically, what kind of internal tensions would distract the Iranians from the nuclear program, cause them to divert resources from it, or convince them it wasn't worth the candle or at least make their behavior more costly?

Iran has fault lines; it is far from a homogenous society. Persians make up only about 60 percent of the population. There are large Kurdish and Azeri minorities and smatterings of Arabs, Baluchis, and Turkmen. Would it be possible to exploit or deepen the unhappiness that these groups already had with the government? The small Arab population was neuralgically discontented under Persian rule. The substantial Azeri population comprised a good chunk of the *bazaari* merchant class, who had their issues with corrupt clerical rule and had the magnet of a self-governing national homeland just to the north. One in ten Iranians were Kurds, who wanted to carve out just such a homeland for themselves. What kind of messaging could mobilize these groups and energize these disputes? What kind of actions could inspire or appear to reflect heightened dissidence?

There were groups, though, with genuine issues, that we would never touch. There was a raging insurgency under way in Baluchistan in southeastern Iran spearheaded by a terrorist gang called Jundallah. They were effective but brutally violent. We never even considered them, contrary to press accounts of an ongoing CIA-Jundallah relationship.

The Mujahedin-e Khalq was another group. They were Persian dissidents who had opposed the clerical regime since the 1970s. They had fought *against* Iran in the Iran-Iraq War and were in Iraq under Saddam Hussein's protection when American forces rolled them up and disarmed them in 2003. They were still designated a terrorist group by the State Department, though, so they were never on our list.

They had publicly revealed the Natanz facility as nuclear related in 2002, but my analysts were never sure how much independent sourcing they had and how much information they might be passing on behalf of other actors.

There were also cultural, class, and age fissures in Iran. Could the hard-liners be discredited? How would messaging about clerical corruption or government ineffectiveness (of which there was a lot) affect the public? How would the public react to outing the IRGC's massive corruption and control of key elements of the Iranian economy? How would shortages of goods and services—real, imagined, or engineered—affect popular attitudes? Would a less compliant population feed factional infighting among the hard-liners themselves?

Urban Iranian youth are high tech and wired in. They are in a constant skirmish with authorities trying to limit their Internet access. Could trade policies make it harder for the government to do that? Was there a way to share technology and software to protect Web privacy? What of embargoed American IT? Would a flood of high-tech goods more threaten the regime than their denial? Conversely, would a real or even perceived heavier government hand increase dissatisfaction even more?

It was a given that we would confront the Iranians in Iraq and Afghanistan, where they were helping to kill our soldiers. The same globally, especially when it came to terrorism. But beyond such defensive measures, was there more that could be done in these areas that would really stress the regime?

So we did our homework and reported our potential courses of action to the Principals Committee (the NSC minus the president) in the summer of 2008. They (and we, frankly) were underwhelmed. We judged that the impact of most measures would be difficult to predict and problematic. Effects, if there were any, would be long delayed. The potential for miscalculation or an Iranian crackdown would be forever present. And there was no way of knowing if any level of dissent would dissuade the Iranians from their nuclear efforts. Early, vague sentiments of enthusiasm melted in the face of hard realities.

We were also now in the last months of the Bush administration. No fair launching a major initiative whose effects only your successor would have to live with. The PC thanked us and moved on.

There was, of course, always a third option. If you can't change the regime's mind, why not change the regime? Our best assessment was that the Supreme Leader, Ayatollah Khamenei, believed that this was really our purpose all along. Our ranting about the nuclear program, he believed, was just a smoke screen to enlist international support for the first stages of our true intention, getting rid of him.

We would have loved a different regime. After all, we weren't so much opposed to Iran having a nuclear program as we were opposed to *this* Iran having one. We visualized two clocks, one marking the nuclear program's progress, the other ticking down the life of Ayatollah Khomeini's 1979 revolution. We were obviously trying to slow down the nuclear clock. In a theoretical sense it would have made sense to accelerate the regime survival timepiece.

Except that we weren't, at least not much beyond publicly calling the regime to account for its many failings. Regime change is tough, and the presence of any American hand might have strengthened the mullahs rather than weakened them.

And there was always the possibility that the regime would indeed change, but in the wrong direction. As bad as Iran was, it could always get worse. After all, their tightly controlled elections were more open than most in the region.

The Obama administration faced this issue starkly in the summer of 2009 as the Green Movement filled the streets of Tehran with three million protesters after it was announced that Mahmoud Ahmadinejad had won the presidential election. Signs, written in English for the international TV cameras, pleaded for external assistance as the Basiji busted heads and demonstrators were gunned down. The Iranian government already believed that we were fomenting the unrest, but the opposition knew better. They begged for help. To no avail. No actions were forthcoming, and even American verbal condemnations were tepid and late. If ever there was a moment for regime change, this was it. But that moment, such as it was, is past.

By the way, in his inaugural address President Obama had already distanced himself from President Bush's freedom agenda—the belief that only democracy offered the hope for long-term stability: "To those who cling to power through corruption and deceit and the silencing of dissent, know that you are on the wrong side of history, but that we will extend a hand if you are willing to unclench your fist." Translation: We won't threaten your *internal* system if we can make our *external* relations right.

Now, in the summer of 2009, the administration was not going to allow a chancy bet on the Iranian street to threaten its approach to Tehran on the nuclear question.

In the three weeks I served as President Obama's CIA chief while awaiting Leon Panetta's confirmation, we discussed Iran twice in the Situation Room. At the first session the new team laid out its proposed opening to Tehran. I offered no views on the merits (not in my job description), but I did opine that such an offer would create stresses in the regime. "Might make their brains explode," I said, since much of what was left of the diminishing legitimacy of the government rested on its heroic opposition to the Great Satan. "Could be instructive to watch," I added.

At the second meeting, attended by the president, he began by turning to me and asking how much enriched uranium the Iranians now had.

"Mr. President, I actually know that but let me offer you a different frame of reference. In one sense, it almost doesn't matter. There isn't an electron or a neutron at Natanz that's ever going to end up in a nuclear weapon. They'll spin *that* uranium at some secret military facility beyond the eyes of the IAEA."

We already knew about the secret facility under the granite mountain at Fordow near Qom, but had not yet made that public. That wouldn't happen until White House aides briefed the *New York Times*'s David Sanger in a Pittsburgh hotel room in September.

"What they're building at Natanz, Mr. President, is knowledge. They're building technology. They're building confidence. They're mastering this process and once they have, they can turn it on whenever or wherever they want to."

That was why someone was killing their scientists. And later that was why someone was destroying their centrifuges with a cyber weapon. And that's why any nuclear program in the hands of this regime that allows centrifuges to continue to spin constitutes a standing danger.

The current deal negotiated between Secretary Kerry and Iranian foreign minister Zarif allows such a program. It preserves Iranian facilities, Iranian centrifuges, and Iranian nuclear research.

Even if the deal is honored, it legitimizes Iran as an industrial-strength nuclear power and as a permanent nuclear weapons threshold state. The near-impenetrable facility at Fordow, big enough for a weapons program but too small for creating fissile material for a civilian energy effort, remains even if uranium is not being enriched there. The agreement after eight years removes restrictions on Iran's ballistic missile program, which, absent weapons of mass destruction, has little utility.

There will also not be an accounting of Tehran's past nuclear activities, including its warhead weaponization program. Turns out that "access" to suspect facilities does not mean invasive physical entry into them by inspectors, and there is no chance that there will be a thorough debriefing of Mohsen Fakhrizadeh, the Robert Oppenheimer of the Iranian weapons program.

The White House has talked about the most intrusive inspection regime in history. That is probably a bit of hyperbole, but there may indeed be a tough regime for Iran's known facilities. Frankly, though, the IAEA smothering locations we know about isn't all that comforting. The inspectors need to be able to go anywhere at any time, since American intelligence has always assessed that weapons-grade enrichment would take place at some covert location. If inspectors cannot quickly go to military or Revolutionary Guard facilities, there will be a gaping hole in the inspection regime. The agreement gives the Iranians at least twenty-four days to "rope-a-dope" any requests.

The agreement's impact on future counterproliferation efforts will also be profound, as a struggling, isolated regional power has challenged the world and clearly won. After all, the starting point for all of this was a series of UN Security Council resolutions that directed Tehran to suspend all enrichment activities, and President Obama himself declared earlier that the facilities at Fordow and Arak were not legitimately part of a peaceful nuclear program.

The final deal goes out of its way to point out that none of its concessions to Iran should be considered precedent-setting for other states party to the Nuclear Non-Proliferation Treaty. That should tell you something.

And even with an accord in hand *and honored*, Iran remains the duplicitous, autocratic, terrorist-backing, Hezbollah-supporting, Hamas-funding, region-destabilizing, hegemony-seeking theocracy it has been. (No wonder Khamenei always thought we were all about regime change.) A nuclear agreement will end the regime's isolation, and the return of frozen funds and the ability to sell oil will underwrite a host of troubling activities.

So Iran may have little incentive to cheat on an agreement.* Many of us in the intelligence community, myself included, were always skeptical that Tehran would build or at least actually test a nuclear device. Unlike the North Koreans, who had to cook off a bomb to achieve the desired political effect, the Iranians get most of what they want with few of the downsides by parking themselves with an acknowledged nuclear capability always within striking distance of a weapon—precisely where they will get in ten to fifteen years *by adhering to the agreement.*

Chalk all of this up as observation, though, rather than condemnation. I don't think the Bush administration would have bought this deal, but it wasn't like we had created a lot of better choices, either.

---

* They *will* cheat, of course. It's what they do. But here I'm talking about cheating with strategic significance.

SEVENTEEN

A GLOBAL ENTERPRISE

LANGLEY, VA, 2007–2009

In early August 2008, Steve Hadley's concerned voice was very clear on the secure Red Switch from the White House. Mikheil Saakashvili, the president of Georgia, had just been on the phone with him and Saakashvili was excited, even desperate. Russian armor was clearing the crossroads town of Tskhinvali in northern Georgia, and he had every reason to fear that the tanks wouldn't stop until they got to him in Tbilisi, his capital.

Saakashvili had had a hand in generating the crisis. He had allowed his troops to rocket and move into South Ossetia, a breakaway part of his republic that was under the protection of Russian "peacekeepers." And he had done it when a division-plus of the Russian army was just finishing up a summer exercise near there. Now those and other units were bearing down on him.

We knew Saakashvili well, and we owed him a lot. As a student, he had done postgraduate work at Columbia and George Washington in a State Department program, and as president he was an unflinching friend of NATO and the West. He had dispatched a brigade of Georgian infantry to Iraq and was trying to pull his country toward a market economy and democracy. But now he was in danger, and Hadley wanted to know what he could tell Saakashvili about Russian capabilities and intentions.

After promising Steve I'd get back to him quickly, I walked into the outer office and barked at my executive assistants, "Get our Georgia people up here right now!"

As they were making their calls, I turned to Larry Pfeiffer, my chief of staff, and only half-jokingly asked, "We got Georgia people, right?"

Turns out we did, and they were good. Within the hour I had gotten a detailed lay-down and was back on the phone with the West Wing. Saakashvili wasn't out of the woods, but we thought a Russian push to his capital was unlikely.

Rather than continue south, the Russians hooked west and hived off another breakaway region, Abkhazia, along the Black Sea. Collecting on Russian movement was tough, though. National technical means, spy satellites and such, were less optimized to work against this army than they had once been.

I remember thinking at the time that we had to get better at this before the Russian army showed up, plowing through the rich black earth of Ukraine (which it did six years later).

In 2008 we ended up relying a lot on direct observation rather than technical collection. We deployed a squad of case officers into Georgia; we put them into soft vehicles and essentially directed them to drive northwest until they saw Russian armor and then take a GPS reading and phone it in.

Policy-wise, the United States also came up short. A few navy ships entered the Black Sea to show presence and make whatever observations they could. DOD conducted an emergency airlift of the Georgian brigade (minus its heavy equipment) back home from Iraq. Some American humanitarian supplies also arrived by military aircraft. We toyed with the prospect of reconnaissance flights near or over Georgia, but ultimately rejected that as too dangerous.

After a few days of fighting, the French brokered a cease-fire calling for a pullback of Russian forces to their pre-conflict lines. A few Russian units moved, but trumped-up arrangements with newly independent South Ossetia and Abkhazia allowed Russian troops to remain there indefinitely. No European governments formally accepted the dismemberment of Georgia, but they also weren't in the mood for military or even strong economic measures to contest the remapping. Economies were teetering with the US financial meltdown, and Russia was their source of energy.

American thoughts circled around the concept of inclusion-exclusion. Throwing off the autarkic Soviet model, Russia had fought hard to enter the post–World War II global structure that had been nurtured by the United States: groups like the G8 and the G20 and institutions like the World Bank, the World Trade Organization, and the International Monetary Fund. But these were supposed to be councils of like-minded nations, and Russia's redrawing of European borders hardly fit that description.

If Russia wanted to be treated like a normal country, it had to act like a normal country, or so our thinking went. But we were very late in the administration, and even the mild sanctions imposed by the United States were withdrawn in May 2010 as part of the Obama administration's famous "reset." Russia was eventually suspended from the G8 in 2014 after the invasion of Ukraine, but we let them out of the penalty box far too quickly for Georgia.

From the agency's perspective, Georgia was a mixed bag. We had helped Steve Hadley keep Saakashvili from suffering a meltdown. But we had not given Hadley or anyone else any warning of the conflict, even though it was our friends, the Georgians, who had precipitated it.

The young folks who originally scrambled to my office with their charts and maps certainly were magnificent, and they stood up to the president's direct questions a few days later when he came to Langley for deeper background. But there weren't many Russia House veterans around to divine Moscow's intentions as opposed to just tracking the battle. Counterterrorism and the war on al-Qaeda were gobbling up a lot of agency focus, resources, and talent.

We didn't get much sympathy. We were still expected to be global and to do more than "just" fight al-Qaeda. Our government clearly expected that, as did our intelligence partners, or "liaison," as we call them. Actually, our being global was the basis of any relationship we had with them.

These partnerships are an exchange of capabilities. CIA is large, powerful, tech savvy, blessed with resources and the ability to take locally derived data and give it greater meaning by fitting it into a *global* context. The liaison partner is local, focused, agile, and culturally and linguistically smart. We trade off each other for mutual benefit, even when there isn't much agreement at the policy level between governments.

In fact, these partnerships are remarkably durable, operating below the surface, even when political relations are stormy. That's because they enable mutually valuable exchanges between professionals who face common problems, between intelligence establishments that will still be in business and will still be expected to perform when policies and political leaders change.

These liaison relationships are also based on a large helping of *personal* trust. That's why you invite the head of service to your home for dinner, or spend an extra afternoon in his capital so that he can personally show you the sights. That's why you follow your mom's advice and eat every (exotic) thing on your plate—and like it. And that's why you clear your calendar to meet with liaison despite other demands.

Such friendships were a real bonus, but what we were really doing was building a precious level of confidence—the kind built on shared experience and personal contacts, not on formal memos or minutes.

A case in point involved a CIA station chief accompanying a cabinet officer to a meeting with a major Middle East partner. At the end of the session, it was agreed that some important data would be exchanged, and the cabinet official said he would have his staff draw up some memos on the arrangement. The head of the foreign service leaned forward, smiled at the official while gently putting his hand on the forearm of the CIA escort, and objected, "Friends do not need memos."

Lots of services want to be a friend of the Central Intelligence Agency (and its director) and they go out of their way to show it. Shortly after my arrival at Langley, Bulgaria's intelligence chief told our office there that he had taken my file out of the archives and was keeping it in his personal safe. I doubt that there was very much embarrassing (or interesting) in the dossier, but Durzhavna Sigurnost (DS)—the former Communist regime's state security apparatus—was nothing if not thorough, so I imagine the file was pretty thick.

I had been the air attaché in Communist Bulgaria in the mid-1980s. Attachés are "overt collectors," so hostile intelligence services know to zero in on them. We were so certain that our apartment was bugged that my wife and I had those little toy erasable pads with a plastic stylus—the kind where you pull up on the top plastic sheet to obliterate what you have just written—in every room. Sensitive or just private conversations were conducted via a series of notes passed between us and then immediately erased.

I had been detained twice by the Bulgarians during my time there, each time prompted by my getting too close to their military activities trying to identify an aircraft or observe an exercise. No rough stuff, just stern formalities, although one of my colleagues doing similar work was shot and killed in East Germany while I was in Bulgaria.

That wasn't the result of a nefarious plot, just a nervous Soviet conscript—a Central Asian, I was later told—put into a situation that he was ill-prepared to handle.

We worked hard to avoid that circumstance. Like on one daylong car ride to observe some nondescript installations in central Bulgaria with my French counterpart. We picked up close DS surveillance almost immediately, and their vehicle stayed locked to our bumper. It was a routine collection trip, but there was a party congress under way, so I guess they weren't taking any chances. Since we were just driving by barracks on public roads, there was little they needed to do beyond just following us.

So my French companion and I were a bit surprised and concerned when, while we were stopped at a railroad crossing, the chase car ominously pulled out and came alongside us. I looked to my left to see one of our stalkers pantomime using an imaginary fork to bring imaginary food to his mouth from an imaginary plate. He was right. We had been going for more than six hours without a break. It was time for lunch.

We pulled off the road, spread our picnic lunch on the trunk of the car, and chowed down. So did our surveillance. When we were almost done I walked most of the hundred yards between us, pointed to my watch, and then held up five fingers. It was nearly time to go. They waved, packed up their food, and got into the car ready to resume their tailgating.

Until I got to Langley, that attaché position was the best job I ever had. I experienced the challenge and the importance of learning a second language and a second culture; I observed the absolute value of just "being there"; and I got some valuable exposure to collecting intelligence on the ground in a hostile environment. All pretty useful for the CIA job.

Now, in 2006, the Bulgarian service wanted to be our friend, so much so that their chief was going out of his way to "protect" me.

I would emphasize the importance of these kinds of ties to our station chiefs at every opportunity. When I met with them during their out-bound interviews, I told them to make use of Steve and me to help cement these ties. We were willing to talk to our foreign counterparts at any time of the day or night—on any issue.

When we had a visitor I really went out of my way to read the biography, not just of the visitor, but of the station chief accompanying him. As the party entered my office, I wanted to be able to ask the station chief about his wife and children by name and to make other personal references. It probably made the station chief feel good, but what I really wanted to do was to suggest that he and I were old buddies. That would enhance his stock when he got back to station.

When I spoke to our station chiefs as a group, I gave them the essence of my personal approach to partners: "When you're meeting with liaison," I said, "remember two things. One, you represent the only superpower in the room. And, two, don't act like it. Our partners already know the first fact; that's why you're able to be there. They're checking for the second."

During the thirty-three months I was at CIA, Steve Kappes and I visited about fifty foreign partners, many of them more than once. It had
been a long time (if ever) since a CIA director had swung by Mexico City,
Bogotá, or Brasília in this hemisphere, and another trip through Ethio-
pia, Djibouti, Ghana, and Mali in Africa was equally groundbreaking.
Not surprisingly, there were issues of common interest at every stop: new
drug routes in Ghana, the FARC in Colombia, terrorism in Djibouti,
narco traffickers in Mexico, and so on.

And if we visited fifty-plus countries, we hosted far more than that at
Langley. There were, of course, the expected heads of service. But we
also entertained the likes of Saif al-Islam, Muammar Gaddafi's British-
educated, dyspeptic second son, who at the time was being courted by
our government as a future hope for Libya.

Saif aside, dealing with most of these people was personally rewarding.
And valuable too. When confronting one or another crisis at an NSC
meeting, it's very nearly priceless to be able to say, "I just spoke with the
head of intelligence for [the relevant country], and he tells me that . . ."

Good people, mostly. But you had to be on guard. Even the best
of them would sometimes treat you to what I came to call "creation
mythology."

That's when something in the head of that professional across from
you or on the phone is triggered and almost primordial judgments start
to intrude on what had been to that point a fact-based dialogue. Amrullah Saleh, the young Panjshiri Tajik who headed up the Afghan National
Directorate of Security, was, as I've mentioned, bright, honest, curious,
self-taught, and well read. During an early evening stroll through Colo-
nial Williamsburg—one of those cultural events we relied on to cement
liaison relationships—we passed the old House of Burgesses. Amrullah
looked puzzled and then asked, "Where are the walls?"

"Walls?"

"Yes. To protect them from the people."

Things, of course, were different in Kabul—and in Amrullah's entire
life experience.

Saleh was an absolute delight to work with—even when the subject of Pakistan came up and objectivity was a threatened commodity. (He wasn't totally paranoid; Pakistani behavior *was* troubling.)

Years earlier, when I was head of intelligence for US forces in Europe, I would visit Belgrade to talk with my Serbian counterpart, Branco Krga. We hit it off, not least because in our initial meeting he revealed that his grandfather had worked in the steel mills in Pittsburgh.

Branco and I shared thoughts about the ongoing conflict in Bosnia, where essentially his government and mine were on different sides. It was a purely professional exchange, tinged with some sense of the human cost of the war.

At one point Branco leaned into me over lunch and lamented the deaths of so many young men. He talked especially about Serb grief, with one- and two-child families now the norm, and then it happened. "But these Muslim families," he continued with a wave of his hand, "they are so large, what does it matter to them?"

There is little point in arguing. Just don't agree or even seem to agree. Sit there, expressionless, not allowing yourself the almost instinctive head nod signaling "transmission acknowledged," hoping that the episode passes quickly and you can get back to useful dialogue.

It took a while, but one night as I was preparing for an overnight hop to another destination on a foreign trip, the thought struck me. What of my side of these dialogues did our partners dismiss as American mythology? When I talked about self-determination? Cultural pluralism? The curative effect of elections? And when were my partners patiently waiting while I finished before we got back to "serious" talk? I never figured that out, but the longer I did this, the more certain I was that it had to be going on.

There was another danger that you always had to be alert to. Contrary to specious claims that US intelligence outsources its dirty work, we are not allowed to assist or enable a partner to do things that we ourselves are not allowed to do. We can't even suggest that it might be a good idea.

I was in a private meeting with Gabi Ashkenazi, the thoughtful head of the Israeli Defense Forces. After showing me a large photo of an Israeli F-15 missing-man formation over the Nazi death camp at Birkenau—a stern reminder of "never again"—we sat down on his sofa to discuss Iran. He asked me what I thought might be the best way to slow down the Iranian nuclear program.

As I've noted, besides enriching uranium at Natanz, the Iranians were building confidence and knowledge there. And that confidence and knowledge went home at night in the persons of key Iranian nuclear scientists. Putting any broader considerations aside, the best way to slow the program down was to kill the scientists. I did *not* raise it. I didn't even suggest it as a theoretical possibility or an interesting talking point. I just sat there, with nothing particularly useful to say.

So there were always challenges. American (and CIA) values, laws, interests, and policies are *never* totally coincident with those of an allied service, not even a close one. The job of intelligence is to work in the common space for common goals while minimizing the impact of (or changing) the dissonant elements.

I spent an afternoon on the Nile with Omar Suleiman, the sonorous head of the Egyptian service, listening to his wise counsel on Israel and the Palestinians. He was the most knowledgeable and effective go-between we had on that question, and he was a tough counterterrorism partner to boot. We gained much from the relationship.

I wondered at the time, though, and still do, if we might not have pulled our punches on other questions—like working contacts within the Egyptian opposition, including the Muslim Brotherhood—for fear of alienating Omar on these other critical issues. If we did, it was to the harm of us *and* our Egyptian partners.

During a visit to Egypt in August 2008, Omar asked me to stay longer to visit with President Mubarak, for whom he was as much consigliere as intelligence chief. They were close, coming from military backgrounds, and Omar had backstopped Mubarak against political opposition for more than a decade.

Mubarak wasn't available on Friday, the Sabbath, so we filled our time with taking in the pyramids of Giza, the Sphinx, and the Egyptian Museum. Even with the Egyptian intelligence service smoothing the way, traveling the hot, teeming, and boisterous streets of Cairo was a challenge. It made one wonder how the unity of Egypt, shaped by the country's deep history, would fare against the obvious fractures in the country's modern society.

The next morning was brilliantly clear as our small group made its way to the presidential palace, set in the tony suburb of Heliopolis, which was eerily like a ghost town as shops and restaurants were shuttered and empty, presumably because of Mubarak's presence. Omar ushered us into the president's office, where I sat at the end of a couch near the president's chair, within arm's reach of Mubarak, as he began a long critique of US policy and President Bush's freedom agenda.

We had no idea of the situation here, he began, obviously referring to ongoing US support for pro-democracy activists and to pressure to release political prisoners. This meddling was a misguided and self-defeating strategy, he said. We didn't understand the true nature of his opponents, especially the Muslim Brotherhood. Democracies develop differently, he added, and at different speeds. "His" people were not yet ready.

Mubarak was impressively sharp at eighty years of age, but also decidedly paternalistic, not just toward his citizens, but to me. Occasionally, he would lean forward, put his hand on my arm, confide to me that he knew that we were both military officers (both air force, in fact), absolve me of personal blame, and then resume his tirade. I believe that he referred to Secretary of State Condoleezza Rice as "that woman."

Mubarak had been governing Egypt since 1981 under an emergency law that expanded police powers and limited constitutional rights, and it was clear that he had no intention of stopping. Omar was the primary agent for implementing that, but he was mostly quiet throughout this session. This was the president's show. Omar's job had been to deliver the audience.

A bare thirty months later, events were to prove that neither Mubarak nor Suleiman had as good a handle on the situation in Egypt as they thought. No telling if a little more democracy delivered a little earlier would have spared Egypt its serial revolutions, but it probably wouldn't have hurt.

I never saw Omar again personally, but I did catch him on national television during his brief stint as Mubarak's vice president, a desperate move made at the height of the Tahrir Square demonstrations. Omar's usual confidence was visibly shaken in these appearances, and he slipped from public life after a short, ill-advised flirtation with running for the presidency. He died, suddenly, in the summer of 2012 while at a US hospital in Cleveland.

We rarely visited Egypt, or anywhere else in the Middle East, without stopping in Saudi Arabia. When we did, King Abdullah usually made time for us. He had a purpose. Abdullah was passionate about Iran, urging us to "cut off the head of the snake" and warning us to be careful not to "lose our aura" in the region.

Steve Kappes and I once visited the king at his farm (some farm—gardens, fountains, etc.) in Morocco. I extended an overseas trip and flew there from Brazil; Steve came directly from Washington. The Moroccan service kindly scurried to accommodate us, and we drove from Rabat to Casablanca to await our late-night (actually early morning) appointment with Abdullah. The monarch, moving slowly with cane in hand, quite unexpectedly met us at the entryway to his estate house. We had a lot of time for the king. He obviously had time for us.

Steve and I had left a few members of our staff on the corniche in Casablanca as we departed for the royal farm. They filled the time shopping the kiosks and souvenir stands. When they discovered that they were in the section of the souk hawking bin Laden dolls and al-Qaeda T-shirts, they decided that they had shopped enough.

Adel al-Jubeir, the savvy Saudi ambassador in Washington, would usually translate for the king. Adel knew America and CIA well; he was a graduate of the University of North Texas and Georgetown, and since his home was just down Chain Bridge Road from Langley, he was always a welcome guest at CIA for tea and conversation. In one such session he related how Abdullah had deep concerns about America's troubled Iraq policy. In what was clearly a bow to American pragmatism, Adel told us that he had responded, "Your Majesty, these are Americans. If it's not working, they'll change it."

During one trip to Jeddah, we dropped in on one of Adel's predecessors, Prince Bandar bin Sultan, who had served over twenty years as the kingdom's emissary in Washington. Bandar was then secretary general of Saudi Arabia's recently created National Security Council; he apparently wanted to sustain his American connections, and we were more than happy to meet with the garrulous, USAF-trained ex–fighter pilot.

It was a delightful and informative evening (once again, it was actually early morning), capped off by Bandar gifting me with a large, framed photo of President Roosevelt meeting King Abdul Aziz bin Saud, the founder of the kingdom, on the cruiser *Quincy* in Great Bitter Lake along the Suez Canal in February 1945. Roosevelt was returning from Yalta and was obviously near death (he died two months later), but the scene commemorated the unspoken contract between the two men and the two countries: oil for security, security for oil. Bandar was messaging.

I hung the photo in my Langley office, not least because the uniformed translator kneeling between the two leaders was Colonel Bill Eddy, a member of OSS, CIA's organizational ancestor.

My actual counterpart in Saudi Arabia was Prince Muqrin, the youngest surviving son of Abdul Aziz. Muqrin was head of the General Intelligence Presidency, the external intelligence service. He had been an air force pilot, schooled in Great Britain with some later military education in the United States. He was very comfortable in English and a good friend, but the GIP was short on resources.

Muqrin did manage to convene a meeting of intelligence chiefs from regional Sunni states to talk about Iraq. I hesitated: it would be a tough, short trip; the session would comprise prepared formal statements rather than dialogue; and no one was going to share any real secrets. But I really had to attend. Our final work product was an undramatic description of the situation in Iraq and some modest statements of support for the US and coalition effort there. Before we adjourned, I suggested that maybe next time we could invite the Iraqis. The intel chief in Baghdad *was* a Sunni, after all.

Prince Mohammed bin Naif (MBN, as we referred to him) was head of the all-powerful Mabahith, the kingdom's internal intelligence and investigative service and our primary point of contact in Saudi Arabia. Mohammed had been educated in Oregon with additional professional classes with the FBI and Scotland Yard. He was an incredibly tough counterterrorism professional; he ruthlessly dismantled al-Qaeda in the kingdom following AQ's attacks on Western housing compounds in 2003. But he also established the best jihadi rehabilitation program in the world, relying on faith and family to recapture souls. And when Mohammed briefed me on the program at his seaside villa near Jeddah, he insisted that my wife—who has a master's degree in counseling—accompany me.

MBN will likely be the next king of Saudi Arabia. He is now crown prince behind his uncle, eighty-year-old King Salman.

Another near-mandatory stop in the region was Amman. Actually, it was always a welcome stop: Arab hospitality, great food, and a society broad-minded enough that you could order a glass of good wine at the hotel without guilt.

Abdullah II of Jordan was as approachable as his Saudi counterpart, Abdullah bin Abdul Aziz, was regal. At a small informal lunch at the royal residence in Amman, we had to dodge the tricycles and other toys spilling out of the children's playroom. When the king is in the United States, he motorcycles our back roads in the company of a close American friend, a former CIA senior.

Deep Jordanian-American security cooperation flowed from 1951, when Abdullah's father, Hussein (then fifteen), witnessed the assassination of Abdullah I, Hussein's grandfather, at the hand of a Palestinian terrorist as the royal pair was leaving the Al-Aqsa Mosque in Jerusalem. Within the year Hussein succeeded his mentally ill father to the throne, and Jordan's intelligence service, the General Intelligence Directorate (GID), was established—the latter with significant American help. Keeping the moderate Hashemite dynasty safely on the throne was in the interest of both countries.

Cooperation continues to this day. During one of my visits to Amman I accompanied the king for the formal opening of GID's counterterrorism center, a facility built with American advice and assistance and within which American work spaces had been provided. After I had left government, the tragedy at Khost in December 2009, which cost the lives of seven CIA officers and contractors, also took the life of a GID case officer (a royal, in fact, cousin to the king) with whom the agency had been working.

I never got the sense that relations between Abdullah and the Bush administration were particularly close. Given its history with Jordan, the agency was happy to step in. Like his Saudi counterpart, Abdullah spent a lot of time talking to us about the dangers posed by Iran, both in Iraq and throughout the region. He was particularly forceful about the underlying pathology and ultimate folly of trying to win Sunni hearts and minds with an Iraqi army dominated by Iran and Iranian-backed militias and steeled with augmentees from the Quds Force and the Iranian Revolutionary Guard.

These weren't just empty complaints; Abdullah paid his dues. At our strong urging and against the advice of some of his leadership, the king in August 2008 became the first Sunni head of state to visit Baghdad. He also welcomed Iraqi prime minister Maliki to Amman that same year. Operationally, GID was the only Sunni intelligence service that pulled its weight in Iraq. With Sunni tribes straddling the border, it was an invaluable partner.

Some of this was self-interest. Iraqi refugees were a threat to stability in Jordan. The poor who were displaced from Iraq were a social burden and a potential security threat; the rich who had fled were driving housing prices in Amman out of the reach of Jordanians. Both groups were problems.

Abdullah also wanted to talk about the Palestinians, who now comprised about half of his population. Failure of the Middle East peace process, he said, made everything—like Iran and terrorism—harder. He argued that there was a destructive downward cycle whenever we missed an opportunity: the Palestinian Authority's credibility was weakened; its status as a viable negotiating partner was undercut; violence then spiked as confidence in the PA waned; Israel then felt justified in taking harsher measures (security, settlements, etc.); and the two sides were then further apart than ever.

Relations between Jordan and Israel weren't so bad, though, that GID couldn't hand me off to Mossad at the famous Allenby Bridge over the Jordan River during one of my trips. (I opted for that in lieu of the sixty-six-mile C-17 ride from Amman to Tel Aviv.)

There were other services who turned to us for help. In July 2007, twenty-three very young, very sincere, and very foolish Korean Christian missionaries were kidnapped in Afghanistan. Korea is the most Christian country in Asia, exceptionally devout, and these young Presbyterians had allowed their zeal to outstrip their judgment.

The head of the Korean service was charged with getting them freed, so he flew immediately—*not to Kabul, but to CIA headquarters*—to ask for our assistance. He needed help on the ground in Afghanistan and knew where to find it. I think I surprised him when I offered him a full-time US officer to accompany him. The young man had deep Afghan experience, but the real trump was played when the chief asked through his interpreter if our officer knew any Korean. Without waiting for the translation, the Korean American case officer responded in the affirmative and in Korean, bringing the first smile of the day to the chief's face.

Sometimes liaison was a pure joy. In July 2008 the Colombian armed forces staged a dramatic rescue of fifteen hostages, including three American contractors who had been held since their observation plane went down five years earlier.

I had visited Bogotá on one of my liaison trips. A long, hard war against the FARC, an insurgency fueled by drug trafficking, was turning the government's way. Colombia's tough president, Alvaro Uribe, had made a big difference since assuming office in 2002, but this was also the product of constant, long-term, unheralded, hard-slogging intelligence work. The kind of stuff that never made the papers or evening news.

When I read of the Colombians' proposed rescue plan, I thought I was reviewing a grade-B movie script. Two helicopters masquerading as NGO aircraft. A fictitious transfer of the prisoners to senior FARC leadership. Colombian military playing the role of FARC guards. I just shook my head. "Oh, yeah. This'll work. Sure."

But it did! The three rescued Americans, whose location was our highest intelligence priority in Colombia for years, were so taken in that one of them resisted the transfer and refused to go. Only after one of the "guards" leaned into him and whispered into his ear, "Trust me, trust me," did he agree to cooperate.

The rescued Americans visited the agency shortly after their release. Even more touching was the insistence of the Colombian rescue team that they visit Langley as well. I sat with them in my conference room as they informally reviewed the whole operation for me. We took a lot of photos, and they gave me some memorabilia that I still have in my home office. The gratitude ran strong both ways.

One of our most unusual (and productive) liaison relationships wasn't with a foreign entity at all—it was with the New York City police department. These ties later became controversial, but all along we viewed New York as a special case, an international as well as an American metropolis. Over a third of the city's residents were born abroad. And New York was certainly at the top of al-Qaeda's target list. Mayor Bloomberg and his tough police commissioner, Ray Kelly, seemed to agree with us.

Cooperation began informally with a CIA counterterrorism analyst in the city passing threat data to the NYPD. It really took off when Kelly hired Dave Cohen, former head of CIA operations and deputy head of analysis who had also worked in New York, to set up his intelligence division. Cohen built a familiar structure: a directorate for operations (collection) and a directorate for analysis.

Domestic intelligence collection has always been countercultural in America. CIA doesn't do it; it's beyond the agency's charter. Law enforcement is reluctant to do anything without a criminal predicate. No crime, no investigation. Without new attorney general guidelines (which were not forthcoming until December 2008), the FBI would be forever constrained. Besides, NYPD was better qualified for this. They knew their domain cold; they could map threats by zip code.

We decided to embed an analyst within Cohen's organization. Just like with our other partners, he could help put locally derived information into a global context. He could also engage with the NYPD on the daily threat matrix, which was an almost no-threshold catalogue of dangers. Together with NYPD he studied the local threats to New York and rated them. After all, false positives to industries like fiscal services would lead to the wasteful expenditure of millions of dollars. The threat had to be real.

A lot of this was more or less in place before I arrived, and I saw no reason to change it. I agreed to formal headquarters approval of the ad hoc arrangements in 2007. The bureau wasn't happy, and I'm sure that we were squeezing more than a paragraph or two of our memorandum of understanding (MOU) with them, but as one of my seniors put it, "This is the right thing to do and, besides, there is no such thing as MOU jail."

We actually gave NYPD a training slot in our field tradecraft course at the Farm. The idea was to help them develop the tools they needed (since they did have liaison relationships overseas), give them some situational awareness for the counterterrorism business, and sensitize them to counterintelligence threats.

When I was in New York I always tried to drop in on Commissioner Kelly. We struck up a friendship on my first visit as he was proudly showing me the massive desk of one of his predecessors, Theodore Roosevelt. Kelly and I were of like mind on many issues (like the *New York Times*). To this day I wear NYPD cuff links on occasion; I trust he wears the CIA links that I gave him.

In 2012 two industrious AP reporters won the Pulitzer Prize for Investigative Reporting for a series of stories on the NYPD's overall counter-terrorism effort and CIA's role in it. The stories intentionally raised all sorts of civil liberties concerns, but although the agency admitted that its effort could have benefited from closer supervision, CIA seemed to reflect the national and city consensus when it responded, "The CIA stepped up cooperation with law enforcement on counterterrorism after 9/11. It's hard to imagine that anyone is suggesting this was inappropriate or unexpected."

And we never suggested that this was a generalized model. New York is unique—unique in demographics, unique in size, unique in threat. The NYPD had its main job, fighting crime, under control, and its sheer size (35,000 uniformed officers, about three times the size of the next largest force, Chicago) gave it sufficient scale. NYPD also had strong, veteran leadership in Kelly and unflinching political support from Mayor Bloomberg.

By Dave Cohen's count, New York City was the target of seventeen terrorist plots between 2002 and the 2011–2013 kerfuffle generated by the AP reporting. Al-Qaeda was 0 for 17. A lot of things contributed to that. One of them was this program. All in all, NYPD was one of the best liaison relationships we had.

It's probably not surprising that China wasn't in the same league when it came to intelligence relationships, though it was important enough that I traveled there to meet with a counterpart. In this case it was the head of what we called 3-PLA, the chief of the Third Department of the Chinese general staff, the office responsible for signals intelligence. My host could not have been more gracious, the banquets were spectacular, and we really did have items of common concern—Russian intentions and technical developments, for example.

We also met some political figures in the Great Hall of the People adjacent to the infamous Tiananmen Square. The Great Hall is divided into rooms named after Chinese provinces. Pointedly, we met in the Taiwan room and in the Tibet room, provinces over which Chinese sovereignty is contested. The Chinese never miss an opportunity to make a point.

Although my counterpart was gracious, I couldn't say the same thing about our security guards. In one instance a balky Chinese driver would not get out of the way of our small convoy as we were speeding toward a meeting. When we finally passed him, I could see in the mirror that police in one of the trail vehicles had stopped, pulled him over, and were starting to beat him as they dragged him from the car. During a later tour of the Forbidden City, a phalanx of large, dark-suited escorts shoved Chinese tourists out of the way to clear a path for us. We feigned fatigue and asked to leave as quickly as possible.

It caused me to wonder how the Chinese thought we would react to all that. Did they know so little about us that they thought we wouldn't mind? Or maybe they did know us, and didn't care. Or maybe they were trying to send another message. If they were, I didn't get it.

With all this liaison activity, it's surprising that neither Steve nor I went to Moscow during our time together. Old habits die hard, I guess. We had little trust in the Russians and in the one area where we should have had common interests: terrorism. Moscow often conflated violent extremism with legitimate dissent.

The Russian resident, the senior intelligence officer at their Washington embassy, came to the agency once for lunch and discussions. It was pleasant enough, but my chief of staff had the security folks sweep the dining room and my office for bugs after the Russian left.

Our bad. Russia stormed back onto the international scene with a vengeance under Putin. Meeting with them would not have stopped any of that, but it would have given us useful insight into how the Russian Federation was thinking and created equally useful contacts in the Russian services, which we knew were feeding Putin's paranoia about America's and the West's intentions. Liaison sometimes means more than just working an intelligence exchange.

George Tenet had proved that. He had been the go-to guy in a complex relationship with the Palestinians and Yasser Arafat. My deputy, Steve Kappes, when he was director of operations, had negotiated a big chunk of Libya's WMD disarmament with Moussa Koussa, the head of Gaddafi's service.

I later got my chance with the Pakistanis (chapter 18).

REVOLUTION IN EGYPT. Hostages along the Andean Ridge and in the Hindu Kush. Russian armor in the Caucasus. The United States has the only intelligence service in the world that is, and is expected to be, global in its field of view. CIA has always tried to live up to that role, but after 9/11 it was a particularly difficult task. As I later told Leon Panetta, we were also America's combatant command when it came to al-Qaeda.

Years after I left government, I reviewed my Thursday morning briefing scripts for the president and was struck by how much they focused on terrorism, and within terrorism how much they were about South Asia—Pakistan and Afghanistan. And during the last six months of the administration, I was struck that we covered the hunt for HVT-1 (High-Value-Target-1, i.e., bin Laden) and HVT-2 (Zawahiri) in practically every session. We were certainly focused.*

The CT obsession was on my mind when Dave Petraeus came to visit us at our home as he was preparing for his CIA confirmation hearing in 2011. He and his wife, Holly, peppered Jeanine and me with a variety of questions about life at the agency over coffee cake and juice in our kitchen.

As Dave and Holly were leaving, I pulled him aside for one last observation.

"Dave," I said, "CIA has never looked more like OSS than it does right now." The reference was to the Office of Strategic Services, the World War II direct action unit under William "Wild Bill" Donovan.

"But it's not OSS," I continued. "It's the nation's global espionage

---

* Focus pays off. We briefed President Bush in December 2008 about closing in on Abu Ahmed al-Kuwaiti, bin Laden's courier and the eventual key to finding him at Abbottabad.

service. And you're going to have to work every day—like I had to and I'm sure Leon had to—to impose that reality on yourself and on the agency."

And make sure you do it without making the country any less safe against terrorism, I silently thought. Tough order.

EIGHTEEN

"THERE WILL BE NO EXPLAINING OUR INACTION"

WASHINGTON, DC, 2002–2009 AND BEYOND

A*re you sure sure they're there?"* the one who will make the decision asks.

"Yes, sir."

"And you're sure it's them?"

"We've got good HUMINT. We've been tracking with streaming video. SIGINT's checking in now and confirming it's them. They're there."

"How long have you had capture of the target and who else is around?"

"A couple of hours. The family is in the main building. The guys we want are in the big guesthouse here."

"They're not very far apart."

"No, sir. But far enough. And there's another outbuilding here. Small. In the past we've seen AQ people use it when they stop here. We're here a lot. So are they. It's a really dirty compound."

"Anyone in that little building now?"

"Don't know. Probably not. We haven't seen anyone since the Pred got capture of the target."

"What's the PK [probability of kill] *on the big guesthouse look like with a GBU* [that would be a GBU-12, a laser-guided five-hundred-pound bomb]*?"*

"These guys are sure dead. We think the family's OK."

"You think they're OK?"

"They should be. We've done the bug splat, but you can never be sure. Structural weakness. They walk out of the house or something."

"What's it look like with a couple of Hellfires [a much smaller weapon with a twenty-pound warhead]*?"*

"We'd bring them in this way. All the energy away from the family quarters. The family quarters are fine. If we hit the right room in the guesthouse, we'll get all the bad guys. But these internal walls can be thick. If we don't hit the right room or if one of them is up taking a piss . . ."

There's a long pause in the room.

Finally, the one responsible for the decision speaks. *"Use the Hellfires the way you said."*

An officer leaves the room en route to the ops center with the message.

There is another long pause.

"Tell me again about these guys."

"Sir, big AQ operators [he recounts names and history]. *We've been trying to track them forever. They're really careful. They've been hard to find. They're involved in homeland plotting. They're the first team. They sure as hell have a track record."*

There is another pause. A long one.

"Use the GBU."

Another, more senior operator jumps from the table and sprints after the first one.

"And that small building they sometimes use as a dorm . . ."

"Yes, sir."

"After the GBU hits, if military-age males come out . . ."

"Yes, sir?"

"Kill them."

Less than an hour later the decision maker is briefed once again.

"Sir, the two targets are dead. There was no damage to the family quar-

ters, but they've all left the compound. Pretty upset. They left quick. No effort to see if there were any survivors in the guesthouse. No one came out of the small building. We didn't hit it."

"*Good.*"

Targeted killing has become a core part of the American way of war, and to do that legally and effectively requires the kind of exquisite intelligence reflected here. It also requires some very difficult operational and political decisions.

CIA plays a part in that, and the agency has acknowledged that it has an intelligence interest and an operational role in the US government's use of drones. Many details on the extent of that interest and that role remain classified, of course, but I can say that during my time at CIA I was exposed to various aspects of this effort and that I witnessed the kind of decision making described here. Although I won't discuss details, I can also say that—given my nearly forty years as an air force officer and other senior positions I held in the intelligence community—I was in a unique position to understand, appreciate, and advocate for this effort. I am as much an airman as an intelligence officer, after all.

WITHIN TWO WEEKS of arriving at Langley I got a handwritten note from Stan McChrystal, commander of JSOC, the Joint Special Operations Command. CIA and American special operations claim a common bloodline back to World War II's Office of Strategic Services and its founder, Wild Bill Donovan. A statue of Donovan stares down at the entrance to CIA's Original Headquarters Building.*

---

* As I was about to leave CIA, my British counterpart John Scarlett presented me with a framed replica of the cable that the wartime MI6 station chief in Washington had sent to London introducing Donovan to his headquarters. "*Impossible to over emphasize importance of DONOVAN's visit. He has (been) controlling influence over KNOX, strong influence over STIMSON, friendly advisory influence HULL and President. A Catholic, Irish American descent, Republican holding confidence of Democrats, with an exceptional war record, places him in unique position to advance our aims here.*" Our British allies have an appreciation for history (and bloodlines).

Coalition forces had just killed Abu Musab al-Zarqawi, the ruthless head of al-Qaeda in Iraq. McChrystal understood better than most the importance of intelligence in the hunt for AMZ. His note was simple. "Mike, Thanks to all of your people. Stan." "Taking terrorists off the battlefield" was the euphemism the United States used when it killed or captured an al-Qaeda member. Either technique worked, but we obviously preferred capture so we could mine the potential intelligence value of a detainee. That was getting increasingly difficult, though, even in Iraq and Afghanistan, where the American military controlled the environment, and beyond those locations it was getting downright rare.

We were ready to recommend more frequent direct action. We knew that the threat had increased to intolerable levels, both to US forces in South Asia and to the homeland. We were watching terrorist trainees leap off motorbikes, steady themselves, and then begin firing against simulated targets.

We were also confident that the quality of intelligence was good enough to sustain a campaign of very precise attacks. We weren't claiming perfection. In late 2006 intelligence had enabled a strike on a suspected terrorist, a one-legged chieftain in the Haqqani network. It turned out that the man killed was affiliated with Haqqani, but he wasn't the senior leader we believed he was. With all the land mines over the past decades, there were a lot of one-legged terrorists in South Asia.

I demanded a full explanation for the misidentification. There was no dodging or excuses. People were thoroughly, maybe even excessively, contrite. He was a bad man, but he wasn't the target.

I reflected a short time, then told them to study what went wrong and make corrections, but to keep their focus looking through the windshield. "I'll take care of the rearview mirror." Later that day I sent word that "if you find another target to nominate this afternoon, I'm still interested." It was a vote of confidence. I later learned that it was a very big deal for the targeting crew.

I knew we could do this. By early 2008 I was convinced that the IC could routinely provide exquisite intelligence to enable precision targeting. Our task was to convince the rest of the government that we could and that they should take advantage of it.

We had one other thing going for us that we knew would not last forever. As director of CIA, I got to talk to *this* president every week without any filters. Who knew what it would be like in a year?

I briefed President Bush every Thursday morning on sensitive collection and covert action, and I began to use these sessions to point out the growing al-Qaeda footprint and brazenness in Pakistan's so-called Federally Administered Tribal Areas, or FATA. My chief analyst on this was a lanky Notre Dame graduate who lived and breathed this work. He educated me almost daily, and I tried to pass this on to the president. The main point was that as bad as this might be for Afghanistan and our forces there, this was fundamentally becoming a threat to the *homeland*.

I never uttered the following sentence to the president, the vice president, or to Steve Hadley through the first half of 2008, but if we had boiled down all of our briefings to just a few words, the essence would have been: *"Knowing what we know now, there will be no explaining our inaction after the next attack."*

I pretty much hit the same theme in the summer of 2008 when I briefed the threat, the intelligence, and potential responses to a large gathering of agency, State, and DOD officials in Dubai. In the federal bureaucracy, that's called "socializing an idea." They seemed to get it.

The US government slowly started to put its toe in the water against al-Qaeda in the Afghanistan-Pakistan border region. A charismatic al-Qaeda operations chief was killed early in 2008. The strike was clean and the target so important that even regional reaction was muted.

Later in the year another AQ senior, active in planning attacks in the West, was killed along with several lieutenants in a similar strike with similar precision and with a similarly restrained response.

In between, a terrorist-affiliated compound was hit as a group gathered. Same result. Same response.

In midsummer, Hellfire missiles ripped through the body of yet another senior AQ operative (who had been active in their WMD program and who had a $5 million price on his head in the US Rewards for Justice program) and a group of his assistants as they were sleeping in a courtyard to beat the oppressive summer heat.

The United States had finally begun a sustained and robust campaign of targeted killings in South Asia from unmanned aerial vehicles.

Progress had been good, but we knew that we had to proceed carefully. Steve Hadley reminded everyone that mistakes, especially early mistakes, would be devastating. He added that all of this had to be at a digestible pace for domestic and especially for foreign audiences.

And it became clear very quickly that some things would *not* be digestible. In early September, American forces made a shallow penetration into Waziristan in pursuit of militants. Although the raid was successful, it had not gone cleanly, and there were claims of civilian casualties. Islamabad responded very forcefully, lodging a formal protest, with Parliament passing a resolution condemning the action, while Ambassador Patterson was called to the Foreign Ministry for a dressing-down. It was reported that the usually dispassionate director general of military operations, Ahmed Shuja Pasha,* completely "lost it" when discussing the raid. The Pakistanis also closed the crucial Torkham highway for a day, an unsubtle reminder that the United States and NATO depended on Pakistani forbearance to use this critical supply route to Afghanistan.

In a perverse (but welcome) way, the raid may have made targeted UAV strikes along the border more acceptable from the Pakistani point of view. Pakistani tolerance also seemed to increase later in September when a suicide truck bomber killed over fifty people in an attack on the Marriott hotel in Islamabad. Some there even went so far as to say that the war on terrorism now had to be Pakistan's war too.

Based on publicly available sources, there were nearly three dozen attacks like the one on the senior WMD operative in the last seven months of the Bush administration, almost three times the total of the previous

---

* Later the head of ISI, the Pakistani intelligence service.

four years combined. Those same sources report that eighteen named senior and mid-level Taliban and al-Qaeda leaders were killed.

The intelligence on which these strikes were conducted was exquisite, based on human intelligence, technical collection, and the near-continuous unblinking stare of the Predator itself. The strikes were particularly telling on al-Qaeda's operational leaders, who had to move and communicate. They couldn't afford to hunker down like bin Laden and Zawahiri, whose main contribution to the movement was pretty much just staying alive.

Not that we weren't interested in the top leaders. We worked hard to locate them; I still remember the briefing I got in late 2007 or early 2008 from our bin Laden cell saying they had a promising lead on a courier they believed might lead them to bin Laden. We didn't lack for executive emphasis either, as President Bush began most of my Thursday morning briefings for the last six months of his administration with the simple question "Well?" followed by reminding me how many days he had left in office.

My only defense was to show him the chart that we had drawn up of the important operational leaders we were chasing and point out the increasing number of *X*s drawn over their faces.

There were other attacks, dubbed "signature strikes" by the press, that were designed to disrupt known al-Qaeda locations and activities even when specific identities were unknown. Some have criticized these as indiscriminate. They were not.

In fact, intelligence for signature strikes was quite robust, since it *always* had multiple threads and deep history. How else to make a judgment about this compound, at this time, with these visible clues? The data was near encyclopedic.

Many such strikes actually killed high-value targets whose presence may have been suspected but was not certain. And we made no excuses about killing lower-ranking terrorists. The United States viewed these attacks as legitimate acts of war against an opposing armed enemy force, and in warfare it is regrettably necessary to kill foot soldiers too. The signature strikes had the effect of shrinking the enemy's bench and the AQ leadership's sense of safe haven. They also had the indirect effect of protecting intelligence sources and methods, since, from the ground, the strikes may have looked more random than they actually were.

It wasn't long before intelligence reporting began to confirm our success. There was genuine mental anguish in the vulnerable al-Qaeda leadership. The attacks were seen as brutal and unrelenting and there was no obvious solution to them. There was literally no place to hide.

Years later, in 2015, an American court case against an al-Qaeda member prompted the government to release eight documents from the trove of bin Laden letters captured in Abbottabad in 2011. Bin Laden's correspondence with his chief lieutenants in 2010 is remarkable in its candor and in its confirmation that we got the intelligence right both before (the targeting) and after (the intended effects) the strikes began.

The letters also confirm that we got the threat to the West and to the homeland right. They are filled with references to foreigners supporting al-Qaeda or undergoing training and preparation. The list includes citizens or residents of Uzbekistan, Turkey, Azerbaijan, Tajikistan, Germany, Bulgaria, Britain, Australia, Canada, the Maldives, Kurdistan, Libya, Syria, Lebanon, Algeria, Iran, and the United States.

The centrality of America as a target is never forgotten. In one correspondence bin Laden emphasizes that "operations inside America are some of the most important work of the Organization, as long as they are possible, because they affect the security and economy of the American people as a whole."

Bin Laden recommends that a German brother give "an idea about how work is done inside America." Then he identifies an American (Azzam al-Amriki) "who can follow up on research posted on the Internet by Western centers, especially the American ones. He could also translate whatever is useful to the brothers in this field, and write his opinions about work inside America." Bin Laden even suggests he conduct English-language classes for some.

The letters reveal the incredible stress being felt within the organization as a result of the strikes. They read like a running eulogy of senior AQ figures with whom bin Laden was familiar. "I convey my condolences regarding our great brother Sheikh Said . . . [who] died as a martyr during a spy plane attack. . . . We think we must announce his death because he is a senior person who had addressed the Ummah [the community of believers] and the Ummah knows him."

"The strikes by the spy planes are still going on. . . . Our brother Al-sa'di [Ihsanullah] . . . was the latest to become a martyr. He was killed about a week ago, also by air raids. . . . The mid-level commands and staff members are hurt by the killings. Compensating for the loss is going slowly."

"I am informing you about the death of brother Hamzah Al-Jawfi. . . . It came at the hands of spy planes in southern Waziristan; others were killed with him but we are not sure who yet."

"The issue got more complicated after the killing of Muhammad Khan and Brother Mu'awiyah Al-Balushi. . . . They went to find out about places . . . and upon their return they were also martyred in an air strike."

The signature strikes were also taking a toll, physically and psychologically. A bin Laden lieutenant complained after "the killing of twenty brothers in one place on the day of Eid" that they had "gathered for the holidays, despite our orders and our emphasizing to avoid gathering in one place . . . but sometimes they discuss matters and take their own decisions."

Al-Qaeda acquired a healthy respect for American intelligence. "As we see it, based on our analysis, they are constantly monitoring several potential or confirmed targets. But they only hit them if they discover a valuable human target inside, or a gathering, or during difficult times (like revenge attacks for example)." The last wasn't true, but it didn't hurt that they thought so.

The seeming ubiquity of reconnaissance and the suddenness of strikes were wearing them down. "As you know," went a report to bin Laden, "everybody is threatened—as long as he moves—by a missile." And, "The strikes by the spy planes are still going on. . . . The planes are still circling our skies nearly every day."

Folks in the field entreated bin Laden: "We would like your guidance. Especially on this idea: reduce the work; meaning stopping many of the operations so we can move around less, and be less exposed to strikes."

A suggestion was raised. "There is an idea preferred by some brothers to avoid attrition (the loss of staff, leaders, and the organization's old elites). The idea is that some brothers will travel to some 'safe' areas with their families, just for protection. They would only stay for a time, until the crisis is over, maybe one or two years." The author offers some ideas for safe havens: Sind, Baluchistan, Iran.

Two months later bin Laden agrees they should be taking refuge in safer areas and "calming down and minimizing movement."

All of this correspondence released from the Abbottabad haul was from 2010, but it is consistent with the intelligence picture we were building as 2008 wore on. The strikes were having the impact we desired and the impact we expected. The al-Qaeda main body along the Afghanistan-Pakistan border was spending a lot more time worrying about its own survival than it was planning how to threaten ours.

Still, there was nervousness in our government that this campaign would shred an already tattered relationship with Islamabad. Others suggested that this could create chaos on the ground. I once coldly responded, "Maybe, but chaos is not a safe haven. Remember, this is about threats to the homeland."

But chaos wasn't our objective. Al-Qaeda was. Collateral damage was a continuing concern, and the United States worked hard to avoid it.

In that strike against the WMD operative noted earlier, his grandson was sleeping on a cot near him in the compound. The Hellfire missiles were carefully directed so that their energy and fragments splayed away from him and toward his grandfather. They did. But not enough.

His grandfather was a very dangerous terrorist. He had a garage full of chemicals and an intent to use them. He was hard to locate and people were risking their lives to find him. The United States took the shot. We sincerely regretted the child's death.

We always tried to get better. Carefully reviewing the video after one very successful strike, one could in retrospect discern—as a GBU was in the air hurtling toward an arms cache—an obviously frightened woman, responding to an earlier weapon that had just detonated, bolting with some young children into the path of the incoming bomb from a place of relative safety. That resulted in our putting more eyes on targets *as they were being struck* to avoid such things.

Despite such incidents, I think it a fair assessment that the targeted killing program has been the most precise application of firepower in the history of armed conflict.

The accuracy and effectiveness of this US government campaign was one of the things that I was asked about by President-elect Obama in December 2008. He was very attentive. Greg Craig, the president's incoming counsel, later told me that my views had convinced the president-elect of the program's utility. I'm not sure how much convincing he needed, but once in office President Obama doubled down on targeted killings, to great effect, as the Abbottabad documents attest.

Al-Qaeda prime, that original organization in Afghanistan and Pakistan, was made a shell of its former self and that was well before the bin Laden kill. All the whooping and hollering on Pennsylvania Avenue and in Lafayette Square the night of bin Laden's demise probably represented a sense of closure for much of the public (and for intelligence professionals, too, based on the phone calls I got that night). But the United States had been killing al-Qaeda operations chiefs routinely and serially for three years by then.

The longer they have gone on, though, the more controversial drone strikes have become. Part of that has been the inevitable claims (exaggerated, but not wholly inaccurate) of collateral damage. Part of that has been the traumatizing effect of these killings on local populations (true enough, even in the face of intelligence and other reporting that suggests most Pashtuns rarely shed tears for the deaths of bullying Arabs and

Uzbeks). Part of that was also the product of a troubling American habit, confined largely to political elites, of complaining that intelligence agencies have not done enough when they feel in danger and then complaining that they have done too much when they are feeling safe again.

In truth, though, targeted killings have always had multiple effects, and some of those were bad—effects like straining relationships with allies (especially Europeans who legally did not support this) or seeming to confirm al-Qaeda recruiting narratives about the perfidy of the Crusaders. Then there was indirectly incentivizing al-Qaeda to put more emphasis on the franchises away from the FATA. Indeed, the very success of targeted killing in South Asia accelerated al-Qaeda's efforts to metastasize into its now more dispersed, albeit less capable, affiliates.

But in 2008 (and apparently continuing into 2009 and 2010) these effects were all trumped by the first order effect of killing those who were already able and willing to do us harm. And as far as the strikes helping al-Qaeda to recruit, nothing would have prompted more flocking to the black banners than a spectacular AQ success.

I usually thought of this in terms of the deep fight and the close fight. The close fight in this war meant dealing with those already committed to killing us. For handling them, targeted killing was ideal. The deep fight, on the other hand, was about the production rate of those who would intend us harm in one, three, five, or ten years. That was a tougher fight, largely ideological, and how we conducted the close fight could affect the deep fight, especially if it accelerated recruitment or deepened sympathy.

Even as we waged the close battle, we always had the deep fight in mind. In those three weeks when I was Barack Obama's CIA chief, I discussed a successful strike on al-Qaeda on the margins of a White House Situation Room meeting. After the session Rahm Emanuel, the blunt new chief of staff, surprisingly congratulated me on CIA's role in the kill. I thanked him, but felt compelled to add, "Rahm, remember. That was a CT success. Unless we change conditions on the ground, we're going to get to kill people forever."

Concerns over the "foreverness" aspect of this eventually began to show up in presidential comments, culminating in a major presidential speech in May 2013. It seems that President Obama had been wanting to make this speech for some time. Even out of government, I was getting frequent cues of an imminent address on the CT way ahead. One had apparently been penciled in for a date right before the Boston Marathon bombing but had been cancelled, no doubt much to the later relief of the president's communications team.

With Boston and the Tsarnaevs bundled up, the president finally went onstage at National Defense University to reflect and direct. It was a remarkable speech, long and deeply personal, more Hamlet than Patton (or even Marshall), but truly reflective of a personal ambivalence over the dilemmas we face.

It was about ending what one of the president's top advisors called the "forever war." The president himself said, "[T]his war, like all wars, must end. That's what history advises. That's what our democracy demands."

A president who at that point had conducted 85 percent of all secret drone strikes in human history called for limits, transparency, oversight, and the near elimination of collateral damage from such strikes. A president who had been conducting global war for more than four years then called on Congress to refine and eventually eliminate his authority to conduct that war by withdrawing and then reissuing a much more confining Authorization for the Use of Military Force.

The analytic premise of the speech was, of course, flawed. Although it correctly assessed that core al-Qaeda was "a shell of its former self," it badly downplayed emerging threats: "In the years to come, not every collection of thugs that labels themselves al-Qaeda will pose a credible threat to the United States." That was a high-end version of his later description of the Islamic State of Iraq and Syria as the JV [junior varsity] team. That was all terribly wrong, but that realization would only become (painfully) clear later.

What seemed obvious at the time, though, was that the president was uncomfortable with his own actions. A not unfair summary of the one-hour talk might have been, "Even if you think I've acted a lot like the other guy, surely you can see that I'm troubled by it and I intend to stop."

Inconsistencies between campaign rhetoric and executive action are easily understood, since national security looks a lot different from the Oval Office than it does from a hotel room in Iowa. But this was different. This seemed to be about inconsistency between the president's deeds and his own deepest beliefs.

Of course, the emergence of ISIS, the meltdowns in Yemen, the disintegration of Iraq and Syria and Libya, and the growth of al-Qaeda wannabes have put most of these discussions on hold. No one is currently enthused at the prospect of the United States voluntarily staying its hand.

But these questions will eventually resurface. At some point the debate on targeted killings will be rejoined.

In my view, the United States will need to keep this capacity and be willing to use it. Islamist terrorism thrives in places—Pakistan, Somalia, Yemen, Syria, Libya, Mali, the list goes on—where governments cannot or will not act. In some of these instances, the United States must.

And unmanned aerial vehicles with precision weapons and exquisite intelligence offer a proportional and discriminating response when one is judged necessary.

What we need here is a dial, not a switch.

PAKISTAN WAS THE ONE AREA where all the dilemmas of the war on terror seemed to play out in their most extreme form.

CIA had actually had good success working with Pakistani ISI sweeping up al-Qaeda in the settled regions of that country: Abu Zubaida in Faisalabad (2002); Ramzi bin al-Shibh in Karachi (2002); Khalid Sheikh Mohammed in Rawalpindi (2003); Abu Faraj al-Libi near Peshawar (2005). Success good enough, it seemed, that senior al-Qaeda no longer frequented the settled regions and opted for the relative safety of the Federally Administered Tribal Areas, the FATA.

Nobody has ever ruled the FATA, not the British Raj and certainly not the Pakistani government. Tribal law, custom, and kinship still govern there. I recall a conversation I had with then ISI chief Pasha in 2008. I was preaching cooperation and partnership, so I was going out of my way to emphasize how much we relied on ISI expertise to understand things like the tribal region. All the while I was thinking that Pasha, a Punjabi, was as much a foreigner in Waziristan as I was.

In September 2006, retired Pakistani general and former corps commander Ali Jan Aurakzai, a Pashtun and hence a member of the region's dominant ethnic group, signed an agreement—the Waziristan Accord—that effectively ended Pakistani military operations in the FATA. In return, the local Pashtun tribal leaders (the maliks) promised they would police the region, stop cross-border movements, expel or control "the foreigners" (i.e., al-Qaeda), and clamp down on Talibanization and paramilitary training.

It was the kind of compact that in simpler times we might have judged to be farsighted, betting on the locals, respecting differences, taking the long view. But these weren't simpler times, and we predicted that decreased Pakistani military activity would result in an al-Qaeda and Taliban safe haven and resurgence.

ISI chief Ashfaq Kayani didn't say anything to ease our concerns when he reported that there was little prospect of the Pakistani military conducting robust ops in the tribal region. He said that it was less a matter of will than of capacity. His army was certainly India-focused. Indeed, one senior Pakistani official told me that his was the only army in the world that sized the perception of the threat (India) to meet the desired end strength of the military. So PAKMIL was big, artillery heavy, and road bound—and ill-suited to navigating mountain trails or dealing with insurgents.

But we didn't see evidence of much will, either. If there is a problem up there in the FATA, Kayani seemed to be saying, it's all yours, not ours.

He was at least partially right. It *was* our problem. The roots of the Taliban comeback in Afghanistan can be traced to late 2006; the same with al-Qaeda safe havens in Waziristan.

I was in Jordan with Jose Rodriguez, head of the National Clandestine Service, in January 2007. By chance Pervez Musharraf, the Pakistani president, was in the Hashemite Kingdom at the same time. We sought and received permission to visit him in his hotel suite in Amman and laid out our case as to why we thought the Aurakzai agreement was a really bad idea.

Musharraf was gracious. After all, he didn't even have to grant us an audience. Gracious, but also immovable. He listened patiently and then sent us on our way. There would be no change in policy. His army was built to fight India, not tribal insurgents, and he wasn't going to bleed it in Waziristan's mountains chasing Pashtun, Uzbek, or Arab jihadists.

Over the next year we continued to press Musharraf and Kayani to do more against the growing militancy in the FATA or to allow the United States to do more. We made little progress. When the US government presented Pakistani officials with intelligence that pinpointed an al-Qaeda leader and a plan of action to "take him off the battlefield," the response was no, maddening delay, or our target suddenly and unexpectedly relocated. Our irreverent and frustrated summary for the year was that the United States was pretty much "0 for '07."

It was a year of what one of my best analysts called "great drift." We needed speed to dismantle the AQ network faster than they could reconstitute it, and we weren't winning. Analytic pieces on the growing threat routinely crossed my desk. We had snippets of plotting, the arrival of Westerners in the tribal region, and evidence that some of these were "graduating" and returning home. Organizationally, the AQ leadership was getting their feet under them, the hierarchy was reforming, committees were regenerating.

This wasn't just bad for us. Musharraf's strategy was ultimately dangerous for him too. Within the year militancy had spread back into the settled areas and he had a raging Islamist outpost within a few hundred yards of his Parliament building in Islamabad.

The Red Mosque had been a hotbed of mujaheddin recruitment and training during the jihad against the Soviets, and by the summer of 2007 it was getting its militant mojo back. Squads of women from the mosque were seizing adjacent land and raiding video stores in the capital; a fatwa from the mosque's imam denied Pakistani soldiers a proper Muslim burial if they were killed fighting the Taliban, and there were rumors flying around Islamabad of suicide bombers being protected in the compound.

Musharraf decided to act. After a short siege, he sent special forces into the massive mosque complex; there was resistance and hundreds were killed. In a national address explaining his actions, Musharraf complained, "They prepared the madrassa as a fortress for war and housed other terrorists in there."

Other wheels were flying off in Islamabad. Within days of the Red Mosque attack, Pakistan's Supreme Court—egged on by demonstrating, briefcase-packing barristers—ordered the reinstatement of the activist chief justice whom Musharraf had sacked for opposing his one-man rule. Musharraf was also under increasing pressure to give up his other role as chief of army staff, which he did in November in favor of ISI chief Kayani. By now the United States was pushing for the return of Benazir Bhutto, the exiled former prime minister, in a kind of power-sharing arrangement with Musharraf.

Granted amnesty for still-pending corruption charges, Bhutto returned to Pakistan in October 2007 to run in the upcoming election. She survived one assassination attempt shortly after her arrival, but she was not as fortunate in late December when a suicide bomber killed her and nearly two dozen supporters at a campaign rally in Rawalpindi.

We gathered in the Situation Room on December 27 as CNN and other outlets played the video of the attack. Bhutto and America's plan for a soft landing for Musharraf were dead. President Bush wanted to better understand the big picture.

"Musharraf made a fatal mistake," I said. "He felt that radicalism in the FATA threatened only us and Afghanistan, not him. He cut the Waziristan deal last year and wrote it off. That allowed Pashtun militancy and al-Qaeda fanaticism to grow and then coalesce in a way reminiscent of the anti-Soviet jihad.

"After he forcibly went into the Red Mosque last summer, bin Laden issued a fatwa against him. Now they're coming out of the mountains into the flatlands and they're coming after him and his government."

A few days later DNI Mike McConnell and I were directed to secretly fly to Islamabad to give this lay-down to Musharraf. We tried to keep the long flight as low profile as possible, and our aircraft stayed on the ground in Islamabad only long enough to drop us off.

Ambassador Anne Patterson allowed us to shower and change at her residence, and then we departed for the presidential palace. We met with Musharraf, new chief of army staff Kayani, and Kayani's temporary successor at ISI, Nadeem Taj, a longtime Musharraf loyalist.

McConnell and I laid it out the way we had played it in the Situation Room. I knelt down in front of a coffee table and stretched out a map and a bunch of images showing militant training areas and safe houses. The message was pretty simple: "They're coming after you, too, not just us."

Musharraf may have believed our description of the *physical* threat. It's hard to say. But Musharraf was a brave man who had survived multiple assassination attempts, and right then his main problem was the fight for his *political life* in Islamabad. Despite some idle talk of gunships and other forms of heavy firepower during our meeting, the Pakistanis were not going to move in the FATA. The political struggle in Islamabad and the settled areas was all-consuming.

It was a long flight home and not just symbolically. It was longer than it should have been because the Pakistanis wouldn't gas up the aircraft that had returned for us and we had to fly to Bagram in Afghanistan to fuel up. The crew had forgotten their government credit card—you can't make this stuff up—and the Pakistanis wouldn't budge. One more bit of evidence that these guys really were the ally from hell.

Back home we refocused on the continuing al-Qaeda buildup in the FATA, especially in Waziristan. It wasn't Afghanistan pre-9/11, but it was pretty bad. We continued to have good intelligence from both human and technical sources. It was the actionable kind, but we had an ally unwilling and unable to act and even less willing to untie American hands.

I went back to South Asia a few months later in the spring of 2008, hitting the usual stops, but lingering longer than normal in Afghanistan. I got to visit some of our locations that were, for security reasons, better approached at night, and I also got to just hang out at Kabul station. The station chief, a veteran of multiple war-zone deployments, made sure I had plenty of time with his officers, informally in his raucous basement "Talibar" and only slightly more formally in his station offices.

Frustration was palpable. We were losing ground because of the Taliban–al-Qaeda safe havens in Pakistan and along the border. What existed of the Pakistani state along the Durand Line, separating Afghanistan and Pakistan, was of little use. On most nights border units and frontier police ignored the enemy's movements; sometimes they aided and abetted them.

I had a long talk with Kabul station's chief targeting officer, Yolanda, an energetic young woman with long brown hair whom the station had dubbed "the Angel of Death." She had a lot of intelligence reporting, most of which she could not act on, and she gave strong individual voice to the collective frustration.

Our putative partner, ISI, continued to support Taliban chieftains like Commander Nazir. They viewed people like Nazir as a hedge to ensure strategic depth in their all-consuming competition with India. For us, people like him cost American lives, including one of our own from Kabul station.

The Pakistanis were badly distracted. As 2008 wore on, Pervez Musharraf's government, such as it was, was disintegrating. General elections in February gave now-deceased Benazir Bhutto's Pakistan Peoples Party (PPP) the largest bloc in Parliament, and by August a PPP-led coalition began impeachment proceedings against Musharraf. He resigned before the month was out and fled to London in November.

Musharraf was replaced by Bhutto's widower, Asif Ali Zardari, put up by the party when she was murdered because the party likely couldn't survive a bruising internal fight over a different successor. Our talented, tough ambassador in Pakistan, Anne Patterson, could see where this was heading and worked hard to nudge Pakistan toward democracy while building a relationship with the incoming president.

On one visit she took a senior CIA officer to background Zardari on what was now happening and what we were doing. Zardari, anxious to keep American support and with plenty else on his plate, took it in stride. He warned that he would have to be publicly critical and admitted that there would be parts of the government that he would not really control (read ISI and the military).

That was certainly true, but politics and policies aside, professional-level CIA exchanges with Pakistan's ISI were usually dispassionate and factual. Mid-level ISI officers seemed to get it in terms of what the United States was doing and why.

But ISI often acted like a plural noun and there were occasional issues, like their trying to squeeze the manpower that CIA could get into the country. The United States was clearly getting some very good intelligence there, a reality that must have made ISI incredibly uncomfortable. They may or may not have had a clear window into how we were developing intelligence, but they correctly judged that it would be harder to do if we had fewer people in the area. So ISI began to quibble, question, delay, and ultimately deny visa requests for multiple officers we were trying to dispatch. It was petty. It was a pain. And it didn't stop what we were doing.

We were personally lobbying Zardari too. In September 2008 Steve Kappes and I spent a day in New York during the UN General Assembly session. The UNGA multiplies the normal chaos of Manhattan, so Steve and I and our security detail moved around largely on foot for the day. It was worth it. We were there to meet the new Pakistani president.

Zardari was engaging, hyperactive, and allegedly so corrupt that Pakistanis had labeled him "Mr. Ten Percent." We met him in his suite at the Waldorf and quickly consumed the time that had been allotted. Zardari had to run to see the Indian prime minister, but insisted we stay until he returned. He wanted to continue talking. So we stayed, surrounded by the new president's staff, who tried to make us feel at home by offering us some juice and South Asian sweets.

We gave Zardari the same macro lay-down we had given Musharraf nine months earlier. He wasn't disinterested, but this was a man who clearly valued relationships more than data. He just wanted us to stay there and "relate."

The US government had a bone to pick, though. Pakistani government "sources" were getting into the habit of routinely claiming massive harm to innocent civilians in South Asia. It may have satisfied some internal Pakistani political need that wasn't obvious to us, but it wasn't true. And if the purpose was to put pressure on the American government to stop anything we were doing, we assured him that it wasn't going to work.

"Mr. President," I explained, "we know the truth and frankly we think these lies are ultimately going to make it harder for you. What's the benefit of feeding this story line?"

I began to spread out some materials in front of Zardari to explain to him "the great care that the US government takes—" He quickly interrupted me, grabbed my arm, and with a half smile said, "General, I am not an American. I don't care about such things."

Well, I guess that was some sort of license, but not one that we welcomed or needed. Steve and I left Manhattan marveling at the personality we had just encountered and went back to our work.

Pakistan was never far from our focus, and two months later it imposed itself on us again in the ugliest of ways.

The day before Thanksgiving, I was chopping celery for holiday stuffing while watching unblinking news coverage of the magnificent Taj Mahal Palace Hotel in Mumbai burning while Lashkar-e-Taiba (LET) terrorists roamed the streets killing or maiming nearly five hundred people in India's commercial center.

The attack in Mumbai was troubling on multiple levels. Of course, there was the human cost: innocents gunned down in a hotel restaurant, at a train station, and at a Jewish center. Then there was the fear that our counterterrorism partner, Pakistan's ISI, was involved. And there was the character of the attack itself. Fewer than a dozen fanatics with cell phones and automatic weapons had just pulled off a terrorist event with strategic effect. What did that mean about future threats to the homeland? What if al-Qaeda went to school on this?

There was also another, more immediate problem. How would India react? There already seemed to be so many Pakistani fingerprints on the atrocity that a sharp Indian response seemed inevitable. And then what?

Even as the administration prepared for the presidential transition, American diplomacy worked feverishly to defuse the situation. The last thing a new president needed was another war in South Asia.

I began routinely harassing my counterpart in Pakistan, now Ahmed Shuja Pasha (the former director general of Military Operations, the Pakistan army's top operational post), on the phone, urging him to get to the bottom of the attack and to discuss it frankly with us. We had no doubt that the attack was the work of LET, and there was mounting evidence that preparation for and direction of the attack took place from within Pakistan, where LET enjoyed the protection and support of ISI.

Pasha had come to ISI only a few weeks earlier and had no previous intelligence experience. ISI was a heavily compartmented organization, so I wouldn't have been surprised if a lot of what he was now picking up was discovery learning on his part.

He flew to the United States on Christmas Day and spent most of the next afternoon in my office. He worked carefully from notes. His investigation had revealed that some former ISI members were involved with Lashkar-e-Taiba (no surprise there). Pasha admitted that these unspecified (and still uncaptured) retirees may have engaged in some broad training of the attackers, but he was characteristically vague about any detailed direction the attackers had gotten during the attack via cell phone from Pakistan. No admission of more formal ties between LET and ISI, either, even though the former was an intelligence service creation to contest Indian control of Kashmir. And ISI did not seem to know much about LET's recent movement from a Kashmiri-focused terrorist group to one with more al-Qaeda–like global ambitions, a migration easily traced through the group's Web activity.

I took to passing sufficiently sanitized intelligence to Pasha on what we believed was going on in order to try to goad him into action. If he knew that we knew . . . perhaps we could get some movement.

We didn't have a whole lot of success. Many Pakistanis viewed LET (like the Haqqani network and the Taliban) as some sort of strategic reserve rather than the strategic liability and regional danger they really were. Attempts by Pakistan to limit LET in the past had been short-lived and incomplete. This proved to be no different.

Pakistani intelligence officials agreed that the Mumbai attack was indeed a tragedy, but they had had nothing to do with it and really couldn't find out much about it.

Thank God the Indians showed remarkable restraint.

And thank God that two successive presidents have decided to act unilaterally when American safety required it.

NINETEEN

TRANSITION

CIA, NOVEMBER 2008–FEBRUARY 2009

I think that the intelligence community consensus was that the election of John McCain would have been more disruptive to the way America produced intelligence than the election of Barack Obama.

Senator McCain was a known quantity. Patriotic. Heroic. Forceful. Emotional. He once angrily stormed out of a meeting I was having on Capitol Hill for Senate Republicans, accusing me of covering my ass while exposing theirs (my summary, not his). He later returned to the session and apologized.

Barack Obama was an unknown. I had been scheduled to meet with him in the spring of 2008, at his initiative, for purposes that remain unclear to me to this day. The candidate got tied up in Tim Russert's remarkable memorial service at the Kennedy Center, though, and he personally called me to cancel the engagement and promise we would get together soon. The campaign predictably swept him up, and the promised meeting never took place.

There were some at CIA who viewed the upcoming election with great concern, fearful that a new president would try to prosecute CIA officers involved in renditions, detentions, and interrogations. Indeed, both candidates had expressed strong negative views on the programs, and Eric Holder had specifically promised a reckoning while campaigning for Senator Obama.

I was approached by a senior CIA lawyer with a package recommending a preemptive presidential pardon for everyone involved. To be clear, he was in no way imputing guilt to his fellow officers. He just feared politically motivated investigations and litigation that would disrupt lives and destroy savings. Given what Holder did once he was in office, he was damn prescient.

I sympathized with what he was trying to do, but saw that this was fraught with difficulties. There was already an active investigation under way on the destruction of the videotapes. I doubted that the president would even consider pardons and our even asking would be read by some as an admission of guilt. It would also moot the efforts we had under way to convince a new administration that these programs should continue.

I wanted a second opinion, so I grabbed Fred Fielding, the White House counsel, on the margins of a Sit Room meeting and briefly explained what I had. Fred and I had struck up a friendship since his arrival in early 2007. His savvy, avuncular style was welcome and calming. There was no better barometer of the political and legal wisdom of pushing this, and after a brief conversation, it was clear to me that Fred was markedly unenthusiastic. Although I didn't know it at the time, he was also then advising against a full pardon for Scooter Libby, the vice president's former chief of staff.

I let the matter drop. There was no need to put the president in an impossible position. Nor to act like we needed pardoning. But I would often parse this decision in the coming years as Eric Holder did indeed try to go after CIA officers.

On election night we had teams in Phoenix and Chicago. Barring a repeat of the long count eight years earlier in Florida, *someone* was going to get the PDB—the President's Daily Brief—in the morning. Early in the evening it became pretty clear that that *someone* was Barack Obama.

The process would have been the same for either man. Like the rest of the government we would work to get access to him and then create as many of what we crudely called "aw, shit" moments as possible.

That implied no disrespect. In fact, it was designed to protect the president-elect. This would be the folks who were around before the election and would be around after the next one telling you about the world as they saw it, not through the lens of campaign rhetoric, tracking polls, or the world as you wanted it to be. The "aw, shit" count simply reflected how many times they had been successful, as in "Aw shit, wish we hadn't said that during that campaign stop in Buffalo."

I had to wait until December 9 to get direct access to the president-elect and vice president–elect. The incoming team was getting its threat and situation briefings from the DNI, who was by law the president's senior intelligence advisor. I needed to talk to them about covert action, which remained the province of CIA.

The December date was obviously a long time coming, and no sooner had I landed in Chicago than I was told that our long-sought appointment might be at risk. As I walked into the darkened lobby of our downtown hotel (we had arrived very late to low-key our presence), my chief of security whispered to me that we had a problem. The venue had been changed; the secure facility at the FBI office in the Federal Building was no longer available, but we had been able to book a smaller room at another location.

A bit exasperated, I asked, "Why?"

Leaning into my ear, the security chief whispered, "Because the FBI is arresting the governor in the morning."

The next morning at the new location, the first time I saw the president-elect he was quietly repeating to himself, "The governor was trying to sell my seat. The governor was trying to sell my seat."

The new venue was tight. We sat across a narrow table from the president-elect; vice president–elect; incoming chief of staff Rahm Emanuel; national security advisor–designate Jim Jones; Tony Blinken, national security advisor to the VP; and Mark Lippert, a navy reservist who had been with the campaign since before Iowa.

I laid out a global map between the president-elect and myself. Its annotations highlighted all ongoing covert actions, some geographically focused, others organized around global issues. I began, "Mr. President-elect." (Yes, it's an awkward term, but shortening it to "president" is constitutionally presumptive and reverting to "senator" ignores an important constitutional reality—he *had* been elected president.)

"Mr. President-elect, I'm going to brief you on all the covert actions currently under way. These have all been authorized by the president. But the authorization comes from the office—not the person—of the president, so absent any action on your part, all of these will be going forward on the afternoon of January 20 [Inauguration Day]."

I then stepped through everything we were doing. The president-elect was focused, absorbing things with little visible reaction. The vice president–elect was his usual garrulous self, so one of my challenges was to get both men to the bottom of each page at about the same time.

The president-elect was more animated when we talked about proliferation. He wanted to know our division of labor, specifically how much did we focus on Iran? He accepted without comment my estimate of 80 percent.

We also explored how targeted killings along the Afghanistan-Pakistan border had ticked up in the last half of 2008 and how their results were now outpacing al-Qaeda's ability to replace key personnel.

I saved the controversial bucket—renditions, detentions, and interrogations—for last.

Once there, I started with rendition—the extrajudicial transfer of someone to a third party. I broadly explained that we had done a series of these in the previous eight years, that they were not something newly created by the Bush administration, and what our moral and legal responsibilities were to the detainees, even in their new location.

"Oh, come on, General," the VP-elect suddenly interrupted, "you shipped them to these places to rough them up so you could get information."

The president-elect was attentive, but silent (as he was for most of the briefing) as I responded, "Mr. Vice President–elect, that's simply not true.

And now that I've told you that, you need to stop saying it." No sense letting an opportunity pass.

When we got to detentions and interrogations the president-elect took control of the narrative. No sooner had I started than he asked, "What are the techniques?"

I asked David Shedd, the DNI's chief of staff, to stand next to me while I demonstrated on him the two grasps and the two slaps we were permitted. As we were sitting down, I added that we also manipulated sleep and diet and gave the president-elect a sense of our limits and authorities there.

I think he was underwhelmed, because his immediate response was, "What were the other techniques?"

I listed them, and he then said that I would have to get together with Greg Craig, soon to be his White House counsel, to work on a way ahead.

Flying back from Chicago, I still had no idea about my personal future, other than a vague comment from Denis McDonough (close advisor to the president who later filled a variety of trusted roles for him) that eventually the transition team would "reach out" to me. We had never had a presidential transition under a DNI before. DCIs, who were head of the American intelligence community as well as head of CIA, routinely swapped out with a new administration (George Tenet was an exception with the incoming George W. Bush), but the DNI now headed the community and I was "just" head of CIA. I was determined *not* to self-identify my post as political (it wasn't), so I did nothing to suggest that I believed I *had* to leave.

The president-elect thought I should go, though, and by early January, Leon Panetta's name was being informally floated as my replacement. Steve Kappes, my deputy, called John Brennan (head of the intelligence transition team) to ask if anyone was ever going to talk to me. The president-elect called me at home that night, told me that he was basing his choice on the need to turn the page (and not look backward), and asked me to stay on until Leon could be confirmed. I readily agreed. I could use the time, since I had not begun any real transition planning.

It was a mistake not to have been better prepared. I was taking a principled position to act like the CIA director position was apolitical, but it wasn't a practical one. And President Bush's endorsement to his successor that I stay on probably hurt more than it helped. I was leaving and I should have seen it. Intelligence is about good analysis, after all.

But if the transition was awkward for me, it was even worse for John Brennan, who had advised Obama during the campaign and was now the intelligence transition team chief. For the most part, his team was composed of intel veterans whom we knew and respected, and their apolitical approach was a perfect complement to President Bush's direction to us to conduct a professional turnover. John confided that one of their directives was to make no news, which was fine with us.

Although he had told us that no members of the transition team were in it for future jobs, John clearly wanted to replace me as head of CIA. But the blogosphere was exploding at the very thought, with the likes of Andrew Sullivan (consistently anti-Bush) and Glenn Greenwald (pretty much anti-everything) in the lead and with human rights lawyer Scott Horton in strong support. They pointed to John's senior roles under George Tenet (chief of staff, executive director, head of the Terrorist Threat Integration Center), when detentions were at their height as inherently disqualifying. They also pulled up quotes from as little as a year before in which John claimed that interrogations had saved lives and that renditions were a vital tool.

A little before Thanksgiving, John wrote a Shermanesque letter to the *Washington Post* withdrawing himself from consideration for a post with which the incoming team had never publicly associated him. He also took the opportunity to distance himself personally from previous CIA policies and practices.

The whole thing played out publicly, and it was pretty ugly. When John came to visit me the next day with Jami Miscik (former head of CIA Analysis) on routine transition business, I tried to lighten the air a bit. After greeting them in the outer office, I allowed myself a "Well, so much for keeping this low-key."

When we sat down, I turned to John directly and sympathized, "I'm sorry, John. I know how you feel." The reference was to the unfair press treatment.

John paused a second, then tersely answered, "With all due respect, Mike, no you don't!"

There was a pause in the conversation. Miscik stared straight ahead. I tried to stay calm by silently counting to ten. Well, f— you, John (one). Well, f— you, John (two). Well, f— you, John (three) . . . and so on till ten. We then resumed the meeting as if nothing had happened.

(John eventually did become director in 2014, and his previous time at the agency did indeed continue to be an issue as he manfully defended CIA from scurrilous accusations.)

And John's experience wasn't isolated. For all the personal unpleasantness, this was a serious policy issue. A personnel structure that effectively had Greenwald, Sullivan, Horton, and the like vetting senior administration officials looked like trouble.

A later visible casualty was Phil Mudd, the nominee to be the under secretary of Homeland Security for intelligence and analysis. Phil was a thoroughgoing professional, a career CIA analyst with superb credentials and extensive experience in counterterrorism. When I was PDDNI, I pressured him to leave his CIA comfort zone to take on a challenging task as deputy head of the FBI's fledgling National Security Branch. Phil's task there was to expand the office and move FBI's forensics-based and law enforcement–focused analysis toward a true intelligence function: predictive, disruptive, and working the "spaces between cases."

No easy task, but Phil thrived. He earned the respect of the broader FBI and tirelessly moved his workforce toward the mainstream of the intelligence community. Along the way he became knowledgeable of and accepted by law enforcement officers at all levels of government. A national intelligence professional with credentials among cops, Phil Mudd was made for the Department of Homeland Security job, which was the key interface between national capabilities and the needs of state, tribal, and local defenders and first responders.

It was not to be. The blogosphere had already begun to light up about his unsuitability for the job. His sin? Phil had been the deputy director of CIA's Counterterrorism Center and its chief analyst at the height of the agency's counterattack against al-Qaeda.

As Mudd made the rounds of Hill staffers, he was told that this aspect of his past, rather than his credentials for the future post, would be the focus of his hearings. Phil calmly (and wisely) said no. He would not become the meat in the sandwich, being badgered to answer what his definition of torture was or whether he agreed with President Obama's description that this had been a dark period in our history, or with the former vice president's assertion that hundreds of lives had been saved, or with the Speaker of the House's judgment that they "mislead us all the time," or with my public statements that the CIA interrogation program produced valuable intelligence. Beyond what personal psychic costs such an inquiry would impose on him, Phil would simply not feed the partisan beast and create yet more distractions for the community he loved. And so the country did without the officer clearly most qualified to fill the head intelligence position at DHS.

The White House issued a short, pro forma statement of regret at Phil's decision. I wrote an op-ed about the self-destructive absurdity of it all and quietly hoped that the purge would soon run its course.

Leon Panetta's nomination raised some eyebrows. Senior Democrats on the Senate Intelligence Committee were angry they weren't consulted on the choice by the new president's team and a little nervous about Leon's lack of intelligence experience. Senator Feinstein had quietly been sounding out my deputy, Steve Kappes, about his interest in the position. That being said, Leon's confirmation was never in doubt.

I had my first meeting with him in downtown Washington at the transition team's headquarters. I went into the session with Steve Kappes, and had the key members of the CIA leadership team in the next room ready to brief. The game plan was simple. I would brief the nominee with Steve for about fifteen minutes and then depart to allow Panetta to talk to Steve about staying on as his deputy. After that session, the leadership team would enter, introduce themselves to the incoming director, and hit the high points of their work.

I built a short list of points to make in my quarter of an hour and jotted them down on the back of a single note card. After congratulating him on his nomination, I told Panetta that he would be, once confirmed, America's combatant commander in the war on terrorism. He would be making the kinds of operational decisions that are usually associated with combatant commanders, and he would be making these decisions at all hours of the day and night. I also told him that he was inheriting a great leadership team.

I then leaned forward and, implicitly referring to some of his comments while out of government, advised that he should never again use the words "torture" and "CIA" in the same paragraph. Torture was a legal term, I said. It has specific meaning. It was a felony. Associating it with the agency was inaccurate and would set in motion things that would be difficult, if not impossible, to control. There were lots of words available if he wanted to condemn any policy or practice of the past, but this shouldn't be one of them. It was the only time during a warm and friendly exchange that I could not read his reaction.

Weeks later, during his confirmation hearing in front of the Senate Intelligence Committee, Panetta was asked directly by Senator Carl Levin whether or not he agreed with the president and the attorney general that waterboarding—a practice I had previously confirmed the agency had used on three people—was torture. He quickly responded that it was: "I have expressed the opinion that waterboarding is torture and that it is wrong."

The nominee was under considerable political pressure to say what he had just said. The president had taken that position in his campaign, as had the Democratic leadership in Congress. And it was inevitable that any nominee for attorney general in the Obama administration was also going to take that reflexive position in his confirmation hearing, as Eric Holder did (without, of course, knowing the details of CIA's waterboarding technique and how important the technique had been in securing valuable intelligence from terrorist detainees). Likewise for the CIA nominee. It was disappointing nonetheless.

Judge Michael Mukasey had faced the same line of questioning during his confirmation hearing for attorney general in 2007. Democratic senators were angry with Mukasey for refusing to answer, but he was just reflecting the reality that the legal question depended on the details and could not be decided in the abstract. This was especially true, since Congress had rejected Senator Kennedy's amendment to explicitly outlaw waterboarding in the Military Commissions Act of 2006.

So Panetta's answer, like Holder's before him, was more political than legal but would nonetheless discomfit agency officers. The incoming director had just said that the workforce he was about to inherit had participated in what he viewed to be a felony.

Earlier, DNI-designate Blair (after a phone conversation with me similar to the one I had had with Panetta) had declined to answer the same question, and told the same senators that it would be awkward for him to head a workforce if he had accused them of doing something illegal.

To his credit, Panetta—on at least four occasions during his hearing—emphasized that CIA officers operating under then-existing legal opinions should not be prosecuted.

Near the end of the day, Senator Wyden asked Panetta whether he believed the United States had "rendered" people to third countries *for the purposes of torture*. Panetta said that he believed that we had: "I suspect that that has been the case . . . that we have rendered individuals to other countries, knowing they would use certain techniques." After admitting that he had limited knowledge on the subject, he concluded by saying, "Every indication seems to be that we used this extraordinary rendition for that purpose."

Like a lot of the CIA workforce, I was watching the testimony on C-SPAN. Rendered "for the purposes of torture"—not that we were deficient in how we got assurances about treatment or that a partner had betrayed our confidence—no, *for the purposes of torture*!

I immediately picked up the secure phone and called the head of the

Counterterrorism Center, an experienced field operator, a student of Islam, as candid as he was terse. "Are you watching this?" I said.

"Oh, yes."

"And how's it going?"

"Not well."

"Have we ever rendered anyone to a third country for the purposes of torture?"

"Never."

"Not just on your watch. Ever?"

"Never."

"And you use all the tools available to us to ensure that a partner lives up to his commitment?"

"Always."

"Thanks. Just wanted to be sure one more time before I did anything."

The Senate had a lot of votes that day, and the hearing did not begin until midafternoon. Chairman Feinstein had to adjourn the session and agreed to reconvene in the morning. That gave us a chance to try to correct testimony that was as damaging as it was wrong.

We lit up the phones to the transition team's handlers around the nominee. The conversation was simple. Walk back the "renditions for the purposes of torture" testimony the next morning or the current director of CIA would issue a public statement that the incoming director had been misinformed.

The transition team felt that the day had gone well, so I'm sure that our fuming wasn't particularly welcome. But several team members did recognize that the "renditions for the purposes of torture" language was at least ill-advised, and they didn't want a public spat to mar the day's achievements.

The next morning, in the "extra time" session dictated by the Senate's heavy schedule the day before, the incoming director did not take up Chairman Feinstein's offer to add to or clarify any statements from the day before. But later, in response to some sharp questioning by Senator Bond, he did admit that renditions for the purposes of torture "was not the policy of the United States" and that he wanted to "retract that statement" from the day before. That pragmatic stance effectively defused the situation.

Leon was a quick study. The more he was briefed up by the agency, the more he discarded views he had formed from popular accounts while he was out of government. He became a staunch agency defender with both the White House and the Hill. He was a better defender than I would have been with the Hill, given that he was a member of the governing party and had personal experience and acquaintances in the institution.

He also had a politician's gift for human relationships. It wasn't lost on me. In the midst of all this he left a voice mail on my home phone wishing my Steelers the best in the upcoming Super Bowl.

The meeting that the president-elect promised me with Greg Craig was a month in coming, but on January 9, Craig, former Oklahoma senator (and mentor to George Tenet) David Boren, and other members of the transition team gave us a full morning at Langley to explain our position on detentions and interrogations.

We met in the director's conference room on the seventh floor, transition team on one side of the table, the agency's counterterrorism staff and myself on the other, with agency subject matter experts in the chairs behind us.

I spent a lot of time preparing for this, but before I began, I told Greg that if this was just theater, we would happily give him and his team their morning back. He assured me that it was not.

"Good. Well then, our objective here is to make you understand what we really are doing and have done, as opposed to the urban legends out there on which people are making judgments and making speeches." We weren't there to defend *torture*. We were there to defend *this* program.

I laid out some of the language that critical senators had used and then wondered aloud why, if they were so certain of their position, they would think they had to mischaracterize what we had done.

Then I continued, "And as far as making changes to this program, we believe that what you think you have to do, we actually took care of in 2006."

I knew that one of the administration's key motivators was to "get us right" with our allies, so I pointed out that about 90 percent of our reporting from detainees had been shared with many of them, that we had directed hundreds of questions at detainees based on liaison queries, and that we had also shared hundreds of finished intelligence products that included detainee information.

I also pointed out that for all the huffing and puffing, Congress had had the opportunity in 2006 to stop the program, and it had not.*

I emphasized how many times CIA had gone to the Justice Department in the history of the program and how Justice had been supportive, not just in the infamous and overreaching "Bybee memo" at the beginning of the program but in later, more limited opinions.

I had a lot of details. There were twenty-two pages of text and briefing notes in front of me on numbers and techniques and reports and intelligence. But the core argument was straightforward: "Be careful. Don't arbitrarily give up something you might need someday."

Senator Boren later told the *Washington Post* that he felt like he needed a shower after the briefing. He didn't tell the paper that at one point in the discussion—in response to our "don't take it off the table" reasoning—he told us that in some future *in extremis* circumstance the president could order us to do something and that we would do it based on the president's authorization alone.

"Wow," I responded, "I haven't heard even David Addington and his unitary executive theory come up with that one. I know that you only have to worry about this for the next couple of weeks, but forget it. I won't support it."

---

* To be fair, the Intelligence Authorization Act of *2008* would have confined all US government agencies to the interrogation techniques in the Army Field Manual, but the bill was vetoed by President Bush.

At this point, the head of the Counterterrorism Center sitting to my right added, "And I won't order it."

And in the uncomfortable silence that followed, a voice from the back row spoke out: "And it doesn't matter what those two guys might say, we're not doing it."

Finally, a member of my personal staff, showing some real anger, said that he thought this theory had been shot down in the 1970s.

Talk about feeling the need for a shower.

The meeting actually *was* theater, of course. The Justice Department transition team was already beavering away on an executive order closing the CIA black sites and limiting any American interrogation to the techniques listed in the Army Field Manual. In front of a phalanx of retired flag officers, the president signed the executive order along with one committing to the closure of Guantánamo two days after the inauguration.

That morning, prior to the president signing the executive order, I made one last try with Craig, even though we had not officially been provided with a coordination draft of the EO.

"Greg," I began, "not that you asked, but this is CIA officially nonconcurring."

"We figured that, Mike."

"And Greg, you could buy back most of what we need if you would just add 'unless otherwise authorized by the president' to the paragraph limiting us to the Army Field Manual. We need ambiguity and doubt in the mind of the detainee more than we need *any* particular technique."

Greg said he would "take it under advisement."

Later that day the EO was published, without my amendment. However we might have disagreed over details, the president had given the agency what it needed and what he owed its officers: clear guidance. I hit the send button on a message to the workforce that we had ready to go.

The legal and policy landscape under which the Agency has conducted itself in the global war on terror has changed in the past and we have consistently and scrupulously adjusted our efforts to reflect these changes. This Executive Order is no different. We will review the order carefully and issue appropriate guidance to ensure that we continue to act in consonance with the law and with policy direction. . . . [Y]ou, the men and women of CIA, will make the best possible use of the space the Republic has given us. . . . I have every confidence in your enduring ability to do so, honoring, as always, the laws and values of the democracy we faithfully serve.

I couldn't resist one additional comment.

When our government changes its law or policy, we will follow that direction without exception, carve out, or loophole.

Outside the government, that was probably read as a further warning to the workforce not to test the new limits. But we knew better. That sentence was for the new administration. You wanted it. Now you are going to have to live with it. No back doors here. Don't even bother calling.

Someone asked me if we would now train CIA officers in the authorized techniques of the Army Field Manual. I replied that if they needed people trained on the Army Field Manual, I could point them down the Potomac to the headquarters of an organization where literally thousands were so trained. CIA would still provide subject matter experts, but we had detained and interrogated because we had had special authorities. Now we didn't. We were out of that business.

We had better luck with the incoming team on renditions, the extrajudicial movements of subjects from one point to another. John Rizzo, CIA's acting general counsel, scanned the very late-arriving draft executive order on detentions and quickly noted that its language was so broad that it would have taken us out of the rendition business too. In a panic he called Greg Craig to ask if that was the intent. "Absolutely not," Greg replied.

We had been explaining to the incoming team that we could neither ask nor support another nation doing something that was beyond our legal authorities to do. It wasn't hard to suggest a variety of scenarios where they would want someone to quietly (even covertly) detain someone and transfer him to a third party. Picture a bomb maker fleeing Afghanistan en route to Yemen through the Persian Gulf or a terrorist financier transiting the Emirates between Gulf donors.

The next day, when the EO was launched amid much fanfare, there was a new phrase tucked into it authorizing detentions "on a short-term transitory basis." In other words, renditions—although that magic word was avoided, and of course, the incoming administration made much about guarantees against torture or cruel treatment as distinguishing it from past practitioners. We simply pocketed the continuation of a valuable tool and tolerated the claims of moral superiority. (That many of the actual movements since 2009 appear to have been in the Horn of Africa suggests the continued challenge of working with dicey partners.)

And renditions were but one example of continuity. Despite some caustic rhetoric, there was surprising persistence between the two administrations in the politically freighted area of countering terrorism. Much more than many expected. CIA black sites were closed, but targeted killings continued and even increased dramatically. Electronic surveillance pressed on unabated. Military commissions were revitalized. The administration routinely invoked the "state secrets" privilege in court cases. And the United States continued to define itself as a belligerent in a global conflict with al-Qaeda and its affiliates.

There were arguably more changes between President Bush's first and second terms than there were between him and his successor. President Obama suggested as much in one remark buried in a lengthy interview with Peter Baker of the *New York Times* six weeks into office.

I think that I would distinguish between some of the steps that were taken immediately after 9/11 and where we were by the time I took office. I think the CIA, for example, and some of the controversial programs that have been a focus of a lot of attention, took steps to correct certain policies and procedures after those first couple of years. I think that Admiral [*sic*] Hayden and Mike McConnell at D.N.I. were capable public servants who really had America's security interests in mind when they acted, and I think were mindful of American values and ideals.

The shout-out was genuinely appreciated (although he could have been a bit more generous to the administration that Mike and I served). In any event, the comment got no bounce in the press, and the president never really returned to the theme, choosing instead to rhetorically stress the differences between himself and his predecessor (see especially chapters 12 and 20).

Correspondent David Sanger got a lot of access to administration officials, and he revealingly titled his perceptive book on the Obama administration's security policy *Confront and Conceal*. A *New York Times* story on counterterrorism in 2012 echoed the thought when it described Obama as "a realist who, unlike some of his fervent supporters, was never carried away by his own rhetoric." The campaign team, according to the *Times*, characterized all this as a victory of pragmatism over ideology.

Hence the continuity between administrations and also the rhetoric designed to disguise that continuity as much as possible. And also the later stresses on the intelligence community when it came time to reconcile apparent word and actual deed, most dramatically demonstrated with the revelation of NSA's metadata program in 2013.

The formal inauguration ceremony imposed a pause on all the frenetic transition activity. For one thing, the security for the event itself had to be tended to by both the incoming and outgoing teams. There was limited specific threat information, but we weren't taking any chances, and there was a delicate dance not to let the old guys' security concerns unduly limit the new guys' desire for a truly popular spectacle for the historic event.

For Inauguration Day itself, Jeanine and I had to decide where to be. Since I was still in government, we were offered two seats on the Mall for

President Obama's formal swearing-in. We had also been invited to Andrews Air Force Base to say goodbye to President Bush.

People forget that I was a Clinton appointee to the NSA job. In 2001 the Bush folks were the new guys on the block and we were settling into *that* new team. It wasn't particularly hard, except for one issue. Somebody in the new crew wanted to review and vet all the members of our advisory boards. Although it was never explicitly stated, I suspected that party affiliation was the issue. These boards are pretty carefully picked (I did mine personally) and they're pretty busy; there isn't room for honorific or emeritus status. I was looking for balance, expertise, and a willingness to work. Now I feared that the criteria would resemble something reminiscent of the 1950s: "Are you now or have you ever been a member of the —— Party?" I decided to ignore the call for names for the new people to vet for as long as we could, and then, post-9/11, this just went away.

I had not met President George W. Bush prior to 9/11. I had met his father when I served on his National Security Council staff, and Vice President Cheney had visited Fort Meade early in the administration, but my first encounter with the president was that September 2001 morning when George Tenet ushered me into the Oval to discuss what more NSA could do. After another meeting or two, Stellarwind was under way. I went back periodically to update the president on the program, but the more detailed briefings to Congress over the next years were always in the vice president's cramped office just down the hall.

I got to know the president a little better when he came out to Fort Meade to encourage and thank the workforce in June 2002. I was alone to greet him on the post parade ground when Marine One landed, and he invited me into the car with him and Andy Card for the short ride to NSA. The route passed the post's golf courses, prompting speculation that the president might be able to run on the secure 3.5-mile jogging trail that snaked through them.

Once at NSA headquarters, the president jumped into the role of personally thanking folks and listening to them explain their work. His advance team willingly agreed to a press availability under one of our near-ubiquitous "We Won't Back Down" banners. After stops that included the Stellarwind shop and the operations center, the president mounted a stage we had constructed in the sun-drenched parking lot to a massive roar from the crowd of over five thousand that had gathered.

The president's message was simple: I appreciate what you do—an important message in the face of congressional inquiries trying to affix blame for 9/11. He was the first president to come to NSA since his father visited after the first Gulf War; "W" visited again in 2006 a few weeks after the *New York Times* revealed aspects of the Stellarwind program.

President Bush worked the rope line for twenty minutes after his remarks. He autographed notepapers, dollar bills, and NSA access badges (which we then had to replace). It was a great day, marked by genuine emotion on both sides. They were his kind of people. He was their kind of president.

When I became director of CIA, I more routinely met with the president. He poked at my loyalty to the Steelers and took to calling me Mikey in lighter moments. That had actually been my handle growing up, as there were two other Mikes in the house, my grandfather (Big Mike) and my uncle (Brother Mike).

His informality often took me off guard. I was hanging in the small outer office of the Oval, waiting to go in, when the president bellowed, "Mikey, get in here!" As I entered, he gestured toward the fireplace and said, "You know Tony, don't you?" I turned to see the prime minister of the United Kingdom extending his hand toward mine.

There is a plotline held by some that the real center of power in the Bush administration was the vice president. A more benign version of the story is that a young, untested president was fortunate to have surrounded himself early on with experienced old hands like the vice president, Don Rumsfeld, Colin Powell, Condi Rice, and the like.

I really had little insight into the inner workings of the administration until the second term. From that perspective, though, there was never any doubt in my mind who the president was. I never left a meeting with

George Bush wondering what it was he wanted me to do. And I rarely had an important meeting with the vice president that did not end with the vice president saying, "We'll have to take that to the president." And if there was ever any truth about a new president benefiting from older, wiser hands, it was clear to me that the president had grown beyond *all* of his advisors by the time I approached his inner circle.

People learn and absorb information in different ways. George Bush was an avid reader, as evidenced by the scorecard kept in the office just outside the Oval with a running count of books and number of pages read by him and Karl Rove. But in terms of intelligence, the president really learned in the conversation. It didn't take long for any briefing with him to go interactive. Questions. Alternative views. Comparisons with past presentations ("That's not what you told me six months ago"). He was never rude, not even brusque, but he was challenging, and he had an appetite for details. Near fanatic about being punctual, he allotted a lot of time for intelligence briefings so as not to go long and create a domino effect on the rest of his schedule. And he acted on the intelligence.

I participated in my share of substantive intelligence discussions with the president, but the DNI was his principal intelligence advisor. My special relationship with him was through covert action, which we discussed weekly. It included conversations on the specifics of renditions, detentions, and interrogations. I don't think that later charges by some Democrats that the president was in the dark about such matters were ever true, but they sure as hell weren't true on my watch. I also updated him weekly about terrorists that were being taken off the battlefield one way or another, and I told him when things didn't go well too.

For the last six months of the administration he often began these sessions by reminding me how much more time I had to get bin Laden while he was president. He must have been as angry as I was when his successor attributed the successful raid in Abbottabad to his personal reprioritization: "And so shortly after taking office, I directed Leon Panetta, the director of the CIA, to make the killing or capture of bin Laden the top priority of our war against al-Qaeda." That night, watching President

Obama's speech in our kitchen, I turned to Jeanine to mockingly comment, "Damn. Why didn't they tell me this UBL guy was important?"

Covert actions are always edgy things. In one, we were controlling a plot that included an al-Qaeda bomb maker who had been brought in to attack an American facility. I was getting briefed daily and had good confidence this was all under control; the president was markedly less sanguine, based on his weekly updates. He leaned on me. Hard. Multiple times. The plan worked, though. A talented bomb maker was taken out of circulation. It all showed a level of presidential trust.

Some covert actions are particularly edgy. One such operation was going to have to thread a very narrow needle in every imaginable dimension: law, politics, ethics, operations, diplomacy. Steve Kappes and I wanted one final gut check with the president, which Steve Hadley arranged. We talked for about an hour. The president was patient. Steve Hadley later told me that the president characterized the session as two good Catholic boys clearing the air with him. When we left, we knew that the president believed that if we thought we should and could do this, we would. If we didn't, we wouldn't. He was happy with that. He didn't speak to us about it again.

We did do it. The morning afterward the president walked into a crowded Sit Room, looked my way, and yelled, "Mike!" He gave me a barely perceptible nod, which I returned, and then he turned to the meeting as if nothing had just transpired.

Much later the president invited Jeanine and me (along with the Hadleys and some friends of the First Family) to Camp David for a weekend. Folks arrived midday Saturday, had lunch with the president and First Lady, and then got a few hours of free time while the president pounded the Catoctin Mountain bike trails. We reconvened for a showing in the theater of *The Great Debaters*, a 1930s Texas period piece about a small black college challenging the Harvard debate club.

Dinner followed shortly. All meals were informal and family style, and the president stimulated conversation by asking everyone what they were reading. In truth, all I was reading were intelligence cables, but the last book I *had* read was *Friday Night Lights,* a controversial account of a football season at a high school in Odessa, Texas. Odessa is just down the road from Midland, where the First Lady was born and the president was raised. If the president thought I was just sucking up, he didn't let on as he filled in the background on how the book had divided the town.

More important, as we were walking in for one of the meals on the weekend, the president pulled me aside for a private moment. "Mike, how are you doing?" he asked.

"Fine, Mr. President," I honestly answered.

"I mean spiritually," he continued, as I slowly understood the nature of his question.

"Mr. President, I'm really fine," I once more honestly (and firmly) answered.

"Good. Good."

It's hard to go through some of this stuff without building some personal bonds, so we really wanted to be at Andrews to say goodbye. I still hesitated for just an instant, though. I still felt that the CIA job should be and be seen as apolitical, which suggested the Mall or just staying away. But the incoming president's decision to replace me pretty much lightened that load for me. If anyone had made this political, it wasn't me.

We arrived at Andrews early and were lucky enough to be in the group that could wait in the DV lounge for the arrival of the helicopter from downtown. I knew that lounge well from countless trips in and out of the capital, but the scene this time was markedly different. The usually quiet, spacious, and well-appointed room was packed with folks in what resembled a somber (but not quite funereal) Bush administration reunion. Current and former officials were everywhere.

Most people were in small groups conversing, with one eye on the TV screens as the events downtown unfolded. With the words "So help me God," spontaneous, polite applause filled the lounge and we then prepared to walk the short distance to the hangar where the now former president would shortly arrive.

The temperature in the hangar was in the high twenties, but we were at least shielded from the blustery winds as the Bushes and the Cheneys disentangled themselves from the ceremony downtown and made their way to the helicopter for a last ride to Andrews.

The crowd there was pretty evenly divided: one part GIs who had served the president in his travels; one part young White House staffers; and one part senior (including cabinet-level) officials. The first two groups ensured that there would be a lot of hooting and hollering when the party arrived from downtown. They didn't disappoint.

Vice President Cheney had hurt his back, so he entered in a wheelchair with a blanket over his legs, unfortunately looking like he was audition-ing for Lionel Barrymore's role of Mr. Potter in some as yet unannounced remake of *It's a Wonderful Life.* The president bounded onstage, acknowl-edging the loud applause as he scanned the crowd. He noticed Jeanine and me off to one side, made eye contact with a slight hint of surprise in his face, and gave me that almost imperceptible nod he had given me in the Sit Room a year before.

The ceremony, such as it was, was short. The young folks afterward rushed the rope line around the stage, and I turned to leave but was stopped short by my wife, who said she wanted to go up for one last goodbye. So we waited at the very end of the rope line as President Bush made his farewells. When he got to us, Jeanine was in front of me and got a hug. Then President Bush reached beyond Jeanine, grabbed my shoul-der, and pulled me toward him. At which point the forty-third president of the United States gave me a warm embrace, practically kissing my forehead, and then wordlessly began to walk toward the waiting 747 for the trip to Texas. Andrews was the right choice.

As the Bush family went to Texas, I went back to work. I would be President Obama's CIA director for the next three weeks. We continued to make our adjustments to the new team. The president's staff demanded brevity in written intelligence products, so much so that one analyst la-beled what we were writing for the morning briefing as PDB haiku. I gave an operational update, scaling back the detail I knew President Bush had liked, and I was still told never to brief the president on such minutiae again. Given how much President Obama later got into the details of programs like targeted killings, I suspect the early fretting was more from his staff than it was from him.

But that was going to be somebody else's problem now. I was leaving and sent one final message to the workforce. It read, in part:

> Our Agency has chosen a quotation from the New Testament to underscore its core mission: "And ye shall know the truth and the truth shall make you free."
>
> Today, though, the Old Testament offers relevant guidance: "To everything there is a season and a time to every purpose under the heaven." It is the season and the time for Jeanine and me to say farewell to you, the wonderful men and women of the Central Intelligence Agency. We have been here for nearly three years and consider ourselves privileged to have been a part of you and your work. . . .
>
> You have . . . carried out your duties with integrity and in a manner that respects American law and reflects America's values. The Nation could ask no more.
>
> You may catch a glimpse of me later in the week but that will largely be me moving out. That's physically moving out. We will be with you spiritually and emotionally for as long as you will have us.
>
> With Deepest Respect,
> Mike Hayden
> 18th Director of CIA

There was nothing left to do but go. Midafternoon on a cold February Friday, Steve Kappes accompanied Jeanine and me through the front lobby to a waiting car for the drive to our house.

Once home, I turned my mind to preparing for the May Pittsburgh Marathon, for which I had signed up, one of the better life decisions I had ever made. I was hopeful that running ten, twelve, fifteen miles or more a day would ease any transition. I was right.

TWENTY

"GENERAL, THEY'RE GOING TO RELEASE THE MEMOS"

MCLEAN, VA, 2009–2014

J im, you're about to spend at least the next forty-six months without a National Clandestine Service."

When I was a junior officer, the air force taught me to begin a briefing with an attention step. That was the best one I had ever come up with, and I had just used it on the national security advisor.

Jim Jones was an old friend. We had been neighbors at European Command in Germany in the early 1990s and Jim and I had traveled together to Bosnia to coordinate US support to the UN mission in that country.

I was right to call the national security advisor, even if I was out of government now, but I was also trading on friendship. Jim was gracious, took the call, gave me the time I needed to explain my concern, and thanked me (genuinely) for raising the issue.

The issue was this: President Obama—at the urging of Attorney General Eric Holder and White House Counsel Greg Craig—had decided to stop fighting an ACLU Freedom of Information Act (FOIA) lawsuit and had agreed to release four Justice Department legal opinions that laid out in detail the techniques that had been authorized for CIA's interrogation of high-value terrorists.

Only days before, agency lawyers had been working with Justice and other departments sorting out which of the many available FOIA exemptions they would use to protect various parts of the documents.

The memos had been a bone of contention for years. They were heavily classified as well as protected by legal privilege, and the Bush administration had only reluctantly shared them with an expanding circle of congressional members and staff.

Now Greg Craig was telling John Rizzo, CIA's acting general counsel, that Justice would be telling the ACLU and the court that the government would release the DOJ memos with minimal redactions.

Rizzo was no stranger to the issue. He was the *acting* general counsel because the Senate Intelligence Committee had denied him the head post after he refused in his confirmation hearing to condemn these same DOJ opinions.

Rizzo related the Craig phone call to Deputy Director Steve Kappes, who was equally stunned. He began his own inquiries downtown while directing Rizzo to alert several former directors. That was pretty much standard practice when formers were going to be implicated in breaking news.

Rizzo called me, still with a tone of disbelief in his voice: "General, they're going to release the memos." I couldn't believe it either. In the very same ACLU FOIA suit, CIA had been in front of the court the year before on an almost identical issue. Based on a declaration I signed, the judge had agreed to allow us to continue to protect—on grounds of national security—the specifics of waterboarding, an interrogation technique that had not been used since 2003, that the agency had not authorized for potential use in years, and that we had publicly acknowledged might now very well be illegal under laws recently enacted by Congress. Despite all that, the court agreed that revealing the details of the technique would tie the hands of a president in a future emergency, since, after all, laws and policies could change.

Releasing the memos would also be inconsistent with an administration commitment *not* to look backward. During the transition, the new president and his team assured me there would be no retrospectives, no witch hunts, no persecution.

Indeed, when I finally got my "Dear John" phone call from the president-elect, he told me that my departure from CIA would help reinforce that message. A new director would make it easier for the president to stick to his policy and his pledge to move ahead.

After mulling the situation for a few hours, I called Jim Jones from the parking lot of a northern Virginia shopping center after dropping my wife off at her book club. The next day I spoke with White House Counsel Greg Craig and the following day, with Jim's deputy, Tom Donilon.

I challenged the Justice Department's presumption that the government was going to lose the case. I pointed to the successful 2008 defense of the details of waterboarding.

I emphasized that the White House could not expect to control events in the aftermath of a release. Despite the administration's commitment to look forward, the release would fuel *more* requests for documents, and there was no natural firewall now that the details of the techniques themselves were *voluntarily* declassified.

There would be calls for prosecution—of the authors of the opinions, those who requested them, those who carried them out, those who gave them their policy approval. Calls for disbarment of lawyers and sanctions of medical and psychological professionals involved in the program would follow.

I described the decision as a "betrayal of trust" and a "fundamental dishonesty." Good men could disagree on the merits of what the agency had done, and the president's policy decision to ratchet back interrogation practices was the kind of decision that the agency expected the commander in chief to make. But this decision was different. This was pushing good people—doing what they did out of duty rather than enthusiasm—into the bus lane and seeming indifferent to what would happen next.

More substantively, I argued that revealing these techniques would teach our enemies the outer limits of what they could expect in any future interrogation session with Americans. The Army Field Manual, the Department of Defense's guidelines for interrogations, was unclassified and already available on the Web, where it was being used by al-Qaeda to teach how to resist American interrogation.

I reminded Greg Craig that the president's executive order that limited government agencies to the Army Field Manual had also directed a government-wide study to judge whether or not the techniques authorized in the manual were sufficient to guard against future threats. Now the president's own study was being mooted by this decision to reveal a detailed description of all our alternative techniques. Removing an enemy's uncertainty by telling him the precise limits of what you may do, how, and for how long would only steel his ability to resist and make any exposed technique ineffective. That meant they were off the table. Period.

Craig pushed back. The president was *never* going to authorize any of the thirteen techniques that were about to be revealed. My first response was that—as popular as the president was currently—he was not president for life, and he had no right to foreclose options for his successors.

But I pressed the case more directly. "Let me get this right," I said. "There are no circumstances of threat under which the president will allow us to interrupt the sleep cycle of a terrorist even if it would help get at lifesaving information?"

Administration officials frequently reminded me that the ICRC's summary of interviews with fourteen former CIA detainees (chapter 12) had recently been leaked. The argument was that, since so much was already out there, it would be impossible not to declassify almost all of the DOJ memos.

I couldn't fathom how the unauthorized disclosure of the ICRC report, which was based entirely on one-sided prisoner debriefs, could possibly lead the US government to conclude that it had no choice but to declassify and inventory for the world the details of our past enhanced interrogation program. There was a difference between speculation (informed or ill-informed) and formal confirmation by the US government.

And that brought my discussions to the core point, a point I emphasized to Jones, Craig, and Donilon: the disclosure of these memos would have a terribly negative impact on the *future* actions of CIA.

With the details of a previously authorized covert action being revealed, declared criminal and disavowed by an incoming administration, every case officer in the agency would now hold any government assurance up to the light and ask if any pledge to them would last longer than one election cycle.

Later, on *Fox News Sunday*, I had a chance to spell this out by suggesting a conversation with a fictitious case officer who is asked to carry out an edgy covert action. The director assures the case officer, "Well, it's authorized by the president. The attorney general says it's lawful. And it's been briefed to Congress."

I then had my fictitious case officer respond: "[Okay, but] have you run it by the ACLU? What does the *New York Times* editorial board think? Have you discussed this with any potential presidential candidates?" I concluded, "In short, you're going to have this agency—on the front line of defending you in this current war—playing back from that line."

Who could blame current officers and the generations to come after them if they never again risked such exposure?

Greg Craig knew that releasing the memos would have an impact. He told me that this decision would "hurt our relationship with the agency."

"Hurt?" I replied. "I think you're *really* lowballing this, Greg."

A sincere attempt by Director Panetta to buck up the spirit of those most affected by this was described by one participant as resembling a "pep rally in the Führer bunker."

I was told that one officer asked the director if the people doing the things currently authorized by the Obama administration would be dragged through this same kind of knothole in five years. Panetta was honest. He couldn't guarantee that they wouldn't. But, he added, that wouldn't happen under this president. Everyone in the room must have appreciated the candor, but they also realized that the durability of support for any of their actions might not be more than one or two election cycles.

We were working to avoid such an outcome. I was making calls. So was George Tenet. So was Porter Goss. So was John McLaughlin. So was John Deutch. That's an uninterrupted string of directors and acting directors reaching back to 1995.

Each of us touched someone in the administration we knew. George called John Brennan, his former chief of staff and at this time deputy national security advisor for Homeland Security. Deutsch called Tom Donilon, an old friend and Jones's deputy. McLaughlin called Denny Blair.

Late Friday afternoon, Craig told me that the train had stopped for now. He had asked the National Security Council to hold a principals meeting the following week. That meant that the national security advisor, the secretary of state, the secretary of defense, the chairman of the Joint Chiefs, the attorney general, the secretary of Homeland Security, the director of National Intelligence, and the director of CIA would consider the issue. We welcomed that, since in our view, the arguments against releasing the documents had not been addressed and the arguments in favor of releasing them had gone unchallenged.

All of this movement about the DOJ memos—pending Department of Justice decisions, CIA angst and anger, former directors weighing in, multiple phone calls between and among multiple actors—was kept from the public eye until Saturday, March 21, an eternity by Washington standards, but about five days according to the way time is reckoned in the rest of the country. And then the story was outed in *Newsweek*—sourced explicitly to administration officials and clearly (if implicitly) from the Department of Justice. The story claimed that the release of the memos had already been decided. The piece asserted that "the White House has sided with Holder." A "senior Obama official" called the memos "ugly" and said they would "embarrass the CIA." The official also claimed that I was "furious" in my phone calls to administration officials trying to reverse the decision.

By putting it out that the decision had already been made, those supporting release were leaning on the president, since any no-go decision would now be portrayed as walking back a decision under pressure from the intelligence community. Later stories described the battle over the memos as a major test of the Obama administration's commitment to transparency.

I told Craig that the administration sources for the articles were doing the agency (and the truth) a disservice by claiming that the agency would be embarrassed by the memos. That maliciously mischaracterized our objections—which had to do with national security, not shame or humiliation. In fact, the memos' release would display the agency's emphasis on continuing dialogue with Justice for the life of the program and would counter many of the ridiculously extreme accusations being made.

Over the course of the next weeks, the NSC did indeed meet on several occasions to try to come to consensus. From all accounts, the agency had opportunities to present its views, and Director Panetta was forceful in expressing them.

Public arguments swirled around the contention that CIA's program had made America less safe by serving as a recruiting tool for jihadists.

It was an easy argument to make. It fit the narrative that American actions created many of our current problems. It just wasn't all that true, or at least all that simple. Lots of things motivated Islamic extremists to take up arms against the United States, but I never encountered any evidence to suggest that CIA's detention of about a hundred terrorist leaders and the tough interrogation of about a third of them had filled the ranks of al-Qaeda.

There were many factors. The spring 2006 National Intelligence Estimate assessed that the war in Iraq had become a "cause célèbre" for jihadists. Radical Web sites routinely cited US support for Israel or conservative Arab governments in their recruitment pitches. The abuses committed by US military personnel at Abu Ghraib had clearly accelerated al-Qaeda recruitment after those images were played and replayed around the world.

But I never encountered a radical Islamist argument that was based on how CIA handled Khalid Sheikh Mohammed or Abu Zubaida or Abd al-Rahim al-Nashiri; I never found an Islamic partner who raised the issue or said that it was an impediment to our cooperation.

In fact, sensitive to how our relationship might be affected after we had very publicly moved fourteen high-value detainees to Guantánamo in 2006, I raised the subject privately with an important Middle East partner. He simply reassured me that he, his service, and his government knew who these people were and what they had done. This was not an issue, he told me.

It would be useful to keep in mind that even if such things—Abu Ghraib, Guantánamo, black sites, Iraq, Israel—might serve (in different degrees) as convenient symbols, they are not at the core of the jihadist narrative. Sayyid Qutb, the Egyptian whose writings form the theological base of modern jihadism, visited the United States in the late 1940s. He described it as a soulless, materialistic place and equated green lawns with greed, and jazz with bestiality. He criticized church socials in conservative Greeley, Colorado, for what he saw as their overt sexuality and condemned our emphasis on civil over divine law. Such beliefs reinforce a worldview where the corruption of modernism itself, represented by Jews and Crusaders, threatens the harmony of Islam. In such an all-defining Manichean universe, American actions might, at the margins, affect the power of the jihadist message, but if they do, we might look to our sexual mores as much as how we choose to defend ourselves.

I will admit that how we choose to defend ourselves *does* affect *European* elites and *European* government and media circles. But those groups do as much huffing and puffing over American targeted killings (which expanded after 2008), renditions (which continued), and electronic espionage (which became less secret) as they do over detentions (which were curtailed) and interrogations (which stopped). And all their objections are anchored in a broader belief system that challenges the current American view toward the utility and legitimacy of force in the modern world. In short, it, too, is part of a much larger conversation.

Another of the "facts" being contested was whether or not the techniques worked; if they didn't, there was little reason to protect them now.

I argued publicly that they did work and had been vital for national security. In a Fox News interview the Sunday after the release of the memos, I said, "The facts of the case are that the use of these techniques against these terrorists made us safer. It really did work. . . . President Bush, in September of '06, outlined how one detainee led to another, led to another, with the use of these techniques."

Indeed, following the release of the DOJ memos, DNI Blair confirmed in a message he sent to the entire intelligence community that "high-value information came from interrogations in which those methods were used and provided a deeper understanding of the al-Qaeda organization that was attacking this country." Even though those words were mysteriously removed from the version of Blair's note that was released to the press, the administration could not contradict his or CIA's conclusions on this point without exposing themselves to a charge that they were politicizing intelligence.

(Five years later Democrats on the Senate Intelligence Committee aggressively challenged the effectiveness argument, but in 2009 the president did not.)

At a press conference marking his first hundred days in office, the president defended his January executive order banning enhanced techniques. "I am absolutely convinced it was the right thing to do, *not because there might not have been information that was yielded by these various detainees who were subjected to this treatment.*"

That put some distance between the president and the program's more strident critics. As I said in the Fox interview, "Most of the people who oppose these techniques want to be able to say, I don't want my nation doing this (which is a purely honorable position), *and they didn't work anyway.* The back half of that sentence isn't true." I continued, "The honorable position has to be, even though these techniques worked, I don't want you to do that. That takes courage. The other sentence doesn't."

From all accounts, even after considerable deliberation, the NSC principals had been divided on the question of releasing the DOJ memos. Some reports suggest that there had been talk of releasing a heavily redacted version of the opinions (the CIA position) balanced by a commitment to launch a presidential commission to review the whole history of interrogation techniques (a concession to "transparency").

In the end, though, the president was faced with a binary choice: release the memos largely intact (the DOJ position) or decide to substantially protect the documents and fight their release in court (the CIA position).

According to the *Washington Post*, with his counselors divided, the president held a late-night meeting in which he assigned one advisor to argue for release of the memos (Greg Craig) and another to argue against (Denis McDonough). At the end of the mock debate, the president opted for release and personally dictated a draft of his public announcement for the next day.

This decision was the same one that Greg Craig had announced to CIA four weeks earlier. Nothing had changed but the date.

I got a call on the morning of April 16 from Director Panetta's chief of staff telling me that the DOJ memos would be released with minimal redactions. That was followed by a call from John Brennan, former CIA senior and now Jim Jones's deputy for Homeland Security. John was in Mexico City awaiting the president's arrival there. I gave him little comfort, decrying the decision as a "fundamental dishonesty" toward the officers of the agency.

Within the next hour, I was called by Jim Jones from Air Force One en route to Mexico with the president. The best I could offer Jim was that I knew how to respect the person and the office of the president but that "I could not just make stuff up." He easily acknowledged that. It was a bad connection. We lost contact at least three times, and I'm sure Jim was as frustrated with the circumstances of our dialogue as I was.

I called former attorney general Mike Mukasey. He and I had drafted an op-ed laying out our objections to the president's decision. We hit the core of our case very early in the piece:

The release of these opinions was unnecessary as a legal matter, and is unsound as a matter of policy. Its effect will be to invite the kind of institutional timidity and fear of recrimination that weakened intelligence gathering in the past, and that we came sorely to regret on September 11, 2001.

We struck out against the arguments in favor of release:

Proponents of the release have argued that the techniques have been abandoned and thus there is no point in keeping them secret any longer; that they were in any event ineffective; that their disclosure was somehow legally compelled; and that they cost us more in the coin of world opinion than they were worth. None of these claims survives scrutiny.

We had held off publishing the op-ed until the president's final decision, since we didn't want to make it harder for the president to do the right thing (as we saw it) by attaching the names of two Bush administration formers to arguments against release.

Although the piece was about twice the length of a normal op-ed, the *Wall Street Journal* agreed to fit it into the next day's paper.

It was important that they did. Both Judge Mukasey and I believed that the public debate needed a calm, coherent counterpoint to what the administration was sure to lay out. I also felt very strongly that the agency workforce needed to hear this voice as quickly as possible, especially since Director Panetta was in no position to make any of the points himself.

I was right. One career operations officer told me, "Friday was an incredibly dark day but I was very proud when I read your piece." Another said, "I read your piece, which captured the moment and the stakes with precision and clarity. Thank God someone is saying what must be said."

The president knew that the release of the memos would hit the agency hard, so the following Monday he visited Langley. He privately met with and answered questions from members of the CTC before the public event in the concourse. By all accounts it was a lighthearted affair with a series of friendly questions until the call went out for "one more question" and a CTC veteran who had been standing in the back of the room with two others raised a hand. Steve Kappes motioned to Director Panetta to recognize the officer, which he did.

The officer thanked the president for coming, conceded that the RDI (rendition, detention, and interrogation) program raised controversial moral and legal questions, but then asked if the president agreed that they could go back and tell their workforce that what they had done in the program had saved lives.

The president, who had been standing at a lectern, came out from behind it, changed his tone, and—waving his finger in the air—began a short lecture on the need for morality.

The agency has a secure instant messaging system called Sametime. Shortly after the session ended, the network was lighting up with comments supportive of the officer as word of the exchange spread.

The president then went to the concourse to speak to about a thousand agency employees, many of whom had been waiting for hours to see him.

Standing in front of the wall of stars for the agency's fallen, the president praised the agency's work and said he knew that "the last few days have been difficult." He justified the release "as a consequence of a court case that was pending and to which it was very difficult for us to mount an effective legal defense." He also asserted, "So much of the information was public—had been publicly acknowledged. The covert nature of the information had been compromised."

The president then urged agency officers not to be "discouraged by what's happened in the last few weeks. Don't be discouraged that we have to acknowledge potentially we've made some mistakes. That's how we learn."

One officer told me that the agency consensus was that that last passage sounded a lot like *Mister Rogers*. The president apparently saw this as one of those teachable moments, while the agency's counterterrorism workforce continued to believe that the past policies were not mistakes at all, but were a central reason why the country had not suffered an attack in more than seven years.

The president was right to go to Langley, and there is no doubt that the agency's officers appreciated his offer of support. But this episode raised issues that could not be fixed by one visit or one speech or one photo op.

Washington Post columnist David Ignatius writes frequently about CIA. He is often a critic, but his comments are rarely without affection or respect for the agency and its people.

Two days after the president's visit, Ignatius—who has always been well wired into the CIA alumni association—published a savage column in the *Washington Post*. "Sad to say," he began, "it's slow roll time at Langley after the release of interrogation memos that, in the words of one veteran officer, 'hit the agency like a car bomb in the driveway.'"

Ignatius noted that the president had tried in his personal visit on Monday to reassure the agency workforce: "He said all the right things about the agency's clandestine role. But it had the look of a campaign event, with employees hooting and hollering and the president reading from his teleprompter with a backdrop of stars that commemorate the CIA's fallen warriors."

Ignatius's judgment was that "Obama seems to think he can have it both ways—authorizing an unprecedented disclosure of CIA operational methods and at the same time galvanizing a clandestine service whose best days, he told them Monday, are 'yet to come.' Life doesn't work that way—even for charismatic politicians."

Many Langley veterans now believed that it was only a matter of time before the long knives were out for the agency and perhaps for its officers as well.

The day after his Langley visit the president refused to rule out legal action against lawyers who crafted the DOJ memos; human rights groups handed Attorney General Holder a petition with 250,000 signatures demanding a special prosecutor; and UN officials and human rights law-yers were predicting that—absent US prosecutions—European courts would investigate American officials suspected of violating the ban on torture.

In the media and political frenzy that followed the release of the memos, charges and countercharges were hurled about. When a CIA-prepared timeline of congressional briefings on interrogation techniques was leaked to the press, the question of who in Congress was briefed, when, and what they were told became a critical subplot to the whole drama.

About a month after the release of the memos (which, remember, was done to put the whole issue of interrogation behind us), a headline in the Capitol Hill daily *Politico* screamed, "Democrats: CIA Out to Get Us."

Two days later the Speaker of the House explicitly accused the agency of lying to Congress—both with respect to the use of enhanced interro-gation methods ("The CIA comes to Congress, withholds information about the timing and use of this subject") and more generally ("They mislead us all the time").

Senator Feinstein, chair of the Senate Intelligence Committee, has-tened to back up Pelosi, charging, "The CIA is not an agency that is above not telling the truth," and Congresswoman Anna Eshoo, of the House Intelligence Committee, chimed in, "You have to play twenty questions with them. They are not forthcoming with information."

In a letter to the workforce designed to be made available to the press, Director Panetta shot back, "It is not our policy or practice to mislead Congress. That is against our laws and our values. . . . [O]ur contempo-raneous records from September 2002 indicate that CIA officers briefed truthfully on the interrogation of Abu Zubaida, describing 'the enhanced techniques that had been employed.'"

To say that the whole mess had now become quite ugly was an under-statement. And it wasn't over.

The driving force within the administration for making the memos public was Eric Holder.

While campaigning for the president, Holder had identified CIA in-terrogations as torture, even though he had never been briefed on the specifics of the program. He also promised a reckoning of CIA activities. That pretty much put him on the same ground as candidate Obama. As president, though, Obama had softened his views. When the Bush-era DOJ opinions were released in April, for example, he cautioned, "This is a time for reflection, not retribution."

Holder apparently never got the memo. He and his staff, according to published accounts, expected release to lead to "a groundswell of support for an independent probe."

When it didn't, they persevered. By summer the AG was pushing to release the CIA inspector general's 2004 classified report on the interro-gation program and to reopen investigations of agency officers.

For the agency, this was like a recurring bad dream. The entire IG re-port had been available to the leadership of the intelligence committees since 2004 and to all members of the committees and an extensive num-ber of staffers since 2006.

The agency had cooperated extensively in the prosecution of an agency contractor who was convicted for manslaughter following the death of one detainee. The agency had also referred other findings of inappropri-ate behavior to the Department of Justice, where they were reviewed thor-oughly by career prosecutors in the Eastern District of Virginia, who ultimately declined further prosecutions. (Holder later admitted that he had not read the career prosecutors' declinations.) Finally, following the prosecutors' decision not to act, the agency took its own disciplinary ac-tion, where appropriate.

Leon Panetta reportedly opposed further DOJ actions in a series of profanity-laced outbursts in the Situation Room. He also took the un-usual step in early August of penning an op-ed in the *Washington Post*. He reported, "Last month, at a meeting overseas of intelligence service chiefs, one of my counterparts from a major Western ally pulled me aside. Why, he asked, is Washington so consumed with what the CIA did in the past, when the most pressing national security concerns are in the present? It was a very good question."

To no avail. Within a few weeks the administration released a lightly redacted version of the CIA inspector general's 2004 report, more Department of Justice legal opinions, as well as a stack of correspondence between CIA and the Office of Legal Counsel. Holder also announced that he had directed John Durham, who was already investigating the agency's destruction of videotapes (see chapter 12), to expand his inquiry to determine whether a full criminal investigation of agency conduct was warranted.

The president had at least tacitly sided with his attorney general. Leon had been unable to stop the train. Now seven of his predecessors stepped forward to try their hand. In mid-September we wrote the president urging him to reverse Holder's decision to reopen the criminal investigations. The letter rehearsed the usual arguments: foreign services will be more reluctant to collaborate; agency officers will become more risk-averse; public disclosures will help al-Qaeda elude US intelligence.

The core argument, however, was one of fairness. "If criminal investigations closed by career prosecutors during one administration can so easily be reopened at the direction of political appointees in the next, declinations of prosecution will be rendered meaningless. . . . [Officers] must believe there is permanence in the legal rules that govern their actions."

Former CIA directors are not an especially close-knit group. They may get together once or twice a year to hear from the current director, but they served different presidents in different times, under different circumstances. It would be hard to get them all to agree that a certain day was Tuesday.

But, once we got the language down, getting agreement to sign the letter was not a heavy lift. All but three former living directors signed the document. Bob Gates was serving as secretary of defense, so we didn't even inform him. George H. W. Bush was a former president, and it would have been inappropriate for us to ask him to comment on the actions of a successor. Admiral Stansfield Turner, who was approaching his eighty-sixth birthday, simply deferred on the grounds that he was not current on the issue. We didn't press him.

It was axiomatic that three of us—Goss, Tenet, and I—would sign; after all, we ran the program. But Woolsey and Deutch were long gone, after having served in the Clinton administration. William Webster was a former federal judge and head of the FBI. And Jim Schlesinger's body of work included an investigation into DOD's abuse of prisoners at Abu Ghraib.

All that said, we did not impress. The president noted our concerns with a fairly dismissive, "I appreciate the former CIA directors wanting to look out for an institution that they helped to build." Although he repeated his preference to "look forward and not backward," he declined to intervene.

The investigation lasted a full three years, during which scores of agency officers were interviewed and many appeared before a grand jury.

The whole affair created a sense of siege at the agency. In February 2010, after the death of seven agency officers and contractors in the suicide bombing at Khost, the agency held a memorial service in a large tent in front of the Original Headquarters Building. The president attended, as did other political leaders like Speaker of the House Nancy Pelosi.

Several eulogists were from the Counterterrorism Center, the very people most affected by Holder's and the president's decisions and by Pelosi's accusation that the agency routinely lies. One eulogist may have signaled the sense of the "them vs. us" estrangement when she highlighted "the privilege of being part of a real band of brothers and sisters engaged in a common struggle." There was an almost unspoken, "We're glad you're here but this is really about us. We were doing this before you got here and we will be doing this after you leave."

The disclosures and renewed investigations were even the cause for some dark humor at the agency. At General Counsel John Rizzo's retirement in late 2009, the emcee was reading a series of letters—testimonials to John's work. As he was closing, he said that he had one more. While reaching for a document in his pocket, he described it as being personally for John from Attorney General Holder. "John," he read, "you have the right to remain silent." It was several minutes before the laughter had died down enough for the ceremony to continue.

But the impact of multiple investigations was no joke. CIA was servicing Durham's investigation into the destruction of the tapes, the reinvestigation into incidents detailed in the IG report, and accelerated congressional inquiries on a variety of fronts. Beyond the impact on morale, foreign relations, and the willingness to embrace risk, there was just a raw manpower bill that the agency had to pay. And it was a high-end manpower bill, to boot. Responding to all those inquiries required some of the best talent the agency had to offer. A permanent office was set up on the seventh floor opposite the director's suite to manage the flow.

Three years and six days after the attorney general reopened investigations, he and prosecutor John Durham announced that they would not pursue criminal charges against anyone in CIA's RDI program. The bloodletting, at least inside the executive branch, appeared to be over.

Holder had been consistent throughout: messianic in his focus, politically tone-deaf, and indifferent to contrary evidence and views.

Panetta was equally consistent, warning that by focusing on the past, we were risking the present and the future.

The president seemed to want to have it both ways. He came out looking inconsistent to people on both sides of the issue.

He may have viewed splitting the difference as his best principled alternative, but it also had a political appeal. The president had a problem. To the disappointment of many, he had doubled down on much of his predecessor's counterterrorism programs. Telephone metadata. State secrets. Renditions. Targeted killings. Military commissions. Frankly, there was a bigger difference between President Bush's first and second terms than there was between him and his successor.

And that was a political problem for President Obama, who campaigned fundamentally on not being George Bush. Let me show you how different I really am, the president must have reasoned. Let me show you what I stopped. And so he released the interrogation memos and allowed (perhaps supported—the record is not clear) his attorney general to release more documents and reopen already closed cases.

The folks at CIA paid a heavy personal price, but perhaps they shouldn't have felt surprised or offended. Personally the president had showed them some appreciation, but this was business and they were props.

And there was more to come.

About the time in 2012 that Holder was standing down the Durham inquiry, my cell phone rang and George Tenet asked me if I had heard about the "SSCI report." I was vaguely aware that Democrat committee staff had been working on something, but I truly had to plead ignorance. "Haven't we seen this movie before, George?" I asked.

In fact, we hadn't, which became really clear two days after the 2012 presidential election. George, Porter Goss, John McLaughlin, and I (directors and acting directors during the RDI program) had arranged for an agency update. Michael Morell, the deputy director and a good friend to all of us, took the meeting and outlined the draft SSCI Democrat report that the agency had recently received. It was an unrelenting prosecutorial screed that accused us and the agency of going beyond our authorities and lying to everyone about that and about the effectiveness of the program. We were all more than a little stunned. And angry. We asked how the Democrat staff could arrive at those conclusions without talking to any of us.

We also asked why this was being done. We were told that the SSCI staff director had said because Senator Feinstein wanted to be sure that this would never happen again, which struck us as a conclusion that then launched a search for data.

The agency was as livid about the report as we were, and they were going to push back hard, since the draft had been selective in citing documents, had errors of fact, and seemed ignorant of the way that intelligence really worked.

It was obvious that this was really going to be interesting when the public pissing started just a few weeks later over (of all things) a movie, *Zero Dark Thirty*, that dramatized the intelligence work that led to the killing of Osama bin Laden. There were complaints that the intelligence and special operations communities had leaned too far forward helping director Kathryn Bigelow and screenwriter Mark Boal. Several members of the Senate demanded that Sony Pictures issue a disclaimer on the role of CIA interrogations in the hunt.

It took two more years of arguing between CIA, the White House, and the SSCI Democrat staff about data, analytic tradecraft, and classification before a five-hundred-plus-page summary of the Feinstein report finally saw the light of day. During that time, the former seniors implicated in the report met or teleconferenced periodically to stay updated and to prepare a response.

It would be hard to overstate our anger, but responding to the calumny was going to be challenging. We were only given a two-week window in August 2014 in which we could actually access the summary report, the agency's 130-plus-page response, and the SSCI Republicans' 150-plus-page rebuttal. With prior travel commitments, I managed to squeeze in about four hours of reading one afternoon.

Undeterred, we submitted our own Freedom of Information Act requests to CIA to get other documents to buttress our case. Bill Harlow, George Tenet's superb public affairs chief, built a Web site, ciasavedlives .com, so that we could make documents available to the press and public. We offered background briefings to any print or video journalist who would care to listen. John McLaughlin crafted a magnificent 2,300-word op-ed that we pre-positioned with the *Wall Street Journal*'s Web site along with a shorter version for the print edition. The op-ed was signed by the three directors and the three deputy directors who had managed the RDI program. I wrote a companion piece for the British press, all to be triggered by the release of the Feinstein report itself, which finally took place on December 12, 2014.

John's argument in the *Journal* summarized our case:

> The Senate Intelligence Committee's report on Central Intelligence Agency detention and interrogation of terrorists, prepared only by the Democratic majority staff, is . . . a one-sided study marred by errors of fact and interpretation—essentially a poorly done and partisan attack on the agency that has done the most to protect America after the 9/11 attacks.

He challenged the report's findings that CIA routinely went beyond the authorized interrogation techniques and misled the Justice Department, the White House, Congress, and the American people. He pointed out that the report chose to ignore the context of the time in which the program was launched and the fact that the agency was not operating alone (he noted more than thirty briefings to Congress).

Most important, he (like the agency and Republican rebuttals) challenged the "claim that the CIA's interrogation program was ineffective in producing intelligence that helped us disrupt, capture, or kill terrorists," citing multiple examples of its effectiveness, including the bin Laden takedown.

One agency wag put it more bluntly: "The Feinstein report would have you believe that the people who got bin Laden just didn't know how it was they got bin Laden."

I received special mention in the Feinstein report, being cited more than three times as often as any of my predecessors. That was not because of the number of detainees I had (two in a total of about a hundred), but rather because I was the director who briefed the entire committee on the full scope of the program.

They particularly focused on my April 2007 testimony, dedicating all of appendix three to pointing out what they believed to be inaccuracies.

A lot of the issues had to do with the still raging argument over what Abu Zubaida (the first detainee to be waterboarded) told us, when, and why. Other issues could fairly be described as my briefing the standard and their searching through millions (literally) of pages to find the deviations, most of which were early in the program.

Then there was the issue of what constituted the program. I said that the program I was briefing was created, at least in part, because of the poor agency performance with early battlefield captures—as thoroughly documented and shared with the SSCI by CIA's inspector general. The committee knew that Gul Rahman had died in agency custody, for example, but CIA never considered him part of *this* program.

And finally, there is the very real possibility that in two hours of testimony discussing things five years distant and separated from me by the administration of two other directors, I may have just gotten some things wrong. It's possible.

Most important, our purpose for the 2007 session—as well as similar sessions with the HPSCI—had *not* been to narrate a definitive history of the RDI program, but to explain its *current* status as a first step in building a consensus on a way ahead. That never happened, of course.

I got wrapped around another axle in the report concerning the number of detainees. According to the report, I "instructed a CIA officer to devise a way to keep the number of CIA detainees at the same number that the CIA had previously briefed to Congress." The report says that was ninety-eight; I think it was actually ninety-nine.

The alleged "incident" took place in January 2009 as I was getting ready to step out the door. One CTC officer suggested that the right number of detainees in the program could be as high as 112. There had always been questions as to who should be counted in the program, and early bookkeeping had been sloppy, but I couldn't resist offering a half smile and saying, "You people have pushed me out there for three years with ninety-seven or ninety-eight [as we added detainees]."

The agency rebuttal reflects the consensus from that meeting that the new CTC numbers were still "somewhat speculative and incomplete." I said that if there really were new numbers, they better make sure and then tell the new director to pass them on to Congress.

The Feinstein report settled on "at least 119" (not 112) as the right number of detainees to book under the program.

That said, Attorney General Holder, at the conclusion of the Durham investigation, confidently announced that "Mr. Durham examined any possible CIA involvement with the interrogation and detention of *101 detainees* who were alleged to have been in United States custody." Looks like it was always a hard number—99, 101, 112, 119—to pin down.

I've since reflected on the Feinstein report and what lessons to draw from it. One positive take-away was the clear need to brief Congress fully and contemporaneously on sensitive activity. No fair relying on a director five years later to reconstruct events.

I'm close to drawing a second, darker conclusion too. Be careful what you tell these people. Some are less interested in honest dialogue than listening to rebut and accuse and discredit.

Which, I suppose, again raises the question of motive. Why the report? CIA was out of the interrogation business. It wasn't going back.*

Here, too, my darker angels suggest an answer. I picture those who really pushed the release thinking that this earned for them a sense of expiation. They get to say, and say publicly, "See. This wasn't about us. It was never about us. We're not like that. Those people, those people over there. The ones who lied. It's about them. Let me show you."

Senator Rockefeller was an especially strong advocate for the Feinstein report. He issued his own sharply critical statement at its release in December 2014.

In March 2003, following the capture of Khalid Sheikh Mohammed, the senator's tone was somewhat different.

---

* In the summer of 2015 I met with presidential candidate Jeb Bush. When the subject of interrogation techniques came up, I opined that—after the memos being released, the techniques being exposed, and CIA officers seemingly abandoned—any future president who would want to resurrect the techniques had better practice up because he would have to administer them himself.

CNN's Wolf Blitzer asked him what would happen to KSM.

ROCKEFELLER: *Well, happily we don't know where he is. . . . He'll be grilled by us. I'm sure we'll be proper with him, but I'm sure we'll be very, very tough with him.*

That raised the question of torture for Blitzer.

ROCKEFELLER: *That's always a delicate question. . . . On the other hand, he does have the information. Getting that information will save American lives. We have no business not getting that information.*

Blitzer again raised the question of torture.

ROCKEFELLER: *We do not sanction torture, but there are psychological and other means that can accomplish most of what we want.*

Blitzer then asked about handing him over to a third country "where the restrictions against torture are not in existence."

ROCKEFELLER: *I wouldn't take anything off the table where he is concerned, because this is the man who has killed hundreds and hundreds of Americans over the last ten years.*

Hmmm. You could see how the folks at the agency might have been confused.

They, of course, disagreed with the report, its narrative, its method, and its conclusions. And they especially disagreed that this was all just about them. If it was just about them, congressional Democrats (those who had been briefed) would have begun their protest in 2002—when the trauma was recent, the threat seemed imminent, and the future was in doubt—and not in 2014, when it was not.

Americans agreed with the agency. Poll after poll following release of the Feinstein report sided with CIA by a wide margin. Pew put the split at 51–29 that CIA's actions were justified. The split was even larger, 56–28, that intelligence from the program prevented attacks. For those who said they were closely following the issue, the numbers were even stronger.

They supported the program 59–34. CNN had similar numbers, 66–34 overall.

Brookings, a highly regarded Washington think tank, led its coverage with the headline "Americans Have Taken Ownership of the CIA's Interrogation Program," pointing out that CIA tactics were approved both retrospectively and prospectively and concluding that "future presidents who refrain from doing what the Bush-Cheney administration did may well find themselves politically exposed—especially if terrorists once again manage to kill large numbers of Americans."

Not quite the outcome intended by the Democrats on the intelligence committee.

But not quite the final word, either. The RDI program cries out for an accurate, dispassionate history. The six of us said as much in that *WSJ* op-ed, calling the Feinstein report "a missed opportunity to deliver a serious and balanced study of an important public policy question. . . . The country and the CIA would have benefited from a more balanced study of these programs and a corresponding set of recommendations. The committee's report is not that study."

We still await that dispassionate history.

TWENTY-ONE

THE PRIVATE SECTOR

WASHINGTON, DC, 2009–2014

In early June 2013, I was settling into a comfortable hotel in La Jolla, California, when I got an e-mail from Mark Hosenball, intelligence beat reporter for Reuters. "Is this real or nuts?" was his subject line. The text was a few words and a hyperlink to an article by Glenn Greenwald that had just been posted on the Web site of the London *Guardian*.

The *Guardian* headline screamed, "NSA Collecting Phone Records of Millions of Verizon Customers Daily," and a subhead pointed to a court order authorizing the operation.

I liked Hosenball, but I didn't answer his e-mail. This wasn't nuts. This was real. But I wasn't going to talk about it. This was the follow-on program to the telephone metadata we had gathered in Stellarwind, now done via a court order, but it wasn't anything I could confirm or even try to explain. I did wonder, though, How the hell did *that* get out?

The next day Greenwald in the *Guardian* and Bart Gellman in the *Washington Post* claimed that NSA had free access to the US-based servers of Microsoft, Google, Yahoo, Skype, YouTube, Facebook, AOL, and Apple under something called PRISM.

The unfolding press coverage was fast taking on the look of a journalistic version of Tommy Franks's "shock and awe" campaign in the second Iraq war.

Before long we all learned that the leaks were the product of a boyish-looking twenty-nine-year-old Booz Allen contractor, Edward Snowden, who was then on the lam in Hong Kong trying to arrange transit through Russia en route to South America.

By the summer of 2013 I had been out of government for more than four years. I was enjoying being a principal at the Chertoff Group, a security consulting firm launched by former DHS secretary Mike Chertoff, and teaching at George Mason University's Graduate School of Policy, Government and International Affairs in northern Virginia. The Chertoff Group kept me around like-minded and like-experienced folks. It was always good to routinely share thoughts with the likes of Charlie Allen, an agency legend. The George Mason position was the product of a casual conversation with a faculty member at former senator Chuck Robb's 2008 Christmas party. Noting what he called my "scholarship of practice," the faculty member shepherded my forty-year-old master's degree through GMU's administrative wickets to land me a distinguished visiting professorship. I enjoyed teaching the course, "Intelligence and Policy," which routinely filled up within a minute or two of online registration, although I suspect that had something to do with the hope I was going to spill some secrets.

I was also doing the routine postgovernment thing of signing on to some boards and consultancies. I often wondered what in particular I had to offer, but the invitations were numerous and steady. At one such encounter, Charlie Allen and I spent several hours with some corporate leaders explaining the structure and dynamics of the intelligence community. It wasn't anything exotic, and we remarked in the elevator after we were done that neither of us could believe that they wrote all that stuff down. Maybe we were underestimating what we had picked up in the near century of IC experience between us.

An active speakers' bureau rounded out my postgovernment portfolio and managed to fill in most of the empty spaces on my schedule.

I missed government work less than I thought I would. When asked, I would respond that I missed the mission and I missed the people (and would occasionally add that I missed the jet), but that was about it. Most mornings I would roll over, grab my iPad, and read the CIA press clips before getting out of bed. When I later delivered my wife her coffee, she would often ask, "Anything in the clips?" and I would just as often respond, "Yet another great day to be a *former* senior intelligence official."

That said, I had taken to writing and commenting on intelligence matters since I left government, so I was quickly pulled into the debate that was swirling around Snowden.

An early point I made was that this debate had actually been long in coming. By the late 1990s, NSA was well aware that legitimately targetable foreign communications (like those of the Soviet Union's strategic forces) were no longer confined to isolated adversary networks. Modern targets (like al-Qaeda's e-mails on the World Wide Web) were coexisting with innocent and even constitutionally protected messages on a unitary, integrated global communications network.

The dilemma only got more acute after 9/11, since the enemy had demonstrated that he was already inside the gates and—even when he physically might not be inside the United States—his communications often were, as terrorists opted to use e-mail services based in this country.

The sins that Greenwald, Gellman, and others were attempting to portray were efforts by NSA and other intelligence services to deal with these new realities. Some of the efforts did indeed raise important questions about the right balance between security and liberty, and Snowden's disclosures no doubt accelerated and intensified that discussion. But the disclosures, and especially how they were rolled out, badly misshaped it as complex stories were misreported or, worse still, purposely pushed to the darkest corner of the room.

Take the PRISM program, for example, disclosed on day two of the campaign. Rushing against deadline, some outlets reported (inaccurately) that NSA had direct and free access to the servers of American communication service providers and it was a short step from there to near-libelous accusations that NSA was routinely rummaging through the e-mails of ordinary Americans. In truth, under court supervision, NSA was requesting specific e-mail accounts of designated foreign intelligence targets from the providers.

Take this hypothetical. NSA is targeting the communications of a known terrorist in Yemen. It discovers that the Yemen-based terrorist is communicating electronically with another individual; he could be in Pakistan, elsewhere in Yemen, or even in the United States. They are using a US-hosted Internet service; they send e-mails back and forth.

Similar contours could apply to e-mail traffic detailing the delivery of dual-use chemicals to a state suspected of developing chemical weapons. Or to other communications that provided information on potential cyber attacks.

In each of these cases, the only thing "American" about the communication is that it is physically in the United States and being hosted by a US-based Internet company. The target of the surveillance is a foreigner outside the United States.

Director of National Intelligence (and former director of NSA) Mike McConnell saw this and convinced Congress to amend FISA (Section 702) in 2008 to make it easier for NSA to grab these kinds of communications. Access is still overseen by the FISA Court (which also compels firms to turn over the data), but the process no longer requires time-consuming, cumbersome, individualized warrants.

NSA treats PRISM as just another collection point, an admittedly new and particularly valuable one, but still one among many designed to acquire *foreign* communications of *foreign* intelligence value.

PRISM didn't light up domestic protests as much as the metadata gathering, called the 215 program, because that was the section of the Patriot Act that underpinned it. PRISM was focused on foreigners; 215 was all about Americans. NSA kept a repository of American calls—not content, but facts of calls like from whom, to whom, when, for how long. It was massive, but access was tightly controlled, not just by limiting the number of people who could touch the data, but also by limiting their purpose to only counterterrorism.

When NSA acquired a new terrorism-related phone number overseas, say, by Yemeni forces nabbing that terrorist mentioned above, a key question was always whether or not that heretofore unknown number had ever been in contact with a US phone. It's a simple matter to query that massive 215 database and, if such a number is identified, NSA gets to ask about the other numbers with which it is in contact. Anything after that is in the hands of the FBI.

As reasonable and constrained as that sounds to me, it sure as hell didn't go down that way. Lots of Americans were upset, and not all of them were wearing tinfoil hats. Pockets of Congress were livid. Part of the issue was that many refused to believe that the program was constrained. They suspected that the data was being used for other purposes or that massive algorithms were being launched against it to divine personal patterns of behavior.

Others made claims that, if true, had NSA not only violating the laws of the United States but the laws of physics as well. I even heard one commentator posit that NSA could, if it suspected something of interest, click on a number in order to go back and hear what was said during a call. Huh? Click on what in reality is a phone bill to hear what was said in the past?

I pushed back strongly against a similar notion in a discussion on *Fox News Sunday* with Tea Party freshman congressman Justin Amash. I advised him that he needed to be telling his constituents the truth rather than whipping them up with scaremongering.

> AMASH: And it's important to understand that it then goes beyond metadata. So, we start with metadata but the government is not suggesting that it can't collect your actual communications. Under this doctrine, they certainly can collect your content just as they can collect your metadata. . . .

HAYDEN: . . . I've got to add, Chris [Wallace], it doesn't make Americans more comfortable about the program to misrepresent it. This does not authorize the collection of content, period.

An early NSA defense of the 215 metadata program was that the executive, the Congress, and the courts were all witting and supportive. In a post–Church Committee intelligence-reform era, that should have been sufficient. It wasn't.

The controversy created strange alignments. Fox News abandoned its usual national security credentials for a chance to beat up the president and strengthen its populist Tea Party brand. The network couldn't address the issue without the lede "NSA scandal," a lede that brought with it its own conclusions.

In midsummer, the 215 program came within a whisker of being shut down. By a bare twelve-vote margin, a bipartisan coalition of more or less centrist Republicans and centrist Democrats defeated an equally bipartisan coalition of their more ideological brethren, the latter an incredibly improbable alliance of far left and far right. In a rare show of bipartisanship, nearly 60 percent of Democrats and over 40 percent of Republicans voted to defund the program. One Hill participant described the hours before the vote as hand-to-hand combat.*

To be fair, there was always a small number (especially in the Senate) who were thoroughly knowledgeable of and thoroughly opposed to 215. Take Ron Wyden of Oregon, a member of the Senate intelligence panel. Well before Snowden, Wyden tried to entrap DNI Jim Clapper into publicly revealing the 215 program by asking him in open session if NSA collects "any type of data at all on millions or hundreds of millions of Americans." Of course, Wyden and his fellow committee members knew

---

* In the June 2015 USA Freedom Act, Congress gave NSA six months to end its acquisition of American metadata, although the agency could still access it by going directly to American telecoms with its queries.

the answer to the question, as did all of their staff. Suddenly on the spot, Clapper clumsily answered, "No, sir. Not wittingly."

Really bad answer. But really bad question too. Rather underhanded. If Wyden wanted to reveal state secrets in an open hearing, he should have just manned up and dumped them himself. After the Snowden revelations, Wyden took a victory lap for asking his question and many were genuinely angered by Clapper's response. Good to keep in mind, though, that Wyden was pressing the issue in open session because he was getting nowhere in closed sessions, where he consistently lost committee votes on the 215 program by wide margins. In fact, the strongest supporters of 215 after it was revealed were the leadership and most members of the two intelligence committees.

That most members who were most knowledgeable of what NSA was doing were supportive was heartening. But there were members of the executive branch who were (or should have been) equally knowledgeable, and their silence was puzzling.

If the vice president made any public defense of NSA, I must have missed it. So, too, with the secretary of defense, for whom the director of NSA works.

The same applies to officials like the national security advisor and the secretary of state, who actually help set intelligence requirements and receive reports based on that tasking. Where did they think this stuff came from?

Curiously, after the Snowden revelations, there were more Bush than Obama administration officials on the networks defending the current administration's programs.

President Obama defended NSA . . . to a point. Shortly after the Snowden deluge began, he took a single (and obviously planted) question right before meeting Chinese president Xi Xinping in California. His extemporaneous response was carefully crafted, technically accurate (not an easy matter), and calmly, but forcefully, given.

The president continued his "response to query" defense in interviews with CNN and with Charlie Rose, defending NSA programs along similar lines, although he was now admitting that "the capabilities of the NSA are scary to people."

By September, when he was asked a question before a foreign audience in Sweden, the president's response had become even more apologetic and defensive. He was willing to walk some things back and took pains to point out that "what I've said domestically and what I say to international audiences is . . . just because we can do something doesn't mean we should do it."

When President Bush launched the current metadata program in 2006 and the PRISM effort in 2008, he told Keith Alexander, the NSA director, to take these authorities and defend America. If they ever became politically contentious, he said, it would be his job to defend the agency (which is exactly how he dealt with the programs for which I was responsible).

When President Obama embraced these efforts in 2009, he should have embraced that social contract as well, even though it might be more difficult for him to fulfill. More difficult because it would cut against his base more than it would have for President Bush. Even more difficult later because such seemingly intrusive surveillance cut against his narrative of "al-Qaeda is on the run" and "the tide of war is receding."

It was also made more difficult by the president's 2008 campaign, which sought to put distance between himself and the Bush administration. There is no doubt he intended to be judgmental in his first inaugural when he said, "As for our common defense, we reject as false the choice between our safety and our ideals."

Compare that with his June 2013 explanation of NSA activities: "But I think it's important for everybody to understand . . . that there are some trade-offs involved. . . . You can't have a hundred percent security and then have hundred percent privacy and zero inconvenience. You know, we're going to have to make some choices as a society."

The president seemed to be splitting the difference again, as he did with the release of the DOJ memos on CIA back in 2009 (chapter 20). But he was in a tough spot. Both his foreign and domestic agendas were in tatters as the failure of his intelligence agencies to keep their secrets roiled constituencies here and overseas. The usually phlegmatic president reportedly showed visible anger in small group settings.

And the Snowden revelations kept on coming, often timed for maximum embarrassment and crafted for maximum impact. The *Los Angeles Times, USA Today,* and the *Washington Post* all piled on a September Glenn Greenwald–Laura Poitras screecher in the London *Guardian*: "NSA Shares Intelligence Including Americans' Data with Israel," the clear implication being that NSA was casually handing off US person information to a dicey ally.

Those kinds of articles seemed to regularly catch the administration flat-footed as responses were forced to go through a cumbersome interagency vetting that often produced a response that was tepid, stripped down, late, or nonexistent. In fact, in this particular case, for someone with *any* knowledge of how signals intelligence works, there was an obvious alternative story line, but one not even suggested in the coverage.

I claim no operational knowledge of this alleged activity, but in my experience—when working with an ally and forwarding SIGINT "take" to them—a memorandum of understanding is usually drawn up so that US privacy is protected even in the unlikely event that US person data is incidentally swept up. The MOU is actually a plus for US privacy. But *that* interpretation never quite made it to the public story.

Another page-one headline in an August 2013 edition of the *Washington Post* blared, "NSA Broke Privacy Rules Thousands of Times per Year, Audit Finds." I parsed the data for that one in a short piece for *USA Today*, pointing out that

all the incidents were inadvertent; no one claimed that any rules were intentionally violated. All of the incidents were discovered, reported and corrected by NSA itself.

Fully two-thirds of the incidents were composed of "roamers"— legitimately targeted foreigners who were temporarily in the United States (and thus temporarily protected by the Fourth Amendment).

I explained a "roamer" in more detail. Picture a legitimate foreign intelligence target who, unbeknownst to NSA, enters the United States. Now the target makes a cell phone call from the States, not collected in the air here, but made in such a way that it is routed back to its home network (for billing purposes) before heading to its intended recipient. It looks every inch like a foreign call and is collected as such, until it becomes apparent, because of the content of a particular call or certain aspects of the intercept itself, that the call originated in the United States. At that point collection is stopped and the inadvertent collection (the "privacy violation") reported—even though the caller remains a legitimate target and NSA will be all over him again once he leaves the United States.

I added that other "violations" included database queries, searches of data already collected. The document the *Post* relied on revealed that in one three-month period, *there were 115 incidents of queries being incorrectly entered, mistakes like mistyping or using too-broad search criteria. That's 115 out of 61 million inquiries.*

I didn't put it into the op-ed, but I did have an alternative headline for the *Post* piece: "NSA Damn Near Perfect."

The backstory on my *USA Today* op-ed was instructive. The *Post* broke its story on Thursday. *USA Today* wanted to run competing point-counterpoint editorials the following Monday. It invited NSA to write the contrary view, an opportunity that the agency embraced. By late Saturday night, though, I had heard that NSA was despairing of getting interagency (read White House) clearance for its response. Shortly afterward, *USA Today* turned to me.

I wrote the piece on Sunday morning and had it cleared for classification that afternoon. That NSA was prevented from doing the same is beyond explanation, and the fact that someone—ten years out from NSA—could muster a coherent argument suggests that this wasn't akin to splitting the atom.

The administration really didn't want to take this on, and the president pointedly did *not* make a morale visit to Fort Meade as George Bush did six weeks after the exposure of Stellarwind.

But the administration's reticence did not save it from criticism at home or abroad. Foreign leaders were weighing in as much as the president's domestic political opponents, since Snowden and his journalistic accomplices hadn't confined their broadsides to questions of US privacy. They alleged US penetration of Chinese computers and US coverage of Russian president Dmitry Medvedev's satellite phone, and they did that early while Snowden was on the run in Hong Kong en route to Sheremetyevo Airport, outside Moscow. They later added charges of spying on foreign leaders in Germany, Brazil, Mexico, and elsewhere.

Europe seemed especially outraged, echoing the turn-of-the-century kerfuffle over the alleged Echelon program (chapter 2). The president must have been personally stung when a writer in *Der Spiegel* effectively announced the end of Europe's love affair with him: "Before, we could at least think, it's just Bush. There is a better America. But now we know; there is only one America." Quite a change in European sentiment, since the president was awarded the Nobel Peace Prize after only a few weeks in office largely for not being George Bush.

The president likely took no comfort when Stewart Baker, former NSA general counsel, summed up a lot of American intelligence community views when he observed that the only surprising aspect of the European response was their ability to recycle their outrage without any obvious sense of embarrassment. In their private moments, most IC veterans were irritated that neither their own nor European political leaders would publicly admit the obvious: that espionage was an accepted international practice and the US Constitution's Fourth Amendment protection against unreasonable search was *not* an international treaty.

At one point there were so many foreign leaders—or intelligence heads on behalf of their leaders—coming to Washington for "explanations" that there were actually scheduling challenges for the IC leadership.

Actually, President Obama had nailed it when he once complained to a foreign audience that "some of the folks who have been most greatly offended publicly, we know privately engage in the same activities directed at us." And he got to the heart of the matter when he pointed out, "So even though we may have the same goals, our means are significantly greater."

But it also became clear that the administration was rethinking how NSA targeted global communications. In addition to the "just because we can doesn't mean we should" concession, the president admitted that there were "questions in terms of whether we're tipping over into being too intrusive with respect to the—you know, the interactions of other governments."

The president went on to add, "We are consulting with other countries in this process and finding out from them what are their areas of specific concern."

Let me attempt to restate that. We were asking other countries what of our possible espionage against them made them most uncomfortable?!

Clearly policy and politics demanded that the president take a conciliatory tone. There is necessarily at least a little bit of theater involved here. *Public* allegations of specific espionage require "victims" to be outraged. They also require "perpetrators" to look into the matter.

Fine. But overachieving here would be dangerous. Director of National Intelligence Clapper bared a bit of his soul when he said he was facing a demand for exquisite intelligence that he had to collect without risk, without embarrassment, and without threat to anyone's privacy or commercial bottom line. He labeled it "immaculate collection."

And 2014 was indeed the year of rolling back.

Following Snowden's allegations that the United States was listening to German chancellor Angela Merkel's cell phone, a senior US official told reporters that the United States had "made a decision not to pursue surveillance on dozens of heads of government." Dozens. That's at least twenty-four and probably more.

The president announced, "If I want to know what [foreign leaders] think about an issue, I'll pick up the phone and call them." Okay, but that sounds naive or disingenuous, since what foreign leaders tell the president may not be exactly what they tell their foreign minister or defense minister or intelligence chief after they hang up.

Even before that announcement, Reuters was reporting that the presi-

dent had ordered an end to electronic surveillance of international organizations like the United Nations, the World Bank, and the International
Monetary Fund. Many understandably applauded those reports. After
all, they reasoned, these institutions were not adversaries.

Whatever the truth of the reports, though, we should be careful with
that argument. It smacks of the Greenwald-Poitras-Snowden theme condemning alleged suspicionless surveillance. That attitude conflates law
enforcement and intelligence. Intelligence collection is not confined to
the communications of adversaries or of the guilty. Rather, it's about
gaining information otherwise unavailable that would help keep Americans safe and free. There's a difference.

American intelligence suffered mightily in the 1990s when human
intelligence collectors were told to stand down and not talk to "bad" people. We would create the same effect again if we tell signals intelligence
collectors they cannot listen to "good" people.

Then there was a flood of stories that CIA had "curbed spying against
friendly governments in Western Europe." That was in response to
charges that CIA had suborned an officer in Germany's intelligence service. I have no special knowledge about the truth of that allegation or the
supposed American response, but the currency of the story was proof
enough that there was a high level of skittishness in American espionage.

The intelligence community was also working hard on the president's
commitment to extend to foreigners overseas US person–like privacy protections on holding and using data collected on them. From all accounts
it was slow going. One observer only half-jokingly commented to me,
"We don't even know what that means." Little surprise there. The American intelligence community and American law had never before extended the concept of the Fourth Amendment to foreigners abroad.

Traditionally, American SIGINT has been limited by the demands of
the Fourth Amendment and defined by the demands of American security. Absent political guidance to the contrary, if you were not protected
by the US Constitution and your communications contained information
that would help keep America free and safe, information that would not

otherwise be available to the US government, it was game on. In those circumstances, the privacy of foreigners overseas was not in the job description of the director of NSA.

When I was at NSA I received my fair share of political guidance to stand down on particular targets. There are indeed factors other than optimal intelligence collection that should influence our actions. But those were retail exceptions. This looked wholesale.

So, before we lock ourselves in, it might be wise to think through the long-term implications. President Obama reflected current and historic reality when he said that "the United States only uses signals intelligence for legitimate national security purposes and not for the purpose of indiscriminately reviewing the e-mails or phone calls of ordinary folks."

Why shouldn't that operational reality be standard enough? What additional administrative burdens can we afford to place on a system that is already stressed keeping up with the demands of a very turbulent world? And what unneeded caution would such a legal and policy regime impose on a bureaucracy that we cannot afford to be risk averse?

We've actually seen a version of this movie before, pre-9/11, when intelligence and law enforcement agencies played back from the "wall" that had been erected between them. As fateful as that was, it at least had the merit of being about *American* constitutional rights. This is not.

And a final question. Is anyone traveling with us? Is any other nation working to extend its domestic constitutional protections to foreigners when it comes to foreign intelligence collection?

I didn't think so.

I GOT TO DELIVER a little of this hard message personally at the Munich Security Conference in February 2014. I was on the agenda (and I'm serious here) at ten-thirty at night onstage in the bar of the host hotel. My copanelists included former congresswoman Jane Harman and my old German counterpart, August Hanning. With everyone swilling Pils and such a touchy topic, it promised to be an interesting session.

Without confirming any US intelligence operations, I talked about how leadership intentions were a high-priority target for any nation. I then freely admitted that Angela Merkel was a true friend of the United States, but asked the audience about her predecessor, Gerhard Schröder, who did a variety of things inconsistent with the American view of the world. We had different points of view on the Iraq war and with regard to his approach to Russia. Then there was the Gazprom billion-euro loan guarantee that seemed to be rewarded with a lucrative board appointment shortly after he left office. "Intelligent statecraft," I asked, "or something more?"

I then recounted an American episode. In 2008, when President Obama was elected, he had a BlackBerry. We thought, Oh, God, he's got to get rid of that. But he refused, so we did some things to make it a little more secure.

"But what's the backstory on that?" I asked my German audience. "We were telling the guy who was soon going to be the most powerful man in the most powerful country on earth that if in his national capital he used his smartphone, a countless number of foreign intelligence services were going to listen to his phone calls and read his e-mails. We didn't feign outrage or claim some moral high ground. We simply explained, 'That's just the way it is.'"

I did learn something at Munich, though. Even if I thought that the German reaction to Snowden was unwarranted, it was clear to me that it was genuine, not the faux outrage that we often saw elsewhere. We underestimated the depth of feelings that the German people—not just the chancellor—felt about the question of privacy given their historical circumstances. At Munich it was clear to me that Germans regarded privacy the way we Americans might regard freedom of speech or religion. We didn't appreciate that enough.

And that had costs beyond hurt feelings. I worked hard at NSA to support the strategic relationship with Germany. An impediment to that was Bad Aibling Station in Bavaria. BAS wasn't just an overhang from the Cold War, it was an overhang from the occupation. No Germans allowed. It didn't target Germany, but its mere existence on German soil complicated the relationship.

There was always an American argument for keeping BAS open, and when one aged off, the army, which ran the facility, excelled at thinking up new ones. The local community was incredibly supportive, and everyone loved being assigned within sight of the Bavarian Alps. Letting go would be hard.

I closed BAS in 2004 to clear the political decks in Germany for deeper and more sustained cooperation. I was trying to buy long-term capital. The German political reaction to Snowden put all of that at risk.

The Germans were friends, and the interaction at Munich was more dialogue than confrontation, but I got to look the devil in the eye a few months later when I debated advocacy journalist Glenn Greenwald in Toronto on the whole Snowden episode. It was actually a team affair, and I was paired with famous trial lawyer Alan Dershowitz (yet another of the odd alignments on this issue), while Greenwald was accompanied by young Internet entrepreneur and Reddit cofounder Alexis Ohanian.

On the morning of the debate, Greenwald was quoted in the *Toronto Globe and Mail* with this characterization of us: "I consider [Hayden] and Dershowitz two of the most pernicious human beings on the planet. I find them morally offensive. There's an element of hypocrisy to being in the same room with them, treating them as if I have outward respect, because I don't."

Even allowing for a little pregame taunting to get into the head of the opposition, it occurred to me that the evening's debate might not be a respectful give-and-take between people of broadly shared values on the difficult balance a free people have to make between their liberty and their security. And I was right.

I lost count of the number of times that Greenwald and Ohanian just declared as a given the existence of an all-knowing, all-pervasive, oppressive "surveillance state." Certainly far more often than Dershowitz and I referred to what Greenwald called our "pretext" of fighting terrorism.

Dershowitz hammered the pretext argument and was relentless in not allowing the presumption of ill intent to stand unchallenged. Motives matter, he declared, even when people might be wrong—a rebuttal to Greenwald's dismissal of our moral worth and the worth of any of our arguments.

Ohanian argued passionately for the survival of the global, ubiquitous, unitary Internet that we know today.

I agreed that perhaps the worst result of the truths, half truths, and untruths in circulation would be to put wind in the sails of those who would destroy the Net, not because of espionage concerns, but because they feared the free movement of ideas and commerce. It would be an easy matter for the Russians, Chinese, Iranians, and a host of other autocrats to now claim that American arguments for an open and free Internet were merely covers for enabling American espionage.

The debate organizers "helpfully," and with almost no advance notice, parachuted in Edward Snowden in a specially taped commentary that reinforced the surveillance-state meme. "It covers your e-mail, it covers your text messages, your Web history, every Google search you've ever made and every plane ticket you've ever bought, the books you buy." The list went on.

Alan and I were pissed at the prerecorded intervention, not the least because it made us look like chum to attract Snowden's commentary. And then there was the question of no advance notice.

But I mishandled it. As soon as the new Muscovite was finished, the moderator turned to me for comment, which I dutifully provided. I shouldn't have. I should have leaped up, turned to the massive fading image, and shouted, "Wait! Don't go! Wait! I've got questions. Now that you're here (he wasn't, of course) can you clear up a few things for me?" And then I would have asked:

> You've cited Jim Clapper's response to Ron Wyden on NSA surveillance as motivating your actions. That was March 2013 but you began offering documents to Greenwald in December 2012 and to Laura Poitras in January 2013. Weren't you already committed?

While you were in Hong Kong fighting extradition, you told the press that NSA was hacking into Chinese computers. On the surface that looks like you were trying to buy safe passage. Were you?

The week before you fled Hong Kong, the London *Guardian* (based on your documents) claimed that the United States had intercepted Russian president Medvedev's satellite phone while he was at a G20 summit in England. What's the civil liberties issue there or is this just trading secrets for passage again?

You said that you raised your concerns within the system and that you were told not to rock the boat. NSA can't find any evidence. You took hundreds of thousands of documents. Do *any* of them show your raising concerns? A single e-mail, perhaps?

You sound pretty authoritative, but the first PRISM stories were wrong, claiming NSA had free access to the server farms of Google, Hotmail, Yahoo, and the like. The *Washington Post* later walked that back. Did you misread the slides too?

Le Monde and *El País*, based on your documents, claimed that NSA was collecting tens of millions of metadata events on French and Spanish citizens each month. It turns out those events were collected *by* the French and Spanish in war zones and provided to NSA to help military force protection. Did you get that wrong too?

God, I still feel bad at letting the opportunity pass. To date, Snowden has been interviewed by adoring acolytes like his ACLU lawyer or perennial NSA critic Jim Bamford. Even Brian Williams's NBC session felt more like hagiography. Damn.

Alan and I held our own in the debate. There were several thousand in the audience, mostly young and almost all Canadian. It was truly a road game for us. Going in, the audience split 40–60 against us, with a little less than a quarter undecided. At the end of the evening, when everyone was forced to vote, the split remained 40–60. Afterward I exchanged cards with Ohanian. I didn't even exchange glances with Greenwald.

THE SNOWDEN REVELATIONS WERE COSTLY. I have characterized them as the greatest hemorrhaging of legitimate American secrets in the history of the republic. I know that all intelligence advantage is transient, particularly in signals intelligence. A casual business decision to upgrade a network that has been successfully penetrated can mean loss of access that was years in the making. Snowden's revelations—across the board— cost the United States dearly in the accesses it had already gained. And, with targets now alerted to American tactics and techniques, recovering those accesses will be more time-consuming and more costly.

I am no doubt betraying my own background when I say that I think Snowden is an incredibly naive, hopelessly narcissistic, and insufferably self-important defector. In early October 2013 at a Washington panel, moderator David Ignatius began by pointing out that Snowden had been nominated and was on the short list for the European Parliament's Sakharov Prize for Freedom of Thought. (It eventually went to Pakistani teenager Malala Yousafzai.) I couldn't help commenting that "I must admit in my darker moments over the past several months, I'd also thought of nominating Mr. Snowden, but it was for a different list."

That comment lit up the blogosphere as Snowdenistas accused me of wanting to put him on a kill list, a thought as ludicrous in my mind as suggesting he should join previous Sakharov awardees like Kofi Annan, Nelson Mandela, and Aung San Suu Kyi.

Not that I—or almost anyone else in the American intelligence community—wasn't viscerally angry with him and what he had done. They tell a story in England of a young man who was condemned by his family for shirking military service during World War II by filling some civilian position in Bletchley, a small, nondescript town safely north of London. Rather than violate his oath of secrecy, the young man allowed his parents to go to their graves ignorant of the contribution he had made to breaking the Germans' Enigma code. That's what people in the intelligence community mean by "keeping the secrets."

Despite that, though, there is one narrow way in which Snowden has been, in his own peculiar manner, a gift. Although I didn't actually wish him the fate of a canary in a coal mine, he has performed like one—he is the visible effect (not the cause) of a broad cultural shift that is redefining legitimate secrecy, necessary transparency, and what constitutes consent of the governed.

Long before Snowden, I was asking CIA's civilian advisory board, "Will America be able to conduct espionage in the future inside a broader political culture that every day demands more transparency and more public accountability from every aspect of national life?" The board studied it for a while and then reported back that they had their doubts. Really important answer.

American intelligence routinely assumes that it is operating with at least the implied sanction of the American people. Its practitioners believe that if the American people knew everything they were doing, they would broadly have their support. We have always believed that we worked with some manner of consent of the governed.

Now the governed are reconsidering how they want to grant that consent. And many are saying that fully and currently informing the intelligence committees in Congress is no longer enough. "That's consent of the governors," they seem to be saying, "not of the governed. You may have told them, but you didn't tell me."

Snowden's "gift" was to make that dilemma clear to everyone. If we are going to conduct espionage in the future, we are going to have to make some changes in the relationship between the intelligence community and the public it serves.

That will be difficult. Espionage thrives in the shadows, and secrecy is an essential component of its success. Despite a latent plus side (legitimacy, support, understanding), American intelligence has traditionally judged the minus side of going public (decreased effectiveness) to be determinative.

It's a noble calculus and one the community rarely gets credit for. Dutifully, the IC responds to leaks by hunkering down, neither confirming nor denying, and hoping for the best. Even when there might be a plus side to a more accurate story being out there, traditional thinking has held that this is outweighed by the operational cost of *anything* being out there at all.

But that is (or should be) changing, and American intelligence is going to have to say and show more and especially do that *before* someone is accusing the intelligence community of wrongdoing. If we continue this debate with one side muted, the outcome will not be in doubt: intelligence will be mismanaged or misdirected or crippled, and in the end neither liberty nor security will be served.

To be sure, the intelligence community doesn't control the "openness" agenda. Things that are better kept hidden now routinely enter the public domain beyond the control of the IC. Often they enter via political masters who see gain in a supportive press story. Other, less official leaks enter the public consciousness, usually via someone who is disgruntled, in a slanted and piecemeal fashion.

Put another way, American intelligence is already paying a lot of the operational cost of this stuff being out there, but is still denying itself any potential upside to a cogent, (more) complete description of what is actually going on. The result is that American intelligence is losing both effectiveness (through leaks) *and* legitimacy (through its own reticence).

Before any of my former colleagues hyperventilate, let me admit that there are limits to openness. Some things have to be secret. And there are other things that should not be confirmed by the government even though they are "known."

Even when justified, transparency has its dangers.

For one thing, this could be a slippery slope. Once started, where or when do you stop? Specifically, once having put some facts out there, the "*Glomar* defense"* becomes problematic. We could also see a weakening

---

* Neither confirming nor denying the existence of something, as the government did in 1975 in response to a *Los Angeles Times* story on the recovery of a Soviet submarine from the bottom of the Pacific by the Hughes Corporation's *Glomar Explorer*.

of state-secrets claims, even in frivolous lawsuits. A coherent public story line also creates a baseline for aggressive reporters to start pressing their sources for additional information. Voluntary disclosures could also seem to legitimize claims that this or that leak really doesn't harm national security.

We also need to explain to those with whom we intend to be more open that with that will come some increased risk. It can be no other way. You can't expand the window of 300 million–plus Americans into US espionage without simultaneously informing those on whom we intend to spy.

So perhaps the goal here should not quite be transparency, but what Mike Leiter (former head of the National Counterterrorism Center) calls translucence. Mike says (and I agree) that the American intelligence community owes the public it serves enough data so that people can make out the broad shapes and broad movements of what intelligence is doing, but they do not need specific operational details. The former should suffice to build trust, while the latter would be destructive of espionage's inherent purposes. Former national security advisor Steve Hadley echoed the theme when he told me that we can distinguish the policy framework from the operational details of an action.

Doing this will be hard. And doing it stupidly could be incredibly damaging. But, at the moment, we are living with the strategic impact of individually justifiable decisions to remain silent, and that impact is an intelligence community that is both less trusted and less effective than we need it to be.

We seem to be trending toward a bit more openness, but we don't seem to be in a big hurry about it. The IC is posting more documents on its public Web site (icontherecord.tumblr.com, which was designed to be read as IC-ON-THE-RECORD but which opponents have dubbed I-CON-THE-RECORD). The FISA Court is also making public redacted versions of some of its decisions. Intelligence community officials continue to make public speeches.

But, no breakthroughs. In fact, the DNI's inexplicable March 2014 guidance—as the intelligence community was being buffeted by near-daily Snowden-sourced allegations—made it more difficult for IC members to talk with outside audiences and counter the innuendo. Even people like me who continue to hold a security clearance were theoretically required to phone in, ask "Mother, may I?" and get guidance before responding to any journalist's sincere request to explain some unfolding event or alleged scandal. And, remember, the directive applied to *"all intelligence related matters,"* not just to classified questions. The strategic effect of that will be further isolation of an intelligence community that desperately needs a richer and better-informed dialogue with the nation.

The Obama administration's rigid control over messaging doesn't help, either. General Mike Flynn's early departure from the Defense Intelligence Agency in 2014 was a complex event, but there is no doubt that Mike's testimony to Congress was more alarmist (and more accurate) than the administration's preferred story line. Matt Olsen, as head of the National Counterterrorism Center, had his bureaucratic ears pinned back after he identified the Benghazi attack as terrorism in open session.

At the height of the Snowden kerfuffle, with allegation piling on allegation, I got frequent unofficial requests from intelligence community members to defend them and what they were doing because they were not allowed to do so by the administration. At one point, as I sat on the set of CBS's *Face the Nation*, Bob Schieffer took advantage of a pause in the show to thank me for being there and then to ask, "Why are *you* here? The only people out here defending the current administration's surveillance policies seem to be people from the previous administration."

In that seminal speech on terrorism at National Defense University in May 2013, President Obama promised to ratchet up transparency when it came to targeted killings and drones. That still hasn't happened, even as the strikes have become more contentious. And the official veil of secrecy has made it more difficult for knowledgeable people to contribute to mature public debate on the subject.

In April 2015, after American counterterrorism operations resulted in the death of two hostages in South Asia, multiple commentators trotted out condemnations of targeted killings and the drone program. I wrote an op-ed for the *Washington Times* supporting such operations, using only official government statements. Since all my writing has to be cleared for classification, I dutifully submitted the piece and was told that no articles about drones would be cleared *regardless of the content.* I actually think that's a misuse of the review process, but beyond that, it's just plain stupid. That it took two days to convince the government of that fact says a lot.

I think the US government's program of targeted killing is lawful, certainly within our technological competence, and effective for our purposes. As director of NSA, when explaining the backdrop to Stellarwind (chapter 5), I would use three Venn ovals labeled "Technologically Feasible," "Operationally Relevant," and "Legal." The area where the ovals overlapped was the operating space that NSA worked in, I said.

By the time I was director of CIA, I had added a fourth Venn oval—one labeled "Politically Sustainable." Presidents (and their intelligence agencies) get to do some things one-off based on raw executive authority. But no president, even a popular one, gets to do anything forever without bringing in the other political branches and, directly or indirectly, the American people.

Beyond a narrow base of lawfulness and just raw effectiveness, actions need to have political and policy legs, and they have to be created by *informed* debate. So sustaining an RDI program (chapters 10 and 12) simply required me to be more public about it. It's hard to build a political consensus if people think you aren't leveling with them.

OF COURSE, all of this is premised on the belief that American espionage is worth doing and worth defending. In my class at George Mason, I usually begin each semester by asking the students if espionage and all of its secrecy is compatible with a democracy. They usually say that it is. I'm pretty sure they believe it, too, even allowing that the guy asking (and ultimately grading) them is the former head of CIA and NSA.

I conclude the discussion with a more challenging proposition. "Rather than just being compatible with a democracy, espionage is essential to it. Frightened people don't make good democrats. No spies. Less security. Less freedom."

I then tell the class about the Washington premiere of the first episode of AMC's miniseries *TURN*, a dramatized version of the espionage exploits of George Washington's Culper Ring on Long Island during the Revolution. Jeanine and I were invited, and we enjoyed the showing, which was at the National Archives, and I got to participate in a panel following it. On the panel I celebrated the fact that the Culper Ring was being memorialized in popular culture and being memorialized there, at the archives, within twenty-five yards of the Constitution and a copy of the Magna Carta.

I admitted that "the American public has an uneasy relationship with espionage agencies. It's just back and forth." Part of that (not surprisingly) is the public's incomplete knowledge. "You know about Benedict Arnold. You know about Nathan Hale. . . . [But there is] an absolute, iron rule about espionage: You know about the spies who fail. You don't know about the spies who succeed."

And that's why I welcomed the moment (and the TV series), since it gave me the opportunity to note that the nation's first spymaster was its first president. He even insisted on and got a covert-action budget from Congress. The point was that this was thoroughly American: "Espionage is as old as the republic," I said. "Baseball, apple pie . . . it goes back to our roots."

But being necessary and traditional doesn't make it easy. I end that first session with my GMU students with a reading of Plato's parable of the cave and its probing questions about appearances and realities and the challenges of discovering truth.

"Can we ever really know the truth?" I ask and then continue by describing a conversation I had three decades earlier with a political officer in Communist Bulgaria. Frustrated by some of his remarks during a lengthy discussion (the subject of which I have long forgotten), I blurted out to him in frustration, "What is truth to you?" and he just as quickly answered, "Truth? Truth is what serves the Party."

Which sets the stage for talking about the true nature of intelligence, or at least the nature of intelligence in a modern democracy. I liken the intelligence-policy dialogue as a room with two doors, one labeled intelligence, the other reserved for the decision maker. Since the decision maker can range from a tactical commander, to a cabinet secretary, to a president, the "room" can range from a canvas-covered tactical operations center, to an ornate office, to an oval one.

In any case, the dynamics are the same. Even though the two enter through separate doors, the intelligence professional must connect with the decision maker. Ideally, that would be in the center of the room, but even if it is not, the job of intelligence is to impose itself on the thinking of the other, no matter how far one has to walk to capture him.

And that can be hard, since to legitimately enter through the intelligence door, one has to be fact-based and see the world as it is, while the policy maker is rightly vision-based (taking us somewhere) and picturing the world as he/she would like it to be.

The intelligence door demands thinking based on inductive reasoning. Swimming in a sea of particulars, the intelligence officer is working to create the general, be that a judgment, a conclusion, or even just the controlling narrative (*Sir, what we thought was an insurgency in Iraq is now clearly a civil war*). The policy maker trends powerfully deductive, trying to apply his or her first principles (the ones that swayed the electorate) to a specific circumstance (*Give me the prisoner-by-prisoner plan to close Guantánamo, as I promised to do*).

The intelligence professional trends pessimistic. Bob Gates once quipped that when a CIA analyst stops to smell the flowers, he always looks around for the hearse. If the policy maker isn't an optimist, he or she wouldn't pursue the job. (Remember, they said they would make things better.)

The trick is for the fact-based, inductive, world-as-it-is pessimist to get into the head of the vision-based, deductive, world-as-we-want-it-to-be optimist without betraying his own roots (and his legitimacy for being there in the first place). And to do it knowing that with every sentence, he is making the policy maker's day worse than it would otherwise have been (*Mr. President, looks like we may have a near-complete nuclear reactor in eastern Syria* or *Mr. President, given what we know, I would NOT characterize ISIS as the JV team*).

Intelligence does not set policy, but when done right, it sets the right- and left-hand boundaries for any rational policy discussion. That is its critical contribution.

On balance, American intelligence masters the art and science of this process pretty well. It is the only intelligence community today that is or is required to be global, and how well it performs that task is best reflected in the number of foreign intelligence services that routinely make the pilgrimage to Langley to enlist support and cement cooperation. There have been mistakes and failures, and I have participated in my share of them, but it is also a truism that there is only so much even good intelligence can do in the service of flawed policy.

But now there are bigger questions than just the competency of American spying. Despite the roots going back to Washington, espionage has never sat easy on the American psyche. At NSA I was fond of saying, "The agency requires only two things to be successful. We need to be powerful and we need to be secretive. And we live in a political culture that distrusts only two things."

Power and secrecy, of course.

We are seeing that play out today in dramatic tones, many of them dark. There are many who, on learning what measures have been taken to deal with new flavors of threat (like terrorism) or new technologies (like a single global integrated cyber grid), have assumed the worst and have been unrelentingly critical of what they have dubbed the "surveillance state."

Others have unfairly labeled any such concerns as perforce emanating from the permanently paranoid, black-helicopter-fearing, tinfoil-hat-wearing crowd.

I really do try to point out that this is NOT a struggle between the forces of light and the forces of darkness, as some seem to assume. This is the normal job of balancing that free people assume when they are serious about both their security and their liberty. We have a history of tacking back and forth on this issue as broader conditions (like the nature and level of threat) dictate.

I am fond of reminding audiences that soon after throwing out George III for his overbearing rule, we became disenchanted with the successor government under the Articles of Confederation, since it was too weak to protect the country or do much of anything that we expect governments to do. The miracle of Philadelphia fixed that with a much stronger centralized authority—strong enough to be feared, actually, so that almost immediately it was constrained by the quick passage of ten amendments to limit its power, the Bill of Rights. We've seen this movie before. In fact, we've been in it.

Fears of the "surveillance state" and "rogue agencies" are now emanating from the impassioned right as much as the impassioned left. In early 2015 I agreed to appear at CPAC, the Conservative Political Action Conference—the annual rally/convention/revival in Washington. I was to debate Judge Andrew Napolitano, Fox News' resident libertarian jurist, on NSA's 215 program. The judge and I know each other and actually are friends. I expected it to be fun, and it was.

After the judge opened with a predictably harsh diatribe dripping with emotive constitutional references, I stood up and began by saying, "Judge Napolitano is an unrelenting libertarian," to the cheers of many of the thousands of twenty-something libertarians in the crowd.

As the cheering died down, I continued, "And so am I," a remark that generated some catcalls, some booing, and at least one shouted, "No, you're not!"

Undeterred, I then added that I was a libertarian who, for most of his adult life, was charged with fulfilling another part of that foundational document, the part that said, "Provide for the common defense." And I reminded the young crowd that *their* favorite part didn't protect them from all searches, just *unreasonable* ones. And so it went for thirty more minutes.

As I was walking offstage I didn't turn as I heard a female voice shout, "You're a liar, Hayden. You have blood on your hands." I didn't turn because I judged her to be unpersuadable. No sense trying. She had her world. The rest of us had ours.

Or I, at least, had mine.

I HAVE SPENT my adult life working in American intelligence. It has been quite an honor. Generally well resourced. A global mission. No want of issues.

And it was a hell of a ride: from the DMZ in Korea to Masada in Israel; from war-ravaged Sarajevo to hyperelegant Geneva; from Baghdad under siege to Sofia under communism; from ancient Addis Ababa to modern London; from isolated Guantánamo to teeming Bamako.

I got to meet the likes of a criminal Ratko Mladić (Bosnian Serb commander), an imperturbable Li Chan Bok (North Korean negotiator), a tough Alvaro Uribe (president of Colombia), a heroic Abdullah II (king of Jordan), a subtly urbane Mohammed bin Zayed (crown prince of Abu Dhabi), a frenetic Nicolas Sarkozy (president of France), a distasteful Saif al-Islam (son of Libya's Muammar Gaddafi), and a whole lot more.

Mostly, though, what stands out is the mission—defending a republic as worthy as ours is—and the people, those noble individuals who mentored me as a junior officer, those I befriended, those I may have helped along the way, and all those who still toil in the shadows and keep the secrets.

Washington's spy ring on Long Island was called the Culper Ring after the alias of its chief agent. It was formed after a previous attempt at espionage on Long Island and in New York City had tragically failed with the execution of twenty-one-year-old Nathan Hale. There is a statue of Hale in a quiet, shaded spot on the CIA campus between the Original Headquarters Building and the Bubble, the agency's auditorium.

Every CIA director gets to design a personal coin that he can give to top performers. The front side is standard, the agency shield, but the back side is up to each director. As a history major, I toyed with the idea of putting an imprint of Hale's statue there. My deputy, Steve Kappes, immediately objected. "You realize he was killed on his first mission, right? And never got any useful information for Washington?"

As usual, Steve was right. I dropped the idea, but held close the thought that success in this business was not guaranteed and failure brought with it a great price. Hale was executed, after all, and the British held New York for the rest of the war.

My daily routine as CIA director began at 5:30 a.m. with a three-mile run along the Potomac, a quick shower, and a thirty-minute drive to Langley in the back of an armored SUV with my PDB briefer. We went over what would be shown to the president at eight o'clock, and then a whole lot of reporting not yet ready for prime time, plus a stack of operational cables from CIA stations and bases. The whole drill took a little more than an hour on average, half in the car, half after we got to the office. Reading that book every day made it hard to maintain a positive view of human nature. It was clear that there was evil afoot in the world.

Facing that evil, sharing a responsibility to prevent or at least deflect it, I sometimes contemplated what the twenty-first-century equivalent of Hale's failure might be.

That conjured up some very dark thoughts, some very dark thoughts indeed.

ACKNOWLEDGMENTS

One of the joys of this project was reestablishing contact with dozens of old friends who freely gave of their time to chat, to reminisce, and to correct both my memory and my prose.

My methodology was pretty straightforward: take advantage of a long domestic or international flight to hammer out (from memory) the summary of a chapter and then identify the people and documents I would need to make sure I got it right, got it complete, and (I would hope) got it interesting.

Over the course of eighteen months I conducted over seventy interviews. I am deeply grateful for all the cooperation, but for fear of leaving someone out and, frankly, to spare my former colleagues the danger of unwarranted editorial abuse or legal harassment by a small fraction of the people they have worked so hard to protect, I have chosen not to mention specific names.

Special thanks, though, to groups like the NSA professionals who set up the Stellarwind program and operated it so professionally and came to my interview with stacks of documents detailing the program's effectiveness. The same for those involved in the CIA detention program, equally anxious for the chance to tell their side of the story. Not surprisingly, the legal staffs at both agencies were also enthused by the opportunity to set the legal record straight. Everyone I spoke to was willing to be judged on what he or she had *actually* done and wanted *that* record out there.

I had wonderful staff support while at CIA, NSA, and ODNI, and I relied heavily on the extensive contemporaneous notes of my executive assistants, chiefs of staff, and others. Kudos to all of them, too, for helping me decipher their handwriting and for the rich verbal detail they willingly provided on nearly forgotten episodes.

Real practitioners of the craft of intelligence rarely get a chance to step outside of themselves and talk about and grade their own work. CIA station chiefs and NSA SIGINT collectors and analysts from both agencies did exactly that during my discussions with them. They were candid about what worked and what didn't, where they were right and where they were wrong. I have tried to reflect their honesty in the narrative.

Of course, not every officer was willing to talk to me. Two folks, both *very* prominent in the counterterrorism effort, politely declined. I consider them both good friends, but true to their own code, they just don't talk to *anyone*, not even a friendly former director writing a book. Ya gotta respect that.

Requests to interview serving intelligence officials were handled by NSA and CIA headquarters, as were my many requests for documents. Special thanks to all for the responsiveness. Frankly, I was surprised how much of a director's daily routine is chronicled and archived and retrievable. These were largely the same folks who had to judge what I could and couldn't say when it came to classification. They were firm when they had to be, but understanding and helpful where they could.

To make sure that I reflected policy debates accurately I also checked in with my executive branch colleagues, cabinet officers, and White House officials. All were generous and candid. My thanks.

I have also drawn on other writing I have done since leaving government, especially my more or less regular columns for CNN, the *Washington Times*, and *World Affairs Journal*. Being able to further develop thoughts first mentioned there added much to the current narrative.

That narrative ended up being a solo work, but I need to mention Vernon Loeb, former *Washington Post* reporter and metro desk editor, who first proposed we collaborate on this project. Before we were barely under way, Vernon opted out in favor of an editor's desk in Houston, but it was his initiative that got me moving.

Finally, I really wanted all of this to be readable, so I tried out chapter drafts on my wife and our adult children. They were generous in sharing their thoughts on my prose, grammar, organization, and logic. They also were very encouraging, sometimes explicitly pointing out the responsibility to leave *my* story for the grandchildren.

The family's inputs really helped the storytelling. If anything remains that is wrong, inelegant, redundant, or superfluous, the fault is fully mine.

INDEX

MORRIS AUTOMATED INFORMATION NETWORK

0 1004 0308388 2

WITHDRAWN

DATE DUE

APR - - 2016